Forging China's Military Might

Forging China's Military Might

A New Framework for Assessing Innovation

Edited by
Tai Ming Cheung

Johns Hopkins University Press
Baltimore

© 2014 Johns Hopkins University Press
All rights reserved. Published 2014
Printed in the United States of America on acid-free paper
9 8 7 6 5 4 3 2 1

Johns Hopkins University Press
2715 North Charles Street
Baltimore, Maryland 21218-4363
www.press.jhu.edu

Library of Congress Cataloging-in-Publication Data

Forging China's military might : a new framework for assessing innovation /
edited by Tai Ming Cheung.
     pages cm
   Includes bibliographical references and index.
   ISBN 978-1-4214-1157-6 (hardcover : alk. paper) — ISBN 978-1-4214-1158-3
(pbk. : alk. paper) — ISBN 978-1-4214-1159-0 (electronic) —
ISBN 1-4214-1157-1 (hardcover : alk. paper) — ISBN 1-4214-1158-X
(pbk. : alk. paper) — ISBN 1-4214-1159-8 (electronic)
     1. China—Armed Forces—Weapons systems.   2. China—Armed
Forces—Operational readiness.   3. China—Defenses—Technological
innovations.   4. Defense industries—Technological innovations—China.
5. Military-industrial complex—China.   6. China—Military policy.
I. Cheung, Tai Ming, author, editor of compilation.
   UA835.F67 2013
   355'.070951—dc23   2013013508

A catalog record for this book is available from the British Library.

Special discounts are available for bulk purchases of this book. For more
information, please contact Special Sales at 410-516-6936 or specialsales@
press.jhu.edu.

Johns Hopkins University Press uses environmentally friendly book
materials, including recycled text paper that is composed of at least
30 percent post-consumer waste, whenever possible.

Contents

Introduction

Tai Ming Cheung

China's leaders see science, technology, and innovation as essential ingredients in the pursuit of power, prosperity, and prestige. This is especially the case in the military realm, where the possession of homegrown innovation capabilities is deemed vital to national security. A concerted effort is now under way to lay the foundations and conditions to meet the goal of China's becoming a world-class defense science and technology (S&T) power by the next decade.

How successful China will be in this ambitious endeavor has profound implications for the rest of the world, and especially for competitors such as the United States. If China is able to catch up and begin to match the technological standards of other world leaders, this could lead to a destabilizing and costly long-term arms race with the United States and other major powers. On the other hand, if China is unable to narrow the technological gap and remains dependent on external sources for critical technological needs, this will undermine its ability to compete for strategic influence and safeguard its expanding security interests in the Asia-Pacific region and beyond. Most likely, though, China will only be successful in a limited, although gradually expanding, number of niche areas, such as precision-strike missiles, space and counter-space systems, and cyber-security. China's progress in these areas is already posing major regional military challenges for the United States and its allies, which will not only become more severe over time but will be coupled with China's growing potential for disruptive surprises in other areas, such as lasers and emerging technologies.

This volume explores how the Chinese defense science, technology, and industrial base is endeavoring to transform itself from an industrial latecomer into a technological frontrunner. While the nine chapter contributions from leading and up and coming Western scholars and policy analysts on defense innovation and Chinese defense S&T issues provide a rich and multifaceted range of insights, they in particular address two research themes. The first is an effort to provide a framework for the analysis of defense innovation, which, as a concept and subfield of study, has been hampered by a lack of common and detailed definitions about what it is, how it compares across countries, and what is occurring in China. The second area of attention is the examination of aspects of the structure and process of the Chinese defense S&T system that are critical to the development of innovation capabilities but have so far been overlooked. These include key organizations, industrial sectors, and policy initiatives.

The chapters in this volume were first presented at a conference on the Chinese defense economy held by the University of California's Institute on Global Conflict and Cooperation (IGCC) in the summer of 2011. The conference was part of a research project led by IGCC and funded by the US Defense Department's Minerva Initiative: The Evolving Relationship Between Technology and National Security in China, which examines China's drive to become a world-class defense and dual-use technological and industrial power and the security, geopolitical, economic, and technological implications of this transformation.

Defining and Applying Frameworks of Analysis to Chinese Defense Innovation

A critical weakness in the examination of Chinese defense issues is that much of the research output tends to be descriptive, non-theoretical, narrowly focused on China, and without much comparative perspective.[1] Moreover, with the rapid pace of change taking place within the Chinese defense economy, studies done in the 1990s and even the first half of the next decade look increasingly dated. For example, one of the ground-breaking studies done by the RAND Corporation in the early 2000s argued that certain parts of the Chinese defense industry were beginning to make discernible progress in reform and modernization after prolonged stagnation during the 1980s and 1990s. This was at odds with the conventional analysis at the time, which was highly skeptical of China's defense S&T capabilities.[2]

The study of the political economy of Chinese defense issues has advanced considerably since the late 2010s, although it is struggling to keep pace with the rapid changes taking place on the ground in China. More effort has been made to apply methodological approaches from other areas of study to the Chinese case, such as national innovation systems and organizational models.[3] There is greater awareness of the need for more precise definitions of critical terms and concepts, and more work is being done to compare Chinese defense technological and innovation developments with other countries and to place them in a more historical perspective.[4]

An important goal of this volume is to develop and make use of conceptual frameworks of analysis from other fields of study to help define the nature of Chinese defense innovation, understand the key drivers shaping its evolution, and locate China's place in the sectoral, national, and global defense industrial and innovation systems. These issues are explicitly addressed in a number of the chapters.

In Chapter 1, on analytical approaches to defense and military innovation, Tai Ming Cheung, Thomas Mahnken, and Andrew Ross[5] put forward a framework to capture the nature, dimensions, and spectrum of innovation in the military and broader defense spheres, drawing from disciplines such as history, social science, business, and strategic studies. The framework incorporates various lenses through which to view the inputs, process, and output of innovation: (1) the components of innovation: technology, doctrine, and organization; (2) the capacity to innovate; (3) the process of innovation: speculation, experimentation, and implementation; (4) the degree of innovation from duplicative imitation to radical innovation; (5) the scope of innovation; and (6) systems of innovation.

A key contribution of this chapter is the development of a rigorous definition of defense innovation and the suggestion of a typology of different innovation types and how it might apply to China. Defense innovation is the transformation of ideas and knowledge into new or improved products, processes, and services for military and dual-use applications; and military innovation is intended to enhance the military's ability to prepare for, fight, and win wars. Cheung offers seven types of imitation or innovation models that can be used to track the evolution in China's defense technological development, ranging from duplicative imitation to radical or disruptive innovation. How states and their defense innovation strategies fit into this typology depends on a few structural factors: their level and approach to economic and technological development, their external security situation, and the nature of their integration in the global economy and technological order. In applying the framework to China, Cheung argues that China's progress in the development of its innovation capabilities is more incremental than discontinuous. However, areas that could yet yield disruptive surprises include anti-ship ballistic missiles, information warfare, and anti-satellite weaponry.

In Chapter 2, on China's defense research, development, and acquisition (RDA) system, Tai Ming Cheung uses analytical approaches from the study of regulatory policy and industrial management to assess the state of reform and to determine whether the Chinese defense economy is in danger of becoming caught in a trapped transition. He argues that the defense economy is struggling to shift from a classic command and control regulatory system to the more independent regulator model that is typically employed in Western countries. While noteworthy progress has been made towards the establishment of a more indirect, rules-based regulatory system, Cheung believes that serious bottlenecks continue to exist and the defense industry, and the defense RDA system in particular, faces a real risk that key legacy segments may not be reformed and may continue to operate according to outmoded practices dating from the central planning era. The negative effects of this partial reform effort have so far been muted because of soaring budgetary and other resources coming into the defense industry since the late 1990s. But a tightening in these resource flows, from a possible economic downturn, for example, could expose how fragile the Chinese defense industry's economic performance and innovation capabilities may be.

Chapter 6, on the Chinese defense innovation system, by Kathleen Walsh employs the concept of national innovation systems. While the Chinese construction and implementation of a defense innovation system (DIS) is opaque and still in its infancy, the Chinese authorities consider it to be an important policy tool, and it is listed as an objective in the country's 2006–2020 Medium- and Long-Term Science and Technology Development Plan. Walsh points out that the Chinese DIS is focused on enhancing integration and interaction among key defense industry actors, institutions, industry sectors, and regions, both domestically and internationally. These actors include enterprises that are regarded as linchpins of the DIS and of state-sponsored research institutes and universities, the science and technology intermediate service system (such as science parks, industry associations, and technology transfer and product promotion centers), and regional geographical clusters.

Walsh puts forward several elements that define the nature of the Chinese DIS strategy. First, China is putting emphasis on the central role played by the state in guiding innovation strategies and policies, perhaps like the top-down approaches of Japan and South Korea. A second feature is that the strategy is long-term and extends to the 2020s. Third is the notion of civil-military fusion, in which integrating the civilian and defense economies is paramount. Fourth is a focus on clustering that encourages the building of DIS development zones, S&T parks, incubation centers, and other technology—and industry—clustering efforts. A fifth element is leveraging global technology and knowledge transfers, as well as cultivating domestic human capital. Walsh's assessment is that, although serious obstacles remain to China's ability to realize an effective DIS, it is laying the foundation for a dual-use DIS that both employs top-down development strategies and fosters greater bottom-up, market-driven, innovation dynamics.

In another methodologically and empirically rich contribution (Chapter 7), Richard Bitzinger, Michael Raska, Collin Koh Swee Lean, and Kelvin Wong Ka Weng seek to locate China's place in the global defense-industrial hierarchy by assessing its relative and comparative progress in three key defense sectors: naval shipbuilding, fighter aircraft production, and space-launch vehicles. Currently available methodologies for comparative assessments are sector-specific but employ the imitation-innovation typology put forward in Chapter 1.

Bitzinger argues that the global defense industry can be divided into three tiers. At the top are "critical innovators" able to engage in comprehensive development and manufacture of advanced conventional weaponry. Only the United States, Britain, France, Germany, and Italy occupy this tier, although the United States is far more technologically capable than the European states. In Tier 2 are "adapters and modifiers," which can be split into: (1) an upper segment of industrialized countries with advanced but niche defense production, such as Israel, Japan, and Sweden; (2) a middle subgrouping of developing or newly industrialized countries with modest military-industrial complexes, such as Brazil, South Korea, Taiwan, and Turkey; and (3) a lower segment of producers, such as India, that are developing industrial states with large, broad-based defense industries that lack sufficiently capable research and development and industrial capacities to develop and produce sophisticated conventional arms. At the bottom are Tier 3 states, the "copiers and reproducers," like Egypt or Nigeria, that have rudimentary defense industrial facilities able to produce small arms or to license the assembly of foreign-designed systems.

China currently languishes in the lower parts of the Tier 2 category, because its defense industry "demonstrate[s] few capacities for designing and producing relatively advanced conventional weapon systems," according to Bitzinger. But Bitzinger says that China may be due for recategorization as a Tier 1 state because of major improvements in the quality and capabilities of the new weapons systems its defense industry is producing, along with the accelerating tempo of overall defense modernization.

Bitzinger puts forward a general framework for conceptualizing the defense innovation trajectories of states that can be used to evaluate China's place in the global defense industrial hierarchy. He argues that innovation trajectories can be projected by an examination of the paths (emulation, adaptation, and innovation), patterns (speculation, experimentation, and implementation), and magnitudes (exploration, modernization, and transformation) that countries pursue. States that are imitators or importers of foreign ideas, practices, and capabilities are in the emulation/speculation/exploration phase while those that engage in advanced development of high-end innovation capabilities would be in the innovation/implementation/transformation category.

This framework is applied to the Chinese aerospace, naval shipbuilding, and fighter aircraft industries, and the assessment is that these three sectors have moved from emulation/speculation/exploration to experimentation/adaptation/modernization over the past one or two decades. The question now is whether China is starting to become an innovator/implementer/transformer. Bitzinger notes that China's ability to catch up with Tier 1 states depends not only on China's development efforts but also on global trends. The slowdown in defense RDA intensity in leading European defense economies and other industrialized states may provide a strategic opportunity for China to close the gap on the global technology frontier in certain areas.

Case Studies of Key Sectors and Organizations

Another important contribution of this volume is several original and detailed studies of key facets of science-, technology-, and innovation-related activities, from the macro to the micro level and within different parts of the defense economy and the People's Liberation Army (PLA). Two of these are the already discussed defense innovation system by Walsh and the defense RDA system by Cheung; also included are studies of technical advisory groups and contract and procurement administrative organizations belonging to the PLA General Armament Department (GAD), an emerging dual-use civil-military economy, and the space and missile industries.

Chapter 4, on the military representative office (MRO) system, by Susan Puska, Debra Geary, and Joe McReynolds, is the first detailed English-language examination of this unglamorous but critical cog in the military RDA apparatus.

The PLA is undertaking a concerted drive to raise the professionalism, efficiency, and effectiveness of its weapons and equipment contracting and procurement system, which is a serious weakness of its RDA process. Much of this reform effort centers on the GAD MRO system, which is responsible for ensuring that military production meets contract specifications prior to distribution to service units. MRO representatives from the GAD carry out this oversight at the factory and research institute floor in state-owned and commercial production and research facilities.

As the eyes and ears of the PLA high command in Beijing, MRO representatives are a critical source of information and monitoring on defense contractors; but the MRO system has been seriously compromised by decades of underfunding, poor training, high personnel turnover, weak coordination, corruption, and numerous other problems. Moreover, MRO representatives lack effective tools to deal with contractors who do not meet contractual obligations. Puska examines initiatives that the PLA has been exploring to address these shortcomings, in particular a pilot program to reform the PLA Navy's MRO system in 2011.

Eric Hagt's study of the GAD Science and Technology Committee (STC) (Chapter 3) is also a pioneering look at one of the most important but understudied organizations within the defense RDA system. Hagt describes the STC as the most senior advisory organization within the PLA on strategic and defense high-technology programs with direct input into the Central Military Commission. Hagt notes that the STC plays a central role in the early stages of weapons development, which have a major impact on determining the PLA's overall armament needs and the direction of its strategic modernization.

Another important feature of the STC is its role as a coordination mechanism between the PLA and the defense industry. Hagt points out that, while the STC is headed by a small number of GAD officers, it depends heavily on a large network of advisors and expert groups, most of whom are affiliated with defense enterprises. The dependence of the STC and GAD on defense industry technical experts means that these advisors often have the ability to influence the nature of programs to the advantage of their employers, according to Hagt. This is a major Achilles heel in the PLA's efforts to reform its defense RDA process.

This volume contains two case studies of the Chinese aerospace and missile industry. Kevin Pollpeter offers an assessment of the manned space program (Chapter 8) while Mark Stokes provides a broad industrywide overview (Chapter 9). The Stokes chapter in particular pays attention to key strategic and operational development drivers, the roles played by the two principal state-owned state corporations China Aerospace Science and Technology Corporation (CASC) and China Aerospace Science and Industry Corporation (CASIC), and a case study of the design and development of its anti-ship ballistic missile program.

Stokes believes that the space and missile sector is the most innovative component of the Chinese defense industry and is able to absorb and disseminate advanced technology for the research, development, manufacturing, and maintenance of advanced weapon and space systems. He sees considerable long-term prospects for technological advancement in the sector and argues that more "effective and efficient defense industrial management could allow China to emerge as a technological competitor of the United States in certain niche areas, such as long-range precision strike." The overall assessment by Stokes is that the aerospace industry is increasingly capable of meeting the PLA's long-term operational requirements.

Pollpeter offers a fascinating comparative analysis of the Chinese and United States manned spaceflight programs. He argues that, because of the unique challenges of manned space programs, far greater emphasis has been placed on the need for reliable technologies, exacting manufacturing processes, and strict quality assurance measures in space projects than in other engineering projects. Furthermore, space programs require long-term support from a country's top leadership and adequate funding.

Pollpeter shows how China's space industry was able to overcome major weaknesses at the outset in the early 1990s and was able to send astronauts into space by the early 2000s. These weaknesses included an aging workforce, poor working standards, backward technology, and a nonchalance about quality control. Among the reasons for the turnaround were top-level leadership support and the cultivation of a rigorous systems engineering program to ensure high quality-control standards, which included extensive testing and adherence by all parties from the prime contractor down to third-tier suppliers. Full development of this system took 13 years, but the organizational and management lessons that were learned in one of China's most complex technology development projects are likely to be invaluable as the country pursues a growing number of large-scale defense and strategic technology projects in other sectors.

In addition to the remaking of traditional industries, Chinese authorities are seeking new sources of ideas, knowledge and technology transfers, and investment to reinvigorate the defense economy. One of the top priorities since the beginning of this century has been forging close ties between the civilian and defense economies in a process known as civil-military integration (CMI). Daniel

Alderman, Lisa Crawford, Brain Lafferty, and Aaron Shraberg investigate the making and implementation of a high-powered CMI policy initiative by the Chinese leadership and the impact this is having on the defense economy (Chapter 5). Alderman points out that the leadership under Hu Jintao has laid out a clear vision for CMI, in which the emphasis is on establishing a balanced and coordinated approach to economic development and defense modernization through integrated planning, to ensure more effective use of overlapping resources. The defense sector in particular has rich opportunities to tap into an increasingly advanced civilian S&T base that has deep ties with the global science, technology, and innovation system. While the vision of coordinated civil-military development is certainly a worthy cause, the reality of deep-seated bureaucratic fragmentation and fiercely competing interests makes this goal virtually unattainable unless there is dedicated long-term, high-level leadership support.

Alderman points out though that CMI is still in its infancy in China, with much of the work focused on laying the long-term foundations of cooperation, such as the establishment of a legal and administrative regulatory regime and the issuance of detailed policy guidance. One significant policy directive discussed by Alderman is Document No. 37, which was issued by the Central Military Commission and the State Council in the run-up to the 12th Five-Year Plan and outlines the near- to medium-term priorities for the implementation of CMI to the mid-2010s, such as the opening up of the defense industry to civilian private companies. This embrace of the civilian nonstate sector is one of the issues that come under the microscope in Chapter 5, along with the research link-ups between civilian academic institutions, the PLA, and the defense industry.

The Broader Context of the Chinese Defense Science, Technology, and Industrial Base

While this volume offers important insights into the state of the field research on Chinese defense innovation and delves closely into a number of critical working aspects of the defense S&T system, it is also valuable to step back and understand the broader context of what is going on in the Chinese defense science, technology, and industrial base. Research results over the past decade show that major progress has been made: the defense industry is consistently posting record annual profits, new generations of weapons systems are in advanced development and production, and a more dynamic research and development apparatus is emerging, staffed by younger and better-trained scientists and engineers.

Key factors behind the improving performance of the defense economy include high-level leadership support, a clear well-defined long-term vision backed up with detailed development plans, a shift from technology-propelled to demand-led innovation, the growing role of defense corporations, the nurturing of a defense innovation system and overhaul of the research and development apparatus, and efforts to promote the integration of the civilian and defense economies.[6]

TOP LEADERSHIP SUPPORT

High-level and sustained support and guidance from the political and military leadership elites is essential to the Chinese defense economy's ability to carry out innovation activities. Leadership backing and intervention has been vital in addressing the entrenched bureaucratic fragmentation, institutional compartmentalization, and chronic project management problems that cause prolonged delays, decision-making paralysis, and cost overruns. Without outside leadership involvement, many achievements of the defense economy probably would not have happened, especially the turnaround in the defense economy since the end of the 1990s. This is a theme explored by Pollpeter in his examination of the manned space program, which points to the critical importance that top-level leadership support played in the launch of the manned space program in the early 1990s. After Deng Xiaoping threw his support behind the project, all opposition faded away.

The central leadership's direct and continuing involvement and oversight in the operations of the defense economy and of critical projects has been essential. This has often been done through the establishment of leadership small groups and special committees. In strategic and defense S&T matters, one of the key mechanisms is the Central Special Committee, a high-powered group reporting to the Politburo Standing Committee, the Central Military Commission, and the State Council.[7]

MEDIUM- AND LONG-TERM DEVELOPMENT PLANS

The PLA, state defense industrial regulatory authorities, and the Chinese defense industry have worked closely together to draw up major plans to guide near-, medium-, and long-term development of weapons, technology, and industry. The 12th Five-Year defense science and technology program, which began in 2011, provides detailed programmatic and procurement guidelines for projects that are in advanced stages of development and are expected to be ready for service during the plan's duration. Some of the defense industry's top development priorities during the 12th Five-Year Plan include the development of the J-20 stealth-like fighter aircraft; research, development, and production of large-sized aircraft carriers; and the aircraft and naval assets required to support carrier-based operations, such as the J-15 naval fighter.

The principal long-term plan is the 2006–2020 Medium- and Long-Term Defense Science and Technology Development Plan (MLDP), which focuses on guiding defense-related basic and applied research and development (R&D).[8] There is also a national medium- and long-term science and technology development plan that covers the same period but includes military and dual-use projects. The principal aspirational goal of these plans is to reach the technological level of first-tier global military powers, such as Western Europe, within the next 10–15 years.

SHIFTING THE DEFENSE ECONOMY FROM TECHNOLOGY-PUSH TO DEMAND-PULL

Major organizational reforms in the late 1990s allowed the PLA to gain primacy in guiding defense science and technology R&D. Previously, the institutional interests of the state-owned defense industry overwhelmingly drove armaments development and the PLA's requirements were secondary. The General Armament Department is responsible for ensuring that military end-users' needs are being served. Hagt's chapter on the key role of the STC offers pertinent insights into the tensions and conflicts that exist in the GAD's relationship with the defense industry.

To ensure that defense companies are in compliance with its requirements, the GAD has created incentive structures and monitoring mechanisms. First, it has imposed tougher competitive and evaluation procedures in the development and procurement of weapons systems. Second, the GAD has been willing to withhold or postpone orders for equipment that do not meet its requirements. Before the 1990s, the PLA had little option but to accept the output of the defense economy. As the quality of indigenous equipment steadily declined, the PLA became increasingly reticent to procure these arms and in the 1990s began to look overseas for weapons, especially from Russia. This practice faded in the next decade, with the improvement in domestic weapons quality.

THE GROWING CLOUT OF DEFENSE CONGLOMERATES

The rise of China's ten major defense corporations since the beginning of the 21st century has had a major impact on shifting the center of innovation gravity from research academies and universities to enterprises. These state-owned conglomerates, each of which has between 100 to more than 200 subsidiaries, have sought to transform themselves from debt-ridden quasi-state bureaucracies into full-fledged, market-driven enterprises. They have been slimmed down, allowed to shed heavy debt burdens, and given access to new sources of capital. Combined with a strong pickup in defense and civilian orders since the late 1990s, these companies have become highly profitable.

The aviation, space and missile, defense electronics, and naval sectors have been the chief beneficiaries of this rising tide of defense procurement, while the ordnance industry has enjoyed considerable success from sales of civilian products. These corporations are now engaged in an ambitious expansion strategy to become global arms and strategic technology champions.

Building of a Defense Innovation System and Research and Development Base

The Chinese defense innovation system, and especially its defense R&D apparatus, has been undergoing a significant overhaul and expansion to meet growing demand for its services from the PLA and also as part of a larger development of the national innovation system. Having a robust defense R&D system is a top priority of defense S&T development plans such as the MLDP. Two goals in service of this end are the shifting of ownership and the funding of key portions of the state-controlled defense R&D apparatus to the country's defense conglomerates. This process will require reducing the dependence of the R&D apparatus on state funding, increasing the amount of investment that firms devote to R&D, especially in applied and commercial development, and speeding up the exploitation and commercialization of proprietary R&D output.

Another high-level priority is the development of an extensive defense laboratory system that would pave the way for long-term technological breakthroughs. Around 90 laboratories belonging to both the defense industry and the PLA have so far been established. It will take some time, though, before these research outfits are able to conduct high-quality R&D, because they lack experienced and top-rated scientific personnel.

A third goal of the MLDP is the breaking down of barriers that have kept the defense R&D system separate from the rest of the national R&D base and the forging of close links with universities and civilian research institutes. Considerable progress has been made in the past few years, with many top research universities,

such as Tsinghua University, establishing sponsored research facilities in cooperation with the defense sector. Large sums have also been invested to upgrade the
research standards of the nine or ten science and technology universities formerly
belonging to the Chinese government's defense industrial regulatory authorities.

CIVIL-MILITARY INTEGRATION

Intensifying efforts have been made since 2000 to forge close links between
the civilian and defense economies, to allow the defense industry to gain access
to more advanced and more globalized civilian sectors. These efforts have led to
the development of some pockets of modest functional and geographical civil-
military activity since 2000. The electronics, information technology, high-
technology, and automotive sectors have been in the vanguard. Alderman carefully
reviews developments in CMI strategy and implementation since the second half
of the last decade.

Barriers to Improvement

Despite these significant improvements, the Chinese defense economy continues to suffer from serious structural weaknesses that could yet frustrate the
goal of closing the technological gap with the West and perhaps lead it to fall into
a transition trap. One overarching problem is the widespread duplication and
Balkanization of industrial and research facilities. The defense industry has
around 1,400 large and medium-sized factories, employing more than 1.6 million workers, scattered across the country, especially in the land-locked interior,
and often possessing outdated manufacturing and research attributes. Because
of intense rivalry, local protectionism, and huge geographical distances, there is
little cooperation or coordination among these facilities, preventing exploitation
of economies of scale and hampering efforts at consolidation.

Weak links in critical technological subsectors is also holding back broader
progress. One of the biggest Achilles heels is the aero-engine sector, which has
struggled to develop and produce state-of-the-art high performance power plants
to equip new generations of military aircraft. This has forced the defense industry and the PLA air force to be dependent on engines imported from Russia for
its latest generation of combat aircraft, such as the J-10 and J-11B.

GAD officials also complain that the defense industry continues to suffer from
excessive monopolization.[9] Reforms in the late 1990s to introduce controlled
competition in key defense industrial sectors appear not to have had much

impact, and this has hampered the PLA in its efforts to counter the domineering authority of the country's ten powerful defense conglomerates.

NOTES

1. The key early scholarship on Chinese defense technological and industrial issues includes Benjamin A. Ostrov, *Conquering Resources: The Growth and Decline of the PLA's Science and Technology Commission for National Defense* (Armonk, NY: M. E. Sharpe, 1991); John Frankenstein and Bates Gill, "Current and Future Challenges Facing Chinese Defence Industries," *China Quarterly*, no. 146 (June 1996); John Frankenstein, "The People's Republic of China: Arms Production, Industrial Strategy and Problems of History," in Herbert Wulf, ed., *Arms Industry Ltd.* (Oxford: Oxford University Press, 1993); Jorn Brommelhorster and John Frankenstein, eds., *Mixed Motives, Uncertain Outcomes: Defense Industry Conversion in China* (Boulder: Lynne Rienner, 1996); and Roger Cliff, *The Military Potential of China's Commercial Technology* (Santa Monica: RAND Corp., 2001).

2. Evan Medeiros, Roger Cliff, Keith Crane, and James Mulvenon, *A New Direction for China's Defense Industry* (Santa Monica: RAND Corp., 2005).

3. For example, see Tai Ming Cheung, *Fortifying China: The Struggle to Build a Modern Defense Economy* (Ithaca: Cornell University Press, 2009), and Evan A. Feigenbaum, *China's Techno-Warriors: National Security and Strategic Competition from the Nuclear to the Information Age* (Stanford, CA: Stanford University Press, 2003).

4. A special issue of the *Journal of Strategic Studies* in June 2011 contains several studies offering comparative, historical, and definitional perspectives. They include Thomas G. Mahnken, "China's Anti-Access Strategy in Historical and Theoretical Perspective"; Samm Tyroler-Cooper and Alison Peet, "The Chinese Aviation Industry: Techno-Hybrid Patterns of Development in the C-919 Program"; Richard A. Bitzinger, "China's Defense Technology and Industrial Base in a Regional Context: Arms Manufacturing in Asia"; and Christopher W. Hughes, "The Slow Death of Japanese Techno-Nationalism? Emerging Comparative Lessons for China's Defense Production."

5. For chapters with multiple authors, all the authors are identified in the first reference but only the first author is mentioned subsequently.

6. For a more comprehensive treatment of these and other factors, see Tai Ming Cheung, "The Chinese Defense Economy's Long March from Imitation to Innovation," *Journal of Strategic Studies* 34, no. 3 (June 2011): 325–354.

7. See Tai Ming Cheung, "The Special One: The Central Special Committee and the Structure, Process, and Leadership of the Chinese Defense and Strategic Dual-Use Science, Technology and Industrial Triangle," paper presented at Conference on the Structure, Process, and Leadership of the Chinese Science and Technology System, University of California, San Diego, July 2012.

8. "Summary of the Medium- and Long-Term Science and Technology Development Plan for the Defense Industry," originally published on the website of the Commission of Science, Technology, and Industry for National Defense, June 20, 2007. The website is no longer accessible.

9. Interviews by the author in Beijing and Changsha, February and November 2011.

Chapter One

Frameworks for Analyzing Chinese Defense and Military Innovation

Tai Ming Cheung, Thomas G. Mahnken, and Andrew L. Ross

Innovation, military or otherwise, is a diverse and multifaceted phenomenon. Broadly conceived, innovation is about change in the multitudinous ways and means employed to accomplish a task. More specifically, it is about the development of new or different instruments (particularly technology), practices (doctrine or operational art in the military realm), and organizations. The term *innovation* conjures up visions of invention, discovery, and breakthrough. It evokes things that are not merely new but novel—change that breaks with tradition, that is bold, groundbreaking, transformational, revolutionary, high risk, and carries a high payoff.[1] In reality, the extent and nature of the change represented by innovation may be located anywhere along a spectrum from continuous to discontinuous, sustaining to disruptive, incremental to transformational, minor to radical, and evolutionary to revolutionary. There is tremendous variation in the originality, complexity, and impact of innovations. Innovation can emphasize technology (i.e., hardware) as well as doctrinal and organizational change (i.e., software) and can be slow or rapid, simultaneous or sequential, modest or profound.

National innovation systems and processes[2] involve a multiplicity of agents and actors, producers and users.[3] Agents of innovation can hail from the public or the private sector and take the form of institutions as well as individuals. The individuals may occupy positions in executive or legislative institutions, be located in research, development, or production enterprises, or emerge from a user community. In the realm of defense, innovation may find champions among military officers or civilians—or a coalition of the two. Intended users may embrace or resist innovation; innovation conceived, funded, developed, and even deployed, is not necessarily innovation implemented.

The diversity inherent in the phenomenon of innovation has posed a challenge to scholars. Like the blind men trying to describe the elephant, scholars have heretofore described only selected aspects of innovation, in particular why and how organizations innovate. The results have at times been less than useful for those who seek to study innovation systematically and for those who seek to apply theory in understanding foreign defense and military innovation.

In this chapter, we seek to develop an analytical framework that captures the nature, dimensions, and spectrum of innovation in the defense and military spheres. To this end, we draw on insights from a range of disciplines, including history, social science, business, and strategic studies. The chapter begins by defining what exactly we mean by the term *innovation*. It goes on to survey the literature on innovation. An analytical framework that encompasses the inputs, process, output, and impact of innovation is developed. We conclude with some tentative observations on Chinese defense and military innovation. Our focus is on developing the conceptual and analytical tools needed to explain accurately the state of Chinese defense innovation and determine which innovations could be most consequential for the United States.

Definitions

Innovation, we have suggested, refers to new ways and means of accomplishing a task.[4] In his work on competitive advantage, Michael Porter embraces a similarly broad conception of innovation. For Porter, innovation includes "improvements in technology and better methods or ways of doing things. It can be manifested in product changes, process changes, new approaches to marketing, new forms of distribution, and new conceptions of scope."[5]

Discussions of innovation typically distinguish between invention—"the first occurrence of an idea for a new product or process"—and innovation—"the first attempt to carry it out in practice."[6] The distinction, however, should not be overemphasized and in reality is often not stark. Both invention and innovation entail the development of new ways and means of doing something, the application of new ideas to practice. More useful for our purposes is the distinction found in business literature between *product innovation* and *process innovation*.[7] Product innovation results in new or improved means or instruments (technologies)—new or improved instruments of war, for instance. Process innovation yields new or improved ways, such as changes in how wars are fought (as opposed to changes in the instruments or tools with which they are fought) brought about by new or improved doctrine and organizations.[8]

In his technology-focused work on, essentially, product innovation, Clayton Christensen provides another useful distinction: that between sustaining and disruptive technologies (or innovation). Christensen employs a broad conception of technology: "the process by which an organization transforms labor, capital, materials, and information into products and services of greater value." For him, innovation consists of "change in one of these technologies."[9] Although Christensen appears to reduce innovation to technological change, the conception of technology he employs includes not only products but also processes.

It is useful to distinguish among three types of national security innovation. First, at the top of the hierarchy, is strategic innovation.[10] Located here is innovation focused on grand strategy (or national security strategy), defense strategy, and military strategy. George Kennan's containment was a strategic innovation of the first order. Post–World War II work on (nuclear) deterrence, compellence, and coercive diplomacy qualifies as strategic innovation, as well. More recently, the post–Cold War US grand strategy debate is one that is essentially about strategic innovation.[11]

Second in the hierarchy is defense innovation, which can take the form of product, process, or organizational innovation in the broader defense establishment.[12] In this application, product innovation refers to new or improved goods and services, process innovation to improvements and new ways to produce these goods and services, and organizational innovation to new and improved ways of organizing activities and institutions.

Defense innovation, broadly defined, is the transformation of ideas and knowledge into new or improved products, processes, and services for military and dual-use applications. To distinguish from its military variant, defense innovation refers primarily to organizations and activities associated with the defense and dual-use civil-military science, technology, and industrial base. Included at this level are, for instance, changes in planning, programming, budgeting, research, development, acquisition, and other business processes. In the United States, Robert McNamara's introduction of PPBS (Planning, Programming, Budgeting System) during the early years of the Kennedy administration is a prime example of process innovation within the defense realm.[13]

Third, at the bottom of this hierarchy, is military innovation. At this level, warfighting innovation, whether modest or profound, is central. Encompassing both product and process innovation and including technological, operational, and organizational innovation, whether separate or in combination, military innovations are intended to enhance the military's ability to prepare for, fight, and win wars.

Some initiatives cut across the levels of the hierarchy. For instance, the National Security Act of 1947, a far-reaching organizational innovation that created the National Security Council, the Department of Defense, and the US Air Force, spanned the entire hierarchy. With its congressionally mandated emphasis on "jointness," the 1986 Goldwater-Nichols Act introduced changes at both the defense and military levels of the hierarchy. More recently, efforts to transform the US military were expanded from the initial focus on military innovation to include defense innovation.[14]

This chapter focuses on defense and military innovation. In it, we will seek to characterize the inputs, process, and output of innovation in the defense realm then apply the framework to China.

Innovation Studies and the Neglected Place of Defense and Military Innovation

The study of innovation has become a thriving academic enterprise over the past few decades. According to one survey, the annual number of publications with the word *innovation* in their title soared from under 10,000 at the beginning of the 1970s to nearly 60,000 by 2005.[15] The topic has received extensive attention across a wide range of disciplinary fields, most notably economics, business and strategic management studies, political economy, geography, and technology and engineering, leading some proponents to argue that this constitutes the rise of a new interdisciplinary field known as "innovation studies."

Although innovation broadly defined has attracted interest among security scholars, their work has been sporadic, diffuse, and compartmentalized in nature.[16] The study of military and defense innovation has been largely excluded from the mainstream examination of innovation, as exemplified by the dearth of these topics in the leading academic journals on innovation issues, such as *Research Policy* and *Strategic Management Journal*. Conversely, those security studies scholars who have examined defense and military innovation only infrequently have integrated the work of scholars who study the civilian sector. This state of affairs is especially ironic given that defense-related issues were among the chief drivers behind the early development of the innovation field. The national innovation systems (NIS) concept, for example, grew out of the examination by leading innovation scholar Christopher Freeman of the development of the military-industrial complex during the Cold War. Indeed, it was Freeman who initially coined the notion of a "military innovation system."[17]

As academic and policy research on civilian innovation activities took off in the 1970s and 1980s, national security–related issues were largely overlooked. In a landmark 1993 comparative study of national innovation systems, Richard Nelson noted that there was surprise among his project collaborators that "national security concerns had been important in shaping innovation systems, in many leading countries."[18] Nelson added that there was no consensus as to whether military research and development (R&D) and procurement had "been a help or a hindrance to the commercial competitiveness of national industry."[19]

There have been occasional efforts to examine the defense and national security aspects of innovation, especially in the post–Cold War era. One early effort in the late 1990s was led by Judith Reppy, who pointed out that the defense-industrial complex had many of the attributes that the national innovation systems framework was most concerned with, such as systems, well-defined boundaries, and robust institutions and organizations.[20] The definition of innovation was also sufficiently broad to include technology transfer and diffusion. Countries with large defense economies such as the United States, Russia, France, China, and the United Kingdom offered the best examples for examination using the NIS approach because of their national and systemic attributes and their extensive role in innovation. A more recent evaluation in 2009 of the role of defense R&D in the US and UK innovation systems pointed to new trends since the beginning of the 21st century.[21] Of particular note has been the accelerating privatization of defense research, especially in the UK, the impact on defense R&D of the 9/11 terrorist attacks in the US, and the shift in the dynamics of technology transfers between the defense and civilian sectors from military-to-civilian spin-off in the 1990s to, increasingly, "spin-on," in which the military sector seeks to draw more broadly upon the civilian, or commercial, industrial and R&D base. While little attention was paid to developments outside of these five nations, some of these key trends, such as privatization and civil-military integration, are also having a profound impact in shaping defense innovation systems in the Asia-Pacific region and other parts of the world.

There is a considerable body of literature on the phenomenon of military innovation.[22] The first wave of this scholarship was focused on the NATO–Warsaw Pact military balance and the prospects that the United States and the Atlantic Alliance would use innovative technology, doctrine, and organization to counter

Soviet forces, as well as Soviet perceptions of an impending revolution in military affairs brought on by the growth and spread of information technology and precision weaponry. In the second wave, which coincided with the end of the Cold War, scholars explored a wide variety of historical cases of innovation as a way of understanding its organizational and doctrinal prerequisites. Over time, it increasingly focused on the organizational barriers to innovation. The third wave of military innovation studies has focused on attempts to innovate and adapt on the battlefield in Iraq and Afghanistan since the beginning of the 21st century.

Scholars have advanced four broad explanations for why and how militaries innovate. One approach, advanced by Barry Posen, holds that civil-military dynamics, and particularly the intervention of civilian policy makers, determine whether militaries innovate.[23] Specifically, Posen argues that military resistance to change may be so entrenched that civilian intervention is required to bring it about. A second argument, whose proponents include Harvey Sapolsky and Owen Coté, holds that the relationship between military services within a state determines military innovation. These scholars argue specifically that interservice competition for roles, missions, and resources drives innovation.[24] A third line of reasoning, which includes work by Stephen P. Rosen, contends that competition between branches of the same military service drives innovation. In Rosen's view, change is the result not of civilian intervention but of the work of singular military visionaries, or mavericks within a particular service who are willing, eager even, to break the eggs needed to make an omelet.[25] A final school of thought, associated with Theo Farrell, Terry Terriff, and others, focuses on the cultures of particular military organizations as the key determinant of military innovation.[26]

Many scholars have pointed to the period between the two world wars as the paradigmatic case of peacetime military innovation.[27] The 1920s and 1930s saw the development of a range of new ways of war, including combined-arms armored warfare, strategic bombing, carrier aviation, amphibious warfare, and strategic air defense, which subsequently shaped the course and outcome of the Second World War.

The advent of nuclear weapons and long-range missiles after World War II has similarly had a profound impact on the character and conduct of war and on the shape of the organizations that plan to wage it. Adaptation to nuclear weapons, the deployment of intercontinental ballistic missiles and submarine-launched ballistic missiles, and the development of space-based reconnaissance satellites all were major innovations.[28] The recent emergence of precision-strike systems has already had a significant impact on the character of warfare, one that is likely to grow as such weapons mature and spread.[29]

Such innovations did not spring up overnight. Indeed, the process of developing novel ways of war may span several decades. Carrier aviation first saw combat use in the closing phases of World War I but did not become the dominant arm of naval warfare until World War II. The first precision-guided munitions (PGMs) saw service in World War II and were widely employed during the Vietnam War, but it was not until the 1991 Gulf War that their full effectiveness became manifest.

Most major military innovations have come out of a pressing strategic or operational problem that could not be handled through improvements to the existing force but rather required a new approach. During the 1920s and 1930s, for example, the expectation of a two-front war helped prod the German army into exploring the potential of combined-arms armored warfare and tactical aviation. During the same period, the possibility that the United States would have to cross the Pacific to defend or reconquer the Philippines from Japan drove the US Navy to explore offensive carrier warfare and the US Marine Corps to develop amphibious landing doctrine.

Unlike the broader analytical literature on innovation, the literature on defense and military innovation tends to equate innovation with major, large-scale change. For instance, Posen, in his work on doctrinal change, views innovation as "large change."[30] Rosen defines major, and therefore "unprecedented," peacetime or wartime operational innovation as "a change in one of the primary combat arms of a service in the way it fights or alternatively, as the creation of a new combat arm."[31] Sapolsky, too, emphasizes major, large-scale change: "by innovation we mean revolutionary change, change that alters significantly military doctrine, the combat role of particular technologies, and the status of groups within the military who specialize in the use of the technology (often called platform communities . . .) and not incremental improvement in weapons or doctrine."[32] More recently, Dima Adamsky focused on the radical, profound military innovation evident in military-technical revolutions or revolutions in military affairs, when "new organizational structures together with novel force deployment methods, usually but not always driven by new technologies, change the conduct of warfare."[33] Michael Horowitz, in another recent work, also focused on major military innovations. For him, "the bigger the change, the bigger the innovation."[34]

The emphasis on major, large-scale innovation, rather than viewing a spectrum from small- to large-scale, excludes much innovation. As Porter noted, "much innovation, in practice, is rather mundane and incremental rather than radical. It depends more on an accumulation of small insights and advances than on major technological breakthroughs."[35]

This fixation in the analytical literature on major, large-scale military innovation is particularly evident in the prominence given to the phenomena characterized as "military revolutions," "revolutions in military affairs (RMAs)," and "military-technological revolutions." These, clearly, are rare events. In a seminal piece, Andrew Krepinevich defined a military revolution as "what occurs when the application of new technologies into a significant number of military systems combines with innovative operational concepts and organizational adaptation in a way that fundamentally alters the character and conduct of war."[36] The character and conduct of war have not often been fundamentally altered. According to Krepinevich, only nine military revolutions occurred from the 14th through the 20th centuries.[37]

For Williamson Murray and MacGregor Knox, a military revolution "fundamentally changes the framework of war." They are upheavals, the political-military equivalents of earthquakes, bringing "systemic changes in politics and society." They are "uncontrollable, unpredictable, and unforeseeable. . . . Military revolutions recast society and the state as well as military organizations. They alter the capacity of states to create and project military power. And their effects are additive."[38] According to Murray and Knox, only five such military revolutions have taken place.[39] In another recent work, Max Boot identifies a mere four RMAs, including what is regarded as the ongoing "information revolution."

Whether considered military revolutions, revolutions in military affairs, or military-technological revolutions, transformations in war feature a combination of (1) new weapons and new weapons systems (technology), (2) new ways of fighting (doctrine/operational art), and (3) new organizational structures. It is the combination of the three that yields discontinuous, radical breakthroughs in the conduct of war.[40] Despite the technologies featured in many of the labels employed to characterize military revolutions or revolutions in military affairs, especially in Krepinevich's roster of military revolutions, technological—or "hardware"—change is insufficient for a revolution or transformation. Doctrinal/operational and organizational—or "software"—change is required as well. As Adamsky also emphasized,[41] it is the *confluence* of technological, doctrinal, and organizational change that makes a revolution.

Such confluences are rare. Despite the attention they continue to generate among practitioners and analysts alike, profound revolutions are not a frequent occurrence. The lists of revolutions compiled by Krepinevich and by Knox and Murray are, essentially, compilations of outliers.[42] This fascination with, or fixation on, outliers should not be allowed to obscure the norm. A far-reaching, profound, radical change that includes each of military innovation's three components is actually relatively rare. It is the allure of the outlier, and perhaps a thinly disguised disdain for the norm, that has prompted military innovators to hold dear a line from Machiavelli: "there is nothing more difficult to carry out, nor more doubtful of success, nor more dangerous to handle, than to initiate a new order of things."[43]

Examining the Chinese defense economy from a national innovation systems approach can help to shed light on critical processes that would otherwise be over-looked in more conventional assessments of defense industry and military modernization issues.[44] Key issues include how the R&D process works, competence building through education and training of the work force, the role of incentives and governance regimes in promoting entrepreneurship and risk-taking, the interactions between technology-push and demand-pull factors, and the integration of complementary knowledge through linkage activities within the system.[45]

A Framework for Understanding Defense and Military Innovation

The section that follows seeks to provide a framework for understanding the inputs, process, and outcome of defense and military innovation.

THE COMPONENTS OF DEFENSE AND MILITARY INNOVATION

The three components of defense and military innovation are technology, organization, and doctrine. Technology, in the form of weapons and weapons systems, provides the hardware dimension of defense and military innovation and its concrete products.[46] Organizational and doctrinal changes, the software of innovation, feature what is characterized in the broader literature as process innovation.[47]

Of these three components of innovation, it is technology that is the most visible component. For the military and the analytical community alike, the allure of new technology can be difficult to resist. Yet, new technology is rarely the *sine qua non* of military innovation. Realizing the full potential of new technology often requires organizational adaptation and the development of new doctrine. Although military organizations tend to want to acquire technology that accords with their culture, new technologies can encounter organizational and bureaucratic resistance.[48] Restructuring of existing organizations or even the development of new organizations to provide new skill sets may be necessary. Similarly, new technologies, particularly those that qualify as breakthroughs, may well require rethinking the principles that shape or guide the employment of military force.

Rarely do these components of military innovation change simultaneously; most often, one leads and the others follow. Technology, for instance, may leap ahead, requiring organizations and doctrine to play catch up, perhaps for decades. The advent of nuclear weapons preceded by years the development of the organizations, such as the US Strategic Air Command and the Soviet Strategic Rocket Forces, and the doctrine to govern their use. Doctrinal visions, such as amphibious warfare in the 1920s and 1930s and ballistic missile defense today, can spur organizational change and drive technological development. The manner in which hardware and software innovation and product and process innovation come together determines whether change is modest or profound, continuous or discontinuous, sustaining or disruptive, incremental or transformational, minor or radical, evolutionary or revolutionary.

These three components of defense and military innovation are at play across the innovation inputs, processes, and outputs highlighted here. The "hard" and "soft" capabilities discussed below are inputs to new or improved technology, organization, and doctrine. Process is about how new or improved technology, organization, and doctrine are generated. Innovation outputs are new or improved technology, organization, and doctrine—or some combination thereof.

Inputs to Innovation

Hard innovation capabilities are input and infrastructure factors intended to advance technological and product development. This includes research and development facilities such as laboratories, research institutes and universities, human capital, firm-level capabilities and participation, manufacturing capabilities, access to foreign technology and knowledge markets, availability of funding sources from state and nonstate sources, and geographical proximity. These hard innovation capabilities attract the most analytical attention because they are tangible and can be measured and quantified.

Soft innovation capabilities are broader in scope than hard factors and cover political, institutional, relational, social, ideational, and other factors that shape nontechnological and process-related innovative activity. This is what innovation scholars such as Moses Abramovitz define as "social capability."[49] These soft capabilities include organizational, marketing, and entrepreneurial skills as well as governance factors such as the existence and effectiveness of legal and regulatory regimes, the role of political leadership, promotion of standards, and corporate governance mechanisms.

For example, the most important soft capabilities for the Chinese defense economy include high-level leadership support, forging a new state regulatory oversight model, cultivating new institutional culture and governance norms, constructing a modern regulatory and standards-based regime, improving technology diffusion and promoting intellectual property rights protection, and enhancing the role and influence of the People's Liberation Army (PLA), through the General Armament Department (GAD), in guiding technological development within the defense economy. Three of these soft capabilities are of particular importance in China's case:

- *Central leadership support:* Active and credible support and guidance from the highest levels of the policy-making elite are crucial factors in the Chinese defense economy's ability to carry out innovation activities. Leadership backing is essential in tackling key structural barriers, which include entrenched bureaucratic inertia, risk-adverse decision making, institutional compartmentalization, and chronic project management problems that cause prolonged delays and cost overruns. Without outside leadership intervention and oversight, many of the key achievements of the Chinese defense economy over the past 60 years might not have happened. This would include the development of the nuclear and strategic missile programs in the 1960s, the turnaround in the fortunes of the defense economy since the end of the 1990s, and the manned space program.
- *Changing industrial culture and governance norms:* One of the biggest challenges in nurturing the innovative spirit of the Chinese defense economy is combatting an insular and conservative institutional mindset shaped by decades of central planning. This legacy has created a strong aversion to risk, a lack of competitive instincts, poor motivation, and weak disciplinary practices. A concerted effort has been conducted since the late 1990s to address these governance deficits by the PLA and the defense industrial regulatory authorities.[50]
- *Growing influence of the military end-user:* The emergence of the PLA as the dominant actor in guiding defense science and technology research and production activities since the late 1990s has been an important factor in improving the performance of the defense economy. Under the watchful eye of the GAD, the defense economy has had to shift from pursuing

technology-push strategies to focusing on demand-pull requirements from PLA end-users.[51]

The technological sophistication of the Chinese military's hard innovation capabilities, especially in certain key areas such as precision-guided ballistic missiles, satellites, and anti-satellite technology, has grown considerably in recent years. What is less clear is the extent to which the PLA has developed the soft capabilities needed to make these instruments truly effective. The much-heralded establishment of the Strategic Planning Department in the PLA General Staff Department in 2011 suggests that the Chinese military's organizational and doctrinal response to its technological progress has been lagging.[52]

PROCESSES OF INNOVATION

A second way to think about innovation is through the process by which innovations are brought into being. Past cases of military innovation show that defense establishments tend to develop new approaches to combat in three distinct but often overlapping phases (see Table 1.1): speculation, experimentation,

Table 1.1   Potential Indicators of Innovation, Divided into Process Phases

Phase	Potential Indicators of Innovation
I. Speculation	• Publication of concept papers, books, journal articles, speeches, and studies regarding new combat methods • Formation of groups to study the lessons of recent wars • Establishment of intelligence collection requirements focused upon foreign innovation activities
II. Experimentation	• Existence of an organization charged with innovation and experimentation • Establishment of experimental organizations and testing grounds • Field training exercises to explore new warfare concepts • War gaming by war colleges, the defense industry, and think tanks regarding new warfare areas
III. Implementation	• Establishment of new units to exploit or counter innovative mission areas • Revision of doctrine to include new missions • Establishment of new branches, career paths • Changes in the curriculum of professional military education institutions • Field training exercises to practice, refine concepts

and implementation.[53] Each phase yields indicators that allow an estimation of the pace and scope of innovation.

Speculation

In the first stage of the process, which may be termed speculation, military innovators identify novel ways to solve existing operational problems or exploit the potential of emerging technology. The most visible indicators of innovation during this phase are often books, journal articles, speeches, and studies advocating new approaches to warfare. These sources may offer the first warning that a state is interested in acquiring new capabilities. In the years following the end of World War I, for example, a handful of European and American military officers speculated on how armored vehicles, aircraft carriers, and land- and sea-based aviation would change the shape of future wars. Debates over the proper composition and employment of tank formations raged on in the pages of British periodicals such as the *Journal of the Royal United Service Institution*, *Army Quarterly*, *Journal of the Royal Artillery*, *Royal Engineers Journal*, and even the *Cavalry Journal*. During the same period, service journals contained numerous articles discussing the proper employment of air power and the relative merits of the battleship and the aircraft carrier.

The primary challenge that foreign observers face at this stage is detecting a military's interest in new approaches to combat. Predicting a service's future actions based upon speculative writings in military journals is a hazardous undertaking. It may be exceedingly difficult to determine which—if any—statements are authoritative. Rarely do military professionals agree on the effectiveness of unproven weapons and concepts. Without in-depth knowledge of both the formal and the informal hierarchy of a country's military organizations, it can be difficult to tell whether an article's statements are one author's opinions or reflect a wider consensus. Nor will discussion of new forms of warfare necessarily take place in public. In 1920, for example, Germany's shadow general staff, the Troop Office (*Truppenamt*), established 57 secret committees to study the lessons of World War I. The army subsequently used their conclusions to develop its doctrine.[54] Great Britain developed its integrated air defense system in utmost secrecy. In these instances, early detection of innovation would have required precisely targeted clandestine collection.

Experimentation

If the seeds of innovation fall on fertile soil, then speculation regarding emerging warfare areas may grow into experiments with new organizations and the development of innovative doctrine. In some cases, this may involve imitating foreign technology, doctrine, and organization; in other cases, it may lead to innovation. Military services may establish experimental units. Between 1926 and 1928, for example, the British army formed the Experimental Mechanized Force to explore armored operations. The US Army created its own experimental forces in 1928 and 1930.[55]

Services may also conduct exercises to examine new concepts. At various times during the 1920s and 1930s, the British, French, German, Soviet, and American armies all held maneuvers to explore the effectiveness of different armored formations.[56] In several cases, they sought to determine the value of new organizations by pitting them against standard formations. During the same period, the US Navy used its fleet exercises to examine concepts for the offensive use of carrier aviation.

War gaming represents another form of experimentation. During the interwar period, for example, war games at the US Naval War College explored the role of carrier aviation in a future conflict. One exercise held in the fall of 1923 depicted an engagement between a US naval force with five aircraft carriers—more than any navy possessed at the time—against an opponent with four. During the game, the US force launched two hundred aircraft armed with bombs and torpedoes in one strike at the enemy fleet, and succeeded in crippling its carriers and a battleship.[57]

Such experimental activities offer clear indicators of interest in new warfare areas. Yet, without a clear understanding of the objectives of such maneuvers, it is easy for a foreign observer to misinterpret their results. The US Marine Corps began conducting amphibious exercises in the early 1920s, only to halt them in 1926. It would have been easy for an observer to conclude that the corps had abandoned the idea of amphibious landings as infeasible. Indeed, a Marine afteraction report describing these early exercises found them "woefully theoretical."[58] In fact, the Marine Corps remained committed to the seizure of advanced bases but had been forced to suspend exercises due to commitments in Asia and Latin America. Conversely, it is not certain that military organizations will adopt experimental concepts, even when they are promising. Indeed, both the British and American armies chose to disband their experimental mechanized forces, even though they had enjoyed considerable success. It is therefore important to understand the level of bureaucratic support for experimentation within a military organization.

Implementation

Successful experimentation with new approaches to warfare may lead military services to adopt new concepts and new organizations tailored to carry them out. Following the British Experimental Mechanized Force's maneuvers, for example, Colonel C. N. F. Broad wrote *Armoured and Mechanized Formations*, the British army's first doctrinal publication to discuss armored warfare. In 1931, he assumed command of the First Brigade of the Royal Tank Corps, with the charge to test methods for conducting deep penetrations of an adversary's lines.[59] In November 1933, the army authorized the permanent formation of the First Tank Brigade and appointed Brigadier Percy Hobart as its commander. Hobart, an advocate of independent tank operations, used the opportunity to test and refine untried concepts of armored warfare. Mechanized infantry and artillery brigades and their supporting units joined the tank brigade to form what was in essence an armored division.

At this stage, a number of indicators of interest to analysts may appear. The establishment of new military formations and the promulgation of doctrine to govern their employment demonstrate a service's commitment to pursuing novel combat methods. In some cases, services may establish new branches, specialties, and career paths to support them. They may also hold exercises and conduct training in these areas, and the curriculum of professional military education institutions may change to reflect new doctrine.

In some cases, the processes of experimentation and doctrinal development overlap. In 1934, for example, the US Marine Corps issued the first draft of its *Tentative Manual for Landing Operations*. Beginning in 1936, it began holding fleet landing exercises to examine a range of new amphibious tactics, techniques, and technology. The corps used the results of these exercises to refine the *Tentative Manual*.[60]

The key challenge for outside observers at this stage is not detecting or recognizing innovation but calculating the merit of practices whose potential is purely theoretical as yet. Predicting the battlefield impact of new weapons and concepts is extremely difficult. Information is often fragmentary, ambiguous, and thus unlikely to challenge prevailing assumptions about warfare. Instead, such incomplete data sometimes reinforce the tendency to ignore new combat methods.

Of course, not all innovations unfold over decades. The Japanese navy developed the concept of launching concentrated carrier air strikes only months before the attack on Pearl Harbor.[61] Similarly, the Japanese army began to study jungle warfare less than a year before its attack upon Southeast Asia.[62] These developments proved much more difficult for Japan's enemies to detect because the experimentation phase had been so short.

When applied to China, this process provides a useful template for gauging the scope and pace of Chinese military innovation. When applied in particular to some of China's potentially most consequential military innovations—precision-guided ballistic missiles, and anti-ship ballistic missiles—the publically available information shows that China has moved from speculating about advanced missiles to at least experimentation, if not deployment and implementation.[63]

THE OUTPUTS OF INNOVATION

A third way to understand an innovation focuses on the nature and degree of the innovative change that is being carried out. Is the outcome imitational or genuinely innovative in nature, and if it is the latter, does it represent incremental or radical innovation? Seven categories of imitation or innovation can be defined:

1. *Duplicative imitation:* Products, usually obtained from foreign sources, are closely copied with little or no technological improvement. This is the starting point of industrial and technological development for latecomers such as China.

2. *Creative imitation:* A more sophisticated form of imitation that generates imitative products with new performance features.

3. *Creative adaptation:* Products are inspired by existing foreign-derived technologies but differ from them significantly.

4. *Incremental innovation:* Existing indigenously developed systems and processes receive limited updating. Such innovation is often the result of organizational and management inputs aimed at producing different versions of products tailored to different markets and users, rather than significant technological improvement through original R&D.

5. *Architectural innovation:* "Innovations that change the way in which the components of a product are linked together, while leaving the core design concepts (and thus the basic knowledge underlying the components) untouched."[64]

6. *Component or modular innovation:* The development of new component technology that can be installed into existing system architecture; emphasizes hard innovation capabilities, such as advanced R&D facilities,

a cadre of experienced scientists and engineers, and large-scale investment outlays.

7. *Disruptive/radical innovation*: Requires major breakthroughs in both new component technology and architecture. Only countries with broad-based, world-class R&D capabilities and personnel, along with deep financial resources and a willingness to take bold risks, can engage in this kind of activity.

Where states and their defense innovation strategies fit into this typology depends on several key structural factors, three of which are: (1) their level of and approach to economic and technological development, (2) their external security situation, and (3) the nature of their integration into the global economy and technological order. Each of these factors contributes to the level of a country's hard and soft innovation capabilities, and the type of imitation or innovation which it is likely to pursue depends upon those capabilities (see Figure 1.1).

For latecomer countries engaged in state-led approaches to catch-up development, of which China and other Northeast Asian countries are classic examples, the principal means of technological advancement in their initial stages of industrialization has been through the absorption of existing foreign-derived technology, because these states lack both hard and soft innovation capabilities. A central element of this absorption strategy is the reverse engineering of available foreign technologies.[65] Of the two distinct forms of imitation that correspond with different stages of development, in the initial phase, duplicative imitation, products are closely copied with little or no technological improvements. This requires only low levels of hard and soft innovation capabilities. In this passive, "black box" form of absorptive learning, technological capabilities for production are provided but not the underlying blueprints or source technologies. The Chinese defense economy went through this duplicative imitation phase during the 1950s and 1960s.

Creative imitation is a more sophisticated form that aims at "generating imitative products but with new performance features."[66] This imitation can come in several forms. The most basic approach, design copying, mimics the style or design of the market leader, but the copier applies their own brand name and engineering specifications. The Chinese *Shanzhai* (guerrilla) model of innovation fits this description; small-scale private Chinese firms, often working closely together in vertically integrated alliances, produce low-cost copycat models of foreign products such as mobile phones and automobiles, but with improved features.[67]

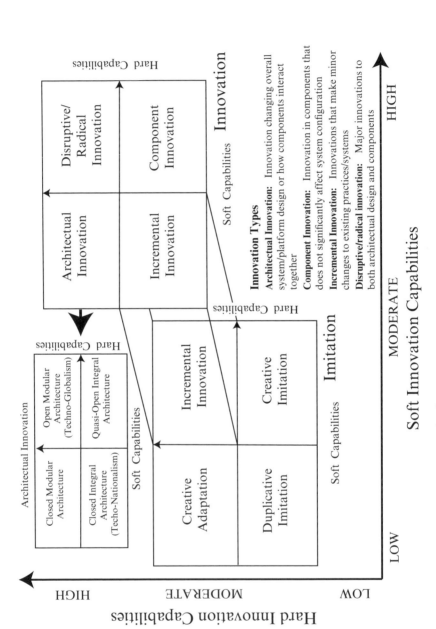

Figure 1.1. The imitation-to-innovation landscape

The next level up is creative adaptation, in which products are inspired by existing foreign-derived technologies but differ from them significantly. These more advanced imitation methods require increasing levels of hard and soft innovation capabilities, especially the ability to conduct R&D and strategic marketing activities. For the Chinese defense economy, this creative imitation phase has spanned from the 1970s to the present day. Design copying was the primary form of imitation in the 1970s and 1980s, but creative adaptation became more prevalent in the 1990s with the development of better innovation capabilities. The Chinese defense industry's sophisticated reverse engineering of Russian weapons systems would fall into this high-end imitation/adaptation category of the model.

Overlapping and complementing these imitation approaches is incremental innovation, which is also extensively practiced by the Chinese defense economy. Incremental innovation and creative adaptation are key elements in the Chinese government's indigenous innovation (*zizhu chuangxin*) strategy. The main difference between creative imitation and incremental innovation is that the former involves the adaptation of foreign acquired technologies while incremental innovation is the limited updating of existing indigenously developed systems and processes. The latter is often the result of organizational and management inputs aimed at producing different versions of products tailored to different markets and users, rather than significant technological improvements through original R&D. Incremental innovation is one of the main pathways of innovation in the Chinese defense economy for the near-to-medium term, because it is the most suited to China's technological capabilities. Several defense subsectors, including the aviation, shipbuilding, ordnance, and electronics industries, have come out with new generations of weapons systems over the past decade, and they have subsequently been updated on a regular basis.

As innovation capabilities become more sophisticated, architectural innovation becomes possible. The primary enablers are improvements in organizational structures, marketing, management, systems integration, and doctrinal processes and knowledge, which are coupled with a deep understanding of market requirements and with close-knit relationships between producers and suppliers and between suppliers and users.[68] As these enablers are the same factors responsible for driving incremental innovation, distinguishing between these different types of innovation poses a major analytical challenge. While many of the soft capabilities enabling architectural innovation may appear to be modest and unremarkable, they have the potential to cause significant, even discontinuous, consequences through the reconfiguration of existing technologies in far more efficient and competitive ways that challenge or overturn the dominance of established leaders. Maneuver warfare and German Blitzkrieg doctrine are historical examples of architectural innovations and architectural breakthroughs triggered by the development of new operational doctrines or the establishment of new organizations.[69] China's efforts to develop asymmetrical warfare doctrine and capabilities are another example of architectural innovation, especially the employment of ballistic missiles as anti-access weapons against the US.[70]

Studies of architectural innovation may offer some clues about which conditions nurture this type of innovative activity. One finding is that architectural innovation requires close integration between first-tier component suppliers and prime systems integrators. Research on the US defense aerospace industry in the 1990s indicated that if producers allowed their chief suppliers to provide major input in product design as early as possible in the concept exploration and definition stage, this could result "in a fundamentally new configuration of how the components in a product or system are linked together" and could offer "significant improvements."[71] Studies of the development of the Japanese automobile industry in the 1980s and 1990s support these findings and show that they have analytical value in various industries, as well as across the civil-military divide.

China's *Shanzhai* model may be slowly evolving into a low-end architectural innovation variant as larger and more established Chinese companies marry some of the insurgent-style creative imitation methods with their more ample R&D and commercial sales capabilities. The combination of these factors would allow these companies to begin to challenge far more advanced foreign competitors in the Chinese marketplace. A few *Shanzhai* companies are emerging to become sizeable players in the Chinese mobile telephone and automobile industries. Geely Group is one example of a young, private company that emerged from obscurity in the first few years of the 21st century to become a top-ten domestic automobile manufacturer through modular production.[72]

The aviation and shipbuilding sectors are spearheading the embrace of architectural innovation within the defense economy. The fledgling commercial aviation industry stands out for designing its long-term development model around this approach. In its development of the ARJ21 trunk liner and C-919 single-aisle passenger aircraft, the aviation industry is concentrating its efforts on airframe design and buying most of its components from foreign suppliers. Local content will account for only 10 percent of the ARJ21 and 30 percent of the C-919, with all the critical technologies being imported.[73] A vital element in this foreign dependence by Commercial Aviation Corporation of China is its willingness to allow these suppliers to assume a prominent role in systems design and integration, including at the concept definition phase.[74] The Chinese commercial shipbuilding industry by comparison obtains 65 percent of its components domestically.[75]

Component or modular innovation, the next step up the innovation ladder, involves the development of new component technology that can be installed into existing systems architecture. While imitation and incremental and architectural innovation depend more on organizational and marketing innovation skills, modular innovation requires hard innovation capabilities, such as advanced R&D facilities, a cadre of experienced scientists and engineers, and large-scale investment outlays. Component innovation is an area of major weakness for much of the Chinese defense economy, especially the higher-technology sectors, such as the aviation and naval sectors. Chinese avionics, radars, fire-control systems, and engines lag one to two generations behind leading international competitors, and the near-term prospects of narrowing this gap are poor, because of the underdevelopment of the country's R&D capabilities.

At the top of the innovation chain is radical innovation, which requires major breakthroughs in both new component technology and architecture. As noted above, only countries with broad-based, world class R&D capabilities and highly skilled personnel, along with considerable financial resources and a willingness to take risk, can engage in this activity. This is the type of innovation that is required for the development of fifth-generation stealth aircraft. Radical innovation has so far been beyond the ability of the Chinese defense economy, but the country has shown, with its strategic weapons programs in the 1960s, that it can engage in such high-quality work, despite the lack of world-class R&D capabilities and despite being cut off from the outside world, if the project is deemed to be of sufficiently high strategic priority by the country's leadership.[76]

It is important to point out that advancements from imitation to innovation do not necessarily take place in a linear, sequential fashion. Many of the constituent processes occur at the same time, and there is plenty of overlap between phases. This is especially the case between creative adaptation and incremental innovation, where the boundaries between these two processes are often blurred.

The Impact of Innovation

As previously noted, most military innovation is distinctly less than revolutionary or transformational. It consists largely of incremental, often near-continuous, improvements in existing capabilities. These fundamentally routine incremental advances in technology, doctrine, and organizational capabilities should not be dismissed in discussions of innovation. On the hardware front, collectively they are what we think of as modernization.[77]

This incremental innovation—often predictable improvement in existing capabilities in support of established performance metrics—is commonplace and sustaining; by contrast, radical innovation is disruptive.[78] Incremental innovation's gradualness does not, however, diminish its significance. It is what military organizations, following standard operating procedures, pursue on a regular basis: technology advances, doctrine is refined, organizations evolve, existing capabilities are optimized. Military revolutions, revolutions in military affairs, and transformations, on the other hand, are extraordinary phenomena that entail profound, fundamental, and disruptive discontinuities (and may enhance rather than reduce uncertainty). Unpredictable, discontinuous, disruptive innovation—a concept reminiscent of Schumpeter's "creative destruction,"[79] which underlies all revolutions and transformations—is extraordinary rather than routine: technology leaps ahead, doctrine is reformulated, organizations are (re)created, and competitors, their capabilities rendered obsolete, are left behind. A wide range of too often overlooked innovation is located between the bookends of the spectrum between incremental innovation and radical innovation. Most innovation fits into one of the three quadrants of the innovation matrix (see Figure 1.2) that do not represent disruptive, revolutionary innovation.[80]

Discontinuous innovation creates the potential for technological or architectural breakthroughs. Breakthroughs, according to Mark Stefik and Barbara Stefik, are rare and surprising; they "create something new or satisfy a previously undiscovered need"[81] and enable us to do something that we didn't know was possible—to fly, to venture into space, to harness the power of the atom or to deliver ordnance with robotic systems. The consequences of breakthroughs may be unintended. They can result in the transformation or even displacement of existing practices.

Discontinuous change to weapons, platforms, or systems, even in the context of incremental doctrinal and/or organizational change, constitutes what in the matrix is labeled a "technological breakthrough." Discontinuous doctrinal and/ or organizational—or software—innovations represent what are depicted as architectural breakthroughs. Architectural innovation redefines how the components of technologies, doctrines, or organizations are linked and features major changes in the relationships, or linkages, among and integration of hardware (technology) and software (doctrine and organization).[82] As Rebecca Henderson

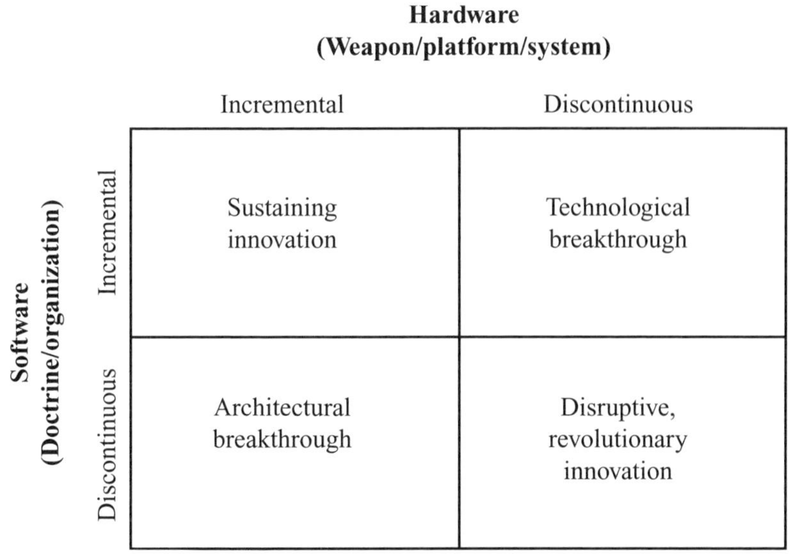

**Hardware
(Weapon/platform/system)**

	Incremental	Discontinuous
Incremental	Sustaining innovation	Technological breakthrough
Discontinuous	Architectural breakthrough	Disruptive, revolutionary innovation

Software (Doctrine/organization)

Figure 1.2. An innovation matrix

and Kim Clark put it, "the essence of an architectural innovation is the recon-figuration of an established system to link together existing components in a new way."[83] Dramatic departures in operational concepts or organizational structure—particularly the development of new doctrine or the establishment of new organizations—that result in new uses of a technology qualify as architectural breakthroughs.

Both discontinuous technological innovation and architectural innovation occur much less frequently than does sustaining innovation. Examples of past discontinuous technological innovations include the introductions of battleships, aircraft, tanks, aircraft carriers, and, more recently, precision guidance. Today, unmanned aerial vehicles (UAVs) and other unmanned, robotic systems are examples of discontinuous technological breakthroughs. The all-volunteer force, "jointness," and maneuver warfare are recent examples of architectural innovation. Blitzkrieg is a well-known historical example of an architectural breakthrough.

Disruptive, revolutionary innovation is the result of a confluence of discontinuous technological, doctrinal, and organizational changes; it occurs when discontinuous hardware and architectural changes coalesce in a coherent, integrated whole. Existing capabilities are not optimized but rendered obsolete and displaced. New dominant technologies, doctrines, and organizations are established and integrated as never before. New performance metrics arise, such as Christensen's "cheaper, simpler, smaller, and, frequently, more convenient to use."[84]

Discontinuous innovation need not require simultaneous technological, doctrinal, and organizational breakthroughs. Indeed, simultaneous hardware and architectural breakthroughs appear to be the exception rather than the rule; one element tends to lead while the other lags and must catch up—if disruptive innovation rather than either a technological or architectural breakthrough alone is to be the result. Breakthrough doctrinal and organizational innovations have often lagged behind breakthrough technological innovations. The technological breakthroughs represented by the development of the tank and the aircraft carrier were not initially disruptive; that awaited the doctrinal and organizational breakthroughs of the interwar period. In the nuclear realm, too, scientific and technological breakthroughs preceded the equivalent doctrinal and organizational innovations (although the immediate technological breakthroughs that yielded the Trinity "gadget," "Little Boy," and "Fat Man" were the result of an unprecedented wartime organizational breakthrough known as the Manhattan Project).[85]

Today, doctrinal and organizational developments trail the development of two disruptive technological innovations: robotics and the information technologies for cyberattack, cyberdefense, and cyberexploitation. The increasingly widespread use of UAVs and other unmanned, robotic systems has outpaced the development of doctrine on their employment; it remains unclear whether centralized control and dispersed firepower or decentralized control and concentrated firepower better exploits the capabilities of this new hardware.[86] Similarly, doctrine and organization have yet to catch up to cyberattack, cyberdefense, and cyberexploitation capabilities.[87] The recently established US Cyber Command (USCYBERCOM) is an attempt to begin bridging the gap between technological and architectural capabilities in this realm.

Architectural breakthroughs need not trail technological breakthroughs. Missile defense doctrine and organization, for instance, have long run ahead of their requisite technological capabilities. Implementation of the concept of network-centric operations, touted by some proponents of the US military transformation during the second half of the 1990s and first decade of the 2000s, awaits either the technological and organizational innovations needed for the doctrine or the doctrinal and organizational capabilities needed for the techonological capability. Either way, on neither the technological nor the architectural front has the innovation thus far progressed sufficiently to qualify as disruptive rather than sustaining, but neither have the technological and architectural innovations yet coalesced into a coherent whole.[88]

Conclusions

The analytical framework developed here, featuring defense and military innovation's technological, doctrinal, and organizational components, innovation capacity or potential (or inputs), the process of innovation, and its outputs and impact, should significantly facilitate efforts to analyze China's military innovation programs and assess their importance. It directs us to the foci—technological, doctrinal, and organizational—of military innovation and to its nature and extent. The framework particularly highlights the need to distinguish among inputs, process, and outputs. Even quantitatively impressive, high-quality inputs will not yield significant outputs in the face of inefficient and ineffective processes.

To date, China's military innovation programs have been more technologically than doctrinally or organizationally focused. Doctrinal and organizational changes appear to lag behind technological advances. This is hardly surprising, however; the development of new capabilities frequently precedes the emergence of new ways of war. It is not clear that the quality of soft capability inputs matches the quality and quantity of hard capability inputs. Thus far, speculation and experimentation have not led to extensive implementation. Duplicative imitation, creative imitation, creative adaptation, and incremental innovation have been more prevalent than architectural and component or modular innovation.

The advances that are most in evidence in China are more incremental than discontinuous and less disruptive than sustaining. Again, this should not be surprising; for every large-scale, disruptive innovation, there have historically been many small-scale, incremental ones. But China's progress on areas as diverse as anti-ship ballistic missiles, information warfare, and anti-satellite weaponry evidence concerted effort in areas that could yield disruptive innovation.

It is important to understand the scope and pace of Chinese developments. There is, on the one hand, the danger of overestimating the extent of Chinese military modernization, of crediting China with capabilities that it does not possess. Overestimation would threaten to increase the pressure for competitive arms dynamics in the region. There is also, however, the danger of underestimating Chinese military modernization. Doing so would open up the United States and other regional actors to surprise in the event of a future crisis or conflict.

An analytical framework such as that described in this chapter will help analysts and policy makers more accurately assess Chinese defense and military innovation. It should guard against both alarmism and complacency.

NOTES

The authors would particularly like to acknowledge Major Steve Fino and Michael Horowitz for their helpful comments.

1. See, for instance, Alan I. Leshner, "Innovation Needs Novel Thinking," *Science* 332, no. 6033 (May 27, 2011): 1009.

2. On national innovation systems, see Charles Edquist, *Systems of Innovation: Technologies, Institutions and Organizations* (London: Pinter, 1997); Bengt-Åke Lundvall, ed., *National Systems of Innovation: Towards a Theory of Innovation and Interactive Learning* (London: Pinter, 1992); and Richard R. Nelson, ed., *National Innovation Systems: A Comparative Analysis* (New York: Oxford University Press, 1993). A useful review of the national innovation literature is provided by Bengt-Åke Lundvall, Björn Johnson, Esben Sloth Andersen, and Bent Dalum, "National Systems of Production, Innovation and Competence Building," *Research Policy* 31, no. 2 (2002): 213–231. For a useful discussion of the US defense innovation system, see Paul Bracken, Linda Brandt, and Stuart E. Johnson, "The Changing Landscape of Defense Innovation," *Defense Horizons* 47 (July 2005). For an application of the national innovation system work to China, see Xue Lan and Nancy Forbes, "Will China Become a Science and Technology Superpower by 2020? An Assessment based on a National Innovation Framework," *Innovations* 1, no. 4 (Fall 2006): 111–126.

3. On users as innovators, see Eric von Hippel, *The Sources of Innovation* (New York: Oxford University Press, 1988).

4. See George W. Downs, Jr., and Lawrence B. Mohr, "Conceptual Issues in the Study of Innovation," *Administrative Science Quarterly* 21, no. 4 (December 1976): 700–714. For Downs and Mohr, innovation is the adoption of new means and ends.

5. Michael E. Porter, *The Competitive Advantage of Nations* (New York: Free Press, 1990), 45.

6. Jan Fagerberg, "Innovation: A Guide to the Literature," in Jan Fagerberg, David C. Mowery, and Richard R. Nelson, eds. *The Oxford Handbook of Innovation* (Oxford: Oxford University Press, 2005), 4. See also Mark Stefik and Barbara Stefik, *Breakthrough: Stories and Strategies of Radical Innovation* (Cambridge, MA: MIT Press, 2004).

7. See, for instance, James M. Utterback, *Mastering the Dynamics of Innovation* (Boston: Harvard Business School Press, 1994).

8. A call for a greater focus on process innovation is provided by Bracken, Brandt, and Johnson, "The Changing Landscape of Defense Innovation."

9. Clayton M. Christensen, *The Innovator's Dilemma* (New York: HarperBusiness, 2000), xvi.

10. On contemporary strategic innovation, see Lawrence Freedman, *The Revolution in Strategic Affairs*, Adelphi Paper 318 (Oxford: Oxford University Press, for the International Institute for Strategic Studies, 1998); and Lawrence Freedman, *The Transforma-

tion of Strategic Affairs, Adelphi Paper 379 (Milton Park, Abingdon, UK: Routledge, for the International Institute for Strategic Studies, 2006).

11. For a survey of US grand strategy alternatives, see Barry R. Posen and Andrew L. Ross, "Competing Visions for U.S. Grand Strategy," *International Security* 21, no. 3 (Winter 1996/97): 5–53.

12. This is true for those defense establishments, at least, in which the military is subordinate to civilian rule.

13. See Alain C. Enthoven and K. Wayne Smith, *How Much Is Enough? Shaping the Defense Program, 1961–1969* (New York: Harper & Row, 1971).

14. For an intriguing discussion of technologically driven diplomatic innovation, see Jesse Lichtenstein, "Digital Diplomacy," *New York Times Magazine*, July 18, 2010, 25–29.

15. Jan Fagerberg and Koson Sapprasert, "Innovation: Exploring the Knowledge Base" (TIK Working Papers on Innovation Studies, Centre for Technology, Innovation, and Culture, University of Oslo, June 2010), 2.

16. For an excellent overview of the literature on military innovation, see Adam Grissom, "The Future of Military Innovation Studies," *Journal of Strategic Studies* 29, no. 5 (October 2006), 905–934.

17. Benoît Godin, "National Innovation System: A Note on the Origins of a Concept," working paper, Project on the Intellectual History of Innovation (Montreal: INRS, 2010), 4–5.

18. Nelson, *National Innovation Systems*, 508.

19. Ibid., 513.

20. Judith Reppy, "Conceptualizing the Role of Defense Industries in National Systems of Innovation," in Judith Reppy, ed., *The Place of the Defense Industry in National Systems of Innovation*, Peace Studies Program Occasional Papers No. 25 (Ithaca: Cornell University Peace Studies Program, April 2000).

21. Andrew James, "Reevaluating the Role of Defense and Security R&D in the Innovation System," *Journal of Technology Transfer* 34, no. 5 (2009): 449–454.

22. See Matthew Evangelista, *Innovation and the Arms Race: How the United States and the Soviet Union Develop New Military Technologies* (Ithaca: Cornell University Press, 1988); Barry R. Posen, *The Sources of Military Doctrine: France, Britain, and Germany between the World Wars* (Ithaca: Cornell University Press, 1984); Stephen Peter Rosen, "New Ways of War: Understanding Military Innovation," *International Security* 13, no. 1 (Summer 1988); Stephen Peter Rosen, *Winning the Next War: Innovation and the Modern Military* (Ithaca: Cornell University Press 1991); Kimberly Marten Zisk, *Engaging the Enemy: Organizational Theory and Soviet Military Innovation, 1955–1991* (Princeton: Princeton University Press, 1993); Peter Dombrowski, Eugene Gholz, and Andrew L. Ross, *Military Transformation and the Defense Industry after Next: The Defense Industrial Implications of Network-Centric Warfare*, Newport Paper No. 18 (Newport, RI: U.S. Naval War College Press, 2003); and Peter Dombrowski and Eugene Gholz, *Buying Military Transformation: Technological Innovation and the Defense Industry* (New York: Columbia University Press, 2006).

23. Posen, *The Sources of Military Doctrine*.

24. Harvey M. Sapolsky, "On the Theory of Military Innovation," *Breakthroughs* 9, no. 1 (Spring 2000): 35–39; Owen R. Coté, "The Politics of Innovative Military Doctrine," Ph.D. diss., Massachusetts Institute of Technology, 1996.

25. Rosen, *Winning the Next War.*

26. Theo Farrell and Terry Terriff, eds., *The Sources of Military Change: Culture, Politics, Technology* (Boulder: Lynne Rienner, 2002); Thomas G. Mahnken, *Technology and the American Way of War since 1945* (New York: Columbia University Press, 2008); Thomas G. Mahnken and James R. FitzSimonds, *The Limits of Transformation: Officer Attitudes Toward the Revolution in Military Affairs* (Newport, R.I.: Naval War College Press, 2003).

27. See, for example, the cases in Williamson Murray and Allan R. Millett, eds., *Military Innovation in the Interwar Period* (New York: Cambridge University Press, 1996).

28. Mahnken, *Technology and the American Way of War since 1945*, 15–59.

29. Thomas G. Mahnken, "Weapons: The Growth and Spread of the Precision-Strike Regime," *Daedalus* 140, no. 3 (Summer 2011).

30. Posen, *The Sources of Military Doctrine*, 29–33, 47.

31. Rosen, *Winning the Next War*, 7, 25. Further, Rosen writes: "A major innovation involves a change in the concepts of operations of that combat arm, that is, the ideas governing the ways it uses its forces to win a campaign, as opposed to a tactical innovation. . . . A major innovation also involves a change in the relation of that combat arm to other combat arms and a downgrading or abandoning of other concepts of operation and possibly of a formerly dominant weapon system" (7–8).

32. Harvey M. Sapolsky, "On the Theory of Military Innovation," *Breakthroughs* 9, no. 1 (Spring 2000): 38.

33. Dima Adamsky, *The Culture of Military Innovation: The Impact of Cultural Factors on the Revolution in Military Affairs in Russia, the US, and Israel* (Palo Alto: Stanford University Press, 2010), 1.

34. Michael C. Horowitz, *The Diffusion of Military Power: Causes and Consequences for International Politics* (Princeton: Princeton University Press, 2010), 22.

35. Porter, *The Competitive Advantage of Nations*, 45.

36. Andrew F. Krepinevich, "Cavalry to Computer: The Pattern of Military Revolutions," *The National Interest*, no. 37 (Fall 1994): 30. Highlights of the extensive literature on military revolutions and revolutions in military affairs include Bernard Brodie, "Technological Change, Strategic Doctrine, and Political Outcomes," in Klaus Knorr, ed., *Historical Dimensions of National Security Problems* (Lawrence: University Press of Kansas, 1976), 263–306; Bernard and Fawn Brodie, *From Crossbow to H-Bomb* (New York: Dell, 1962); Jeremy Black, *A Military Revolution? Military Change and European Society, 1550–1800* (Atlantic Highlands, NJ: Humanities Press International, 1991); MacGregor Knox and Williamson Murray, eds., *The Dynamics of Military Revolution, 1300–2050* (Cambridge: Cambridge University Press, 2001); Murray and Millett, *Military Innovation in the Interwar Period*; Peter Paret, "Revolutions in Warfare: An Earlier Generation of Interpreters," in Bernard Brodie, Michael D. Intriligator, and Roman Kolkowicz, eds., *National Security and International Stability* (Cambridge: Oelgeschlager, Gunn & Hain, 1983), 157–169; Geoffrey Parker, *The Military Revolution: Military Innovation and the Rise of the West, 1500–1800*, 2nd ed., (Cambridge: Cambridge University Press, 1996); and Clifford J. Rogers, ed., *The Military Revolution Debate: Readings on the Military Transformation of Early Modern Europe* (Boulder: Westview Press, 1995).

37. The nine military revolutions Krepinevich lists are infantry, artillery, sail and shot, fortress, gunpowder, Napoleonic, naval, those of mechanization, aviation, and information between the world wars, and nuclear.

38. Williamson Murray and MacGregor Knox, "Thinking about Revolutions in Warfare," in MacGregor Knox and Williamson Murray, eds., *The Dynamics of Military Revolution, 1300–2050* (Cambridge: Cambridge University Press, 2001), 6–7.

39. The military revolutions listed by Murray and Knox are the 17th-century creation of the modern state and its associated military institutions, the 18th-century French Revolution, the Industrial Revolution of the late 19th and early 20th centuries, the First World War, and the nuclear revolution. For Murray and Knox, "revolutions in military affairs" are seen as distinctly lesser affairs: "less all-embracing," "lesser transformations" that "require the assembly of a complex mix of tactical, organizational, doctrinal, and technological revolutions in order to implement a new conceptual approach to warfare or to a specialized sub-branch of warfare" (12). The list of RMAs compiled by Murray and Knox includes the revolutions identified by Krepinevich that didn't qualify as one of their five military revolutions.

40. Mahnken, "Weapons."

41. Adamsky, *The Culture of Military Innovation*, 1.

42. The infrequence of a confluence of new weaponry, new ways of fighting, and new original structures explains why scholars' lists of revolutions are rather short.

43. As quoted in Rosen, *Winning the Next War*, 1.

44. The key Western works have covered issues such as the structure and reform of the defense industry, defense conversion, development of the strategic weapons sector, arms trade and proliferation, Russian military assistance, weapons developments, commercialization, and technology transfer activities. The bulk of work on dual-use-related issues has focused on defense conversion that appeared during the heyday of the Chinese defense conversion drive in the 1980s and first half of the 1990s. For an excellent critique of the state of the field in the study of the Chinese defense economy at the beginning of the 21st century, see Bates Gill, "Chinese Military-Technical Development: The Record for Western Assessments, 1979–1999," in James C. Mulvenon and Andrew N. D. Yang, eds., *Seeking Truth from Facts: A Retrospective on Chinese Military Studies in the Post-Mao Era* (Santa Monica: RAND Corp., 2001), 141–172.

45. See Tai Ming Cheung, *Fortifying China* (Ithaca: Cornell University Press, 2009).

46. On technology and the technological component of innovation, see Colin S. Gray, "Technology as a Dynamic of Defense Transformation," *Defense Studies* 6, no. 1 (March 2006): 26–51; and Andrew L. Ross, "The Dynamics of Military Technology," in David Dewitt, David Haglund, and John Kirton, eds., *Building a New Global Order: Emerging Trends in International Security* (Toronto: Oxford University Press, 1993), 106–140.

47. The distinction between "hardware" and "software" employed here is drawn from Ross, "The Dynamics of Military Technology," 106–140.

48. As Fred Iklé aptly observed, "military services cling to the types of weapons to which they have become accustomed, seeking marginal improvements rather than radical innovation." Fred Charles Iklé, "Can Nuclear Deterrence Last Out the Century?" *Foreign Affairs* 51, no. 2 (January 1973): 384. For an insightful examination of the relationship between organizations, or institutions, and technology, see Timothy Moy, *War*

Machines: Transforming Technologies in the U.S. Military, 1920–1940 (College Station: Texas A&M University Press, 2001).

49. Moses Abramovitz, "Catching Up, Forging Ahead, and Falling Behind," *Journal of Economic History* 46, no. 2 (June 1986): 385–406.

50. This campaign is known as the "Four Mechanisms" and involves: (1) competition, which focused on overhauling outdated contract and project management systems; (2) evaluation, which involved the setting up of an independent and robust evaluation system; (3) supervision, which sought to tackle widespread malpractices and bolster greater disciplinary oversight; and (4) encouragement and incentivization, which aimed to improve motivation among employees through ideological campaigns, better human resource management, and the use of financial incentives. For more details, see Cheung, *Fortifying China*, 129–132.

51. See Chapter 2 of this volume.

52. "CMC Vice Chairman Guo Boxiong Speaks at Founding of Strategic Planning Department," *Liberation Army Daily*, November 23, 2011, 1.

53. Thomas G. Mahnken, *Uncovering Ways of War: U.S. Military Intelligence and Foreign Military Innovation, 1918–1941* (Ithaca: Cornell University Press, 2002).

54. James S. Corum, *The Roots of Blitzkrieg: Hans von Seeckt and German Military Reform* (Lawrence: University of Kansas Press, 1992), 37–38.

55. John T. Hendrix, "The Interwar Army and Mechanization: The American Approach," *Journal of Strategic Studies* 16, no. 1 (March 1993): 78–82; Timothy K. Nenninger, "The Experimental Mechanized Forces," *Armor* 78, no. 3 (May–June 1969).

56. On the development of armored warfare during the interwar period, see Captain Jonathan M. House, US Army, *Toward Combined Arms Warfare: A Survey of 20th-Century Tactics, Doctrine, and Organization*, Combat Studies Institute Research Survey No. 2 (Fort Leavenworth, KS: US Army Command and General Staff College, 1984); Richard M. Ogorkiewicz, *Armor: A History of Mechanized Forces* (New York: Frederick A. Praeger, 1960).

57. Rosen, *Winning the Next War*, 69.

58. Allan R. Millett and Peter Maslowski, *For the Common Defense: A Military History of the United States of America* (New York: Free Press, 1984), 376.

59. Captain B. H. Liddell Hart, *The Tanks: The History of the Royal Tank Regiment and its Predecessors Heavy Branch Machine-Gun Corps, Tank Corps, and Royal Tank Corps, 1914–1945*, vol. 1, *1914–1939* (London: Cassel and Company, 1959), 292–294.

60. Allan R. Millett, "Assault from the Sea: The Development of Amphibious Warfare Between the Wars—the American, British, and Japanese Experiences," in Williamson Murray and Allan R. Millett, eds., *Military Innovation in the Interwar Period* (Cambridge: Cambridge University Press, 1996), 76–77.

61. David C. Evans and Mark R. Peattie, *Kaigun: Strategy, Tactics, and Technology in the Imperial Japanese Navy, 1887–1941* (Annapolis, MD: Naval Institute Press, 1997), 347–352.

62. Colonel Masanobu Tsuji, *Japan's Greatest Victory, Britain's Worst Defeat*, ed. H. V. Howe, trans. Margaret E. Lake (New York: Sarpedon Books, 1993), 1–18.

63. Thomas G. Mahnken, "China's Anti-Access Strategy in Historical and Theoretical Perspective," *Journal of Strategic Studies* 34, no. 3 (June 2011).

64. Rebecca Henderson and Kim Clark, "Architectural Innovation: The Reconfiguration of Existing Product Technologies and the Failure of Established Firms," *Administrative Science Quarterly* 35, no. 1 (March 1990): 10.

65. Linsu Kim and Richard R. Nelson, eds., *Technology, Learning, and Innovation* (Cambridge: Cambridge University Press, 2000), 3–5.

66. Ibid., 5.

67. Sheng Zhu and Yongjiang Shi, "Shanzhai Manufacturing: An Alternative Innovation Phenomenon in China," *Journal of Science and Technology in China* 1, no. 1 (2010): 29–49.

68. Dieter Ernst, *A New Geography of Knowledge in the Electronics Industry? Asia's Role in Global Innovation Networks*, Policy Studies No. 54 (Honolulu: Honolulu East-West Center, 2009), 10.

69. Andrew L. Ross, "On Military Innovation: Toward an Analytical Framework," in Tai Ming Cheung, ed., *China's Emergence as a Defense Technological Power* (Milton Park, Abingdon, UK; Routledge, 2013).

70. See Mahnken, "China's Anti-Access Strategy in Historical and Theoretical Perspective," 299–324; and Andrew Erickson and David Yang, "Using the Land to Control the Sea? Chinese Analysts Consider the Anti-Ship Ballistic Missile," *Naval War College Review* 62, no. 4, (Autumn 2009): 53–86.

71. Kirkor Bozdogan, John Deyst, David Hoult, and Malee Lucas, "Architectural Innovation in Product Development Through Early Supplier Integration," *R&D Management* 28, no. 3 (1998): 163.

72. Hua Wang, "Innovation in Product Architecture: A Study of the Chinese Automobile Industry," *Journal of Asia Pacific Journal of Management* 25, no. 3 (2008): 509–535.

73. Gao Lu, "Chinese Jetliner Development Is on Track," *Guoji Xianqu Daobao*, June 9, 2009.

74. Michael Mecham, "Yankee Support," *Aviation Week and Space Technology*, July 19, 2010, 59–60.

75. Organization for Economic Cooperation and Development (OECD), *The Shipbuilding Industry in China*, (Paris: OECD, June 2008), 8.

76. See Cheung, *Fortifying China*, 22–51.

77. The material in the following section draws upon and develops work presented in Ross, "On Military Innovation."

78. The distinction between sustaining and disruptive innovation employed here is drawn from Christensen, *The Innovator's Dilemma*. See also Joseph L. Bower and Clayton M. Christensen, "Disruptive Technologies: Catching the Wave," *Harvard Business Review* (January–February 1995): 43–53; Clayton M. Christensen and Michael Overdorf, "Meeting the Challenge of Disruptive Change," *Harvard Business Review* (March–April 2000): 67–76; Clayton M. Christensen, Mark W. Johnson, and Darrell K. Rigby, "Foundations for Growth: How to Identify and Build Disruptive New Businesses," *MIT Sloan Management Review* 43, no. 3 (2002): 22–31; Clayton M. Christensen, "The Rules of Innovation," *Technology Review* 105, no. 5 (2002): 33–38; Clayton M. Christensen and Michael E. Raynor, *The Innovator's Solution: Creating and Sustaining Successful Growth* (Boston: Harvard Business School Press, 2003); and Clayton M. Christensen, Scott D. Anthony, and Erik A. Roth, *Seeing What's Next: Using the Theories of Innovation to Predict*

Industry Change (Boston: Harvard Business School Press, 2004). Peter Dombrowski and Eugene Gholz, "Identifying Disruptive Innovation: Innovation Theory and the Defense Industry," *Innovations* 4, no. 2 (Spring 2009): 101–117, further develop the concept of disruptive innovation.

79. Joseph A. Schumpeter, *Capitalism, Socialism and Democracy*, 3rd ed. (New York: Harper & Row, 1950). The distinction between sustaining and disruptive innovation made by Christensen and employed here echoes that between incremental and radical innovation made by Rebecca Henderson in "Underinvestment and Incompetence as Responses to Radical Innovation: Evidence from the Photolithographic Alignment Equipment Industry," *RAND Journal of Economics* 24, no. 2 (Summer 1993): 248–270.

80. The emphasis in the matrix is distinctly focused upon outputs: technology, doctrine, and organization. The approach developed by Tai Ming Cheung in his insightful contribution, "The Chinese Defense Economy's Long March from Imitation to Innovation," *Journal of Strategic Studies* 34, no. 3 (June 2011), is input oriented. The defense industrialization stages described by Tai Ming Cheung echo those laid out in Andrew L. Ross, "Developing Countries," in Andrew J. Pierre, ed., *Cascade of Arms: Managing Conventional Weapons Proliferation* (Washington, DC: Brookings Institution, 1997), 89–127.

81. Stefik and Stefik, *Breakthrough*, 3.

82. On the concept of architectural innovation, see Henderson and Clark, "Architectural Innovation," 9–30. Terry C. Pierce, *Warfighting and Disruptive Technologies: Disguising Innovation* (London: Frank Cass, 2004), insightfully employs the concepts of sustaining, disruptive, and architectural innovation to great effect, though for somewhat different purposes than here.

83. Henderson and Clark, "Architectural Innovation," 12.

84. These are performance metrics that hold no small appeal to transformation's advocates; see Christensen, *The Innovator's Dilemma*, xviii. On the significance of performance metrics see Dombrowski, Gholz, and Ross, *Military Transformation and the Defense Industry after Next*; and Dombrowski and Gholz, *Buying Military Transformation*.

85. Cynthia C. Kelly, ed., *The Manhattan Project: The Birth of the Atomic Bomb in the Words of Its Creators, Eyewitnesses, and Historians* (New York: Black Dog & Leventhal Publishers, 2007). On the nuclear revolution as a military revolution or revolution in military affairs, see Andrew L. Ross, "You Say You Had a Revolution: The Nuclear Revolution Revisited," presented at the Annual Convention of the International Studies Association, New Orleans, February 16–20, 2010).

86. P. W. Singer, "Wired for War? Robots and Military Doctrine," *Joint Forces Quarterly*, no. 52 (Winter 2009): 104–110.

87. William A. Owens, Kenneth W. Dam, and Herbert S. Lin, eds., *Technology, Policy, Law, and Ethics Regarding U.S. Acquisition and Use of Cyberattack Capabilities* (Washington, DC: National Academies Press, 2009).

88. On just how nontransformational the US transformation enterprise was during these years, see Peter J. Dombrowski and Andrew L. Ross, "Transforming the Navy: Punching a Featherbed?" *Naval War College Review* 56, no. 3 (Summer 2003): 107–131; and Steven Metz, "America's Defense Transformation: A Conceptual and Political History," *Defense Studies* 6, no. 1 (March 2006): 1–25.

Chapter Two

An Uncertain Transition

Regulatory Reform and Industrial Innovation in China's Defense Research, Development, and Acquisition System

Tai Ming Cheung

The Chinese defense science, technology, and industrial base is battling to transform itself from a bastion of central planning into a more open, rules-based system that will allow technological innovation to flourish. Important progress is being made in loosening the deadening grip of the state, nurturing competition among enterprises, and improving the quality of defense output. However, deep-seated structural and governance problems remain, and the Chinese defense economy is in danger of being bogged down in an uncertain transition that could seriously impede its cherished goal of becoming a world-class defense technological power.

A prime arena in this struggle for reform is the defense research, development, and acquisition (RDA) system, which is the backbone of a country's ability to organize and carry out the development and production of weapons systems. As a product of the Maoist command economy, the Chinese RDA system suffers from bureaucratic fragmentation, politicized decision making, nontransparency, ad hoc implementation, and weak market mechanisms. Major organizational and regulatory reforms have been undertaken to address these deficiencies, such as enhancing the authority and influence of the General Armament Department (GAD) of the People's Liberation Army (PLA), but much more remains to be done.

This chapter explores the present state of China's defense RDA system using two analytical approaches borrowed from the fields of economic regulatory policy and industrial management. Using these two approaches, we look at various aspects of the structures and processes of the Chinese RDA system that are critical to addressing the question of whether the Chinese defense science, technology, and industrial base (DSTIB) can become truly innovative and effective in producing advanced weapons. The first perspective examines changing models of regulatory reform, especially efforts to shift from a coercive command and control regulatory model to a more Western-style indirect, independent regulatory regime. The second approach focuses on the evolving nature of push-pull interactions between technology developers and military end-users, viewing them with insights from the academic literature on models of industrial innovation.

Defining the Defense Research, Development, and Acquisition System

Using the RDA paradigm to assess a country's DSTIB has considerable analytical merit, because the defense RDA system encapsulates the way a country and its defense establishment organize and provide the economic, technological, human, and industrial resources and capabilities to meet its present and future defense needs. The defense RDA apparatus refers to the complex ecosystem of organizations and rules responsible for the conceptualization, design, engineering, testing, production, and operation of weapons systems.[1] Numerous actors are involved in this process, ranging from scientific research institutes and defense contractors to military end-users and state regulatory bodies. This system can include both domestic and foreign entities as many countries participate in both national and international defense RDA projects.

The RDA process can be defined as the approach that a country uses to acquire weapons, whether indigenously or with foreign assistance, and which involves multiple phases of development and related activities.[2] The current Chinese defense RDA process resembles the five key phases of the U.S. defense RDA approach (see Figure 2.1):[3]

1. Comprehensive Feasibility Study Stage (综合可行性阶段): Joint undertakings by military end-users and defense industry research and development (R&D) entities occur to examine the operational needs of war-fighters for the equipment, tactical and technical requirements and specifications, and acquisition, and the life-cycle costs of producing them. The feasibility study provides the basis for drawing up R&D work contracts. This stage is also referred to as the Project Development Stage (研制立项阶段).

The Stages of the Chinese Defense RDA Process

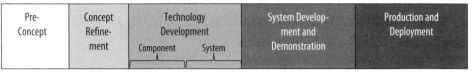

The Stages of the US Defense RDA Process

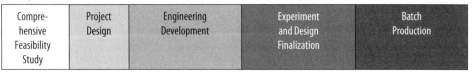

Figure 2.1. Stages of the Chinese and US defense RDA processes compared

2. Project Design Stage (项目设计阶段): R&D entities are contracted to carry out comprehensive project design, model development, full life-cycle analysis, and the scientific and practical demonstration and verification of the new equipment. The GAD then reviews the results for approval to enter the development phase. The second stage is also known as the Project General Requirements Determination Stage (确定研制总要求阶段).

3. Engineering Development Stage (工程研制阶段): Full-scale development takes place, which includes full-scale design, trial manufacturing, and development and evaluation of test models. Preparatory work also begins for small batch production and computer simulation of production processes. Once design requirements are met, final reports are submitted for finalization tests.

4. Experiment and Design Finalization Stage (试验和设计定型阶段): Final inspection of the designs and standards of the equipment is carried out. This includes testing of both development and batch production equipment. Both specialized testing centers and frontline military units carry out this testing.

5. Batch Production Stage (批量生产阶段): This is when weapons systems complete their research and development process and receive final approval for serial production and entry into service.

Approach 1: Regulatory System Reform in the Chinese Defense Industry and RDA System

The Chinese defense RDA system is a prime example of a classic command and control (CAC) regulatory system, in which authorities rely on administrative coercion and threats to achieve compliance, state agencies are responsible for direct micromanagement and rule making, and the primary focus of rules and regulations is on enterprises' performance and outputs.[4] While this top-down regulatory approach may work in a centrally planned system, it is ill suited to market-based environments. One major reason is that activity-based intervention requires regulatory agencies to have adequate information to monitor what is going on, but their access to data is limited in more open markets, where they play a less direct regulatory role and enterprises have greater autonomy and privacy. When the Commission for Science, Technology, and Industry for National Defense (COSTIND) was restructured in the late 1990s and its responsibilities were shifted from direct to indirect management of the defense industry, its ability to carry out CAC-style regulatory oversight was fundamentally compromised.

Another drawback to using a CAC model in an open-market economy is that rulebooks governing CAC regulatory behavior would have to be extremely detailed and difficult to enforce in a market-based or an increasingly developed economy. The Soviet Union's State Planning Committee, or Gosplan, exemplifies the folly of CAC management; it required a huge bureaucracy—50,000 employees—to administer an ever-expanding list of regulations in overseeing millions of products.[5] COSTIND also was a sprawling bureaucracy, and it was only concerned with managing activities, not also performance.

These glaring deficiencies in the CAC model led some civilian sectors in the Chinese economy to begin to search for alternative models of regulatory control, starting in the early 1990s. Two very different approaches vied for attention. One followed an East Asian state development regulatory model and the other an independent regulator system model; the latter is the standard in developed market economies, especially in Western Europe and North America. The East Asian development model is based on Japan's post–World War II regulatory model and is tolerant of state intervention to manage markets, favors well-connected firms, supports the creation of national champions, discourages excessive competition, and involves limited public accountability or transparency.[6] In contrast, the independent regulatory system emphasizes the importance of political independence, impartiality, and transparency.

While the independent regulator model is regarded as the international standard, Chinese policy makers and regulators were attracted to the developmental model because it fit closer with their preexisting regulatory practices and thinking. The 21st-century Chinese regulatory state model appears to be a hybrid, featuring elements of both the independent regulator and the development frameworks, although with a bias towards the latter model. This hybrid system includes nurturing the building of national champions, protecting favored state firms, and allowing only limited competition. Moreover, when new regulatory bodies are established, they inherit the norms, biases, and institutional interests of their predecessors and employ the same personnel. These practices are especially noticeable in areas of the economy that the Chinese authorities have deemed to be strategic in nature, such as energy, financial services, and telecommunications.[7]

The state-owned defense industry began to take concrete steps towards the establishment of a more independent regulatory structure in the late 1990s. One of its principal initiatives was downgrading the authority and reach of COSTIND. The commission's overarching and intrusive micromanagement of the defense industry was significantly curtailed after the late 1990s, allowing defense corporations more independence and the PLA a greater voice and involvement in the RDA process. COSTIND's status suffered another blow in 2008 when it was demoted by two administrative ranks, first from a state commission to a state administration and then subsumed into the newly created Ministry of Industry and Information Technology (MIIT).[8]

Hand in hand with these organizational reforms came the building of a multitiered assemblage of laws and regulations covering armament acquisitions and contracts. To pave the way for a detailed legal and regulatory framework, a series of national-level laws had to be enacted first. This included the 1997 National Defense Law and 1999 State Contract Law, both of which were passed by the National People's Congress. At the next level down, the Central Military Commission began to promulgate PLA-wide regulations beginning in 2000. They included the 2000 PLA Armament Regulations, 2004 PLA Armament Research and Development Regulations, and the 2002 PLA Armament Procurement Regulations. Finally, at the working level, the GAD began enacting administrative rules from 2000. They included the 2003 Provisions for the Management of Armament Procurement Plans and the 2003 Provisions on the Management of Armament Procurement Contracts.[9]

While these reform initiatives look impressive, they have so far had only limited impact in fundamentally moving the ingrained central planning institutional norms and operating principles, routines, and habits of the defense industry towards a more rules-based governance culture. Key aspects of the defense RDA system and process continue to operate in the same manner as during the command economy period. PLA acquisition experts point to a long menu of key difficulties. Four of the biggest and most intractable issues will be discussed here.

First, there is little competition for the award of major contracts for weapons systems and defense equipment because of the monopolistic structure of the defense industry. Contracts continue to be awarded through single-sourcing mechanisms to the small coterie of dominant state-owned defense corporations. Competitive bidding and tendering takes place for only noncombat, support equipment, such as logistics supplies. An effort in 1999 to inject more competition by splitting in two each of the companies in charge of the six defense industrial subsectors did little to curb monopolistic practices. PLA and civilian defense acquisition specialists believe that the defense industry's continuing monopoly structure represents the biggest obstacle to a transition away from its central planning legacy.[10]

Second, the PLA continues to rely on outdated administrative tools to manage projects with defense contractors, in the absence of the establishment of an effective contract management system. The PLA did implement the use of contracts on a trial basis in the late 1980s, introducing a contract responsibility system.[11] These contracts are administrative in nature, though, and have little legal standing because there is no developed legal framework within the DSTIB. Consequently, contracts are vague and do not define obligations or critical performance issues such as quality, pricing, or schedules. Contracts for complex weapons projects can be as short as one or two pages, according to analysts.[12]

Moreover, the PLA acquisition apparatus is woefully backward in many other management approaches and tools that it uses compared to its counterparts in the United States and other advanced military powers. It has yet to adopt total life-cycle management methods, for example, and many internal management information systems are on stand-alone networks that prevent effective communications and coordination. One analyst interviewed in 2011 said that this often meant that the only way for project teams to exchange information was through paper transactions.[13]

Third, bureaucratic fragmentation remains a serious problem and afflicts a number of critical coordination and command mechanisms within the PLA and RDA systems. One glaring flaw is that the GAD is responsible for managing the armament needs of only the ground forces, the People's Armed Police, and the militia.[14] The navy, air force, and Second Artillery have their own armament bureaucracies, and competition is fierce for budgetary resources to support projects favored by each of these services. This compartmentalized structure serves to intensify parochial interests and undermine efforts to promote joint undertakings.

Also problematic are coordination gaps and bureaucratic rivalries between the GAD, the General Staff Department (GSD) and General Logistics Department (GLD) in areas such as policy planning, resource allocations, and drafting of longer-term development plans.[15] This led the military authorities to establish the Strategic Planning Department (SPD) in 2011; it is charged with "strengthening the strategic management functions of the Central Military Commission," according to CMC Vice Chairman General Guo Boxiong.[16] However, the nascent SPD is struggling to assert its presence in the face of the reluctance of the GAD and GLD to allow any diminution of their authority and influence over key management, budgetary, and planning issues.[17]

The RDA system also suffers from compartmentalization along many segments of the RDA process. Responsibilities for research and development, testing, procurement, production, and maintenance are in the hands of different units, and under-institutionalization has meant that linkages among these entities tend to be ad hoc in nature with major gaps in oversight, reporting, and information sharing.[18] The fragmented nature of the RDA process may help explain why Hu Jintao was apparently caught by surprise by the first publicized test-flight of the J-20 fighter aircraft, which occurred during the visit of US Defense Secretary Robert Gates in January 2011.[19]

Fourth, the Chinese pricing system for military equipment is broken, and deep-seated institutional competition between the PLA and the defense industry has stymied efforts to fix it. The existing armament pricing framework is based on a cost-plus model that dates to the planned economy, in which contractors are allowed 5 percent profit margins on top of actual costs.[20] There are several drawbacks to this model, which holds back efficiency and innovation. One is that contractors are incentivized to push up costs, as this will also drive up profits. Another problem is that contractors are not rewarded for finding ways to lower costs, through more streamlined management or more cost-effective designs or manufacturing techniques, for example. Contracts rarely include performance incentives, and this discourages risk taking and willingness to adopt innovative approaches. Contractors are also discouraged from making major investments in new technological capabilities or processes because of the low, 5 percent, profit margin that is available.

To address this long-standing problem, the PLA, Ministry of Finance, and National Development and Reform Commission held a high-level meeting on armament pricing reform in 2009, at which it was concluded that the outdated pricing system had seriously restricted weapons development and innovation.[21] Several reform proposals were put forward, three of which were: (1) provide incentives to contain costs, (2) switch from accounting procedures that focus on ex post pricing to ex ante controls, and (3) expand from a single pricing methodology to multiple pricing methods. Some of these ideas were incorporated in a document issued after the meeting, entitled "Opinions on Further Pushing Forward the Reform of Work Concerning the Prices of Military Products." Little concrete progress appears to have been made, however, in implementing these policy initiatives in the past few years.

This discussion of the obstacles that continue to plague the defense industry and RDA system shows how much further they have to go on the journey from the Maoist past to a more market-oriented, rules-based future and how uncertain future progress will be. There is a real risk that the defense industry could find itself trapped partway through a transition in which key segments are left unreformed or partially reformed because of strong opposition from various interest groups. The negative consequences from such selective reform has so far been masked by the abundance of resources that have flowed through the defense industry and RDA system since the late 1990s. But any tightening in budgets because of slowing economic growth could expose the fragilities of this deeply fragmented and flawed system.

Approach 2: Models of Industrial Innovation and Their Application to the Chinese Defense RDA System

Another useful way to examine the defense RDA system is through the conceptualization of technological innovation in industrial systems. This approach has made considerable progress over time and reflects the evolving technological and industrial landscapes as well as academic, policy, and industry debates and inputs as to what are the critical drivers of success and transformation. Successive generations of models have become increasingly more sophisticated and holistic in analyzing the structure and process of industrial innovation.[22]

The first analytical framework emerged in the 1950s and 1960s and viewed industrial innovation as linear in nature. "Technology push" became the first widely adopted analytical explanation of industrial innovation. It broke down the process into sequential steps: basic research, applied research, development, and production and diffusion.[23] In the middle to late 1960s, as more investigation took place into how innovation occurred, especially at the operational level, the "market-pull" model gained prominence. The defense RDA system played a role in promoting this shift, because it was responsible for funding a significant proportion of scientific research during this period. An influential Pentagon-commissioned study in the mid-1960s found that 95 percent of 700 key military innovations had occurred because of an actual need and less than 1 percent had come from "undirected" basic science.[24]

These push and pull variants were combined into a third generation, "coupling" model in the 1970s that incorporated feedback loops to allow for interactions between R&D and market needs. While this model offered some functional integration between the push and pull processes, it remained a linear, sequential framework of analysis. The coupling model has been refined in recent years. One version widely employed within the US defense RDA apparatus is the stage-gate model, which organizes the innovation process into successive stages with reviews (feedback loops) at predetermined milestones to evaluate whether work can progress onto the next stage or needs to be revised (see Figure 2.2).[25]

Borrowing from supply chain management theory on the relationships between buyers and suppliers, this coupling model can be further developed by defining different degrees of coupling between R&D/supplier and buyer/demand-pull parties.[26] A loosely coupled relationship allows suppliers and buyers to be relatively independent of each other and to conduct their interactions through open market bargaining. In a tightly coupled relationship, there is close cooperation

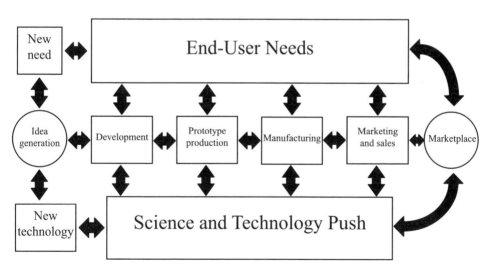

Figure 2.2. Model for coupling of industrial innovation and product development. Adapted from Roy Rothwell, "Successful Industrial Innovation: Critical Factors for the 1990s," *R&D Management* 22, no. 3 (1992): 221–239.

between the buyer and supplier and their interests are aligned. In a fully coupled relationship, the buyer and supplier are completely integrated and committed to each other (see Table 2.1).

Tightly coupled relationships are common in defense RDA processes in the United States and Europe because of their monopsonistic structures. These relationships are also characterized by credible commitments from each side based on their shared interests. By contrast, loosely coupled relationships are often adversarial in nature, and the buyer will use threats of competition and termination to enforce supplier performance and compliance.

A critical limitation of these linear models was revealed in the inherent lack of functional integration among the different activities. In response, a fourth-generation model was developed in the 1980s; it viewed the innovation process as consisting of parallel but integrated activities across the organizational functions. Activities such as idea generation, R&D, testing and evaluation, manufacturing, and marketing would occur in parallel but with close coordination through integrated product teams made up of representa-

Table 2.1 Types and Attributes of Buyer-Supplier Coupling Relationships

	Loosely Coupled Relationship (Competitive Open Market)	Tightly Coupled Relationship (Cooperative)	Fully Coupled Relationship (Vertical Integration)
Nature of overall relationship	Adversarial	Cooperative	Captive
Supplier base	Numerous	Select suppliers	Single internal supplier
Enforcement of relationship obligations	Credible threats	Primarily credible commitments with secondary use of threats	Credible commitments
Dispute resolution	Adversarial (win-lose) negotiations	Cooperative (win-win) negotiations	Trade-offs
Information exchange	Minimal	Extensive	Extensive

Sources: Adapted from Robert Landeros and Robert M. Monczka, "Cooperative Buyer/Seller Relationships and a Firm's Competitive Posture," *Journal of Purchasing and Materials Management* 25 (1989): 9–17; and Carl R. Templin, "Defense Contracting Buyer-Seller Relationships: Theoretical Approaches," *Acquisition Review Quarterly* 1 (1994): 114–28.

tives from all these different activities working together. This model, which is also known as concurrent engineering, was first popularized in the commercial automobile industry in Japan and was adopted by a growing number of US firms during the 1990s. The US Defense Department also embraced the approach, in the mid-1990s, although the track record of the model has been mixed.[27]

As the general study of innovation shifted towards a more systems-oriented approach in the late 1990s, more recent models have focused on comprehensive frameworks of analysis that seek to capture the complex interactions between networks. Different versions of this systems model include open- and closed-innovation models.

Development of the Chinese Defense Industrial Innovation System

China has traveled a very different path of defense industrial innovation than have Western countries. Its opening development phase began in the 1950s and extended to the early 1980s and can be characterized as a top-down sequential model. The central authorities maintained pervasive control over all aspects of the process, from R&D to manufacturing. Innovation came overwhelmingly from foreign technology and knowledge transfers, and technology-push and demand-pull factors played a peripheral role. The strategic weapons industry was a notable exception, though. In this sector, which was responsible for China's development of nuclear weapons and strategic delivery systems such as long-range ballistic missiles, technology-push was the dominant model of innovation (see Figure 2.3).[28]

In the second stage, starting from the mid-1980s, demand-pull drivers began to assert growing influence as the PLA's role in defense RDA grew, but the top-down model persisted because of the dominance of COSTIND. Moreover, as the defense industry underwent a prolonged downturn during this period, amid a sharp drop in military orders and a large shift to civilian output, these pull factors had little impact in improving innovation (see Figure 2.4).

Since the late 1990s, the push-pull coupling model has emerged as the principal model of Chinese defense industrial innovation. There have been intensifying efforts to forge closer interactions between the RDA apparatus and military end-users. The establishment of the GAD and its active involvement in weapons research and development have been a pivotal development in allowing the military apparatus for the first time to occupy a central role in the defense industrial

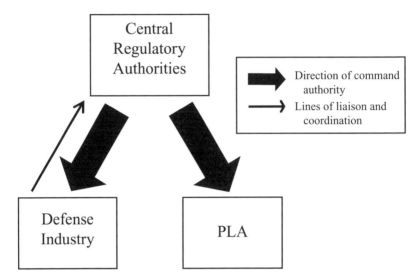

Figure 2.3. Top-down command model of Chinese defense industrial innovation, 1950s–1970s

innovation system. Allied with this has been the curtailment in the authority and role of the COSTIND and its successor, the State Administration for Science, Technology, and Industry for National Defense (SASTIND) from a direct to an indirect regulator (see Figure 2.5).

From its inception, the GAD's relationship with the defense industry has been loosely coupled in nature. Interaction between the two parties was often adversarial and lacked trust. The defense industry's abysmal performance and inability to meet the PLA's needs led military chiefs in the 1990s and the early 2000s to introduce competitive mechanisms into the acquisition process, by looking overseas for arms to meet some of its critical needs. Efforts were also made to inject competition into the RDA system, by overhauling the traditional practice of spreading funding across large numbers of projects with little consideration for performance and a turn to concentrating research budgets instead on fewer, high-priority projects. Efforts were also made to corporatize large numbers of R&D institutes, by allowing major defense conglomerates to take them over. Defense corporations are estimated to have absorbed 90 percent of the defense industry's 300-odd R&D institutes by 2011.[29]

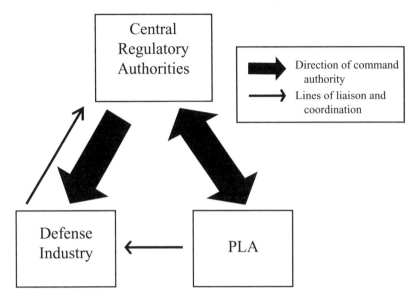

Figure 2.4. Weakening top-down model of Chinese defense industrial innovation, 1980s–1990s

As the defense industry undertook major reforms and the GAD's involvement in the RDA process grew, the relationship between the two began to shift towards a more tightly coupled framework of interaction. Cooperation increased as the PLA's trust in the defense industry began to be restored by the new generations of weapons finally emerging from the development pipeline. Domestic orders rose while foreign imports fell.

An important dimension of this coupled relationship is the role of defense firms. Before the late 1990s reforms, defense enterprise groups that controlled each of the six key defense industrial sectors were state-owned bureaucratic monopolies that had little independence from the central government. The post-1998 reforms have turned around the fortunes of these conglomerates and they have been transformed into profit-oriented, shareholding entities that enjoy operational autonomy while remaining wholly state owned. Moreover, each defense conglomerate was divided into two entities in an effort to promote competition within their industrial sectors. This arrangement was intended to foster friendly cooperation between these firms and the PLA through credible

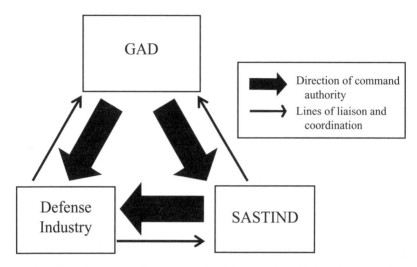

Figure 2.5. Emerging model for coupling of Chinese defense industrial innovation and product development, 2000s–present

commitments, extensive information sharing, and other hallmark features of a tightly coupled relationship.

While the nature of these linkages between defense corporations and the PLA has yet to be fully mapped, these enterprises appear to have benefited handsomely from improved cooperation with the PLA. Revenues and profits for the entire defense industry have grown strongly since early in the first decade of the 2000s. In 2012, total industry profits are estimated to have been around 85 billion renminbi, the highest in its history.[30]

The deepening cooperation and coordination between the PLA and the defense industry appear to be occurring at multiple levels ranging from high-level strategic and doctrinal planning and policy making to factory floors around the country. PLA, civilian defense industry officials, and science and technology (S&T) experts have been cooperating on long-range S&T development plans since early in this century, including the drafting of the 2006–2020 Defense Medium-and Long-Term S&T Development Plan, which was one of the first long-range national plans for defense technological innovation drawn up since the 1950s (see Table 2.2).[31]

A longer-term question is whether the PLA and the Chinese defense industry will adopt integrated parallel models to help further advance the innovation

Table 2.2   Distinguishing Features of the Supplier-Buyer Coupled Relationship
in the Chinese Defense Economy since the 1990s

	Loosely Coupled Relationship (Late 1990s–Mid 2000s)	Tightly Coupled Relationship (Late 2000s–Present)
Competitive structure of defense industrial base	Monopoly structure (single conglomerate for each industrial sector)	Monopsony (two conglomerates for each industrial sector)
Nature of producer-procurer relationship	Adversarial, lack of trust	Cooperative
Information sharing	Limited	Extensive
Integration of R&D base with acquisition and manufacturing base	Compartmentalized	Integrated
Role of regulator	Direct	Indirect

process. These approaches, such as the integrated product and process development at the US Department of Defense, appear to offer faster, more effective, and perhaps more creative solutions to the development of new technological capabilities.[32] But they can also carry substantial risks, especially if management systems are lacking or if product designs are subject to change and uncertainty because of their immaturity or changing end-user requirements.[33] The reworking caused by such circumstances is costly and time-consuming. Some PLA weapons analysts believe that China's deeply entrenched traditional, compartmentalized organizational and management practices are major obstacles to the adoption of new and more efficient parallel processes, such as integrated product teams.[34]

A noteworthy feature of the Chinese defense RDA system is the need for close collaboration among the PLA, defense industry R&D, and industrial entities throughout all the stages of the RDA process. In principle, feasibility studies are a joint undertaking by PLA end-user units and civilian defense R&D entities. While civilian organizations are responsible for project design and engineering development, PLA units led by the GAD review and approve work before it is allowed to progress to the next phase. Testing is also undertaken by defense and PLA organizations. The extent to which this process is actually implemented in practice is far from clear, but the adoption of this tightly coupled arrangement is a promising and important step forward in the development of the Chinese defense industrial innovation system.

Conclusions

The regulatory regime and industrial innovation frameworks of analysis not surprisingly offer contrasting outlooks in assessing the state and future prospects for the Chinese defense RDA system's capacity to conduct innovation. The two frameworks focus on different aspects of the structure and process of the RDA system. From the regulatory systems perspective, the Chinese RDA system is still going through a wrenching reform drive and the prospects for success are far from certain. While important structural and process-related reforms have occurred since the late 1990s, helping to reinvigorate the defense industry's performance and innovative capabilities, these measures have tended to be "low-hanging fruit" reforms that are less controversial and easier to sell to the different constituencies involved. Harder reform targets, such as overhauling the pricing system and breaking up corporate monopolies, are proving far more difficult, if not impossible, to tackle because of the deeply entrenched and powerful political, bureaucratic, and corporate interests that stand in the way and have proven to be highly adept in fighting and winning rear-guard actions. The continuing presence of monopoly structures, absence of competitive pricing mechanisms, bureaucratic fragmentation, lack of incentives, and other legacy problems of the central planning economy seriously undermine the defense industry's innovation capabilities.

The industrial innovation perspective offers a more positive assessment. The foundations for sustainable and increasingly sophisticated forms of innovative activity are being laid, and the deep-rooted barriers inherited from the days of central planning are now being addressed. The relationship between technology push end-user pull has become increasingly tightly coupled, which has led to the gradual reestablishment of more cooperative relationships between the PLA and the defense industry following decades of acrimony and distrust in the 1980s and 1990s.

Taken together, these two perspectives show that the defense industry and RDA system have made steady if uneven progress over the past 15 years to become significantly more innovative and effective. This progress has enabled the defense industry to move beyond a primarily imitation-led model of technological development and to also engage in original, homegrown innovation since the turn of this century.[35] Incremental innovation is becoming an important dimension of this innovation activity, which consists of routine improvements to existing capabilities. There is also evidence that more advanced forms of innovation, such as architectural innovation, are beginning to occur in select areas, such as space, missiles, and cyberwarfare. High-end, disruptive innovation, though, will be problematic as long as the defense industry is still struggling to carry out fundamental reforms in the RDA process and other important parts of the defense industry.

If the Chinese defense industry is to meet its aspirational goal of catching up to the global technology frontier by the beginning of the 2020s, it will need to make a successful transition to a market-oriented, rules-based system or, perhaps more likely, a hybrid model that incorporates elements of both the CAC and independent regulator models. For this to happen, the defense industry will need to make a decisive break from its Maoist past. This will require replacing the incremental, consensus-based process that is currently driving the reform agenda with a far more bold approach that is able to aggressively tackle the root causes of the defense industry's underlying weaknesses. The prospects of this happening appear slim, as the leaders in charge of the defense industrial portfolio within the PLA and defense industry, and their constituencies, firmly favor the present cautious, gradualist approach.

NOTES

1. No universally accepted definition for defense RDA exists as yet, but the US Defense Department captures all the key elements in its definition of defense acquisition, which "includes design, engineering, test and evaluation, production, and operations and support of defense systems." Bradford Brown, *Introduction to Defense Acquisition Management,* (Fort Belvoir, VA: Defense Acquisition University, August 2010), vol. 10, p. 1.

2. See National Air and Space Intelligence Center (NASIC), *People's Liberation Army Air Force 2010* (Wright-Patterson Air Force Base, Ohio, August 2010), 119.

3. The PLA describes the RDA process as the "armament development procedure" (装备研制程序). See Tu Hengzhang, ed., *Military Armament Development [军事装备发展]* (Beijing: Encyclopedia of China Publishing House [中国大百科全书出版社], China Military Encyclopedia, 2nd ed. [中国军事百科全书第二版], 2008), 74–76. The PLA Armament Command and Technology Academy was in charge of organizing this volume. See also Lu Yu, chief ed., *Introduction to Military Equipment Secrecy Work [军事装备工作保密概论]* (Beijing: National Defense Industry Press [国防工业出版社], 2008), Chapter 5. See also Wei Gang and Chen Haoguang, eds., *Introduction to Defense Acquisition Systems [武器装备采办制度概论]* (Beijing: National Defense Industry Press [国防工业出版社], 2008), 188–196; and Shen Jianming, chief ed., *Chinese Defense Project Management Body of Knowledge [中国国防项目管理知识体系]* (Beijing: National Defense Industry Press [国防工业出版社], 2006). The US process is: preconcept (basic research), concept refinement (applied research), technology development (advanced development), systems development and demonstration, and production and deployment.

4. See Anthony Ogus, *Comparing Regulatory Systems: Institutions, Processes and Legal Forms in Industrialized Countries* (Manchester, UK: Centre on Regulation and Competition, University of Manchester, December 2002), 21–22.

5. USSR: *Role of the State Planning Committee (Gosplan)*, Central Intelligence Agency, April 1975, http://www.foia.cia.gov/docs/DOC_0000308042/DOC_0000308042.pdf.

6. Margaret Pearson, "The Business of Governing Business in China: Institutions and Norms of the Emerging Regulatory State," *World Politics* (January 2005): 296–322.

7. See Roselyn Hsueh, *China's Regulatory State* (Ithaca: Cornell University Press, 2011).

8. See Mao Guohui, ed., *Introduction to the Military Armament Legal System [军事装备法律制度概论]* (Beijing: National Defense Industry Press [国防工业出版社], 2012), 58–60.

9. See Tai Ming Cheung, *Fortifying China* (Ithaca: Cornell University Press, 2008), 132–134; and Mao, *Introduction to the Military Armament Legal System*, 4–12.

10. Interviews with PLA acquisition specialists, Beijing and Changsha, November 2011 and June 2012.

11. Cheung, *Fortifying China*, 83–85.

12. Interview with PLA acquisition specialist, Beijing, November 2011.

13. Ibid.

14. Mao, *Introduction to the Military Armament Legal System*, 46.

15. Ibid., 45.

16. "Chairman Hu Jintao and Central Military Commission Decide on the PLA to Organize the Strategic Planning Department," *Liberation Army Daily [解放军报]*, November 23, 2011, p. 1.

17. Interviews with PLA officers who interacted with the SPD within the first six months of its establishment, Beijing, June 2012.

18. See Liu Hanrong and Wang Baoshun, eds., *National Defense Scientific Research Test Project Management [国防科研试验项目管理]* (Beijing: National Defense Industry Press [国防工业出版社], 2009).

19. John Pomfret, "Chinese Army Tests Jet During Gates Visit," *Washington Post*, January 12, 2011; and Elizabeth Bumiller and Michael Wines, "Chinese Army Tests Jet as Gates Visits," *New York Times*, January 12, 2011.

20. Mao, *Introduction to the Military Armament Legal System*, 158–159.

21. Zong Zhaodun and Zhao Bo, "Major Reform Considered in Work on the Prices of Our Army's Armaments," *Liberation Army Daily*, November 13, 2009.

22. See Roy Rothwell, "Successful Industrial Innovation: Critical Factors for the 1990s," *R&D Management* 22, no. 3 (1992): 221–239; and Niek du Preez and Louis Louw, "A Framework for Managing the Innovation Process," Portland International Conference on Management of Engineering and Technology, Portland, Oregon, July 2008, 546–558.

23. For a detailed history of the technology push model, see Benoît Godin, *The Linear Model of Innovation: The Historical Construction of an Analytical Framework*, Project on the History and Sociology of S&T Statistics, Montreal, 2005.

24. See Chalmers Sherwin and Raymond Isenson, "Project Hindsight: A Defense Department Study of the Utility of Research," *Science* 156, no. 3782 (June 1967): 1571–1577.

25. Robert G. Cooper, *Winning at New Products: Accelerating the Process from Idea to Launch,* (Cambridge: Perseus Publishing, 2001).

26. Carl Templin, "Defense Contracting Buyer-Seller Relationships: Theoretical Approaches," *Acquisition Review Quarterly* (Spring 1994): 123–126; and Robert Landeros

and Robert Monczka, "Cooperative Buyer/Seller Relationships and a Firm's Competitive Posture," *Journal of Purchasing and Materials Management* 25 (September 1989): 9–17.

27. The Pentagon issued a directive in 1995 to promote the adoption of this parallel development process in the defense S&T system and published a handbook in 1998. See Department of Defense, *Integrated Product and Process Development Handbook* (Washington, DC: Office of the Under Secretary of Defense Acquisition and Technology, 1998). A 2001 US Government Accounting Office study of the Defense Department's use of the integrated parallel model through the use of integrated product teams found poor implementation. See GAO, *Best Practices: DOD Teaming Practices Not Achieving Potential Results* (Washington, DC: GAO-01-510, April 2001).

28. See Cheung, *Fortifying China*, Chapter 2.

29. Interview with PLA acquisitions specialist, Changsha, February 2011.

30. This estimate is based on annual performance figures released by nine of the ten leading state-owned defense corporations for 2012. Only the China State Shipbuilding Corporation did not release its profit numbers for that year.

31. "China Unveils Plan for Developing Defense Technologies," *Xinhua News Agency*, May 25, 2006.

32. One study that compared the linear-sequential model with an integrative-iterative model suggested that the former was more appropriate for incremental innovation while the latter was more geared to disruptive innovation. See Ravi Jain, Harry Triandis, and Cynthia Weick, *Managing Research, Development, and Innovation* (Hoboken, NJ: John Wiley, 2010), 244–249.

33. Christian Terwiesch and Christoph H. Loch, "Measuring the Effectiveness of Overlapping Development Activities," *Management Science* 45, no. 4 (April 1999): 455–465.

34. Zhang Chong and Cheng Shaoyu, "Organizational Model of Project Management in U.S. Military Equipment Acquisition–Research on IPT" (美军装备采办中项目管理组织模式 -IPT 研究), *Foundations of Defense Technology* (*国防技术基础*), March 2009, 3–6. Zhang and Cheng are both from the PLA Armament Command and Technology College.

35. For a discussion of the changing nature of China's defense innovation models, see Tai Ming Cheung, "The Chinese Defense Economy's Long March from Imitation to Innovation," *Journal of Strategic Studies* 34, no. 3 (June 2011): 325–354.

Chapter Three

The General Armament Department's Science and Technology Committee

PLA-Industry Relations and Implications
for Defense Innovation

Eric Hagt

Over the past decade or more, the People's Liberation Army (PLA) has striven to consolidate an effective defense high-tech innovation system. The Science and Technology Committee (STC) under the General Armament Department (GAD) has been a leading institution in this reform process—producing mixed results. The STC is the most senior body in the PLA advising on high-tech and strategic platforms. As such, the current STC has become more of a professionalized agency, having stronger oversight and management function and being less of a think-tank on cutting-edge technologies compared to its former incarnation under the Commission on Science, Technology, and Industry for National Defense (COSTIND). But, the current STC lacks the ability to provide the PLA with the long-term, strategic vision for future defense innovation that the PLA needs.

In this chapter I examine the linkage between the defense industry and the PLA under the umbrella of GAD's STC and how this relationship shapes defense innovation development in China. I seek to explore the ways in which these two actors influence each other and, in particular, how industry is able to exert its influence and preferences on the PLA's weapons programs. In other words, this is a study of the industrial-technological "push" on the defense research, development, and acquisition (RDA) process.

From a formal organizational perspective, the STC is a focal point for understanding this relationship, especially as it affects weapons programs in high-tech fields. The STC both sits atop the defense science and technology system and has the deepest links to industry. Through the STC, the defense industry provides substantial input into the direction and guidance of S&T developments. Informal networks will also be examined in this chapter, for their role in manipulating the procurement and acquisition system. Based on these findings, an assessment will be made on how this evolving relationship between the PLA and industry is impacting China's efforts to transform defense innovation into a more integrated and dynamic system.

The Science and Technology Committee

Following the reforms of 1998, the General Armaments Department was created as the fourth unit with the title General Department under the Central Military Commission (CMC). It was meant to consolidate into one centralized institution the PLA's procurement and acquisition process, formerly spread out among several bodies in the other three General Departments. While the bulk of defense R&D remained within the industry groups and their subsidiaries, the reforms enabled the PLA to better oversee weapons programs in a coherent fashion. These reforms also provided the PLA with greater leverage to acquire the platforms they needed to meet their military modernization goals.

The success of these reforms and the degree to which they have improved China's RDA system have been mixed. Even given the industry's dismal performance in the 1990s, the quality of major weapons systems produced in the past decade has certainly improved, as evidenced by a range of new and advanced ships, submarines, missiles, aircraft, and space assets. However, as China moves into a phase of developing more complex, net-centric systems, its ability to innovate in more creative ways will test its still evolving RDA infrastructure. The Science and Technology Committee will be key to understanding and measuring the PLA's progress in this evolutionary process of transforming itself into a modern fighting force.

Form: Biography of the STC

A number of features of the STC make it a prime case study for evaluating the impact of industry on the defense S&T and innovation system. The STC enjoys a senior position within the PLA hierarchy. It is described as the leading technical and intellectual brain trust supporting the planning and development of defense S&T.[1] Within GAD, the bureaucratic level of the STC is equivalent to a deputy military region–level entity (副大军区级) and is superior to all of the GAD's other divisions that are army-level units (正军级).[2] Moreover, while the STC formally resides within GAD, it also appears to have direct access to the CMC.

The high rank of the STC leadership and large size of its membership are indicators of its bureaucratic heft within the GAD.[3] The STC is the largest body in GAD. At the apex is the STC's six-member leadership, the most senior of whom is Li Andong, a full general and of equal rank with the director of GAD.[4] Underneath these six STC leaders are ten permanent members, principally from the military, and an unknown number of nonpermanent members. Below the STC leadership are the expert groups, a large base of expertise that consists of an estimated 1,000 technology specialists with 44 expert groups (see Figure 3.1). These expert group members are selected in part from academia, military research centers, and the GAD system, but the majority come from the vast workforce of 400,000 in more than 300 institutes in the defense R&D industry network.[5]

The STC has historically demonstrated a degree of independence from PLA regulations. Many of its members have been immune from age limits, a legacy of the organization under the leadership of Zhu Guangya, when the STC was housed under COSTIND.[6] Following Zhu's retirement in 2005, however, the STC leadership appears to have standardized its age limits and the military ranks of its members.[7] Nonetheless, the committee still holds highly regarded S&T elders, most of whom are either civilians or military with technical rank and are often under a looser association with the STC as senior advisors.[8] While such elderly consultants usually do not hold any military rank, these exceptions within the STC indicate their unique status as senior consultants to the PLA.

Several salient characteristics of the STC leadership help to explain both the nature and the limitations of its role in shaping the defense innovation system. While some of the leaders hold advanced degrees, principally in electronics (Tao Ping, vice secretary general), computer science (Lu Xicheng, deputy director) and aeronautics/space (Li Andong, director), almost all came to the STC from within the greater procurement system that extends down to the military region and service level. This experience provided them with the necessary expertise in armament planning and procurement that is required in their positions, as well as facilitating vertical connections to armament departments throughout the military apparatus. Moreover, all members of the leadership (except Lu Xicheng, who has technical rank) and the vast majority of the permanent members— where the locus of decision-making authority is—have formal military rank. In short, though many in the STC have some degree of expertise, their knowledge in broader S&T issues is likely to be limited. While the STC leadership makes

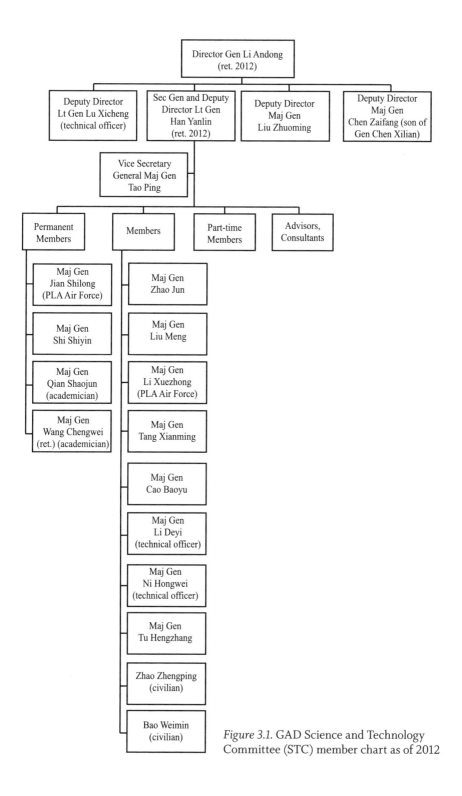

Figure 3.1. GAD Science and Technology Committee (STC) member chart as of 2012

decisions on issues of defense S&T efforts, it clearly relies on its other members and expert groups for support.

The technical expertise that the STC leadership and a majority of its members do possess is heavily concentrated in a select number of fields, suggesting that STC governance is focused on these areas. One concentration is the electronics sector, computer networking, and information systems. As the PLA strives to improve its high-tech capabilities, the ability to operationalize information warfare across the different service branches, integrate forces, and enhance "combat jointness" is a high priority and so appears to be a central focus of STC expertise. A second focus seems to be complex strategic weapons technologies such as ballistic missiles, space systems, and nuclear weapons, which entail the integration of numerous cutting-edge technologies from a wide array of industry players. A number of very senior figures in the STC are leading authorities on these key strategic weapons programs.[9] A third area of concentration is the defense (军口) portions of the 863 Program.

FUNCTION: LEAD SYSTEM INTEGRATOR

The primary role of the STC appears to be advisor and lead system integrator for acquisition projects in focused high-tech fields. The STC does not comprehensively orchestrate all aspects of the defense S&T system. Rather, it is centered on a number of core competencies that are relevant to China's path toward military modernization.

First, the areas of specialization of the STC's leadership fit a pattern of governance over S&T that adheres to the doctrinal priorities established by the CMC. All of the areas are directly relevant to China's drive for greater "informatization" and control over strategic systems. They all relate to key projects that the PLA leadership has given high priority. Moreover, they require a high level of coordination across S&T fields and across industries. As the authoritative body for S&T decision making, the STC is best placed to identify and orchestrate the RDA for these systems. Other areas of S&T development and more routine procurement and maintenance are overseen by other divisions in the GAD or at lower-level armament departments within the armed services and military regions.

Second, the STC plays a central role in the early stages of weapons development. As discussed in Chapter 2, GAD's procurement and acquisition system can be broken down into roughly five stages, beginning with preliminary research and feasibility studies. While all aspects of the procurement system are crucial to understanding China's comprehensive ability to modernize its war fighting capabilities, it is these preliminary stages that are most critical to the innovation phase of weapons RDA. These early stages in the procurement cycle "determine the PLA's armament needs, the direction, goals, key areas, scope, level, and speed of development"; proper planning at these early stages of procurement can have the greatest impact on the direction of strategic modernization.[10] The preliminary stages are also where the greatest gains in efficiency are realized, because while proportionately less time and money is spent on this area of activity in the procurement cycle, it has a disproportionate effect on future weapons development and spending.

Defense economists in China have compared the cost of each stage of a weapon program with its impact on program life-cycle costs. Estimates indicate that while the stage of feasibility determination, preliminary research, and verification constitutes only 3–5 percent of the cost of a major weapons program, it affects 70 percent of the program's total life-cycle spending in terms of deciding whether to pursue a program or not.[11] Recent reform efforts have consequently focused on these earlier stages as keys to deeper reform in the RDA process.[12] This focus is significant because of the STC's primary role in orchestrating the PLA's efforts to identify and develop leading technologies by coordinating these initial stages of procurement. Moreover, it is the bureaucratic entity where the defense industry, and to a lesser extent civilian enterprises participating in the defense sector, has its most extensive connections with the PLA, primarily with GAD personnel.

Leverage of Industry

The small number of professional soldiers who lead the STC depend heavily on the committee's vast network of advisors and expert groups for specific technical support, most of which originates from the defense enterprises. The director and vice directors are active-duty (military or civilian rank) officers, but below them the STC has direct linkages to industry throughout its organization. For instance, at least two of the STC's ten members have positions in state-owned group corporations: Zhao Zhengping of the China Electronics Technology Corporation and Bao Weimin, director of the technology department of the China Aerospace Science and Technology Corporation.[13]

To understand the potential leverage the defense industry may have over the RDA process, it is useful to outline the notional decision-making layers within GAD for S&T projects.[14] At the top, GAD and its managing staff (主管参谋)

maintain overall authority on decisions related to contract review and approval. This means they have general, but overriding, procedural power over all procurement activities. The STC holds a central position in decision making on high-tech programs and technologies and key RDA efforts. The STC leadership and senior GAD leaders also both approve the appointment of key expert group members.[15]

A second tier of authority is composed of mid-level STC experts that head the advisory groups. They are tasked with identifying important technologies in their respective fields as well as in the enterprises and research institutes that will be involved in conducting RDA work. Consequently, they hold a key position in generating ideas, initiating projects, and selecting competent suppliers. They are also responsible for the evaluation of applications to GAD by all enterprises. At the third level—and largest by size—are the S&T leading groups and their composite members. These persons come primarily from defense industry institutes and academic institutions, where the designated S&T applications, the specific plans, feasibility reports, testing, and costing are designed.

As a result, there is a structural equilibrium to the S&T governance system. On the one hand, the expert groups within the STC have significant potential to influence decision making on high-tech projects. According to regulations developed for expert groups, they are convened for a maximum period of three years to study new potential technologies and their applications for weapon systems and, if necessary, to develop the pre-research, draft planning, and feasibility reports for projects.[16] Once the expert groups are formed, they are positioned to shape projects according to their constituent interests. On the other hand, senior GAD and STC leadership maintain ultimate decision-making authority for both contract decisions and the make-up of expert and advisory groups, thereby limiting any orchestrated influence by the defense industry.[17]

In theory, this provides a check and balance condition between the defense industry and GAD decision makers. In practice, however, many complications remain. Most important among these are calls within the PLA to adjust the role and function of high-level S&T governing institutions.[18] The reformers making this case believe that the existing PLA S&T organs are ineffective in macro-level and long-term planning. The technological push within the PLA's current S&T branch is seen as mirroring the pre-1998 COSTIND, which relied too heavily on narrowly specialized scientists and technocrats. The system remains compartmentalized by parochial scopes and focuses on particular technology areas. Reformers argue that the PLA's S&T governing bodies, such as the STC, remain overly involved in routine operations like project management, contract management, and dispersal of financial resources. They argue that the STC should instead become a body with strong executive power that is confined to long-term strategic planning and advising.

One of the key stumbling blocks to the STC's ability to provide long-term strategic planning is insufficient "in-house" expertise on a wide range of S&T areas.[19] The resultant reliance on the defense industry provides rent-seeking opportunities for interest groups both within the defense industry and from other sources of expertise. As a result, the S&T system has failed to serve as a strategic advisor with a strong commitment to the long-term planning of military technological advancement. This has become particularly acute as the PLA has striven to operationalize increasingly sophisticated technologies into its forces and enhance combat jointness.[20] To this end, the PLA has ramped up efforts to recruit into their ranks greater numbers of and higher-quality experts in information technology and other high-tech areas to improve its overall aptitude for S&T innovation.[21] The PLA also appears to be consolidating its R&D capabilities to give it a better basis of knowledge upon which to make sound decisions about cutting-edge S&T.[22]

The challenges associated with reforming the S&T system and dealing with the avenues of rent-seeking in the RDA process are persistent, judging from the Chinese language professional and academic literature, as well as personal accounts.[23] As the complexity of weapon systems grows, so does the number of RDA institutes and production plants involved. Previously, the GAD had to manage only a small number of these actors for the core components of a weapon system. Today, dozens and sometimes hundreds are involved. As the number of actors in a weapon system development project grows, so do the moving parts, transactions, and opportunities to influence the procurement process. The specialized nature of these technologies, the secrecy requirements, and the strict approval process lead to large information asymmetries that thwart a more open, competitive system among state defense contractors and throw up entry barriers to the civilian sector.[24]

Informal Network Influence

Layered throughout the Chinese defense RDA organizational structure are pervasive informal networks and personal ties. There is limited investigative journalism focused on specific weapon programs, due to their sensitivity; however, using what information is available through the literature and through interviews, several case studies can be sketched out that demonstrate a phenomenon of informal channels and patronage which increasingly plagues the defense RDA process.[25]

COMPANY V

The case of Company V illustrates the enduring and pernicious issue of patronage within the RDA sphere.[26] In 2010, Company V, which develops technology in the field of organic light-emitting displays, made a bid for a GAD-funded R&D project. However, the head of the STC expert advisory group in charge of this field, who was a graduate of the Xian Electronics Technology University, advised GAD managing staff (主管参谋) against choosing Company V in favor of a competing company that happened to be associated with his alma mater. After initially losing the bid, Company V hired a relative of the head of GAD's Basic Electronic Information Division (电子信息基础部) as a vice president as well as two temporary consultants who were retired GAD officers. The company then lobbied the GAD through these personal contacts.[27] In the end, a compromise was reached. The GAD did not reverse its decision but instead increased the budget and added Company V to the project.[28]

This actual case is hardly unique, and it illustrates a few of the distortions within the Chinese bidding system. The RDA bureaucratic structure places the STC as a high-level but largely advisory body within the GAD system, giving it a function that is ostensibly separate from final decisions over matters like contracts; yet members of the STC expert groups, many of whom come from industry, are the actors who are identifying new technologies and recommending suppliers. They have the potential to sway contract awards. The PLA could have lost out on procuring superior technology had Company V not circumvented formal channels and availed itself of lobbying avenues to apply persuasion elsewhere in GAD. Under normal regulatory boundaries, the Xian connection would represent a clear conflict of interest, yet in a system where patronage ties stem from common education, bureaucratic, enterprise, family, or friend connections, the networks are difficult to root out.

A second point of interest is the apparent importance of implementing bureaucracies, such as the mid-level staff in GAD that manage the contract awards. In this case, the contract office in the Basic Electronic Information Division (电子信息基础部) was the key point of contact.[29] Company V was able to alter the outcome by lobbying this office.

Third, this case demonstrates a general principle that is widely acknowledged among industry experts. That is, while informal networks are often *necessary*, they are not *guarantees* to winning contracts and are secondary to the institutional and bureaucratic environment in which they operate. Only when competing interest groups are relatively equal in terms of technology and competence do personal connections come into play.[30] In other words, opportunities for rent-seeking of this form are conditional, not absolute. Nonetheless, the apparent necessity of patronage ties distorts the system, not only by disadvantaging those with weaker lobbying potential, but also by erecting prohibitively high barriers to outsiders entering the initial contract competition. The additional obstacles to civilian companies include a rigorous three-tier approval process (confidentiality, quality control, and "product security"—a euphemism for strict requirements to maintain a stable product line over the long term[31]) that few firms are able to pass.[32]

J-20 STEALTH FIGHTER PROGRAM

In a second notable case, the R&D contract for China's J-20 stealth fighter is of interest both in the extent and the limitations of industry manipulation of the procurement system. In reports that have trickled out about this program, it appears that the Chengdu Aircraft Industry Corporation defeated the Shenyang Aircraft Corporation in the competition for the best model, despite the fact that both are subsidiaries of China Aviation Industry Corporation (AVIC) and that AVIC lobbied hard in favor of the Shenyang model.[33] The preliminary R&D for the stealth fighter was reviewed by a GAD expert group that included specialists from the PLA Air Force, GAD, and AVIC. Shenyang has the longest legacy in AVIC and used that to garner support at the AVIC headquarters in Beijing for what would have been a highly profitable project.[34] Despite this lobbying, the Shenyang model did not satisfy the additional technical standards established by the PLA Air Force and thus was not chosen.[35]

This case underscores several issues in the defense industry–PLA relationship. First, despite substantial effort to alter the preferences of the PLA Air Force and the GAD, Shenyang largely failed in the end. This reinforces the principle that, although various competing interests can influence the outcome of a contract award, the GAD reserves the right to make final determination of contracts, and that decision is largely framed by the basic standards of technology levels and competence. In order to ensure a favorable outcome in these terms, the PLA Air Force recently established a Key Projects Office (空军装备部重点型号部), which was deemed necessary to oversee the R&D of the stealth fighter program.[36] These preliminary R&D, feasibility, and initial model and design verification tasks, which would have been left to the principal participating industries in the past, are now under the air force's purview, allowing for greater PLA leverage and oversight for key acquisitions. Yet, in an outcome similar to that in the Company V case, the GAD ended up adding funds to other projects being performed by the Shenyang Corporation to "compensate" it for losing out on the stealth fighter program. This "compensation strategy," as one industry specialist termed it, seems to be an operating principle in the GAD, and it undermines a rigorous competitive environment as well as increasing project costs.[37]

The above cases reveal thorny problems in defense industry lobbying and patronage. They demonstrate monopolistic behavior. The coupling between industry and the PLA is cooperative and close in many respects but often works to the disadvantage of superior suppliers and therefore produces inefficiencies in the system. In both of these examples, PLA procurement of the best and most advanced technologies and weapon systems was potentially undermined.

STC Governance Regime

Since being transferred to the GAD in 1998, the STC has clearly been transformed into a far more rationalized bureaucracy, bringing management over key military RDA programs more firmly under military control. Prior to this shift, the STC, under COSTIND, was co-governed by the PLA and the State Council, but its leadership was shared (even dominated) by the defense industry and academic specialists, a situation that clearly was not optimal for the military.[38] Since relocating to GAD, and especially following Zhu Guangya's retirement in 2005, the STC's top positions have been almost exclusively filled by in-house armament procurement and acquisition careerists. This professionalization and bureaucratization of the STC has helped to strengthen the PLA's hand over the defense industry in the management of critical weapon and S&T priorities. This enhanced role as lead system integrator has borne positive results. The acquisition of greater numbers and more sophisticated indigenously produced weapon platforms over the past decade points to the PLA's success in its bargaining position vis-à-vis industry in the S&T innovation process.

However, there are trade-offs to this transformation. While the GAD maintains decision-making authority through procedural management and implementation of programs, it does not possess the expertise to micromanage the S&T system and so remains largely dependent on the defense industry's ten conglomerates, their subsidiaries, academia, and civilian enterprises. Under this more vertically divided S&T system, in which the GAD is at the top but is dependent on industry for expertise at the base, new problems have arisen. Largely devoid of final decision-making authority, the defense industry has sought to more closely couple itself with the PLA, often to the detriment of competition among suppliers. This pressure has resulted in a lobbying system driven by individual and specific industry interests. Whereas the pre-1998 system may be characterized as a top-down governance of S&T initiatives (though very ineffective in meeting PLA demands), the current system results in bottom-up pressure in which each defense industrial sector vies for programs to its own advantage. Without the kind of comprehensive expertise needed to navigate myriad new and high-technology fields, there is greater room for industry to influence program priorities. Largely acting as arbiters in this competition, the STC and other bodies that govern the S&T system are failing in their role as long-term strategic S&T advisors to the PLA.

A second dynamic that has impacted the defense S&T governance over the past decade is the evolving nature of the weapon systems RDA process. Put simply, the complexity of acquisition has grown in tandem with the technological sophistication of armaments. A fourth-generation stealth fighter, an anti-ship ballistic missile, an unmanned drone able to operate far from China's shores, and a space-based command and control network all involve the integration of numerous, highly advanced technologies. Consequently, there are far more research and design institutes and production facilities participating in the RDA process. This proliferation of "moving parts" means a concomitant rise in transactions and more opportunity for rent-seeking. This is not a defect in GAD's procurement system per se but rather a natural consequence of military modernization. Nevertheless, it is a phenomenon to which the PLA must adapt, ill-equipped as it is to do so.

The current state of China's RDA system clearly implies a problematic relationship between the PLA and the defense industry. The research findings show that the PLA is striving to address some of these issues by implementing various measures beyond merely adding to growing body of standards and regulations.[39] For instance, the PLA is consolidating and even ramping up its own in-house technical expertise with more R&D institutions and recruitment of S&T specialists into its ranks through a variety of programs. The GAD is also attempting to overhaul the military representative system, as described by Susan Puska in Chapter 4 of this volume. In addition, the military services are establishing key project offices in their armament departments to oversee preliminary R&D for critical programs. This work would have been accomplished by the defense industry in an earlier era, but the PLA obviously feels the need to secure greater control over these critical early stages of decision making in key technologies.

Measuring Up: Comparing S&T Systems

The analysis above strives to link China's evolving institutional culture to its defense S&T and innovation efforts. However, a comparison with other national systems can provide a useful metric by which to measure its progress in terms of global military modernization trends. Direct organizational comparisons between nations often quickly break down into irrelevant similarities. A better approach is to disaggregate core competencies and assess how they are managed in different national systems. While the GAD's STC is unique in many regards, other countries' defense establishments exercise many of the same functions through a variety of actors. One of the principal frameworks for contrasting different national systems is the degree to which state and nonstate bodies play central coordinating roles in complex S&T procurement projects—to what extent they are the lead system integrator (LSI), or the prime contractor, that possesses the financial, intellectual, and experiential wherewithal to undertake expensive, long-term, and inherently risky projects.

At the macro level, the GAD seems similar in function and organization to France's Directorate General for Armament (DGA). In fact, the Chinese GAD was inspired by the French organizational model, in which could be combined state-driven policies and industrial initiatives, though the components of each differ in these two systems, as does the nature of the components' relationship.[40] The DGA is responsible for coordinating the operational requirements of the military services with the defense industries.[41] Compared to the GAD, the DGA has a relatively broad area of responsibility, including the development, procurement, and repair of all weapon systems. The DGA also maintains its own network of laboratories, R&D centers, test centers, and engineers (the IGA—General Engineers for Armament).[42] Though private firms have played an increasingly greater role as LSIs, conducting a large share of French defense R&D, those firms are often seminationalized (the government has roughly a 35% stake in them), which tends toward a more centralized or closely managed LSI system. Moreover, R&D funding is provided and managed by the DGA. Within the DGA, those functions accomplished by the GAD's STC are implemented by several different directorates—for example, the now-defunct Centre for Higher Armament Studies, which annually convened a loosely managed group of DGA and industry experts—though the proceedings of these directorates appear to have no direct bearing on the agencies' decisions. The DGA, like the GAD's STC, retains a high level of in-house expertise, though these personnel are distributed throughout its internal labs. The DGA also directs the REI Projects Fund, established in 2004 to provide funding for fundamental and exploratory research. Since 2004, the fund has financed 258 projects, among which 96 were entirely developed by private companies. In sum, while defense S&T systems in China and France are both largely under bureaucratic control, China's system appears more centralized and under tighter GAD control. While the GAD may rely more on industry expertise, those enterprises are state-owned and -controlled to a far greater degree than in France.

Historically, the defense industry of the People's Republic of China bore a strong resemblance to that of the Soviet Union, but the collapse of the USSR and the reforms in the Chinese defense industry have resulted in very dissimilar systems. Despite recent reforms, the Russian system is still characterized by relatively "stove-piped" defense companies that have amassed considerable power because of their reliance on foreign sales for sustenance. Defense S&T requirements are set in the Ministry of Defense's Directorate of Logistics and Joint Supply and Procurement Center,[43] though it is likely that the defense industries and their legacy research institutes have developed significant capabilities to steer these goals independently. In 2006, Russia established the Military-Industrial Commission (MIC), which reports directly to the president and is responsible for supervising the distribution and implementation of the "State defense order." The MIC coordinates between the Defense Ministry of the Russian Federation, the Armed Forces of the Russian Federation, and the defense industry.[44] Though its coordination role is similar to GAD's, MIC controls a much larger and more disparate portfolio of interests, including exports and other tertiary industries.[45] Through recent reforms, increased budgets, and strategic drivers, China has been far more successful in centrally directing and channeling its defense S&T initiatives than Russia has been.

India's military S&T functions are mainly concentrated in the Defense Research and Development Organization (DRDO), which operates nearly 50 labs employing more than 34,000 personnel.[46] The headquarters of the Indian Defense Service issues an overall Defense Capability Plan Document and then meets with representatives of the DRDO and branch services to determine subsequent technology projects.[47] In contrast to the Chinese STC, the Indian military headquarters plays the coordinating role between end-users and suppliers. Moreover, operating through the DRDO, an agency within the Ministry of Defense, the Indian S&T system appears to retain greater expertise within the military establishment than does the system in China. Similarly, the British Ministry of Defense decides S&T goals, though with advice from its defense science and technology labs.

The US defense science and technology system stands in perhaps starkest contrast to China's. On one level, it appears to be more decentralized, with each armed service branch setting its own S&T goals and operating its own network of research labs, though there is some cooperation among the services. R&D projects must be approved at Department of Defense (DOD) level, but only to ensure that they meet Joint Forces Requirements in conforming to the nation's overall defense goals. The Office of the Undersecretary of Defense for Acquisition, Technology, and Logistics is responsible for the overall procurement direction of the military. Within the procurement guidelines, the army, navy, and air force have significant leeway to pursue their own S&T objectives. The S&T objectives pursued by the services do, however, remain under a system of supervision, the Joint Requirements Oversight Council, to ensure that they are in compliance with greater Pentagon and national security objectives. To the extent that S&T is applied to major defense acquisition projects, congressional scrutiny becomes a major factor. In terms of cutting-edge S&T projects, the Defense Advanced Research Projects Agency plays a principal role and is uniquely positioned directly under the Office of the Secretary of Defense, operating independently of the mainstream acquisition system, particularly in the early phases in R&D. In general, this more decentralized system would appear to be more flexible for innovating to meet specific operational demands.

A second fundamental difference is the role of the lead system integrator. Industry plays a key role in the US defense contracting system overall, as it serves as the LSI for most of the major weapon systems under development.[48] With the exponential rise in the complexity of weapon systems, the service branches could no longer maintain adequate in-house resources to play the role of LSI. The difficulties of technical complexity plus the cost pressures and the heavy bureaucratic hand of DOD's procurement system drove the movement of LSIs into the private sector, which became almost singularly responsible for complex defense acquisition programs. Supporters of this system argue that, in the modern information technology era, this is a more sensible arrangement, because the private sector is more attuned to changes in technology and better positioned to spin-on emerging technology. However, several notable failures of this LSI system have led to a rethinking of the arrangement.[49] The general congressional reaction to these failures has been to adjust the LSI role somewhat back to governmental management, to institute greater transparency requirements for private LSIs, and to promote more active coordination between the private firms and the government services.

China has acknowledged the advantages of the American system, and its defense industries have taken on aspects of an LSI role. However, they are state-owned and controlled, with the accounting, transparency, and management regimes that such a system implies. Moreover, the PLA has striven hard in the past decade to increase its control over the acquisition and procurement process more broadly. Thus, while China aspires to move closer to a US-style system, in many respects the state-driven policies and institutional culture remain obstacles that will keep the Chinese system dramatically different from that of the United States.

Conclusions

How do we assess the impact of the PLA–defense industry relationship on the defense S&T system's ability to innovate? With the Science and Technology Committee's focus on informatization-related programs, the PLA is making progress in improving its level of jointness, networking ability, electronics, and cyberwar fighting prowess. The lure of big profits and a more structured S&T governance in the GAD has led to a more coupled relationship between end-user and producer. Progress still appears to be most salient with regard to the development of clearly identified priority programs. The PLA has established a more robust system to ensure oversight in the development of a widening range of big-ticket items that have provided the PLA with important strategic gains.

Beyond the progress being made under these more clearly defined aims, the transformation of the system to diffuse technology in more organic ways remains problematic. The findings of this chapter suggest that obstacles to the adoption of a more flexible, integrated procurement process in China remain. This is particularly acute for advanced and complex technologies, in which the PLA relies more heavily on defense industry expertise for input. The STC and its expert groups are largely populated by industry specialists, so they have an inherent incentive to control the flow of information in favor of the technology field and/or the corporate interests they represent. Since the expert groups play a key role in several early critical stages of the procurement process, from the generation of ideas and feasibility to preliminary research and recommendations of suppliers and producers, the system fails to allow for a high level of parallel integration, which would provide for more creative innovation. For this to happen, the bodies that are responsible for identifying, recommending, and overseeing the development of advanced technologies for defense application must be more neutral and independent. The PLA is undertaking a major effort to enhance its proficiency in S&T in a widening range of areas. Time will tell to what degree it can reduce its dependence on the expertise of the defense industry.

NOTES

1. Li Jinai, preface to *Essay Collection of Academician Zhu Guangya* (Beijing: Nuclear Energy Publishing House, 2004).

2. GAD's other divisions are commonly called the "Eight Divisions, One Office" (八部一办).

3. See *PLA Personnel Directory* (中国军队现任主要负责人名录) (Beijing: China Military Observers Forum, 2011).

4. Li Andong, one of only three full generals (上将) in the GAD (with director Chang Wanquan and political commissar Chi Wanchun), is concurrently the GAD's first vice director, so he is likely the third-ranking officer in the GAD. He received his promotion to full general on becoming head of the STC, which indicates that the STC is clearly a promotional track, perhaps just below the GAD directorship level but above its vice directorship. See "Qian Xuesen: Shining Model for China's National Defense S&T Frontline" (钱学森:国防科技战线的光辉典范), and Lu Xicheng, *Liberation Army Daily*, November 12, 2009; and "GAD Memorial Speeches for Comrade Qian Xuesen" (总装备部缅怀学习钱学森同志座谈会发言), November 11, 2009, XinhuaNet.

5. Other national S&T legends, such as Qian Xuesen (钱学森), Qian Shaojun (钱绍钧), and Mao Erke (毛二可), have held key positions past the age limit. See Li Jinai, preface in *Essay Collection of Academician Zhu Guangya*.

6. Article 16 (Law of PLA Active Officers [中华人民共和国现役军官法]), published by Central Military Commission and State Council in 1988 and revised in 2000.

7. Lu Xicheng (卢锡城) is the one remaining exception with the technical rank of lieutenant general.

8. STC senior advisor Qian Xuesen held a technical rank as lieutenant general until his death in 2009. Qian Shaojun also holds a technical rank as a major general.

9. For example, Jiao Anchang (焦安昌), former STC vice director and director of the Aerodynamic Research Institute under GAD, and Jian Shilong (简仕龙) and Tang Xianming (唐贤明), are both current permanent members and commanders of space bases or branches. Despite this, it is noteworthy that the STC is almost devoid of members with a background in the Second Artillery, whether within its armament department, research institutes, or operations.

10. Niu Xinguang, ed., *Analysis of the Armament Construction of the National Defense System* (武器装备建设的国防系统分析) (Beijing: National Defense Industry Publishing House, 2007). Quote within pp. 1–23.

11. While the author borrows this model from the US defense system, he notes that China spends on average less than the United States on R&D, so China's situation is within these parameters.

12. Zhang Xiaoqi, "Comprehensive Audit and Evaluation of PLA Armament Procurement" (我军装备采购审计和评价试点全面启动), *Liberation Army Daily*, March 17, 2011.

13. For Zhao Zhengping, accessed April 2, 2011, http://memsc.xmu.edu.cn/mems_renchaiduiwu/display1.asp?id=483; for Bao Weimin, accessed April 2, 2011, http://www.rmzxb.com.cn/zxtz/wyjy/t20110318_377927.htm.

14. This formulation of responsibilities comes largely from defense industry expert interviews conducted in Beijing, March–April 2011. There is also some explanation of specific roles and responsibilities of managing staff on the official website of China Aero-Polytechnology Establishment, accessed March 14, 2011, http://www.cape.cn/UserFiles/File/xwzx_old/20061230162747734.asp.

15. There is a managing staff responsible for each technology field, major contract, and expert group. This information comes from interviews with defense industry experts, Beijing, April 2011.

16. Regulations for expert groups were formalized under the 863 Program. See *Notification of Management Measures for the 863 Program* (国家高技术研究发展计划(863计划)管理办法), jointly published by Ministry of Science, PLA GAD, COSTIND, and the Ministry of Finance, December 25, 2001.

17. Yu Gaoda and Zhao Lusheng, *Military Armament Studies* (军事装备学) (Beijing: National Defense University Publishing House, 2000), 342–344.

18. Based on interviews with defense industry experts, March–April 2011. See also Yu Cunguang and Fei Shiting, "The Rise of S&T Talent under the Military Flag" (科技人才方阵在军旗下崛起), *Liberation Army Daily*, December 7, 2009; and Liu Yanxun, Zhang Wenbo, and Li Chuanxun, "Three Effects of Talent Growth in PLAAF Armament Research Academy" (空军装备研究院人才成长三大效应), *Liberation Army Daily*, December 10, 2009.

19. For example, see "Naval Research Institutes to Form Expertise in Armament Feasibility and Research" (中国海军装备研究院打造装备论证研究专业队伍), accessed February 4, 2011, http://mil.news.sina.com.cn/2009-04-09/0737548088.html; and "Equipment Research Institute of Second Artillery: Form Independent Weapons R&D (二炮装备研究院某研究所: 搞出自己的独门兵器), *S&T Daily*, April 17, 2009, accessed February 4, 2011, http://news.ifeng.com/mil/2/200904/0417_340_1112428_1.shtml.

20. See Yu Cunguang and Fei Shiting, "The Rise of S&T Talent under the Military Flag" (科技人才方阵在军旗下崛起), *Liberation Army Daily*, December 7, 2009.

21. An example of these efforts can be found in programs like Implementation Measures for Military High-Level Personnel Project in Scientific and Technological Innovation, established in 2009 with very specific targets to recruit well-established scientists and specialists to undertake R&D for the military and to teach specializations to PLA officers. See "Implementation of PLA High-level Innovation Talents Project" (军队高层次科技创新人才工程实施办法), accessed on April 15, 2011, http://www.docin.com/p-62227762.html.

22. For instance, see Li Chuanxun and Liu Zhuanlin, "PLAAF Academy of Armament Research Undertakes 3000 Research Projects in Past 3 Years" (中国空军装备研究院 3 年来承担科研任务3000多项), accessed February 2, 2007, *Xinhua.com*; He Zhong, Zhou Ming, and Wang Yongxiao, "Creating 6000 Research Projects by Second Artillery" (二炮 6000多项科研成果是如何创造的), *Liberation Army Daily*, February 11, 2008; and Si Yanwen, "PLAN Academy of Armament Research Builds Professional Team for Weapons Feasibility Studies" (中国海军装备研究院打造装备论证研究专业队伍), *Liberation Army Daily*, April 9, 2009.

23. As an example, see Zhong Jian, "Mainland Military to Reform Arms Procurement" (大陆军方改革军火采购), *Fenghuang Weekly*, April 4, 2011.

24. One example is the growing use of closed conferences held by defense industry groups, which bring together GAD officers and other relevant PLA departments and provide the opportunity to network with GAD officers to understand their requirements and operational needs. For example, see Chai Zhifang, "Convening the Defense Industry Science and Technology Meeting of Henan Province in Zhengzhou," February 17, 2009, See http://www.costind-henan.gov.cn/system/2009/02/18/010119930.shtml; and "Convening the National Defense Science and Technology Industry Working Session in Beijing," February 23, 2012, See http://www.587766.com/news1/34109.html.

25. In addition to the case studies outlined above, China Electronics Corporation (CEC) has good personal connections with Senior Colonel Zhang Shuping, the former director of the contract management office under the Basic Electronic Information Division. Before Zhang's retirement, CEC often won contracts over the China Electronics Technology Corporation, despite the latter's reputation for higher-quality, lower-cost products. Based on interviews with defense industry experts, March–April 2011.

26. Company V is a civilian high-tech spin-off from Tsinghua University. The defense branch of the company is the main supplier to the PLA of the organic light-emitting display (OLED) technology used in satellites, combat aircraft, and a variety of communication devices. The company's defense related revenues are tens of millions of renminbi. Based on interviews with defense industry experts, March–April 2011.

27. In fact, Company V's technology in this field was known to be superior to its Xian competitor.

28. Following this outcome, Company V attempted to secure a position in the relevant expert group for a Tsinghua professor who was a strong backer of the company.

29. In further research, we could only find evidence of a "contract management office" (full name is 总装备部军用电子元器件合同管理办公室) in the Basic Electronic Information Division.

30. Based on interviews with defense industry experts, Beijing, April 2011.

31. Ding Feng and Wei Lan, *References of Civil Enterprises Provides Military Products* (Beijing: Ordnance Industry Press, 2008), 267–270.

32. While the 2010 defense white paper states that "civilian industrial enterprises now make up two-thirds of the total licensed enterprises and institutions," this figure says little about the size, quality, or monetary value of contracts awarded to these entities. "China's National Defense in 2010," published by the Information Office of the State Council of the People's Republic of China, March 2011, Beijing. See, http://news.xinhuanet.com/english2010/china/2011-03/31/c_13806851.htm.

33. There are extensive discussions related to the J-20 project and the handling of the model and design contract phase between the various players. This analysis comes mainly from bulletin board sites (BBS) and other military blog–based reports. For example, see "Chengdu AVIC Defeats Shenyang AVIC to Research the 4th-Generation Fighter" (成飞击败沈飞主抓四代机), *Tiexue BBS*, accessed January 3, 2011, http://hi.baidu .com/roomx/blog/item/807b0db36eec32b5d8335a60.html; and, "The Inside Story of Shenyang AVIC: Has It Absolutely Lost the Project for the 4th-Generation Fighter?" (再爆 中国沈飞内情: 四代机已彻底没戏了?), *People BBS*, accessed on October 7, 2010, http://hi.baidu .com/%CE%C0%CA%F9%D6%D0%BB%AA/blog/item/bab1d253e85591000cf3e3aa .html; "Shenyang AVIC Last Ditch Effort: 4th-Generation Fighter Prototype to Be Handed Over to Beijing" (沈飞背水一战: 四代原型机近日提交北京), *Sina.com*, accessed in March 2010, http://blog.sina.com.cn/s/blog_4dacb4240100i00i.html?tj=1; Song Lake and Ji Xiaoduo, "The Head of CAC Research Institute, Yang Wei, Invited to Make Speech at Alma Mater" (航空少帅成都飞机研究所所长杨伟应邀回母校作报告), website of Northwestern Polytechnic University, accessed on October 6, 2008, http://www.nwpu .edu.cn/web/view/news/xyxw/43937.htm; and "Yang Wei Directs Preliminary Research of Next Generation Fighter" (杨伟主持下一代战斗机预先研究等重大项目), *Sina.com*, accessed on December 30, 2006, http://mil.news.sina.com.cn/2006-12-30/1143423656 .html.

34. The Shenyang corporation has more clout in AVIC headquarters because, as its oldest aviation corporation group, promotions from the Shenyang company level to AVIC group corporation level are most entrenched.

35. From the available information, Shenyang apparently proposed its model after the GAD and air force had already awarded Chengdu the contract for R&D based on its model. It remains unclear whether Shenyang did this to maneuver for contracts on components of the stealth fighter or to win compensation for separate contracts in GAD's method of compensation. An alternative explanation is that since this was only for the model phase of R&D, Shenyang believes it still has a chance to compete with a second model or backup model, which could still potentially win substantial contracts.

36. Liu Daijia and Zhou Wenhui, "Jin Wenchun, Deputy Commander of PLAAF Inspects and Guides R&D of Key Projects in Yanliang" (空军副司令员景文春到阎良地区检查指导 重点型号研制工作), *China Aviation News*, August 2, 2010; and "Chengdu AVIC Defeats Shenyang AVIC to Research the 4th-Generation Fighter" (成飞击败沈飞主抓四代机), *Tiexue BBS*, accessed on January 3, 2011, http://hi.baidu.com/roomx/blog/item/807b 0db36eec32b5d8335a60.html.

37. Interviews with defense industry expert, Beijing, April 2011.

38. Under COSTIND, there were a number of civilian STC vice directors, among them Zhu Guangya, Qian Xuesen, and Deng Jiaxian (邓稼先), with no military rank, and many other vice directors had backgrounds in industry with technical military ranks, for instance Ye Zhengda (叶正大), Nie Li (聂力), and Wang Taoyun (王寿云).

39. For a summary of recent regulations promulgated by GAD, the CMC, and other military and state organs, see Eric Hagt, "Emerging Grand Strategy for China's Defense Industry Reform," in Roy Kamphausen et al., eds., *The PLA at Home and Abroad: Assessing the Operational Capabilities of China's Military* (Carlisle, PA: US Army War College and National Bureau of Asian Research, July 2010).

40. I thank Emmanuel Puig for clarifying this point (he is associate researcher at France's National Center for Scientific Research in Paris). See also David Shambaugh, *Modernizing China's Military: Progress, Problems and Prospects* (Berkeley: University of California Press, 2002), 143–145.

41. Nathalie Lazaric et al., "Changes in the French Defense Innovation System: New Roles and Capabilities for the Government Agency for Defense," *Industry and Innovation* 18, no 5 (2011): 509–530.

42. John Birkler et al., *The U.S. Aircraft Carrier Industrial Base: Force Structure, Cost, Schedule, and Technology Issues for CVN77* (Santa Monica, CA: RAND Corporation, 1998), accessed on July 10, 2011, http://www.rnd.org/pubs/monograph_reports/MR948.

43. "Russia: Ministry of Defense," last modified September 7, 2011, http://www.globalsecurity.org/military/world/russia/mo-org.htm.

44. Irina Bystrova, "Russian Military-Industrial Complex," Papers Aleksentari, February 2002, accessed on July 2, 2011, http://www.helsinki.fi/aleksanteri/julkaisut/tiedostot/ap_2-2011.pdf.

45. "Russia: Military Industry Commission," last modified September 7, 2011, http://www.globalsecurity.org/military/world/russia/mic.htm.

46. "Defense Research and Development Organization (DRDO)," last modified May 29, 1998, http://www.fas.org/nuke/guide/india/agency/drdo.htm.

47. See charts starting on p. 163 of "Defense Procurement Procedure," India Ministry of Defense, 2011, accessed July 2011, http://mod.nic.in/dpm/DPP2011.pdf.

48. Valerie Bailey Grasso, "Defense Acquisition: Use of Lead System Integrators (LSIs)—Background, Oversight Issues, and Options for Congress," *Congressional Research Service*, accessed on October 8, 2010, http://www.fas.org/sgp/crs/natsec/RS22631.pdf.

49. Two notable examples are the army's Future Combat System (FCS) and the coast guard's Deep Water acquisition program. The role of LSI for FCS was awarded to a joint arrangement of Boeing and SAIC. However, after both companies made a complete debacle of the contract, Secretary of Defense William Gates ripped the heart out of the program. What's left of FCS will be divided up into smaller acquisitions projects that will be more closely controlled by the army itself. Amid similar cost overruns and delays, the coast guard announced in April 2007 that it would gradually assume the role of LSI on the Deep Water project. See Robbin Laird, "Evolving Defense Business Models: Challenges of Globalization, Systems Integration and National Interests," *RUSI Defense Systems*, June 2008.

Chapter Four

Commissars of Weapons Production

The Chinese Military Representative System

Susan M. Puska, Debra Geary, and Joe McReynolds

The procurement of weapons, equipment, and supplies to sustain a military is an extremely costly and complex enterprise that is extraordinarily difficult to manage. Even advanced military establishments, such as that in the United States, with well-developed acquisition systems and plenty of experience have struggled mightily to master this process, often with disappointing results.

The Chinese approach to the management of its military procurement system has been very different from the systems in the US and other industrialized countries. China's state-owned defense industry remains at the center of military weapons and equipment production, in contrast to the US system, which relies primarily on negotiated contracts with civilian firms. The People's Liberation Army (PLA) is directly responsible for quality control and contract management for military weapons and equipment production and has built a multilayered, redundant, and largely ineffective system staffed by active-duty military officers in military representative offices (MROs). The US military, on the other hand, has developed a large network of civilian and military personnel to ensure that contracts meet military specifications.

This chapter reviews the current state of the Chinese MRO system's capabilities, shortcomings, and ongoing reforms. Gaining a detailed understanding of the MRO system provides a useful benchmark for evaluating the overall effectiveness of China's research, development, and acquisition (RDA) in support of its military modernization.

History and Organization of China's Military Representative System

Since the PLA's founding in 1927, it has relied on military liaison personnel to coordinate civilian provisions and other forms of troop support. In the 1950s, influenced by its partnership with the former Soviet Union, the PLA formalized a military representative (军事代表) system.[1] Military personnel were dispatched to China's newly established military regions and to factories producing military equipment and weapons. The MRO system was suspended during the disruption caused by the Cultural Revolution but was reestablished in the late 1970s.[2]

Despite its relatively long history, the system has remained weak and ineffective, even with repeated attempts at reform. As discussed below, the system has been plagued by personnel problems, which have been aggravated by gaps in regulatory guidelines, standardization, and enforcement. Also, the PLA's development of extensive business enterprises during the 1980s and 1990s spread a corrupting influence throughout PLA institutions, particularly in the PLA logistics and armament systems, which left a negative influence on the MROs.

The absence of an integrated MRO system has been a persistent barrier to professionalization and efficiency, as redundant and fragmented MROs have developed under the General Staffing Department (GSD), General Armament Department (GAD), General Logistics Department (GLD), PLA Navy (PLAN), PLA Air Force (PLAAF), and Second Artillery. Although, as of this writing, the PLA does not appear to be moving toward an integrated MRO system, the GAD does appear to be promoting a stronger oversight role for itself, and there is a general push to raise the quality of MRO personnel through enhanced training and education, while also regularizing their duties, responsibilities, and authority. These reforms support the PLA's overall effort to modernize research, development, and acquisitions processes to improve the production of modern weapons and equipment, reduce redundancies and inefficiencies, and enhance the enforcement of military contract specifications, but questions remain about whether or not the MRO system can be reformed to meet the challenges.

Dissatisfaction among the PLA leadership with the quality of the MRO system is not new. Beginning in the 1990s, regulations and guidelines were enacted to address MRO shortcomings. The establishment of the GAD in April 1998, which was followed by the abolishment of the Commission for Science, Technology, and Industry for National Defense (COSTIND) 10 years later, may have contributed to the professionalization of MROs; but on the whole, the pace of reform has been protracted, and the reality may be that the MRO system is simply inadequate to ensure quality control of weapons and equipment and adherence to military contracts. Overtasked with technical and procedural responsibilities, the military representative officers are essentially commissars of weapons production, who remain in their positions for decades, beholden to the state-owned enterprises that materially support them and lacking up-to-date expertise. Consequently, the outcome for the PLA is that the officers they depend on to ensure quality and meet military requirements are often compromised to rubber-stamp production output, which leads to uneven quality and elevated failure rates.

Efforts to improve the MRO system continue. New and updated regulations governing MROs were promulgated in 2006. Between December 2010 and December 2011, the military experimented with a PLAN military representative pilot program that was heralded as a test model for all services and branches to follow. The test seems to have floundered, however, as the high cost of implementing a significantly improved MRO system became clear.[3]

GENERAL MILITARY REPRESENTATIVE RESPONSIBILITIES

Military representative offices have extensive administrative and technical responsibilities extending across the materiel development process, from the contract bid phase until final delivery, to ensure quality control and to meet the specifications of the contract. In limited cases, staff in MROs also develop and test new equipment, such as when an engineer stationed at a PLAN MRO within a research institute developed and tested electronic warfare equipment at sea.[4] In another case, a senior engineer in an MRO identified and corrected major manufacturing deficiencies at a factory.[5]

ORGANIZATION OF THE MILITARY REPRESENTATIVES

The GSD, GLD, GAD, PLAN, PLAAF, and Second Artillery each have their own military representative system, creating a collection of MRO systems. This study focuses on military representatives who are tasked to oversee military production within the GAD, PLAN, PLAAF, and Second Artillery, in each of which there are three layers[6] of bureaus and offices from the regional level down to the factory or research institute level.

REGIONAL MILITARY REPRESENTATIVE BUREAUS AND OFFICES

The first two levels within the MRO system are the regional military representative bureaus and offices.[7] Regional military representative bureaus (军事代表局) oversee MROs at defense industry factories and research institutes within their assigned region.[8] Each regional military representative bureau is subordinate to a general department of the PLA, a service headquarters, a branch headquarters, or a central military representative bureau. Their basic responsibilities include overseeing MROs at factories and research institutes, conducting military product pricing reviews, and inspecting equipment during the research, production quality control, and testing phases. Regional military representative offices (地区军事代表室 or 地区军代室), which are organizationally below the bureau level, also oversee MROs within their particular geographic area. For example, the Xian regional military representative office manages MROs stationed at more than 20 factories.[9]

Collectively, the regional bureaus and regional offices are responsible for management of MROs in factories and regions. Their primary responsibilities are to provide political, theoretical, and ideological guidance to their subordinate military representative offices, draft standards for and lead the overall development of subordinate factory offices, and organize subordinate military representative offices to carry out their key tasks. Such tasks include carrying out equipment purchasing plans, signing procurement and maintenance contracts with manufacturers (after receiving authorization from the relevant equipment procurement departments), reviewing the pricing for purchase and repair of equipment, and carrying out internal research and assessments for the military. Additionally, the military representatives organize product conversion, spare parts production, technical services, and inspections of equipment during the research, production, and quality control phases. Finally, the military representatives also engage in planning for wartime activities, in terms of both factory mobilization and supply chain continuity in the event that factories are damaged or destroyed.

Under the authority of the end-user, regional military representative bureaus and offices determine which companies can submit contract bids for equipment manufacture.[10] They review each bidder's compliance qualifications based on an assessment of the company[11] and organize the quality control process for equipment development,[12] including participation in new equipment demonstrations, design, and technical review prior to inspection by the military end-user.[13] They are also expected to understand product pricing and production finances for each piece of materiel under their purview.[14]

The GAD, PLAN, PLAAF, and Second Artillery each have separate military representative bureaus across China. The locations have varied over time and according to the particular needs of each service. For instance, GAD has maintained regional military representative bureaus in Shenyang, Beijing, Xian, Jinan, Nanjing, Wuhan, Changsha, Chongqing, and several additional cities at various points; in 2003, GAD's bureaus in Changsha and Jinan were closed.[15] The various services and departments also have bureaus devoted to particular types of equipment, such as armored vehicles, engineering corps equipment, chemical protection, and sea vessels.[16] The PLAN's Equipment Department currently has military representative bureaus in Shenyang, Tianjin, Xian, Shanghai, Wuhan, Guangzhou, and Chongqing.[17] It had a subordinate department devoted to naval aviation, but that has been discontinued and each PLAN military representative bureau now contains an aviation MRO.[18] The PLAAF's Equipment Department has military representative bureaus in Shenyang, Beijing, Xian, Shanghai, Guangzhou, Chengdu, and Guiyang, while the Second Artillery has military representative bureaus in Beijing and Chongqing.[19]

Military Representative Offices at Factories and Research Institutes

The third layer consists of the MROs stationed at specific factories or research institutes (驻厂军事代表室 or 驻厂军代室).[20] MROs are the structural foundation of the system. They help determine which companies can bid on a contract.[21] They evaluate each bidder's past performance for contractual compliance, technical research, and production capabilities, as well as its level of service and support, quality management, and evaluation systems.[22] Military representatives implement the contract bidding invitation instructions and supervise the selection of parts suppliers for the equipment that the manufacturing unit is bidding on.[23] They serve as ground-level liaisons between the military and factories or institutes, where they are expected to carry out inspection, testing, and quality control assessments under the guidance of the military representative bureaus and other higher headquarters.

MROs from different services and branches can be collocated in a single factory; however, they do not appear to be under a joint chain of command or follow a joint reporting channel. For example, if a particular factory has both PLAN and Second Artillery MROs, the PLAN MRO and the Second Artillery MROs will each report to its respective military representative bureau. The degree of communication and coordination between these collocated offices is unknown, but each office appears to operate independently.[24]

Development and Reforms of the MRO System

In 1950, the Central Military Commission (CMC) of the Chinese Communist Party (CCP) Central Committee and the Ministry of Heavy Industry sent the first 24 professional military representatives to several military regions and ordnance factories. Until 1953, these personnel were referred to as "inspection representatives." The PLAN and PLAAF established their own MROs in factories in 1952 and 1953, respectively. However, it was not until 11 years later, in 1964, that the CCP Central Committee and State Council issued the "PLA Military Representative Stationed at Factories Work Regulations" (中国人民解放军驻厂军事代表工作条例), which specified the roles of military representatives in factories. MROs were closed down for roughly a decade during the Cultural Revolution. They were reestablished in 1977 under the 1964 regulations. Military representative work regulations were not revised again until 1989, when the first attempts to modernize the role and procedures of the military representatives began.[25]

The past 15 years have brought a number of changes to the military representative system. For example, military representative bureaus were created to manage the preexisting military representative offices.[26] With the establishment of the General Armament Department in 1998, separate GAD MROs were also created.[27] Additionally, regulations governing the military representative system have been revised on multiple occasions, as seen in Table 4.1.

Recently, regulatory changes have increased. In February 2010, the Chinese government initiated the Military Representative System Adjustment Reform Plan (军事代表制度调整改革方案), and in March 2010 the Central Military Committee announced that the PLAN would carry out a pilot program for procurement that would include a comprehensive reform of its current military representative system.[28] The one-year pilot program officially began in December 2010. To support the program, in March 2011 the GAD opened two new subdepartments, the Armament Procurement Audit Center (装备采购审计中心) and the Armament Procurement Appraisal Center (装备采购评价中心).[29] These recent reform efforts are discussed later in this chapter.

Training and Advancement of Military Representative Officers

Training for military representatives occurs at five major military universities—the Academy of Equipment Command and Technology, the Naval University of Engineering, the Air Force Engineering University, the Second Artillery Engineering College, and the Ordnance Engineering College.[30] The majority of the military representative officer training is conducted at the Academy

Table 4.1   Military Representative Regulations, 2001–2006

Date	Title (English)	Title (Chinese)	Releasing Authority
Jan. 9, 2001	Military Representative Bureau Work Regulations	军事代表局工作规范	GSD, GPD, GLD, and GAD
Jan. 9, 2001	Work Regulations for PLA Military Representatives Stationed at Factories	驻厂军事代表室工作规范	GSD, GPD, GLD, and GAD
Oct. 1, 2006	Requirements for Quality Surveillance of Equipment Development Process	装备研制过程质量监督要求	PLAN Equipment Department stationed at the Tianjin Military Representative Bureau
Oct. 1, 2006	Requirements for Project Expenses of Contractors Supervised by the Military Representatives	军事代表对承制单位型号研制费使用监督要求	PLAN Equipment Department stationed at the Shanghai Military Representative Bureau
Oct. 1, 2006	Working Procedure for the Military Representatives for the Evaluation and Validation of Equipments	军事代表参加装备定型工作程序	PLAN Equipment Department stationed at the Tianjin Military Representative Bureau
Oct. 1, 2006	Work Requirements for Military Representatives for the Invitation of Tenders of Equipments	军事代表参与装备采购招标工作要求	PLAAF Representative stationed at the Beijing Military Representative Bureau

of Equipment Command and Technology. Officers receive training in equipment procurement and mid-level–professional training in specialized fields of study, such as weapons systems design.

There are three levels of training for military representatives. The first level is normally given to either recent college graduates assigned to a particular industry or a military representative who has transferred to a new department. This training focuses on weapons and equipment procurement management, with an emphasis on basic knowledge and skills. The second level is for military representatives who are about to be promoted to a key leadership position at a factory MRO. This training is aimed at improving their general skills and, in particular, leadership ability. The third level of training is for military representatives working at the military representative bureaus, and it involves learning the latest policies in equipment acquisition as well as further leadership and management skills.

The opportunities for advancement for military representatives appear to be slow. The majority of biographies examined for this study showed vertical advancement within the military representative system over a period of decades; experienced military representatives were gradually moved into positions of increasing authority over time.[31] An interesting phenomenon was the multiple instances of unregulated "revolving door" situations, in which military representatives stationed in factories officially retired from their military representative job at a relatively young age (in their 40s or 50s) and were immediately recalled under the "reposting" (返聘) system to work at the same factory in a civilian role or even supervisory position. These arrangements, which in some ways are similar to the post-retirement work of many retired military personnel in the United States and other countries, help retain experience; but they also have a potential downside, for if not carefully regulated they aggravate corrupt practices in weapons and equipment production, which are reported to be endemic throughout the military representative system.

GAD and Service MROs Involvement in the Push-Pull Process

The GAD, PLAN, PLAAF, and Second Artillery MROs serve as links in the "technology-push, demand-pull" process discussed in Chapter 1. First, once the technology-push occurs during the development and production of weapons and equipment, under the guidance of the general departments and service headquarters level down into production, the MROs ensure that military production meets contract specifications of the technology-push prior to receipt by military units. Second, MROs support demand-pull by serving as an avenue through which the concerns and needs of military units for weapons and equipment can be conveyed up the chain of command.

To examine the MRO role in weapons and equipment procurement, we look at MROs at state-owned and commercial production facilities that are linked to the GAD.[32] The PLAN military representative pilot test, which has been associated with organizational developments in the GAD, is included in this discussion as a potential template for continuing enhancements of military representative capabilities, including the potential realization of greater and more joint operational capability.

Figure 4.1 shows the systemic architecture above the MRO system from the GAD[33] down to the Army Armament Scientific Research and Procurement Department, which manages its regional bureaus and offices.[34]

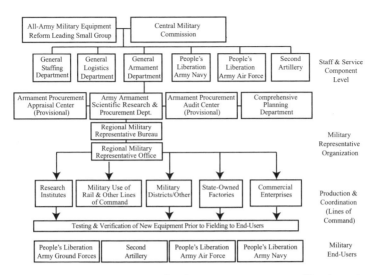

Figure 4.1. Notional diagram of Military Representative Office (MRO) system highlighting GAD linkages

Military Representatives and End-Users

Military representatives have major responsibilities in the RDA process in the development of a contract[35] to ensure protection of military interests and enforcement of quality control,[36] but it is not clear how effectively military end-users (in bottom rank of diagram in Figure 4.1) can promote a demand-pull of concerns and needs through the military representatives. More research is needed to understand this part of the linkage and how it might affect the relationship between end-users and RDA, but the end-user influence through the military representatives appears weak.

What is clearer is that military representatives are tasked to serve as a key node in the enforcement of contractual compliance,[37] including ensuring that "the final equipment delivered to the warfighter will perform as required."[38] MROs are tasked with ensuring quality control through each stage of the development process up to final design and employment, as shown in Table 4.2.[39]

Problems in the Military Representative System

The military representative system has historically suffered from multiple and persistent problems that have inhibited it from achieving its assigned missions and responsibilities. Recent literature identifies several key problems. The distribution of personnel, for example, is often inefficient. Representatives from

Table 4.2   MRO Duties and Responsibilities through Weapons and Equipment
Development Process

Equipment Development Stages	Military Representatives Duties and Responsibilities
Verification stage 核查階段	• Understanding new combat equipment, main mission tasks, operational performances, and the initial overall program • Understand how to inspect the manufacturing units while they develop new projects • Solve main technical problems
Project planning stage 項目規劃階段	• Understand the preliminary design and prototype development • Solve main technical issues that arise • Participate in prototype testing and assessment
Engineering development stage 工程發展階段	• Ensure that the prototype passes test requirements • Supervise the manufacturing units by relevant standards and development design specifications • Participate in the technical design review • Monitor prototype equipment; inspect and accept before delivery • Supervise the manufacturing units so they publish technical materials according to related regulations
Design foundation stage 設計基礎階段	• Participate in and supervise the manufacturing unit in prototype performance testing, environmental testing, reliability testing, and evaluate the test results • Supply the complete set of technical materials for the design foundation, and document the progress of examination approval
Production of final design and employment phase 生產的最終設計和就業相	• Test and evaluate the overall inspection process and evaluation, as well as provide input

multiple headquarters and services are often unnecessarily assigned overlapping duties.[40] Quality control processes are often insufficient or only partially carried out.[41] Pressured by factory owners who control day-to-day operations, military representatives often face difficulties in maintaining their impartiality.[42] The independence of the MROs is further undermined by the requirement that the factories, rather than the services or general departments, provide their salaries and other personnel support.[43]

Other problems are linked to a personnel management system that fails to produce sufficient military representatives capable of carrying out essential functions.[44] Many military representatives have not received education in procurement management.[45] Despite recent improvements in training, the three-tiered training process remains inadequate. Military representatives frequently lack the technical education and military experience to fully understand the increasingly complex equipment produced by the factories they oversee, and the MRO system offers few opportunities for continuing education or on-the-job training.[46] These management problems are exacerbated by a failure to develop effective means of attracting and retaining qualified personnel.[47]

Personnel are often selected from recent civilian college graduates, who then receive training to become military representatives. Some lack operational experience and lack understanding of weapons and equipment the end-users need. Military representatives often remain within one narrow production area, transferring from one job to another without benefit of assignment to any operational units.[48] In addition to hiring recent college graduates, some MROs hire undergraduate interns. For example, the PLAN military representative office stationed in Luoyang hired a group of 30 inexperienced interns from the Naval Aviation Engineering Academy.[49]

The ineffectualness of MROs is magnified because, given the limited operational experience and expertise of many military representatives, they are more easily corrupted and deceived by factory personnel as they try to perform their quality control duties.[50] Additionally, there are few consequences for factories that fail to meet military contractual expectations in delivery time and cost, so the military representatives' oversight role is often ineffective and provisions of the contracts go unenforced at the factory level.

Comparison with US Defense Acquisition Personnel and Procedures

The literature on the Chinese MRO system examines other military representative systems, such as the US defense acquisition system. Training and professional education of acquisition officers in the US defense procurement system has been directly contrasted with Chinese military representative training by Chinese academics.[51] Although the Chinese acquisition training and education are portrayed in a favorable light of centralized management, it is clear that this training is highly fragmented between services and components.

In comparison, the US training is evaluated as providing more rational management and a broader range of topics that allows more opportunity for specialization.[52] US training is seen to make better use of the latest information and network technology.[53] Other analysis cites the US system's extensive regulations, which are regularly updated, and its effective management, which results in greater clarity as to the duties and responsibilities of the American equivalents of military representatives.[54] Since their roles are more clearly defined, confusing and inefficient overlaps are avoided.[55] The writings also assert that Americans more closely monitor the production process, stressing quality control inspection through checking and double-checking to ensure that standards are met.[56] Finally, the US system is seen as more effective in providing timely payment of producers and suppliers and in responding to needed adjustments in production, all of which the GAD appears to be seeking to emulate in its reforms of the military representative and procurement systems.[57]

Recent Military Representative System Reforms

In 2010, the CMC introduced the Equipment Procurement System Adjustment Reform Plan (装备采购制度调整改革方案) and the Military Representative System Adjustment Reform Plan (军事代表制度调整改革方案). These two acts, taken together, aimed to resolve a number of persistent problems with the military representative system. They aimed to ease duplication of effort by multiple military representative offices stationed at the same factory, to increase accountability in contract supervision, and to create checks and balances for the phases of price and contract negotiations that are particularly prone to military representative corruption.[58]

Recognizing the endemic problems and the important role that military representatives can play in the modernization of the PLA, the CMC directed the PLAN to develop and implement a pilot program for comprehensive reform of its procurement and military representative systems in March 2010. As mentioned above, the pilot program was officially launched in December 2010 and ended in December 2011. The CMC directive called for the development of specialized offices to address equipment procurement, evaluation of bids for procurement contracts, management and quality control of procurement projects, and auditing and negotiation of procurement contracts.

A primary aim of this test program was to evaluate how to develop military representatives who were expert in specific aspects of the weapons and equipment development process, rather than to continue to impose a wide mandate on undertrained and unqualified personnel in the research, development, and acquisition process. These reforms also sought to establish independent bodies to oversee the development and production of weapons and equipment. The goal, going forward, is to have military representatives oversee a specific part of the procurement process in various locations, rather than trying to evaluate a variety of processes while being stationed at one factory.

To date, little information on the findings of the PLAN pilot program have reached the outside public. Informal discussions indicate that the pilot may have been a failure in the sense that it would be too costly to improve the MRO system at the sought-after level,[59] but overall procurement reforms may be more successful.

The proposed reforms of the procurement process began to gather wide support in the first half of 2011 and led to organizational changes under the GAD and the CMC. In March 2011, the All-Army Armament Procurement System Reform Leading Group Office (全军装备采购制度改革领导小组办公室) announced that two new offices had been ratified by the CMC and opened within the GAD, the Armament Procurement Audit Center (装备采购审计中心) and the Armament Procurement Appraisal Center (装备采购评价中心).

The two new offices are currently also in pilot program status. Their purpose is to identify new ways to monitor equipment development projects and evaluate procurement decisions in order to determine best practices. The establishment of these two offices has been praised as a significant step forward in the military's procurement reform program.[60] These GAD offices were established to oversee the entire research process, from preliminary research through production, with an increased emphasis on nearly 10,000 projects that are considered of high priority to the military. The provisional offices also underwent a trial experiment for one year, and in the future, if they are judged to be successful, they will become permanent and their programs will be expanded.

The creation of these offices under the GAD could help transform the old MRO practice of stationing ill-trained and inexperienced representatives at the factory level, where they often failed to perform their independent oversight mission, into a structure with greater independence that enhances technical competence. While little is known about the current operations of these provisional procurement offices now that their one-year trial period has expired, they do appear to have reached out to the private sector for consulting expertise on best business practices.[61] The pilot program suggests an admission on the part of the CMC that the costs of corruption and incompetence within weapons and equipment production cannot continue if the PLA is to achieve higher levels of military modernization.

Although there is little information available regarding the leaders and institutions that have advocated for the PLAN pilot program, a number of military institutions appear to be actively participating in the program's development and implementation. Current and former heads of GAD's Comprehensive Planning

Department (CPD) (总装备部综合计划部), for example, have appeared at meetings promoting the reforms. Additionally, the CPD's former head, Major General Liu Sheng, was recently promoted to be a GAD deputy director, where he has continued to promote the reform process.

It is also worth noting that the pilot program is not the only effort in this area. In addition to the PLAN pilot program, GAD has been working with the Ministry of Finance and National Development Reform Commission to issue a leading opinion; the "guidance to further promote the reform of military pricing work" (关于进一步推进军品价格工作改革的指导意见) is aimed at establishing new programs for price control in military procurement, including cost estimates conducted by an independent panel of experts. A pilot program for cost control was launched in 2012 with a one-year time frame.[62]

In the meantime, GAD has issued interim regulations on quality control issues in weapons and equipment procurement, known as the Provisional Measure for Active-Duty Army Weapons and Equipment (现役陆军武器装备技术质量问题处置暂行办法). Given that the PLAN pilot program on procurement reform began in December 2011 and was scheduled to run for a year, these regulations may be intended as a prelude to a full rollout of the PLAN pilot program's reforms and a sign that the reforms may be extended to institutions within the wider military. In the PLA, several years often pass between the conclusion of a test program and the final enactment of reforms based on that program's results.

Representatives from new audit institutions under GAD's Audit Department (总装备部审计局), as well as the head of the GAD Logistics Department, Ren Wangde, have also participated in meetings on the pilot cost control program. Additionally, representatives from both the State Administration for Science, Technology and Industry for National Defense (SASTIND) and the PLAN's political offices have attended these meetings.

The most important office involved, however, appears to be the newly created All-Army Armament Procurement System Reform Leading Small Group Office. GAD director General Chang Wanquan heads the group,[63] which has issued instructions to GAD departments on the implementation of procurement reforms. The issuance of instructions indicates a need to tread lightly and forge cooperative goodwill, to win support of the armed service branches and other general headquarter departments with independent vested interests in their parallel military representatives and procurement systems.

To help popularize the reforms, Chang has made numerous public speeches on the reforms, calling them an important national security priority, which echoes Hu Jintao's language on the topic. In March 2011, Chang went on a joint "fact-finding" tour of PLA military academies with PLAN Commander Admiral Wu Shengli, and advocated for reform with the next generations of officers.

An overarching systemic challenge to professionalizing military representatives is the absence of an integrated system of MROs or other organized quality control and military contract management structure that could work to ensure quality and delivery in accordance with the specifications of the military. The lack of communication and coordination that now exists among the duplicative systems under the GSD, GAD, PLAN, PLAAF, and Second Artillery squanders limited resources and inhibits the development of a cohort of experienced and professional experts in military procurement and production.

Although the PLA has not explicitly pushed for a jointly managed military representative system under GAD, it has been steadily moving in the direction of a more coordinated system, by attempting to centrally raise the quality of military representatives and regularize their duties, responsibilities, and authority across the PLA, with the goals of enhancing the production of modern weapons and equipment, reducing redundancies and inefficiencies, enhancing the enforcement of military contract specifications, and facilitating civil-military integration.

It is not surprising that China's military acquisition process faces daunting challenges. Even the US military's acquisition process has numerous shortcomings. Nevertheless, it is significant that, perhaps for the first time in the PLA's history, there may be an emerging consensus that China cannot modernize its military to promote its national interests without major reform and rationalization of its weapons and equipment acquisition processes. The GAD's efforts to lead this reform and the PLAN's participation in the pilot program may signal a turning point in which the PLA, fresh with operational experiences from its anti-piracy mission in the Gulf of Aden and other nontraditional military missions, recognizes that a concerted effort at acquisition reform is a necessary condition for accelerated military modernization, but the challenges are considerable.

A Comparative View of Chinese and US Defense Acquisition Reforms

To put the current Chinese military representatives and procurement system reforms into perspective, it is important to recognize that many of China's acquisition problems discussed above, such as personnel deficiencies, conflicts of interests, and contract fraud, are not unique to the Chinese defense industries. The US military, which has one of the world's largest and most sophisticated military acquisition systems, has made determined efforts to reform and rationalize its system throughout much of its history.[64] Since 1986, for example, when the Packard Commission and an internal defense management review identified key shortcomings in the acquisition process,[65] the US Department of Defense (DOD) and its armed services have continually sought to improve acquisition processes, including the effectiveness of its personnel, to reduce the frequently cited trio "fraud, waste, and abuse" so as to achieve higher levels of efficiency and effectiveness in the development of weapons and equipment for the US armed forces.[66]

The US government has carried out nearly 130 studies in pursuit of acquisition reform since the end of World War II.[67] Nevertheless, the process of reform has been incomplete, according to a series of reports by the Government Accountability Office (GAO) in 2009, which concluded that "DOD's processes for identifying warfighter needs, allocating resources, and developing and procuring weapon systems . . . are fragmented and broken."[68]

The GAO also identified DOD contract management as a particularly problematic area, noting that a shortage of trained acquisition and contract oversight personnel and the use of inappropriate types of contracts have put the DOD at risk of failing to obtain some needed goods and services and overpaying for others.[69] Partly in order to address these issues, the 2009 Duncan Hunter National Defense Authorization Act (S. 3001 / P.L. 110-417) established the Configuration Steering Boards, designed to control costs and more actively manage the operations of major defense acquisition programs.[70] The law is also intended to help the acquisition workforce attract high-quality officers and civilian personnel. To that end, it establishes a minimum number of billets to be reserved for general and flag officers in the acquisition workforce.[71] These efforts are in keeping with updates made in 2008 to the National Defense Authorization Act, which established a Defense Acquisition Workforce Development Fund to be used for the recruitment, training, and retention of acquisition personnel.[72]

Like its Chinese counterpart, the US military acquisition system is separated by service. The US Navy's acquisition unit is the Naval Air Systems Command, the Air Force's is the Air Force Acquisition Command, the Marines' is the Marine Corps Systems Command, and the Army's is the US Army Acquisition Support Center (USAASC).

The role of the USAASC is similar to that of Chinese military representatives. Officers and noncommissioned officers (NCOs) who are in the Army Acquisition Corps tend to work in one of the five DOD acquisition career fields: program management; contracting; systems planning, research, development, and engineering–systems engineering; information technology; and test and evaluation.[73] A difference between China's military representatives and the US Army Acquisition Corps is that the latter's workforce also includes civilians and NCOs. For example, within the US Army Acquisition Corps, the Army Acquisition, Logistics, and Technology Department consists of more than 42,000 civilians and 1,600 commissioned and noncommissioned officers.[74] Civilians in the Chinese military representative system's workforce appear to be limited to former military officers and a small number of military representatives who were educated in Chinese civilian universities rather than PLA-affiliated schools.

Another problem within the Chinese military representatives is their lack of training and education. At present, although 98.1 percent of PLAAF military representative personnel have a bachelor's degree or above, only 32.2 percent have a graduate degree.[75] Within the US Army Acquisition Corps, by contrast, 98 percent of the workforce have a master's degree.[76] The US Army Acquisition Corps also has ongoing certification requirements and continuing education policies that require personnel to engage in ongoing training over two-year cycles.[77]

As stated earlier, another problem within the MRO system is its unregulated "revolving door" whereby military personnel retire and return to the same office without the restrictions placed on active-duty service members. In contrast, US regulatory guidelines strictly regulate military and civilian personnel who leave government service, to avoid any conflict of interest.[78]

Finally, transparency constitutes another gap between US and Chinese practice. The US is far from perfect in this area; although the Obama administration has stressed the importance of openness and transparency in government bureaucracy, the GAO has found that "departments and agencies in the DOD" were not reporting "complete information on contract awards" or "complying with Defense Federal Acquisition Regulation Supplement (DFARS) requirements," which prevented "full transparency to the public on DOD's contract awards."[79] The Federal Acquisition Regulations require contracting officers to make information on any contract action over a certain dollar amount publicly available on the same day the contract is awarded.[80] China's standards for transparency in military procurement are almost nonexistent, providing a fertile environment for fraud and waste unchecked by any substantial safeguards.

Conclusions

Study of China's military representatives system reveals that fundamental reforms to tackle deep-rooted structural and process problems have only recently been undertaken. Considerable expectation was placed on the PLAN pilot program and procurement reform. The outcome of this pilot program and the trial experiment of the Armament Procurement Audit Center and the Armament Procurement Appraisal Center may help push the PLA toward a military representative system that could facilitate horizontal joint integration among services and general departments and reduce waste, corruption, and inefficiencies within the materiel production and procurement system. Lacking this, the pilot nonetheless shows promise in raising the quality and role of the military representatives. Monitoring the outcome of these reforms and the steps taken to implement new procedures will give a clearer idea of the long-term direction in which the PLA is moving on materiel procurement and production.

Many questions remain, though, in explaining the military representatives' evolving role in the weapons and equipment process. Of particular interest is what role, if any, they currently serve in representing the interests and needs of end-users; their effectiveness appears to be circumscribed by their limited technical and military expertise and experience. More information is also needed on how the military representative system functions within the broader context of the defense RDA stakeholders, including the services and general departments (with the exception of the General Political Department [GPD], which does not participate in weapons and equipment procurement and production). A more comprehensive understanding of the effects and scope of military representative corruption on the MRO system would also help predict whether or not reform of the procurement and military representative system will be sufficient to create the checks and balances needed to address these problems and thus improve the pace and scope of PLA modernization. Although the creation of the PLAN pilot test indicates both a recognition by the PLA that change is needed and a willingness to work with the GAD to secure better weapons and equipment, the entrenched bureaucratic system as well as the high cost of improvements represent formidable obstacles to meaningful reform of China's defense procurement system.

NOTES

1. Studies of the MRO system have been included in larger studies of China's defense industries, such as Tai Ming Cheung, *Fortifying China: The Struggle to Build a Modern Defense Economy* (Ithaca: Cornell University Press, 2009), and Evan S. Medeiros, Roger Cliff, Keith Crane and James C. Mulvenon, *A New Direction for China's Defense Industry* (Washington, DC: RAND Corporation, 2005).

2. Cheung, *Fortifying China*, 96.

3. The authors would like to thank Tai Ming Cheung for this observation, which is based on his research and interviews.

4. Information is based on a review of multiple articles published in *Air Force News* (空军报) and *People's Navy News* (人民海军报) during 2002–2006, and in *Missile Forces News* (火箭兵报) for 2006.

5. Ibid.

6. Information from http://wenda.tianya.cn/wenda/thread?sort=wsmorv&tid=3de 29f0737e5ce0b, accessed on May 9, 2011.

7. "Military Representative Bureau," in Zhang Fuxing, ed., *Military Equipment General Introduction* (军事装备总论), in *China Military Encyclopedia*, 2nd ed. (中国军斯百科全书 (第二版) (Beijing: China Encyclopedia Press, March 2008), 403–404.

8. Ibid.

9. Li Zitong. "Xian Military Representative Office to Achieve Desired Goals" (西安军代室管理实现预期目标), *People's Daily*, September 7, 2005. Accessed May 15, 2011. http://www.people.com.cn/GB/paper53/15647/1384209.html.

10. Ibid.

11. Ibid.

12. PLAN Equipment Bureau Stationed at the Tianjin Military Representative Bureau, "GJB 3885-2006 Requirements for Quality Surveillance of Development Process of Equipment," October 1, 2006. Accessed at http://www.bzfxw.com/soft/softdown .asp?softid=126050 in January 2011.

13. Ibid.

14. Song Haitao, Liu Weye, and Di Xiaohua. "Military Representatives Stationed at a Factory Work Analysis" (驻厂军事代表工作分析), *O. I. Automation* 26, no. 7 (2007): 3.

15. Ibid.

16. Information from http://wenda.tianya.cn/wenda/thread?sort=wsmorv&tid =3de29f0737e5ce0b, accessed on May 9, 2011.

17. Ibid.

18. Ibid.

19. Information from scholarly articles written by Chinese military representatives, as well as http://wenda.tianya.cn/wenda/thread?sort=wsmorv&tid=3de29f0737e5ce0b, accessed on May 9, 2011.

20. Information from http://wenda.tianya.cn/wenda/thread?sort=wsmorv&tid=3d e29f0737e5ce0b, accessed on May 9, 2011.

21. The companies that MROs supervise are primarily under state-owned industries, not commercial companies like those which dominate in the US defense procurement system.

22. PLAAF Beijing Military Representative Bureau, "GJB 3898a-2006 Work Requirements for Military Representatives for the Invite Tenders of Equipment," October 1, 2006. Accessed at http://www.bzfxw.com/soft/softdown.asp?softid=125189 in March 2011.

23. Ibid.

24. There are also representatives for equipment development and production, and some GLD military representatives are assigned to conduct oversight of specific lines of transportation. These offices are tangential to the representative system and are thus not discussed in further detail here.

25. Gu Binghua, "Interview with a Female Military Representative in Charge of China's Surface to Air Missile System (2)" (专访中国最新型地空导弹系统的主管女军代表 [2]), accessed on May 7, 2011, at http://military.china.com/zh_cn/news/568/20050430/12285618_1.html.

26. Ibid.

27. Ibid.

28. Chen Chuandong, Han Yanrong, "The Media Said Military Representatives to Receive Business Favors Yields Hidden Troubles in the Quality of Equipment" (媒体称军事代表接受企业好处给装备质量带来隐患), February 23, 2012, http://www.jfdaily.com/a/2709996.htm.

29. See http://www.chnarmy.com/html/2011-03/12207.html for the closest English version, or http://www.gov.cn/jrzg/2011-03/16/content_1826036.htm for the closest Chinese version.

30. Unless otherwise specified, all information on training is from Liu Hanrong, Bai Haiwei, and Cheng Yanmiao, "US Defense Acquisition Team Working and Thinking: A Comparison of Education" (中美国防采办队伍任职教育的比较及思考), *Continuing Education*, no. 8 (2006): 57–58.

31. Information is based on a review of multiple articles published in *Air Force News (空军报)* and *People's Navy News (人民海军报)* during 2002–2006, and in *Missile Forces News (火箭兵报)* for 2006.

32. While military representatives are primarily assigned to state-owned enterprises, they may also temporarily go to commercial enterprises. Based on a personal discussion with an active duty military officer.

33. In addition to GAD, as mentioned above, the services, Second Artillery, GSD, and GLD all have concurrent networks of military representatives. Sharing an organizational level with military representatives in factories, research institutes, and military districts are military representatives who are assigned to China's lines of communication, particularly rail. They play a key role in national mobilization and training for exercises but are outside the scope of this discussion.

34. Ed Francis and Susan M. Puska, "SASTIND, CMIPD, and GAD: Contemporary Chinese Defense Reform," paper presented at the Conference on China's Defense and Dual-use Science, Technology and Industrial Base, San Diego, July 1–2, 2010, 45.

35. Susan M. Puska, Aaron Shraberg, Daniel Alderman, and Jana Allen, "A Model for Analysis of China's Life Cycle Management System," conference paper prepared for the Fourth Annual University of California Institute on Global Conflict and Cooperation (IGCC) conference on China's defense economy, July 29–30, 2013, 24.

36. Ibid., 34–36.

37. Ibid., 36.

38. Ibid., 34.

39. Ibid., 24–36.

40. Bai Haiwei, Qu Wei, and Bai Fengkai, "Study on the Reform of Military Representative System" (军事代表制度改革研究), *Journal of Institute of Command and Technology*, no. 3 (2004): 7–8.

41. Ibid.

42. Ibid.

43. The authors would like to thank Tai Ming Cheung for this observation, which is based on his research and interviews.

44. Tian Siming, "Equipment with Innovative Means to Strengthen Management Quality" (用创新手段加强装备质量管理), *Technology Foundation of National Defense*, no. 1 (2008): 33–34.

45. Ibid.

46. Bai, Qu, and Bai, "Study on the Reform of Military Representative System."

47. Tian, "Equipment with Innovative Means," 33–34.

48. Liu, Bai, and Cheng, "US Defense Acquisition Team Working and Thinking."

49. Ibid.

50. Zhang Ming and Gong Xiu, "Discussion on Progress Supervision Problems of the Equipment Research and Production" (浅谈武器装备研制生产进度监督问题), *Journal of the Academy of Equipment Command and Technology*, no. 3 (2010): 46–49.

51. Liu, Bai, and Cheng, "US Defense Acquisition Team Working and Thinking."

52. Ibid.

53. Ibid.

54. Ren Zhenyuan and Ni Huayong, "US Equipment Acquisition Reform an Inspiration for Our Military" (美军装备采办改革及对我军的启示), *Technology Foundation of National Defense* (机械工程学报), no. 2 (2010): 55–58.

55. Ibid.

56. Ibid.

57. Ibid.

58. Chen Chuandong and Han Yanrong, "The Media Said Military Representatives to Receive Business Favors Yields Hidden Troubles in the Quality of Equipment" (媒体称军事代表接受企业好处给装备质量带来隐患), February 23, 2012, http://www.jfdaily.com/a/2709996.htm.

59. The authors would like to thank Tai Ming Cheung for this observation, which is based on his research and interviews.

60. "General Armament Department, Equipment Procurement, Audit Center and Assessment Center Set Up" (总装备部装备采购审计中心和评价中心挂牌成立)], Xinhua News Agency (新化社), March 16, 2011, accessed online at http://www.gov.cn/jrzg/2011-03/16/content_1826036.htm on June 15th 2011.

61. "Tendering Center for the Pilot Units of the Army Equipment Procurement System: Naval Equipment Office Provides Management Consulting and Establishes Strategic Partnership" (为全军装备采购制度改革试点单位-海军装备部招标中心提供管理咨询，并建立了战略合作伙伴关系). Taken from the web page "Sinochem Tendering Company, A Member of the Sinochem Enterprise" (中化招标公司—中化集团成员企业), accessed at http://www.sinochemitc.com/business.php?optionid=250&auto_id=250, on April 23, 2012.

62. Zhang Shaoqi and Wang Shizhong, "General Requirements of the Chinese Army for the Initial Target Price of Weapons Development Research and Manufacture Programs" (中国陆军首次把目标价格方案纳入武器研制总要求)], *People's Liberation Army Daily* (解放军报), February 24, 2012. Accessed at http://www.china.com.cn/military/txt/2012-02/24/content_24716987.htm, on April 23, 2012.

63. Ibid.

64. Christopher H. Hanks, Elliot I. Axelband, Shuna Lindsay, Mohammed Rehan Malik, and Brett D. Steele, *Reexamining Military Acquisition Reform: Are We There Yet?* (Arlington, VA: RAND Corporation, 2005).

65. Ibid., p. 6.

66. Ibid.

67. US Congress, House Committee on Armed Services, "The Department of Defense at High Risk: The Recommendations of the Chief Management Officer on Acquisition Reform and Related High-Risk Areas," 1st congressional session, May 6, 2009, p. 8; Moshe Schwartz, "Defense Acquisitions: How DOD Acquires Weapon Systems and Recent Efforts to Reform the Process," Congressional Research Service, No. RL34026, p. 13, http://www.fas.org/sgp/crs/natsec/RL34026.pdf.

68. US Government Accountability Office, High-Risk Series—An Update, GAO-09-271, January 2009, p. 65; Schwartz, "Defense Acquisitions," p. 16, http://www.fas.org/sgp/crs/natsec/RL34026.pdf.

69. US Government Accountability Office, High-Risk Series—An Update, GAO-09-271, January 2009, p. 73; Schwartz, "Defense Acquisitions," p. 16, http://www.fas.org/sgp/crs/natsec/RL34026.pdf.

70. Schwartz, "Defense Acquisitions," p. 20, http://www.fas.org/sgp/crs/natsec/RL34026.pdf.

71. Ibid.

72. Ibid., p. 21.

73. Appendix 14, Statutory Reporting Requirement Career Path and Other Requirements for Military Personnel in the Acquisition Field, accessed June 10, 2012, https://acc.dau.mil/CommunityBrowser.aspx?id=360666.

74. Stephanie L. Watson, "Training the Army Acquisition Workforce," *Defense AT&L: Special Edition* (2011), http://www.dau.mil/pubscats/ATL%20Docs/Mar-Apr11/Watson_mar-apr.pdf.

75. Cui Yongxin, "PLA Air Force Military Representative 60th Anniversary of Outstanding Contributions" (空军军事代表派驻六十周年成果丰硕贡献突出)], *Air Force News* (空军报增刊), April 12, 2012, http://tp.chinamil.com.cn/2012/2012-04/12/content_4833020.htm.

76. "Interview with Dr. Malcolm Ross O'Neill, Assistant Secretary of the Army for Acquisitions, Logistics, and Technology," *Army AL&T* (2011): 4, http://asc.army.mil/docs/pubs/alt/2011/1_JanFebMar/full/00_ALT_magazine_Full_Issue_201101.pdf.

77. US Army Acquisition Support Center, Workforce Management Division, "Acquisition Career Management Workforce Brief," accessed May 20, 2012, http://asc.army.mil/docs/regions/Acquisition_Workforce_Briefing_new.pdf.

78. Personal Finance and Transition Website, "Chapter 13—Employment Restrictions after Leaving the Military," accessed May 20, 2012, http://www.turbotap.org/export/sites/default/transition/resources/PDF/TransitionGuide_RC_C13_Restrictions.pdf.

79. Shay Assad, "DOD Components Are Not Sending Required Information on Contract Awards to the Office of Public Affairs" (Washington, DC: US Government Accountability Office, November 30, 2010). Shay Assad was the director of defense procurement and acquisition policy at the Department of Defense at the time.

80. Ibid.

Chapter Five

The Rise of Chinese Civil-Military Integration

Daniel Alderman, Lisa Crawford,
Brian Lafferty, and Aaron Shraberg

In its latest push to promote innovation in China's defense industries and raise the military's level of advanced science and technology (S&T), the Chinese government has crafted a strategy that is focused on greatly expanding its utilization of civil-military integration (CMI). Hu Jintao signaled the start of this effort in his report to the 17th Central Party Congress in 2007, in which he stated, "We will adjust and reform the national defense S&T industrial system and the weapons and equipment procurement system, and we will enhance the quality, efficiency, and indigenous innovation capability of our weapons and equipment development. We will establish and perfect a weapons and equipment research and manufacturing system that 'combines the military and civilian sectors' and 'locates military potential in civilian capabilities' . . . and we will take the development road of military and civilian integration with Chinese characteristics."[1] At its heart, this statement was designed to provide momentum for formerly tentative efforts to dismantle the structural barriers that have kept China's defense economy and military S&T institutions mostly cut off from the rest of the country. Hu and other Chinese leaders have recognized that the defense industry's relative independence, particularly in its systems of procurement and weapons and equipment research and development (R&D), is counterproductive, preventing the defense industry from effectively tapping into the S&T boom that is rapidly emerging in the rest of the country. Likewise, the defense industry can do more to serve civilian needs, by sharing technological discoveries, producing high-quality goods for the civilian marketplace, and acting as a consumer for new technological products developed in the nonmilitary sector. Reformers hope that increased collaboration between military and civilian actors will be a boon to development within both systems.

China's focus on CMI comes at a time when its policy apparatus is consumed with advancing the nation's S&T capabilities. China's leaders view scientific innovation as a matter of both national security and economic necessity, and they have made it one of the government's highest priorities. Premier Wen Jiabao, at a ceremony honoring Chinese scientific achievements in 2009 stated, "Strength in science and technology decides a nation's fate. In today's world, where technology is developing at a swift and vigorous pace, countries that do not pay attention to science and technology will be weeded out [淘汰]."[2] Similarly, Hu Jintao has proclaimed, "In the current period, science and technology, especially strategic high technology, has already become the focus in the competition for comprehensive national strength. Raising our ability in indigenous innovation is the strategic core of our state development, and it is the key to raising our comprehensive national strength."[3] This imperative has been stressed with equal vigor in China's defense circles, as leaders in the defense industry have acknowledged that China's defense industries face serious challenges in becoming more innovative and keeping pace with rapid technological advances around the globe.[4]

As envisioned, China's CMI reforms amount to a win-win development strategy, with direct benefits that are easy to recognize for stakeholders throughout China's political system. However, China's CMI reforms also involve some fundamental reordering of long-standing traditions and procedures; so, while Chinese actors are publicly unified in their support for the reforms, in most cases the hard part of enacting them still lies ahead. This chapter provides a broad sketch of China's current CMI reforms as they impact the defense industry, paying particular attention to how CMI is trying to enhance civil-military research collaboration and civilian participation in the production of military-use technology. It will also help illuminate some of the key problems that currently hamper China's CMI efforts and the contradictions that are being targeted in the government's current policy debates.

China's Civil-Military Integration Concept

Civil-military integration, broadly conceived, is not a new concept in the People's Republic of China. A number of important elements of Mao's defense policies were centered on taking advantage of mutual contributions by the civilian and defense sectors, and this tradition helped create permissive conditions for the direction that civil-military linkages took after his death. Since the start of the reform era, Deng and his successors have implemented initiatives that sought to improve various aspects of operations in the People's Liberation Army (PLA) by forging closer ties between military and civilian systems. Deng's CMI policies, encapsulated by the slogan "combining the military and civilian sectors" (军民结合), emphasized encouraging China's defense industries to produce goods for the civilian market, as the government wanted to encourage the development of dual-use technologies and maintain defense industry capacities in an era of relative peace. This kind of defense conversion (军转民) continued in similar fashion at the start of Jiang Zemin's tenure as party chairman, but by the late 1990s Chinese civil-military integration had begun to be more openly oriented towards cooperative civilian and military S&T production and towards breaking down barriers that had kept civilian entities from participating in R&D and in manufacturing areas long monopolized by the defense industries.

In its current state, China's CMI strategy under Hu Jintao has developed into a much broader, more complex, and more systemic attempt to blend civilian and military operations than anything that preceded it. Hu has introduced a new way to express the concept ("civil-military integration" [军民融合] instead of "combining the military and civilian sectors" [军民结合]), directed policy makers to learn from past experience and the best practices of other countries, and ordered them to use that knowledge to find new ways to better link military and civilian capabilities. His expanded conception of CMI has specifically pursued "overall coordination" (统筹规划) by merging defense modernization planning with the country's broader economic planning. It aims to join, integrate, and combine planning efforts in economic and military development in order to utilize capital, technology, human capital, facilities, and information most effectively at the national strategic level. In doing so, China hopes to reduce wasteful redundancy in the use of common resources needed by military and civilian actors, improve the overall efficiency of national resource consumption, and improve the central government's ability to direct resources where it wants them to go. The feasibility of integrating the two sectors is based on an assumption that there is considerable overlap between military and civilian S&T needs and that up to 85 percent of technologies have dual-use applications.[5] Therefore, CMI would not only mitigate the severity of the "guns versus butter" dilemma by reducing the amount of resources that the defense sector would squeeze out of the rest of the economy, but it could also foster better use of the defense sector's S&T expertise in overall economic development and the promotion of civilian S&T.[6] For the military specifically, Defense Minister Liang Guanglie has stated that the goals of CMI reforms are to "provide rich resources and sustained momentum for national defense and armed forces modernization, to obtain more effective security guarantees and technological support for national defense and armed forces building from economic development, and to promote the coordinated development and positive interaction of the economy and national defense construction."[7]

Under Hu, the impetus to increase cooperation between the defense and civilian sectors is primarily driven by technological need and the relative strength of the civilian S&T base. For many years the vanguard of the PRC's S&T efforts was the defense sector, which received the lion's share of China's limited S&T talent and development resources.[8] However, since the start of the reform era, the locus of China's S&T activity has steadily moved beyond the military's sole domain. The most advanced technologies are increasingly found in the civilian sector, and China's rapid economic development has created a civilian capacity for S&T innovation that the government expects will be much broader and deeper than anything the defense sector can marshal on its own. Given these conditions, Chinese analysts have concluded that relying solely on the defense sector to provide technological support for the PLA is inadequate and wasteful.[9] Accordingly, China's leaders have begun to craft political strategies that look to the civilian sector to provide key resources for defense-related S&T innovation, in recognition of the fact that the civilian sector's "spin-on" potential is substantial, and that China's defense industries can no longer keep up with the necessary pace of innovation on their own.

In its pursuit of a CMI strategy, China can utilize the growing S&T output from a network of research centers, universities, large and mid-sized enterprises, state key labs, and supporting institutions that collectively form the main sources for S&T innovation. This innovation can then spread to create returns at relevant points throughout the civilian and military systems. At the risk of oversimplification, one could say that the way Chinese innovation spread in the past can be split into channels that transferred technology from the military to the civilian sector and channels that transferred civilian technology and resources to military use.[10] These channels represent the foundation upon which the government's current CMI strategy is being built.

Defense Conversion (军转民)

Throughout the reform era, defense conversion has been the dominant form of Chinese CMI, as China has tried to leverage the defense industry's more advanced S&T capabilities into productive spin-off benefits to the civilian economy. This mode of tech transfer has taken the following forms:

- *Direct transfer of defense S&T advances to nondefense entities.* In this form, described as the most common method of spreading the defense sector's S&T products, defense S&T innovations are passed on to civilian entities via the technology market. Some of this transfer is accomplished through the declassification (解密) of certain defense S&T advances; in other cases it occurs via trade fairs that are held around China every year, in which some of the defense sector's S&T advances are made available to a wider market.

- *Cooperative alliance between defense scientific institutions and civilian scientific institutions on particular civilian- or military-use research projects.* In the course of cooperating in the development of particular research projects, the defense sector's scientific institutions share some of their S&T products with their civilian partners, introducing that technology to the civilian sector. Although this typically happens in large-scale projects, like the Qinshan and Dayawan nuclear power plants, it also occurs in small- and medium-scale projects.

- *Defense scientific institutions establish affiliated enterprises for civilian use.* This has been described as the most effective method for using the defense sector's innovation capacity. When scientific institutions use enterprises as an arena for disseminating and showcasing new products,[11] defense sector scientific institutions can establish a working relationship with suitable, preexisting civilian enterprises (via mergers, contracted work, renting the enterprises' facilities, and so on) or create their own enterprises. The latter strategy is most often employed when the marketable technologies are relatively niche products and the scientific institution needs to establish its own pioneering enterprise.

- *Defense sector scientific personnel engage in research or production management for civilian-use products.* This is a key tech transfer method, in that it is one of the simpler means of moving scientific knowledge from the defense sector to the civilian sector, particularly when it relates to production management. In the past few years, the government has created policies that allow defense sector scientific personnel to work as contractors in the civilian sector, either detailing them to civilian departments on a temporary basis or allowing them to concurrently hold a position in a civilian department.

SPIN-ON TECH TRANSFER (民转军)

China's leaders believe that, due to the special needs of the national security sector—in particular, secrecy imperatives and the need to guarantee national security capabilities independently of considerations like efficiency and the whims of the market—China's defense industries cannot be marketized like a normal industry or opened up to the civilian sector beyond a certain extent.[12] However, they still recognize that there are significant potential benefits to dismantling some of the barriers that impede civilian participation in defense-related S&T production. While the defense sector enjoys some of China's most advanced technologies, facilities, and talent, it can no longer satisfy the PLA's critical need for innovation on its own; and by tapping into the civilian sector's resources, China hopes to capture significant spin-on benefits. This process is still in its initial stages, as will be discussed below, but as envisioned, China's spin-on mode of tech transfer might take the following forms:

- *Adapting civilian technology for military use.* This occurs when civilian-use technologies are adapted for military use and are used in the development of defense weaponry and defense-related scientific production.
- *Providing civilian capital for military use.* This occurs when civilian-use research and production resources are used in the service of defense construction. The defense industry's shareholding (股份制) system reform is an indirect offshoot of this, designed to create subsidiary enterprises that can attract civilian capital and resources.

It is important to note that China's plan for its current and near future civil-military integration is not focused on simply improving spin-on or spin-off strategies in isolation. Instead, it is chiefly concerned with making them part of a dynamic, interconnected innovation system that develops organic links between relevant entities, so that innovation can be initiated from as many different sources as possible and so there can be as many avenues as possible to get innovation on the quickest, most efficient path to production. To these ends, a significant part of China's CMI reforms involve working to break down barriers between actors and to coordinate and harmonize the innovation efforts being pursued in four separate, broadly conceived strata:[13]

- *Top layer:* the administrative and management level, led by the Central Military Commission (CMC) and State Council. These bodies are responsible for providing a supportive environment for CMI-based S&T innovation. They make relevant policies to guide national innovation, direct S&T investments, organize S&T plans, and evaluate S&T progress.
- *Second layer:* the technological innovation receiver layer, made up of civilian and defense enterprises. These enterprises are usually thought of as the main target of CMI and national innovation strategies, because their primary goal is to get technological advances to the production stage.
- *Third layer:* the technological innovation supplier level, made up of scientific institutions and colleges and universities that are engaged in research. This layer is considered the foundation for civil-military technology innovation, since it is the primary source of advanced learning, new technologies, and creative talent.
- *Fourth layer:* the tech transfer intermediaries layer, made up of institutions created by the government, enterprises, schools, and nongovernmental organizations to facilitate S&T development and tech transfer. These entities distribute resources, provide information, and act as bridges linking relevant institutions. Examples from this category include the government's Torch High-Technology Industry Development Center and various university-supported tech transfer centers, like Qinghua University's International Tech Transfer Center (ITTC).

Making CMI Work at the Administrative Level

In order to break down barriers and make the disparate civilian and military parts of the national innovation system work together more effectively, Chinese analyses of its problems and prospects often argue that CMI needs more regulation and guidance. This may appear surprising, considering that the government has produced dozens of CMI-related regulations, guidelines, and opinions in the past few years, at both the central and local levels. However, critics of these efforts within China complain that the clear majority of these documents are little more than broad statements of principle, lacking operational specificity and detailed rules and regulations.[14] Much of this vagueness can be blamed on the fact that the government still lacks a clear sense of how to craft policies that broaden CMI effectively. Its legislation tends to be more aspirational than purposeful, leaving Chinese actors without reliable guidance on numerous aspects of CMI implementation. China's policy making is further complicated by the prevalence of intractable contradictions within the national innovation system. China's leaders are not legislating their idealized vision for CMI from scratch; they must work within a preexisting system full of entrenched interests and competing imperatives, and still try to shape reforms in ways that achieve their goals. Some of the hurdles they face do not lend themselves to easy, win-win solutions.

One of the most difficult challenges for the government is that the traditional segregation between the military and civilian sectors has acted as a fundamental drag on CMI reform. The PLA and civilian systems have for decades operated within their own boundaries, and this isolation has encouraged them to focus narrowly on corporate interests and caused them to develop in ways that are now at odds with the needs of CMI. For example, the PLA has long been accustomed to conducting nearly every aspect of its operations on its own—with its own resources, regulations, and standard procedures—even when the operations overlap with civilian functions. Over the years this has created an entire universe of deep-rooted barriers, redundancies, and incompatibilities between the military and civilian sectors, and they will be difficult to redress. Changing guidelines to integrate civilian and military functions can involve complex untangling of interrelated guidelines on both the military and civilian side, beyond simply making military and civilian guidelines compatible (which itself can be quite complex).

Even the concept of merging civilian and military systems can be a barrier, as resistance to change and entrenched interests favor the status quo, despite what the propaganda outlets say about the great strides that have been made in CMI work. The civilian and military sectors have done little strategic thinking about the needs or interests of the other side, and Chinese analysts worry that the military in particular may have a preference for continuing to do things on its own, to ensure that its core missions are not disrupted.[15] The civil-military divide strikes at the heart of China's latest CMI strategy, because it limits opportunities for cooperation between civilian and military S&T institutions, decreases technology exchanges, hampers the integration of research efforts even when the research areas overlap, and makes optimizing the distribution of resources impossible. It is no wonder that Chinese propaganda outlets have been unrelenting in their insistence that China must unwaveringly support the government's CMI development strategy.

Another complicating factor for Chinese leaders is that some of the defense industry's needs are not necessarily conducive to CMI. The government must guard against the possibility that changing policies to make CMI work better may harm other areas of national concern. For instance, the top-down, highly administrative management method used to govern the defense industries helps to ensure that those industries are not ignoring or deprioritizing national security imperatives. However, it exacts a cost on initiative within the defense industries and does not lend itself to the kind of flexibility and autonomy that innovation strategies often require. If the government gave the defense industries more autonomy to pursue their own interests, or if it integrated defense industries into the civilian sector in a way that made them subject to bottom-up pressures or the whims of the civilian market, defense industries might pursue business plans that did not (or could not) fully meet defense readiness and national security needs. A similar dynamic exists because defense sector technological innovation unavoidably involves secrecy; specs, components, designs, and other aspects of defense technologies are typically kept out of the public eye. Many technical aspects of Chinese military capabilities are classified, and the government must weigh the potential benefits of letting the civilian sector use and learn from military S&T achievements versus the risk that sensitive information could get out in the open. Even when the government decides to make certain technologies available for civilian products, the complex declassification process slows the pace at which the technologies reach the public, and thus still hampers the spread of innovation.[16]

In addition to these kinds of "rob Peter to pay Paul" choices, the government is constrained by the underdevelopment of some basic aspects of China's S&T system, which will require significant improvements before deeper CMI reforms can proceed. For example, despite the existence of information-sharing channels and reams of data, Chinese analysts claim that the government has a generally poor awareness of the supply and demand situation for technological innovation in the country. This is not necessarily a problem in all contexts, but given China's preference to guide CMI from above, this lack of awareness hampers the government's ability to make policies that push integration in preferred directions. The government does not reliably know how many defense technologies are available for potential civilian use, what the specific characteristics of those technologies are, or which technologies and projects the defense industries want to open up to civilian participation. As a result, although government managers are focused on S&T development and CMI, they still lack an accurate picture of the system they are trying to administer. A well-developed statistical S&T data collection system that is geared towards the needs of CMI has not yet been built.[17]

The implementation of China's CMI strategy is also hampered by weak intellectual property protections, particularly for military products entering the civilian market. Where China's patent laws address such transfers, they are mostly concerned with how patented civilian technology is transferred to military use and do not provide enough guidance for military technology that is introduced into the civilian market. This leaves military technological advances vulnerable to intellectual property violations when they are exposed to the civilian market, and this has dampened the military sector's enthusiasm for tech transfer.[18]

One final systemic hurdle is that Chinese civilian and military enterprises are not naturally complementary; they are not quite "like units." This difference presents problems in an environment where they would (ideally) be working in tandem. Most civilian enterprises are relatively small-scale, lacking a reputation and a track record within the military sector. Purely on these grounds, they may find it difficult to find partners or markets in the defense industry. Their size relative to the defense conglomerates' also presents notable entry barriers for civilian companies. China's ten defense industry group companies have a massive advantage in capital, market share, talent, and facilities, making it challenging for any outside company to identify and exploit a competitive niche.[19] Additionally, the military applies its own product standards to any item sold for military use, and they are stricter than corresponding standards in the civilian sector. There is a general concern that civilian companies would chase lower costs at the expense of higher quality, making such companies poor fits for military product development. A final concern within the military is that nonmilitary enterprises without any experience in working with the PLA will be ignorant of the military's quality requirements. Since it is currently difficult for civilians to even find product standards for the military market, military consumers fear that outside companies will be unprepared to offer high-quality services to the defense sector.[20]

Civilian Academic Institutions and Research Support for CMI

Apart from these administrative issues, CMI policies also face problems at the innovation supplier level as the government strives to improve the defense industry's utilization of S&T discoveries. Backed by a deluge of resources and governmental initiatives to promote academic S&T activities and to build up S&T infrastructure, Chinese civilian academic institutions currently serve as research workhorses, producing an enormous volume of scientific product each year. They are critical suppliers of original, advanced research, and they stand ready to provide key support for high-tech innovation in the defense sector. As Chinese analysts have noted, the rapid increase in the level of technology used in the civilian sector, combined with corresponding advances in civilian sector R&D capability, has pushed the civilian sector past the defense sector in a growing number of technological areas. If China were not promoting the military's access to this S&T capability, the defense industry would be left with suboptimal access to the country's most advanced technologies.[21] Duplicated research efforts are also a problem. China's separation of its civilian and defense research systems has meant that a great deal of advanced S&T research has been pursued in both domains without benefit of collaboration, resource sharing, or other policies that would make this research less wasteful.[22] Accordingly, one important focus of China's CMI strategy has been improving interactions between civilian research institutions and the defense industries, particularly in fields where China's civilian research is most sophisticated, like computers and sensing technologies.[23]

The drive to encourage civilian academic institutions to contribute to the development of military technology began in earnest during the 1990s, when the defense industry began to recognize that China's higher learning institutions could act as a source of technical and scientific expertise.[24] To develop this capability, the government established the 211 and 985 Projects (211工程 and 985 工程), in 1995 and 1998, respectively. These programs made top-tier universities the focus of the government's efforts to develop S&T research and expertise at the collegiate level. Over the years, the Ministry of Finance has heavily invested in the more than 100 academic institutions designated as 211 Project schools, spending 2.7 billion renminbi (RMB) during the 9th Five-Year Plan (FYP), 6 billion RMB during the 10th FYP, and as much as 10 billion RMB during the 11th FYP.[25] These schools responded by producing the majority of China's S&T graduate students and are now the site of most of the country's key laboratories and key academic disciplines.[26] The 985 Project is similar to 211, also focusing government resources on key universities, but it is even more distinguished; only about 40 universities have the distinction of being 985 Project schools.[27] This kind of targeted funding on star universities, and on key academic disciplines within those universities, has improved China's facilities for scientific research and made the schools more effective instruments for innovation.[28]

The development of China's S&T expertise has also been helped by a proliferation of new state key laboratories and national defense S&T key laboratories with a particular purpose. These "key" labs are intended to "support cutting-edge breakthroughs as important platforms for cutting-edge technologies," and their construction became a national strategic development objective during the 9th FYP.[29] National defense S&T key labs were opened specifically to provide coverage for new technology areas that were deemed critical to national defense.[30] As the key labs have developed, they have become magnets for funding and talent. By the beginning of 2010, China's government had created 218 state key laboratories and 232 state engineering technology research centers to serve as leaders of research in critical technologies.[31] More than 60 percent of the key labs and 36 percent of the state engineering technology centers were located in China's colleges and universities.[32] According to Ministry of Science and Technology statistics, by 2009 the key labs employed around 13,000 people working on more than 20,000 research topics, and in 2008 they attracted more than 7.8 billion RMB in research funds.[33]

With this foundation in place, the government's challenge has been to create policies that foster mutually beneficial interaction among these S&T actors. China's academic databases indicate that a limited but significant portion of the publicly available articles on high-technology topics are coauthored by researchers from different institutions, and projects involving multidisciplinary teams from more than one institution are not difficult to find. These partnerships can be between civilian academic institutions, between civilian and military academic institutions, between civilian academic institutions and military units, or between civilian academic institutions and enterprises. Key projects are particularly likely to be collaborative, since the expertise needed to carry out specialized, cutting-edge research may need to be drawn from multiple sources.

The problem, as identified in Chinese academic sources, is in successfully "transforming" (转化) this research into real products. On this score, these sources indicate that the discoveries being made in academic institutions are still not effectively making it into the marketplace as new products. They estimate that only 10 to 15 percent of scientific advances are transferred into the product side of the national innovation system.[34] The reasons for this are not because outside units have no need for these discoveries or that the technologies are not viable as commercial products. In 2005, the Ministry of Science and Technology released the results of a survey it conducted on the economic potential of major S&T discoveries (重大科技成果) produced in the academic sector. The conclusion was that only 12 percent of them lacked market prospects.[35] Even if that conclusion were overly optimistic regarding the market potential for new

S&T achievements, the gulf between the apparent product viability of S&T research versus what is actually realized is a source of concern for Chinese policy makers. The inability to get more technological advances to the production stage is quite problematic for a system in which academic research is envisioned as a key source of innovation.

A 2005 Ministry of Education survey determined that discoveries were failing to turn into products because there were no driving mechanisms within academic institutions to incentivize the production of high-technology inventions, and no clear economic and investment mechanisms outside academic institutions to encourage the adoption of academic S&T output.[36] Given the risk inherent in trying to bring new products to the marketplace, and given China's relative lack of enterprises that could regularly take on that risk, more needed to be done from a policy perspective to make up for these deficiencies. On the academic side of the ledger, the most prominent incentives for research personnel were heavily weighted towards publishing (and patent filing, to a lesser extent). As one academic noted, if researchers published their findings and tried to patent their discoveries, this was often all that was needed to advance in one's career.[37] When the government was evaluating academic institutions in terms of their S&T contributions, it was still focused on how well schools were integrating S&T work into their own educational activities, not on whether or not schools were getting their innovations into the marketplace.

An ongoing lack of communication between colleges and universities and the outside tech market has compounded the incentive problem; there is little coordination of supply and demand and a paucity of opportunities for academic researchers to learn how to exploit their inventions. One survey found that most academic researchers had only superficial knowledge of the market environment even in their specialty, and almost none had done any specialized research on relevant market conditions.[38] This lack of market awareness is apparently prevalent in Chinese academic institutions.[39] However, without the ability to understand what technologies are in demand in the defense market, researchers are unlikely to make any special efforts to focus their research in relevant directions. Additionally, because the government still plays a key role in determining research priorities, it employs a relatively top-down, traditional mode of determining national S&T priorities. The expert groups that propose projects consist only of government workers and researchers; they do not include the market analysts and economists who might be able to communicate the needs of the market and help build bridges between the two sectors.[40]

The other key obstacle hindering technology transformation efforts is the country's relatively weak intellectual property (IP) system. China's current system of IP protection is dual track, consisting of a patent system and separate policies for utilizing S&T discoveries (技术成果) until they enter the patent system. However, Chinese analysts note that the latter policies do little to establish concrete legal ownership and financial rights for technological discoveries. Consequently, until patent protections are achieved, individuals often cannot gain effective legal protections for their new innovations.[41] In addition, Chinese researchers are not yet in the habit of filing patent applications for their discoveries, so their ability to find a market for them is severely curtailed. For researchers, military uses of S&T discoveries are particularly unrewarding, because they are inevitably produced in the course of projects that are funded by the state, so any intellectual property derived from them belongs to the state.[42]

Chinese analysts have noted that the government's legislation regarding ownership of IP is still focused on establishing principles, rather than operational rules and guidelines, and it has done little to clarify rights, responsibilities, and interests for relevant parties. In the absence of a more developed protection system, IP has become a common source of conflict between academic institutions and other organizations and has limited the enthusiasm of researchers, academics in particular, to engage in S&T collaborations with other units.[43] Without a robust IP protection system for technological discoveries, cooperative partnerships between researchers and enterprises are vulnerable to disputes about how much the technology is worth, at what stage in the development process IP protections begin, and when a technology should be considered mature (成熟).[44] As it stands, there is already a large body of research that becomes public each year (via publishing and other avenues, like applications for awards) without IP protection, and the lack of IP standardization among different units makes the potential losses even greater.[45]

One of China's major strategies to foster S&T innovation has centered on facilitating formal alliances between industry, academia, and research institutions (产学研),[46] which would be a breakthrough principle for S&T innovation development. These coalitions are intended to spur the creation of joint R&D institutions and technological coalitions within industries, in which universities and research institutions discover technologies and carry out R&D while enterprises commoditize, design, and manufacture products.[47] Such alliances solve a number of problems at once, balancing the key behavioral deficiencies of each institutional type with a partner that excels in those areas. In this fashion, Chinese industry's insufficient focus on indigenous innovation and its general inability to achieve technology innovation are ameliorated by partnerships with institutions that focus on those things, and universities and research institutes are partnered with suitable technology companies, incentivized to produce and distribute new technologies.[48] China's attempts to institutionalize these kinds of alliances are still a work in progress. Critics note that, despite a proliferation of news conferences touting S&T discoveries, the number of actual project agreements that result from them is small. Similarly, although numerous agreements of intent are signed at S&T exchange meetings, most are never realized.[49]

Civil-Military Reforms and Private Enterprise

With respect to CMI's impact on innovation production, one of China's other major CMI-related reforms involves allowing private enterprises to produce goods for the military market. Although piecemeal, these reforms have—for the first time—formally allowed private companies (民营公司 or 非公企业) to enter and compete in the Chinese defense market. This process, which is a part of the effort to "spin-on" civilian innovation into the defense sector, is aimed at dual-use technologies (两用技术) and new products developed exclusively for military purposes (军用).

China's Goals in Allowing Private Participation in the Defense Industry

China's two primary goals in allowing private companies to participate in the defense sector are to increase competition and create spin-on benefits. Private companies also offer alternative channels for raising capital within the defense sector, allowing leaders to address the defense industry's dependence on government investment.[50] The assumption that greater private competition will lead to increased innovation is based in part on lessons that Chinese leaders have learned from abroad. China's extensive research on foreign defense industries and their relationships with private companies has offered assurances that a defense industry open to private enterprise can be more competitive and creative than a more restricted, state-controlled system. Although the implementation of these kinds of systems in other countries has been long and arduous, these examples have shown Chinese military leaders the positive impact of the diversified supply chain allowed by multiple private companies in competition.[51]

The anticipated benefit to opening the defense industry to private competition has made Chinese leaders receptive to the change in precedent, but they recognize that reforms in this area are not without some risk. Critics have argued that there may not be enough safeguards in place to protect state secrets, that private companies are not stable, and that they do not produce products of sufficient quality for such a critical industry.[52] In addition, there is anxiety over the lack of a clear path of communication between private firms and the military, as the two sides discuss their needs and capabilities. This last concern exemplifies the bureaucratic challenge facing private companies, in that the defense market has not yet fully institutionalized structures and procedures to support private participation.[53]

Steps Taken to Allow Private Participation in the Defense Industry

For decades, protected by numerous legal boundaries, the state-owned defense industry acted as a monopoly, devoid of even internal competitive bidding. These exclusions of privately owned companies were codified early on in the reform period by the 1988 Provisional Regulation Number 12 (中国人民共和国私营企业暂行条例 第 12 规定), which stated that private companies "could not participate in the defense sector" because, as elements of a "special manufacturing sector," defense products had to be researched and manufactured by the defense industry's state-owned enterprises.[54]

The process for allowing private companies to contribute to the defense sector began in 2002, when the Central Military Commission issued the PLA Equipment Purchasing Regulations (中国人民解放军装备采购条例), which called for competitive bidding to take place for most of China's military-use goods.[55] After its passage, the General Armament Department (GAD) incrementally released a series of five rules that laid the foundation for a more competitive market for weapons procurement and weakened the arguments for keeping the defense market closed to civilian participation.[56] The final legal breakthrough occurred in February 2005, when the State Council promulgated the State Council Opinions on Encouraging, Supporting, and Guiding the Economic Development of Individual Privately Owned and Other Non-Public Enterprises (国务院关于鼓励支持和引导个体私营等非公有制经济发展的若干意见 [非公经济36条]).[57]

While this opinion opened the door, at first there was a distinct lack of associated guidelines and regulations to condition this activity. Companies outside of the state-owned system had never formally participated in the defense industry; all of the military and government oversight mechanisms had been handled internally within a closed system. No rules were in place to govern how private companies could register for defense manufacturing, communicate with defense enterprises in order to enter bids, receive oversight, or learn about official military standards for production. The responsibility for rectifying these shortcomings has fallen on the State Administration for Science, Technology, and Industry for National Defense (SASTIND) and the GAD. In this division of labor, the GAD is tasked with regulating private companies and overseeing the actual procurement of equipment, and SASTIND plays a primarily regulatory role.

These two agencies act as gatekeepers for private defense firms, by overseeing the application and certification process for would-be defense manufacturing firms. Any private civilian company that wishes to produce military-use goods must receive three certifications. The first is a secrecy certification (保密证), which signifies that the company meets the security requirements for producing sensitive, military-use goods. The second is certification for specific products, indicating that these products must meet military standards for quality. Finally, companies must receive a Certificate for Undertaking Equipment Manufacturing (装备承制单位资格证书), indicating that they meet the corporate requirements (having to do with personnel, capital, etc.) for defense market producers.[58]

Enterprises with these three certificates can then be placed on the two lists maintained by SASTIND and the GAD that name the full roster of companies permitted to manufacture goods for the defense market. These lists offer official assurance to the buyers in the defense market that the companies meet the standards for military grade production.

The GAD's list is the Directory of Certified Organizations for Equipment Manufacture (装备承制单位名录). Inclusion in it is described as "extremely important" and the "ultimate goal" for any company wishing to manufacture military use products; companies wishing to enter a bid or take part in weapons development must be on this list. The only exceptions are companies or special departments that have been given special permission by the CMC or State Council to produce for the defense market.[59] The second regulatory directory that companies must join is the Weapons and Equipment Research and Production Permit List (武器装备科研生产许可目录),[60] previously managed solely by the Commission for Science, Technology, and Industry for National Defense (COSTIND) but now jointly managed by the GAD and SASTIND.

The difference between the GAD list and the GAD/SASTIND list is that the former allows an organization to manufacture military-use products, and the latter determines what types of military-use products it can research and produce. There are two types of permits that companies can receive for the GAD/

SASTIND list. A class one permit is for products that involve "core technology and equipment"; a class two permit is for "subsystems and special auxiliary products."[61] Private companies were initially allowed to seek only a class two permit, but now, in very rare cases, they can hold both.[62] The one publicized example of a dual-permit company is the Baoji Special Vehicles Company.[63] Since nearly all of the civilian sector enterprises with permits to sell on the defense market are limited to class two, they have been characterized as being stuck on the margins of the defense market.[64]

ADDRESSING THE REMAINING PROBLEMS

One of the most pressing problems hampering the government's efforts to open up the defense market is that the state-owned defense industries have enjoyed marked competitive advantages over private firms beyond what they already have in their large size and close government connections. State-owned enterprises (SOE) are entitled to various tax exemptions, such as land tax and value added tax, for undertaking defense-related contracts, but these benefits currently are not available to private-sector firms, even if they perform the same work.[65] SOEs are also entitled to priority consideration in bids on PLA procurement and R&D contracts, even if they are bidding against technologically more qualified private-sector firms.[66] Also, industrial information in the defense sector tends to be excessively classified, making it inaccessible to private-sector firms without the requisite level of security clearance. Even the administrative system in the military market is hostile to nongovernmental enterprises, as the eligibility certification process is particularly onerous and time-consuming for firms without prior defense-sector experience. Indeed, in 2005 many private-sector executives reported that the complexity of the bureaucratic procedures alone was sufficient to deter them from entering the military market.[67] As one commentary stated in 2008, "Most of the present policies, laws, and regulations are directed and designed for state-owned defense firms. . . . [T]his doesn't suit private firms . . . and makes it difficult to have a level playing field"[68]

In the run-up to the 12th Five-Year Plan, the CMC and State Council jointly issued "Some Opinions on Building and Improving a 'Combining of the Military and Civilian Sectors' and 'Locating Military Potential in Civilian Capabilities' Weapons Research and Production System" (关于建立和完善军民结合寓军于民武器装备科研生产体系的若干意见) to provide some guidance in addressing the aforementioned problems.[69] Now known simply as document Number 37, this document describes the government's near-term priorities for CMI, placing special emphasis on reforming how privately held companies and civilian economy entities interact with the defense industry, and it lays out a series of goals for overcoming most of the issues facing private firms in the defense market by the end of the 12th Five-Year Plan, which runs from 2011 to 2015.[70]

The thrust of the document is recognition of the barriers to CMI implementation in the military's weapons and equipment market. These problems, as described in the document, start with the fact that the defense industries remain closed off (封闭) and that there is not enough support for production that "combines the military and civilian sectors." As a result, the degree of resource sharing between defense industries and other actors is not high, the mechanics of institutional interaction are not smooth, and relevant policies, laws, and regulations still need further refinement.

In terms of basic needs, the document outlines two goals for the near term. The first, notably, is establishing a crack defense industry (精干军工) as the center of the government's efforts to serve the needs of weapons development and the socialist market economy. Given that the defense industry is both a problem and a solution with respect to CMI development, this is probably a good place to start. However, as we have seen throughout the long path of defense industry reform, the industry does not move easily. The second basic need described by the document is to cultivate a market system (市场主体) that accords with the needs of the modern enterprise system and the modern scientific research center system. This appears to be targeting the various factors that have inhibited the transfer of technology innovation throughout the system, in recognition that market incentives are still not properly aligned to encourage this movement.

The means the document prescribes to achieve these goals focus on coordination mechanisms and structural incentives. While on paper the government has weakened the barriers that exist between sectors, practical barriers, particularly with respect to traditional modes of doing things, still remain. To address this situation, the document calls for using the next three to five years (essentially the duration of the 12th FYP) to improve coordination and "basically achieve" (基本实现) a host of improvements, including interflow, mutual engagement, and complementarity between defense use S&T and civilian use S&T and between national defense S&T industries and civilian S&T industries. The government will also use this time frame to address the inequities and disincentives that private firms face in trying to enter the defense market, involving a drive to "basically achieve" fairness in financial investment, tax policies, access to markets, and defense industry fixed capital investment. Other tasks outlined by the document Number 37 include better sharing and coordination in the utilization of civilian and military resources; enhancing of market competition without weakening product standards; making progress in the reform of the defense industry's scientific research institutions; further developing competitive purchasing, centralized purchasing, and integrated purchasing; quickly developing industries that "combine military and civilian sectors"; and strengthening the industrial base for weapons development.

The government's awareness of the issues it needs to resolve is helped by efforts to gather information and feedback. For example, the annual All-China Federation of Industry and Commerce's surveys of private industries entering the defense market, now in their third year, ask respondents to list any defense manufacturing certificates and licenses they possess, before asking for detailed information on any technologies or products that they are currently researching and manufacturing or would like to participate in researching and manufacturing in the future.[71] This survey presumably helps the military overcome its communication gap with private companies, as the federation is able to reach a wider audience within the private sector. Another state survey, conducted in 2010, looked at whether private companies felt that the laws redefining the relationship between SOEs and private firms had been carried out successfully, asking respondents whether they were familiar with the loosened restrictions against defense manufacturing by private businesses and whether the legal changes of 2005 had had any impact on their own business.[72]

The government's willingness to continue refining this aspect of CMI illustrates its importance, raising the possibility that major reforms will be undertaken within the next three to five years to further improve the process by which private firms enter the defense industry. One sign that these issues are being addressed would be the creation of a more unified purchasing system that would provide greater fairness for private companies.[73] No single group is now responsible for oversight of private companies, and one might need to be created, to establish more formal channels of communication with defense consumers while also managing the production certification process, processing application fees, determining the quality of military products, and ensuring that secrecy needs are met.[74]

Conclusions

Chinese analysts have demonstrated an awareness that civil-military integration, as a policy-making challenge, is systemic in scope, requiring more than just a few targeted reforms for full implementation. There are many institutions, at various levels, that must bend and align towards the same endpoint and many actors who must shake off old interests to help reshape behavior within the system. At the same time, CMI's nature is such that it encompasses actors, institutions, and processes that are embedded in other systems as well. Those other systems may shape behaviors in ways that are counter to the goals of CMI, or in ways that distract actors from focusing on CMI's imperatives. Therefore, the challenge for China's leaders is to ensure not only that the elements within the CMI policy system are aligned and working effectively but also that countervailing systemic forces are anticipated and addressed. Their experience to this point with CMI has offered them valuable insight into the political difficulties they face.

China's vision for CMI and the role it plays in the country's reform of the defense industry are not the subject of much open debate, presumably because CMI's potential value as a means to more efficient resource allocation and faster S&T development has become well understood. Chinese analysts can also grasp the purpose of CMI and envision the perfect world reforms that are needed to make it work. These factors should help Chinese leaders craft policies to enact CMI more fully. However, as the roadblocks they have encountered in trying to move towards CMI in the last five years suggest, incentives and vested interests do not always align with the government's needs, and these conflicts must be addressed.

One indication of China's broad policy strategy for the next five years was revealed in document Number 37, which addressed CMI with respect to research and production of PLA weapons and equipment. In its preface, it stated, "[D]efense industries have completed a strategic shift from a relatively unitary military product structure towards a complex, civil-military product structure. Production that 'combines military and civilian sectors' has rapidly developed, and the scope of civilian industries participating in the construction of weapons' scientific research and production has steadily expanded. The development structure of 'combining the military and civilian sectors' and 'locating military potential in civilian means' has been basically formed."

This assessment of where things stand is true enough, in the sense that China has created a basic framework and guiding principles to govern CMI activities. It significantly obscures just how immature and underdeveloped this system remains, but it serves as a useful reminder that CMI has taken root and has started laying a groundwork that will help it become institutionalized.

China's problem is that it has not fully aligned the interests of the actors involved towards meeting CMI goals. For example, in the government's push to open up the defense market to greater competition, the most important actors are the defense industries. Current CMI reforms have been beneficial, because they have given the defense industries a more formalized outlet for finding qualified components and parts manufacturers, while exposing them to very limited competition from private companies. The potential danger for defense industries is in what they might be forced to give up if the government's enthusiasm for spin-on potential opens up the defense sector to greater competition from civilian companies. The abandonment of a protected defense market is widely supported in principle, and beneficial to most other actors, but the defense industry itself has repeatedly demonstrated resilience and skill in surviving internal policy battles, and its status as an increasingly wealthy sector may make it hard to move in directions it sees as counter to its interests. With respect to other actors, if the government is able to implement reforms that incentivize their participation in CMI, then the structures will be in place to enable them to start taking advantage of it. However, the government must focus on enabling a smoother process that allows researchers and producers to mutually benefit from innovation. China's CMI and broader S&T development strategies have not reconciled the practical barriers that exist between research and production, particularly with respect to the protection of intellectual property, and this impediment continues to plague efforts to support technology transfer through China's S&T system.

China's drive towards CMI has added a national security dimension to economic and S&T development, and this may provide leverage and added urgency within the defense system when the government tries to make reforms. These policies are still in their infancy and may be adjusted by a new leadership group eager to make their mark, but right now these policies are helping to strengthen the underdeveloped ties between the PLA and China's S&T architecture, and in this respect China's CMI efforts will continue to be an important process to track.

NOTES

1. Hu Jintao, "Hold High the Great Banner of Socialism with Chinese Characteristics and Strive for New Victories in Building a Moderately Prosperous Society in All Respects" (高举中国特色社会主义伟大旗帜，为夺取全面建设小康社会新胜利而奋斗), Xinhuanet,

accessed October 10, 2011, http://news.xinhuanet.com/newscenter/2007-10/24/content _6938568.htm.

2. Wen quoted in Li Bin and Zou Shengwen, "The State Council Solemnly Holds the State Science and Technology Awards Ceremony" (中共中央国务院隆重举行国家科学技术奖励大会), *Liberation Army Daily* (*解放军报*), January 10, 2009: 1.

3. Hu Jintao, "The Talk at the Meeting to Celebrate the Complete Success of the First Lunar Probe Project" (在庆祝我国首次月球探测工程圆满成功大会上的讲话), *Liberation Army Daily* (*解放军报*), December 13, 2007: 1.

4. Unnamed staff reporter, "Miao Wei Requires: Unswervingly Take the Civil-Military Integration-Style Development Path" (苗圩要求: 坚定不移地走军民融合式发展道路), *Defense Science and Technology Industry* (*国防科技工业*) 1 (2011): 14.

5. He Xinwen and Hou Guangming, "Constructing National Defense Science and Technology Innovation Organizational Systems on the Basis of Civil-Military Integration" (基于军民结合的国防科技创新组织系统的构建), *China Soft Sciences Supplement* (*中国软科学增刊 [上]*) 1 (2009): 333.

6. Zhao Yue, "Optimize the Deployment of Information Resources, Promote Civil-Military Integration-Style Development" (优化信息资源配置, 推进军民融合发展), *Defense Science and Technology Industry* (*国防科技工业*) 6 (2011): 48.

7. Liang Guanglie, "Persevere with Taking the Civil-Military Integration with Chinese Characteristics-Style Development Path" (坚持走中国特色军民融合式发展之路), *Seeking Truth* (*求实*) 15 (2011), accessed October 20, 2011, http://www.qstheory.cn/zxdk/2011 /201115/201107/t20110728_98346.htm.

8. Evan A. Feigenbaum, *China's Techno-Warriors—National Security and Strategic Competition from the Nuclear to the Information Age* (Stanford, CA: Stanford University Press, 2003).

9. He Xinwen, Hou Guangming, and Wang Yan, "The Path of National Defense Science and Technology Industrialization From the Perspective of Civil-Military Integration" (基于军民融合视角的国防科技工业化路径), *Military Economics Research* (*军事经济研究*) 4 (2011): 34.

10. This classification method and the description that follows are taken from Hou Guangming, *Military-Civilian Technology Transfer: Organization and Policy Research* (*军民技术转移的组织与政策研究*) (Beijing: Science Press, 2009): 15–18.

11. Ibid., 16.

12. Ibid., 18.

13. Ibid., 22; and He and Hou, "Constructing National Defense Civil-Military Integration," 334.

14. Hou, *Military-Civilian Technology Transfer*, 206–211.

15. Wang Shuping, Zhang Jun, Zhu Xiaomei, and Xu Zhihui, "The Problems We Face in Promoting the Construction of Our Civil—Military Integration System, and Some Solutions" (推进我国军民融合制度建设面临的问题及对策), *Military Economics Research* (*军事经济研究*) 9 (2010): 12.

16. Hou, *Military-Civilian Technology Transfer*, 35.

17. Ibid., 27.

18. Ibid., 35.

19. Han Xin and Liu Shuangshuang, "An Economic Analysis of Private Enterprises' Entry into the Defense S&T Industry" (民营企业进入国防科技工业的经济分析), *Finance and Economics Science* (财经科学) 257 (2009): 95–101.

20. Hou, *Military-Civilian Technology Transfer*, 38.

21. He, Hou, and Wang, "The Path of National Defense Science and Technology Industrialization," 34.

22. Yu Xiangjun and Kuang Ye, "The Problems Facing Civil-Military Integration–Style Weapons and Equipment Scientific Research and Production, and Some Solutions" (军民融合式武器装备科研生产面临的问题与对策), *Journal of Military Economics Academy* (军事经济学院学报) 5 (2010): 9.

23. Hou, *Military-Civilian Technology Transfer*, 34.

24. Tai Ming Cheung, *Fortifying China: The Struggle to Build a Modern Defense Economy* (Ithaca, NY: Cornell University Press, 2009): 208.

25. "Over 10 Billion Yuan to Be Invested in '211 Project,'" People's Daily Online, accessed May 22, 2011, http://english.people.com.cn/90001/6381319.html.

26. Ibid. China's national key disciplines (国家重点学科) are academic programs that are rated by the Ministry of Education as being among China's best. They were created as a way of identifying the institutes of higher learning that have the best programs in particular subject areas.

27. "Project 211 and 985," China Education Center, accessed May 13, 2011, http://www.chinaeducenter.com/en/cedu/ceduproject211.php.

28. Mao Xiaoxong, Qi Yong, and Chen Yaling, "Study on the Establishment of Research Laboratory Systems in Research-Orientated Universities "研究型大学科研类实验室体系建设问题研究," *Experimental Technology and Management* (试验技术与管理) 12 (2010): 211–212.

29. Ibid., 212.

30. Yang Yue, "Enhance Innovation Capability, Promote Sustainable Development" (提升创新能力, 促进持续发展), *Defense Science and Technology Industry* (国防科技工业) 8 (2009): 17.

31. "2009 Annual Report of the State Programs of Science and Technology Development" (2009 年国家科技计划执行概况), State Ministry of Science and Technology, accessed June 18, 2011, http://www.most.gov.cn/ndbg/2010ndbg/201010/P02010 1015519918287667.pdf.

32. "30 Years of Science and Technology Reform and Opening Up" (科技改革开放 30 年), (2009): 233, accessed June 18, 2011, http://www.most.gov.cn/kjfz/kjxz/2008/201003 /P020100304432123439954.pdf.

33. "Science and Technology Resources and Capacity Building" (科技资源与能力建设)," (2009): 46, accessed June 18, 2011, http://www.most.gov.cn/kjfz/kjxz/2008/201003 /P020100304395910319841.pdf.

34. Lin Zhigang and Ning Ruifang, "A Brief Comment on Science and Technology Innovation Work in Colleges and Universities" (高校科技创新工作简论), *Journal of Hunan Institute of Engineering* (湖南工程学院学报) 2 (2007): 106; and Rao Dejin, "In Jiangxi, How Many Science and Technology Discoveries Stay in the Labs?" (江西多少科技成果呆在实验室?) February 28, 2005, accessed June 10, 2011, http://www.jxnews.com.cn/xxrb/system /2005/02/28/000800324.shtml. It is also worth noting that transforming research into

new products has been a problem associated with Chinese research for some time. See Xielin Liu and Steven White, "Comparing Innovation Systems: A Framework and Application to China's Transitional Context," *Research Policy* 30 (2001): 1105.

35. Rao, "In Jiangxi, How Many Science and Technology Discoveries Stay in the Labs?"

36. Ibid.

37. Ibid.

38. Ibid.

39. Zheng Yongping, Dang Xiaomei, and Yu Linfeng, "Study on the Technology Transfer Mode of Research Universities in the State Technology Innovation System" (国家科技创新体系下研究型大学的技术转移模式探讨), *R&D Management* (研究与发展管理) 4 (2008): 113.

40. Yu Zhenfei, Zhang Jun, Du Ning, and Chen Pengwan, "Analysis of the Problems Encountered with Research Universities in Industry-Academia-Research Institute Cooperation" (浅析研究型大学在产学研合作中遇到的问题), *Science Research Management* (科研管理) ZK (2008): 14.

41. Hou, *Military-Civilian Technology Transfer*, 90.

42. Ibid.

43. Yu, Zhang, Du, and Chen, "Analysis of the Problems Encountered with Research Universities in Industry-Academia-Research Institute Cooperation," 14; and Xu Hui, Dang Gang, and Wu Ji, "Promoting Research Universities in the National Defense Innovation System" (促进研究型大学融合国防科技创新体系的思考), *Studies in Science of Science* (科学学研究) Supplement (2007): 52.

44. Yu, Zhang, Du, and Chen, "Analysis of the Problems Encountered with Research Universities in Industry-Academia-Research Institute Cooperation," 14.

45. Lin and Ning, "A Brief Comment on Science and Technology Innovation Work in Colleges and Universities," 106.

46. Xu Feng, "The Defense Industry Holds a Successful Meeting in Ningbo for its Linked Project Activity with Industry, Academia, and Research Institutions" (军工产学研项目对接活动在宁波成功举行), *Defense Science and Technology Industry* (国防科技工业) 8 (2010): 38.

47. Yu, Zhang, Du, and Chen, "Analysis of the Problems Encountered with Research Universities in Industry-Academia-Research Institute Cooperation," 13.

48. Li Qin, "Problems and Countermeasures with Army-Local 'Industry-Academia-Research Institute' Cooperative Innovation in Western China" (西部军地'产学研'合作创新的问题及对策) *Defense Industry Conversion in China* (中国军转民) 12 (2006): 46–48.

49. Ibid., 46.

50. Ma Yuejin and Liu Jingang, "Chief Difficulties and Countermeasures for the Private Economy Participating in National Defense Construction" (非公有制经济参与国防建设面临鹅主要困难和对策), in Yu Chuanxin, ed., *Theoretical Research on the Development of Civil-Military Integration* (军民融合式发展理论研究) (Beijing: Military Science Press, 2008): 297–298.

51. "Access Certificates for Privately Run Businesses Entering the Defense Industry" (民营企业进入军工产品的准入证), Shandong Province Zhejiang Chamber of Commerce, accessed May 12, 2011, http://www.zjsh.com.cn/article_show.asp?id=436.

52. Ibid.

53. Ma and Liu, "Chief Difficulties and Countermeasures," 299–300.

54. "Access Certificates for Privately Run Businesses Entering the Defense Industry"; and Liu Baoting and Jiang Zong, "Reflections on Private Companies Entering the National Defense Science and Technology Industry" (对非公有制企业进入国防科技工业的思考)," in Yu, ed., *Theoretical Research on the Development of Civil-Military Integration*, 326.

55. "Chronicle of Events Regarding Structural Reform within the PLA's Competitive Procurement System" (我军竞争性装备采购体制改革大事记), accessed May 22, 2011, http://www.chinamil.com.cn/site1/xwpdxw/2008-11/20/content_1555030.htm.

56. Ibid.

57. Ibid.; and "The All-China Federation of Industry and Commerce Third Special Questionnaire on Private Enterprise Dual-use High Technology and Product R&D and Production" (全国工商联第三次民营企业军民两用高新技术及产品研发生产情况专项调查表), accessed June 5, 2011, www.acfic.org.cn/publicfiles/business/htmlfiles/qggsl/cmsmedia/document/2011/2/doc4207.doc.

58. "Chronicle of Events Regarding Structural Reform."

59. Bai Haiwei, *Equipment Contract Management Theory and Practice* (装备合同管理理论与实务), (Beijing: National Defense Industry Press, 2010): 211.

60. Ed Francis and Susan M. Puska, "SASTIND, CMIPD, and GAD: Contemporary Chinese Defense Industry Reform," paper presented at Conference on China's Defense and Dual-use Science, Technology and Industrial Base, San Diego, California, July 1–2, 2010, p. 45.

61. "China Opens Weapon Production to Private, Foreign-Funded Businesses," accessed May 19, 2011, http://english.peopledaily.com.cn/200505/28/eng20050528_187195.html.

62. Zheng Shuyan and Tian Yiwei, "'New Star,' Rising from the Qinling Mountain Range" ("新星," 从秦岭升起), *Liberation Army Daily* (解放军报), April 27, 2009, 2.

63. "Shaanxi Baoji Special Vehicles Manufacturing Co., Ltd." (陕西宝鸡专用汽车有限公司), accessed May 20, 2012, http://www.cnnewstar.com/index.htm.

64. Yu Chunlai, "The News That Defense Industry Shareholder Reforms Will Speed Up 'Civilian Enterprises Participating in the Defense Sector' Receives Encouragement" (军工企业股份制改造将加速'民企参军'受到鼓励), *National Business Daily* (每日经济新闻), January 7, 2011, accessed April 6, 2011, http://www.nbd.com.cn/newshtml/20110107/20110107090506540.html.

65. Yu and Kuang, "The Problems Facing Civil-Military Integration–Style Weapons and Equipment Scientific Research and Production, and Some Solutions," 9.

66. Hou, *Military-Civilian Technology Transfer*, 234.

67. Li Yang, "Open the Front Entrance to Greet the Spring—Private Entrepreneurs Discuss 'Civilian-to-Military Conversion'" (打开门庭迎春—民营企业家谈"民参军") *Defense Industry Conversion in China* (中国军转民) 3 (2005): 33–34.

68. Ma and Liu, " Chief Difficulties and Countermeasures," 304.

69. Full text of this opinion is at www.gzjxw.gov.cn/file/001.pdf.

70. Ibid.

71. "The All-China Federation of Industry and Commerce Third Special Questionnaire on Private Enterprise Dual-use High Technology and Product R&D and Production." 2011.

72. "Questionnaire on the Implementation of Opinions of the State Council with Regard to Encouraging, Supporting, and Guiding Individual, Privately Owned, and Other Non-State-Owned Economic Development" (《国务院关于鼓励支持和引导个体私营等非公有制经济发展的若干意见》落实情况调查问卷) accessed April 29, 2011, http://www.xszsh.com/oledit/UploadFile/20103/2010315906232.doc.

73. "Construct a Civil-Military Integration Style Weapons Research and Production System" (构建军民融合式武器装备科研生产体系), accessed May 2, 2011, http://www.mod.gov.cn/gflt/2011-02/14/content_4224759.htm.

74. Ibid.

Chapter Six

China's Emerging Defense Innovation System

Making the Wheels Turn

Kathleen A. Walsh

China's modernization, in both commercial and military terms, is coming into closer focus in the outlines and, increasingly, the details of its overarching innovation strategy, policies, and systemic design. Beijing's present course in support of its long-term goal of "indigenous innovation" (*Zìzhǔ chuàngxīn*) builds on lessons learned through other countries' experiences in developing national and defense innovation systems, and it incorporates aspects that are unique to China's institutional, cultural, political, economic, and industrial circumstances. This chapter outlines the contours of China's emerging defense innovation system, its conceptual foundations, connections, motivations, processes, and prospects for success. While China has a distance to travel before realizing its aspirations for innovation, Beijing's present course suggests that a more vibrant, nationwide, dual-use, defense-oriented innovation ecosystem is beginning to emerge as part of a system of innovation systems (SoIS) and could in time translate into more advanced defense technological innovations.

China's Innovation Concept: A Nested System-of-Innovation-Systems Approach

China's strategy for fostering national and, more specifically, defense innovation is becoming more apparent, and the two efforts are connected. While there is no clear or agreed-upon definition of what constitutes a *defense* innovation system (DIS) in either the Western or Chinese literature on the subject, it is evident that some notion of a DIS (*guófáng chuàngxīn tǐxì*) exists in China; a DIS is cited, for example, among the objectives in the 2006–2020 Medium- to Long-term S&T Development Plan (MLTP) and is being pursued as an extension or subset of the more broadly accepted concept of a national innovation system (NIS) (*guójiā chuàngxīn tǐxì*).[1]

Behind the development of a national innovation system lies a more fully developed and widely recognized concept found in both the science and technology (S&T) literature and in economic growth strategies promoted by international institutions such the Organization for Economic Cooperation and Development (OECD).[2] As stated by the OECD, "the national innovation systems approach stresses that the flows of technology and information among people, enterprises and institutions are key to the innovative process. Innovation and technology development are the result of a complex set of relationships among actors in the system, which include enterprises, universities and government research institutes."[3]

Over the past few decades, with the advent of the NIS concept, the study of innovation has shifted from a linear concept of scientific discovery leading, in turn, to technology development towards today's concept of a more holistic, complex, and systemic approach that features technology clusters and rests on development of a national system of innovation and subvariants thereof (e.g., industry sector-specific, knowledge-oriented, and technological innovation systems, of which the DIS is one subset).[4] Contemporary S&T literature, in fact, increasingly highlights these other macro-, micro-, and subnational layers and systems of innovation as worthy of greater scholarly attention, including the international or global innovation system (GIS), intraregional or regional innovation systems (RIS), and industrial, sectoral, or cluster-oriented analysis.[5] While the primary focus here is China's DIS (generally viewed as a subset, sector, or technology innovation system), it is impossible to discuss this concept absent its place among and in relation to these other systemic layers of innovation ecosystems that China also seeks to develop as a part of its overall innovation strategy, particularly given Beijing's dual-use-oriented technology development strategy. The bottom line is this: China is implementing a series of macro-to-micro layers of innovation at the same time in a complex system-of-innovation-systems model that is aimed at promoting greater dual-use, civil-military innovation and is geared specifically to an age of industrial, technological, and scientific globalization.[6]

In this endeavor, China is not alone. Following in the footsteps of developed countries and spurred on by new opportunities made possible by the information technology and communications revolution, a number of developing states, particularly the BRICS—Brazil, Russia, India, China, and South Africa—among others seek to move up (or remain high on) the industrial ladder by pursuing their own NIS and development of innovative knowledge-based societies. China, too, seeks to build an innovation-based society as both an overall aim and the primary means by which to promote continued, advanced economic growth, as well as defense industrial development and military modernization, in order ultimately to realize a "well-off society in an all-around way."[7] The development of an NIS—and its DIS subset—is a critical component in this endeavor.

Yet, the NIS approach is also a topic of considerable debate as leaders contemplate what type and level of investment in science, technology, education, and innovation is best for today's internationally and informationally interactive society, for each state's own ethno-cultural-geographical-techno-security challenges and characteristics, and for competing in an age of global science and greater environmental consciousness. China is having these same sorts of discussions, particularly in terms of how to pursue economic development and sustainable development simultaneously and in terms of the proper balance between commercial economic development and military modernization.

Nor is the NIS approach to understanding modern innovation processes considered to be a formal, theoretical construct; rather, it serves more as a useful conceptual framework of how states might plan to enhance their overall innovative capabilities.[8] The concept can be applied to any state's own needs and situation. As Judith Reppy points out, one of the key advantages of the NIS approach in understanding innovation is that:

> Whereas conventional economic theory locates innovation in the firm, depicted as an optimizing machine running on automatic pilot, and seeks to construct general models of technology diffusion across firms, the . . . [NIS] approach provides space for the role of government policy, legal institutions, educational and training institutions, and even norms and regimes. Interactive processes and feedback loops are emphasized. Success or failure in innovation can be affected by any of the constituent elements of the system, and weaknesses in one area may be compensated for by strength in another. Human resources get particular attention, and the contributions of well-trained and motivated technicians may be as important as those of Ph.D. scientists.[9]

Evaluating a country's NIS plans, policies, and strategies thus entails acquiring a broad understanding of these various sectors of the economy and the processes by which they interact (or not). In short, in order to understand China's DIS concept, it is essential to first understand its approach to developing an NIS, since the former is nested in the latter.

China's NIS concept consists of innovative linkages between and among key actors, institutions, and ecosystems. As outlined and explained most succinctly in a 2006 brief by a senior researcher at China's National Research Center for S&T for Development (now the Chinese Academy of Science and Technology for Development), the NIS concept is designed around the following core components:

- enterprises as the innovative center and linchpin (with the "defense innovation system combining military and civil use" listed as a subcomponent);
- government or state-sponsored research institutes comprising a "knowledge innovation system" along with universities and colleges (including civilian and military researchers);
- "S&T intermediate service system" (e.g., investment zones, science parks, incubators, industry associations, technology transfer, and product promotion centers);
- "regional innovation system embodying individual features and advantages" (i.e., the Yangtze River Delta region and other geographically oriented clusters); and
- "government system coordinating S&T policies and economic policies." [10]

The study's author, Gao Changlin, identifies six layers among which vital linkages are needed to make this a dynamic, effective national innovation system: (1) actors, (2) knowledge, (3) industrial clusters, (4) regions, (5) environments ("institutions and the legal system, education system, infrastructures, market mechanism, and innovation culture"), and (6) international linkages.[11] In the search for China's concept of a DIS, it is to be found nested within this broader NIS construct and its system of innovation systems.

Finally, China's notion of an NIS bears a striking resemblance to that portrayed by the OECD in a study published in 1999 outlining the notion of an NIS.[12] Yet, China's NIS concept also has interesting and distinct features. For instance, the main actors involved in any NIS or DIS are the state, industry (private- and state-sector), and the academic and research communities (government-sponsored and private). The main actors comprising China's DIS, however, are broader, namely:

1. Industry enterprises, both civilian enterprises *and*, specifically, defense industry conglomerates and their subsidiary enterprises, including both state- and private-sector entities (which are often difficult to distinguish in China) (Foreign-invested enterprises in China, too, play a key role in commercial industrial and technological endeavors in this concept and will play a role in China's defense industrial projects.)[13]

2. Researchers, including state research institutes, academic researchers at military and civilian universities, industry researchers working in both commercial and defense industry sectors, as well as domestic and international researchers working in Chinese industry, universities and state laboratories.

3. Government regulatory and oversight agencies at the central, provincial, regional, and local levels

4. Other government officials and new innovation-promoting bodies, associations, and services supported by key ministries, departments, and innovation centers established at the national, regional, provincial, and local levels in the various investment or industrial zones, parks, technology clusters, incubation centers, and more, all of which are designed to foster and facilitate commercial as well as defense and dual-use innovation

Another key distinction in China's approach is that, while the NIS of some states might focus primarily, if not exclusively, on promoting domestic linkages, China's NIS *and* DIS both emphasize international linkages as a core component.[14] Moreover, the interconnectedness—in design, at least—of both military and civilian (i.e., commercial) enterprises as the center of China's innovation scheme is a marked distinction from the OECD model, which simply lists "firms" and does not appear to address the civil-military divide, suggesting that for China this is a central, distinct design concept. This dual, civil-military approach would fit with China's strategic development plans, which, despite much Western criticism, persist in attempting to establish an "indigenous innovation" capacity and to spin-off as well as spin-on civil-military technological advances, even in the face of the technological and institutional difficulties inherent in this approach. In these ways, China's pursuit of a DIS as nested within its NIS appears in important ways to be distinct. See Figure 6.1 for a notional illustration of China's SoIS approach as centered around the DIS concept.

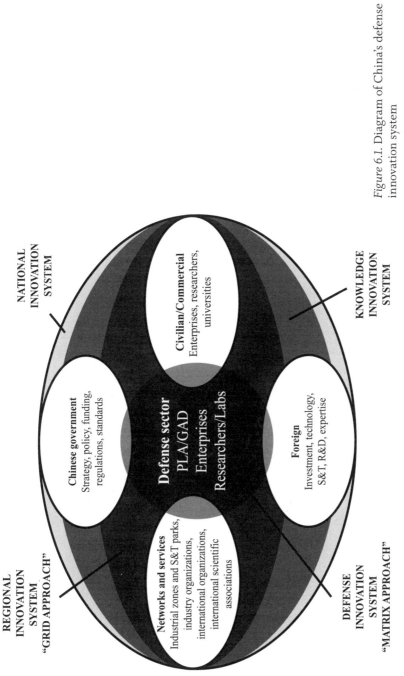

NATIONAL INNOVATION SYSTEM

KNOWLEDGE INNOVATION SYSTEM

REGIONAL INNOVATION SYSTEM "GRID APPROACH"

DEFENSE INNOVATION SYSTEM "MATRIX APPROACH"

Civilian/Commercial Enterprises, researchers, universities

Chinese government Strategy, policy, funding, regulations, standards

Defense sector PLA/GAD Enterprises Researchers/Labs

Foreign Investment, technology, S&T, R&D, expertise

Networks and services Industrial zones and S&T parks, industry organizations, international organizations, international scientific associations

Figure 6.1. Diagram of China's defense innovation system

In terms of understanding China's approach to developing a defense innovation system, the existing literature on defense innovation is of limited use, given its general scarcity in the West and the lack of scholarly treatment in China. The few exceptions, such as studies by Judith Reppy, Andrew James, and Tai Ming Cheung, provide no common definition nor single set of actors or even scope that constitute a uniform understanding of defense innovation systems; on the contrary, each state develops its own defense industrial priorities, strategies, and means of pursuing these capabilities in a way that best serves its national, military, and industrial needs.[15] In addition, most of the DIS-related literature that does exist is based upon Western theorizing, revolves mainly around US, European, or Japanese defense industrial experiences post-WWII, and lacks a formal, empirical approach, theory, or model.[16] Absent a robust theoretical foundation, much of the literature remains based on defense officials', industry experts', and academic views on what has worked or failed, why (or why not), and on what the next stage(s) in defense innovation should therefore be. Nothing succeeds like success,[17] however, which is why many, including China, view the US defense industrial innovation system as the primary model to be emulated. Yet, in typical Chinese fashion, PRC researchers have studied what others around the globe have tried. Among the published reports they have studied are ones by international institutions such as the OECD and those concerning different approaches to developing an NIS and the key subset of interest here, the DIS, as pursued by states such Canada, Australia, and Norway.[18] As a result, China's NIS/DIS strategy appears to be a hybrid of these and of China's own concepts and priorities.

At the same time, around the globe even the traditional concept of how to institute an NIS and DIS is presently being reconsidered, prompted by a number of recent academic studies on the increasingly global connections being made across national innovation systems. These studies suggest that the notion of merely adopting a traditionally laissez faire, market-oriented approach to innovation (which is how US defense innovation is often depicted, though not necessarily accurately) appears to be a necessary but insufficient means of widening economic, industrial, scientific, and technological innovation in an age of expanding globalization.[19] Rather, the studies collectively suggest that what is necessary in such a globally interconnected age is a combination of a state-level national innovation strategy that incorporates a global dimension paired with a vibrant, market-driven, laissez-faire economy bolstered by nationally linked innovation ecosystems, thereby combining a top-down, state-driven strategy with a bottom-up, firm-driven, entrepreneurial approach to fostering innovative connections across national, regional, industrial, and sectoral, as well as global systems. This, in fact, aptly describes what China is attempting to put in place. Consequently, China's approach to developing a DIS—which appears to be a modified version of earlier innovation systems efforts by the United States and others but with even more of a global dimension inherently built in—could well serve as a new, 21st-century NIS-DIS model.

China's Emerging Defense Innovation System: A Work in Progress

The DIS that China is presently working to put in place does not represent Beijing's first, nor likely final, attempt at devising a well-functioning, effective, and efficient DIS. Putting in place a system that promotes advanced defense innovation has been a goal—if not a systemic one or always labeled as such—for more than a half-century, dating back to the early 1950s (shortly after the PRC's founding in 1949) when China's high-tech defense and military modernization efforts concentrated on big science projects, resulting years later in the heralded "two bombs and one satellite" weapons systems. It has been only in the last two decades or so, however, that Chinese strategists have sought explicitly to put in place a more holistic NIS and now DIS subset that incorporate and connect *all* key parts of the economy and society, including international inputs. This is at the same time that Beijing is prioritizing S&T development as the foundation of economic growth *and* military modernization. As a result, China's current efforts, decades in the making but recently accelerated as part of a system of innovation systems, could conceivably usher in a new era in Chinese defense industrialization and innovation. These more systemic efforts, however, remain still in the early stages of development.

The Chinese DIS concept described below is the product of these decades of defense-and commercial-sector industrial and institutional reforms, some of which have had lasting positive effects but many of which have had just the opposite. While it appears today that many of the main, particularly state-controlled, actors in the current DIS are the same, or roughly the same, as in previous eras, how they are meant to interact, with whom, and why has changed fundamentally.[20] Moreover, this latest approach appears to have reaped some successes. The US Defense Department dates a shift toward more advanced Chinese defense industrial capabilities to the mid-1990s, stating, "Defense industry modernization accelerated . . . based on reforms to rationalize military procurement and increase innovation among China's state-owned defense companies. These reforms have enabled the development and production of select weapon systems, such as missiles, fighter jets, and warships, approaching performance parameters in some cases comparable to Western systems."[21] China still has a long way to go before realizing what most would characterize as a fully modernized defense innovation system or technological innovations on par with Western counterparts, yet China's emerging DIS and related strategy, plans, and programs could hasten this realization.

Another novel and important aspect of China's current approach to defense innovation is its systemic nature and the degree of interconnections made to other, ongoing systemic innovation efforts. Much of the current focus is on linking China's traditionally segregated defense industrial sectors to other, already more dynamic, parts of the economy *and* to develop similar innovative communities, cycles, clusters, and regional ecosystems to produce a more dynamic, productive, efficient, and innovative defense industry. Thus, whether China succeeds in its defense innovation aims will depend on how these key actors, institutions, processes, and dynamics function within and across the DIS as well as in connection to the other systems of innovation.

Emerging Themes in China's DIS Systems Development Strategy

There are several important themes apparent in China's present efforts to devise a more modern DIS. Each of these themes is briefly expanded upon below; together they form the basis of China's complex, layered approach to developing a modern, globally connected, and internally integrated defense innovation system.

Theme 1: Continued reliance on top-down, goal-oriented government guidance, highlighting particular near-, medium-, and long-term milestones as outlined in regular five-year plans and longer-term plans and strategies aimed at completion in later years, most in 2020, others (i.e., industrial and S&T "roadmaps") by 2050

The approach to S&T and defense industrial development taken by any state is often tinged with ideological and cultural distinctions that affect the way in which theories and strategies are pursued and implemented. While China in its DIS endeavor is following in the footsteps of the United States and other Western, developed states, Beijing puts particular emphasis on the role of the state as the guiding force for instituting innovative strategies and policies, more so than does the United States but in some respects on par with the European Union's, Japan's, or South Korea's state-led efforts.

In addition, the pursuit of national strategic objectives is traditionally an important driver in defense innovation, as attested to even in the United States, where the Manhattan Project, DARPA Program, and NASA space programs, among others, bear witness to the importance and impact that pursuing long-term, state-generated, strategic goals can have on the broader national and defense innovation systems development. Moreover, given the advent of more globalized scientific collaborations and cooperative, cross-border technological endeavors, having a top-down strategic approach to leveraging such emerging international dynamics is increasingly viewed as an important competitive asset.

The PRC's reliance on the five-year plan (FYP) and longer-term development strategies and policies is, of course, not new. What is novel, however, is the manner in which Beijing is today seeking to both develop and implement such strategies, policies, and plans. In recent years the planning process has become more adaptive and more inclusive. A wider variety of outside expertise (including Chinese academics, industry consultants, and even foreign experts) has been involved in conception and implementation of plans that are more along the lines of guiding principles than the mandated performance measures and quotas that were often the case in the past.[22] While such practices represent a subtle change in process and outlook, they have had a noticeable impact on the tenor of official statements, presumably also on officials' mindset, and perhaps more importantly on the new-found flexibility permitted in the ways in which Beijing's goals are actually achieved at the local level. In short, China has opted to pursue measurable goals but with a focus on attaining more qualitative achievements than on the primarily quantitative-based metrics common in the past. This more flexible but still goal-oriented, top-down strategic approach to innovative technological development resembles that of many other industrialized, market-oriented states.[23] Yet, quantitative goals do remain. Old habits die hard, and the MLTP (2006–2020) and 12th FYP (2011–2015) continue to reflect state planners' desire to accelerate efforts to achieve China's stated goals by their respective deadlines. These goals include achieving certain levels of spending on R&D (2.5% of gross domestic product by 2020), increasing the contribution of S&T and indigenous innovation to China's economy (to 60% or more) while reducing the level of dependence on foreign technology inputs (to less than 30%), as well as achieving higher status in various international competitiveness rankings, among others.[24]

Chinese state planners also have laid out sector-specific S&T plans through 2050, highlighting eight strategic S&T fields in particular; the plans were published collectively in 2010 through a commercial press. This effort was conducted by the Chinese Academy of Sciences (CAS), China's premier national scientific academy that oversees a system of state-run research institutions focused on basic, fundamental research. A CAS report in 2009 entitled "Creation 2050: Science, Technology, and China's Future" outlined a long-term strategy to promote development of select strategic industry sectors and dual-use technology sectors, namely "energy, water resources, mineral resources, marine resources, oil and gas, population and health, agriculture, eco-environment, biomass resources, regional development, space, information, advanced manufacturing, advanced materials, nano-science, big science facilities, cross-disciplinary and frontier research, and national and public security."[25] This strategy and an S&T roadmap were developed by 300 CAS experts through high-level and cross-disciplinary working groups and are expected to be updated and revised every few years, with an interim review set for around 2030–2035.[26] As suggested by this strategic tasking, it appears that the Chinese Academy of Sciences has been given a high-profile charge to coordinate and enhance S&T and R&D collaboration across China's disparate research communities in an effort to expand China's knowledge innovation system.[27] CAS at the same time is pursuing its own *Innovation 2020* plan, along with other efforts under way designed to consolidate existing laboratories and research institutes and develop new forms of collaboration, exchange, and technology transfers between and among CAS institutions and others. One such example is the newly formed Multidisciplinary, Civil-Military Research Centers established to focus on specific S&T development goals and applied research in space, clean coal technology, and geoscience monitoring.[28]

In addition to the changing role of government in promoting innovation, several other strategic themes stand out in China's present efforts to develop its DIS.

Theme 2: Promoting S&T development as a high priority in government strategy, plans, and policies for economic growth and military modernization with an ongoing defense industry doctrine of "combining military and civilian and placing military into civilian"

Under Hu Jintao's leadership, China's official doctrine has shifted to S&T as the foundation for continued economic growth and modernization. The impact of this approach—known as the "scientific concept of development" (*kēxué fāzhǎn guān*)—is evident in China's escalating scientific and research statistics as well as in the continued investment of huge sums into S&T development programs, infrastructures, educational institutions, and other efforts expected to enhance S&T development. What this means in practical and policy terms is that pursuing mere economic growth is no longer sufficient; government, private, and foreign investments must also serve to promote China's S&T advances. At the same time, full-scale military modernization will remain a future priority as S&T development is being pursued as a strategic, interim, priority step. Policy makers in Beijing view S&T development as the institutional and intellectual bridge between economic and military modernization: S&T development is considered a vital cog in building a dual-use defense industrial sector and innovation system designed to serve both commercial and military needs.

China accordingly continues to implement the *Junmin Jiehe* strategy of "combining civil and military needs" but with particular emphasis on "placing military into civilian." This approach is clearly reflected in both the MLTP and the 12th FYP.[29] The MLTP, for instance, specifies a variety of mechanisms by which to promote and integrate civilian and defense S&T for the purpose of defense and dual-use development, reflecting the SoIS approach outlined earlier. For example, the MLTP seeks pursuit of "an enterprise-led technology innovation system featuring the combination of enterprises, universities, and research institutes . . . creating an open, mobile, competitive, and collaborative operational mechanism at the core . . . to promote the collaboration and resource sharing between research institutes and with universities . . . a national defense S&T innovation system highlighting the combination of both the defense and civilian needs as well as a civilianized defense industry by making defense S&T part of the civilian operations . . . regional innovation systems with diverse characteristics and strengths . . . a socialized, networked S&T intermediary service system. . . ."[30] In short, the main focus in developing China's defense innovation system is to integrate the military and civilian S&T communities to foster more collaboration within and across each sector in response to mechanisms established specifically to promote greater cross-sector, cross-disciplinary, and cross-regional collaboration and innovation.

Not all of these ideas are new, however, and implementation appears, at least in some instances, to remain slow. Efforts to cross-pollinate civil-military interactions, for instance, have taken several years to implement and to take hold, with efforts still ongoing. In 2005, leaders announced their intention to issue licenses to civilian firms to "provide subsystems and auxiliary military equipment" to the military, providing government subsidies to many domestic civilian investors.[31] This policy was revised in 2007 to specify that foreign investment in defense enterprises would be limited to those firms *not* involved in development of secret military programs but would be permitted mainly in enterprises involved in dual-production of civil-military technologies and systems.[32] In what might be interpreted as a reversal, a more recent, revised Foreign Direct Investment (FDI) Catalogue reportedly promotes foreign investment in a variety of defense sectors, including helicopters; unmanned aerial vehicles; ground equipment, training, and flight simulation technologies for the aviation sector; gas turbine engines and high-speed diesel engine manufacturing; and marine radars.[33] Clearly, some difficulties have been encountered in the actual implementation of this licensing policy; some reports suggest that industry leaders have raised concerns over an increased reliance on foreign technology and expertise as being more likely to hurt than to help China's domestic defense industry development or simply are concerned about allowing competition with their own interests.[34]

Another recently released policy document outlines measures to reincentivize private-sector investment in China's defense enterprises, based on a May 2010 policy and reiterated in 2011 following approval of the 12th FYP at the National People's Congress.[35] According to press reports, the current push emphasizes new financial incentives for civilian firms to invest in military and defense enterprises, provides new "guidance and support" for firms doing so, and promotes greater overseas investments by defense and civilian enterprises as a means of exploiting international networks and promoting export opportunities. The document states, "Private enterprises need to participate, in accordance with relevant provisions related to military production, in the development and industrialization of dual-use and hi-tech equipment."[36] As rules for participation in the Chinese defense industries generally have been relaxed over the past decade, an increasing number of private Chinese enterprises have indeed begun to engage in weapons and equipment research and development on behalf of the People's Liberation Army (PLA). Chinese regulations require all enterprises, both state-owned and private, to be licensed in order to participate in weapons and equipment research and production. Recent estimates place the number of such enterprises at approximately 300.[37]

Progress on reforming the defense innovation research system itself appears to have been slow, although new institutions have been established specially for this purpose. In 2003, years before the MLTP and 12th FYP, the lead ministry, the Commission for Science, Technology, and Industry for National Defense (COSTIND) articulated its plan to put in place (over 20 years) a new R&D system specifically designed to promote civil-military development and production.[38]

Several years later, in 2007, COSTIND announced its intention to establish a se-ries of new government-sponsored R&D laboratories with the specific aims of accelerating defense-oriented research and development and providing a plat-form through which lab researchers could coordinate with defense industry and other researchers from around the country. According to a then-COSTIND vice minister, the purpose was to "build them into a world-class integrated national-level research base. The laboratories will not be large in number, but we will pilot new management and operation models to achieve big breakthroughs in major science and technology fields."[39] Some such labs have been established, but it is unclear as yet whether they are fulfilling these objectives. As research by Ed Francis points out, for instance, both COSTIND's successor, SASTIND (State Administration), and the General Armament Department (GAD) through its "science and technology research funding programs support and directly tap into the civilian university system's research talent by establishing key point facilities and talent accreditation programs such as the Defense Science and Technology Key Laboratories, Defense Science and Technology Key Discipline Laboratories, and Defense Science and Technology Innovation Talent Teams, of-ten at civilian universities."[40]

In addition, Beijing has established a series of other new or upgraded institu-tions designed to cross-pollinate innovative collaborations across the defense sector and civil-military divide, as well as in foreign-domestic cooperation. These include, for example, Defense Science, Technology, and Industry Technology Research and Application Centers; Multidisciplinary Civil-Military Research Centers; the Dual-Use R&D Integration Institute; provincial-level Civil-Military Integration Promotion Offices; a Lenovo College, a higher-education institution established by one of China's leading computer software firms; Tsinghua (Uni-versity) Institute of Engineering Development; CAS Overseas Talent Recruit-ment Programs; an expanded Shanghai Technology Transfer Exchange; and a China-Italy Technology Transfer Exchange.[41]

Both the defense enterprises and research centers are expected to prioritize their efforts on seven new strategic industry sectors announced under the 12th FYP as an S&T priority for civil-military development. These sectors are: (1) energy and environmental protection (energy saving, recycling, regulations); (2) next-generation IT; (3) bio S&T (agriculture, marine, and pharmaceuticals); (4) high-end assembly and manufacturing (including aerospace, air and rail transportation, and smart assembly); (5) new energy sources (including nuclear, solar, wind, biomass, and smartgrid); (6) new materials; and (7) new-fuel/energy autos.[42]

Theme 3: Putting in place the necessary defense S&T–related infrastructure, services, and resources to serve as the primary means and platform for defense innovation, thereby enabling clusters of innovation to develop, mature, and expand between and among key actors in the DIS while fostering more efficient sharing of S&T resources and infrastructure

Having reaped substantial rewards from opening its doors in the early 1980s to foreign investment and subsequently realizing additional advantages from having experimented with various forms of investment and development zones in pursuit of rapid economic growth, industrialization, and establishment of an NIS, China is now adapting the same overall strategy, policies, and programs to promoting its defense industrial and DIS development. China is effectively overlaying the latter on top of its already existing, more well-established NIS, thereby seeking to expand and share a common, dual-use S&T and innovation infrastructure. As a result of this approach and the expansion to the defense sector of the aforementioned "S&T intermediate service system," there are new defense industry-oriented investment zones, S&T parks and, more recently, regional clusters and defense innovation–related services being established across the country.[43] Two new zones, in particular, are noteworthy. "Over the past several years, numerous 'Civil-Military Integrated Industrial Bases' or 'Civil-Military Integration Industry Zones' have been established in cities across the mainland. These bases are intended to promote innovation in defense and dual-use technologies by encouraging collaboration by physically clustering defense and dual-use technology enterprises. They also serve a local administrative function within the defense innovation system."[44] According to Francis's research, "like other civil-military integration initiatives, these zones build on earlier programs, such as the National Military-Civilian Conversion Science and Technology Zone, established in 2002 around Miangyang City outside Chengdu, and the first provincial-level Military-Civilian Conversion High and New Technology Industry Demonstration Zone, in Guizhou. These military-civilian conversion zones are focused on creating spin-off civilian products based on defense-industry technologies. Since 2008, numerous additional civil-military industry bases have been initiated. In November 2008, for instance, the Zhuhai Aviation Industry Zone formally opened and is intended to be an aviation manufacturing industry base, bringing together industry, academia, and research institutes. That same month, construction began at the Guangyuan City Tashantai Civil-Military Integration Industry Zone."[45]

The Chinese Academy of Sciences, too, is establishing a series of "science parks," to be located in Beijing, Shanghai, and Guangzhou. They are intended to, among other things, "coordinate the deployment of basic research in defense and civilian sectors, and strengthen the integration of research and development efforts in both sectors," as outlined in China's MLTP.

Also being initiated are new types of services to promote defense innovation, such as "technology auctions." These are described in Chinese press reports as "an array of major S&T findings . . . from national S&T programs . . . traded in the form of auction, a brand new mode for S&T findings transfer." A recent auction offered "26 S&T findings, derived from the 973 Program, National 863 Program, National S&T Infrastructure Program, and Special S&T Projects Program . . . auctioned through listing, auction, or bidding, covering the areas of biopharmaceutical, energy efficiency and emission reduction, agricultural technology, and information technology."[46] The idea behind the auctions is to make better use of defense resources, research, and state capital already being expended and to introduce new ideas into various scientific, technological, and industrial communities across the civil-military divide. In this and other ways, Chinese officials are seeking to make more efficient use of government-sponsored research developed in the defense sector, helping in the process to foster a more robust civil-military innovation ecosystem.

In establishing defense or dual-use-specific zones, parks, centers, and services, China is adopting a similar approach to that used in developing the commercial sector and with some success. This is not to suggest that commercial innovation zones and clusters in China are functioning perfectly; serious challenges remain, such as unproductive intermunicipal, interprovincial, and intraregional competition for foreign and domestic investment (at times allowing foreign investors to play regional, zone, or park officials against one another in a reversal of the typical China market advantage). To alleviate this competition for FDI—viewed as wasteful competition from China's perspective—and to promote an expanded, nationwide, and dual-use ecosystem of innovation, China has sought to develop regional innovation clusters built around strategic locations and industries, while taking into account each area's industrial and technological base—both civil and military—its geographic location, culture, and so on, in order to promote greater intraregional collaboration and innovation. There are at least six such regional clusters being developed across China, the latter three being those more recently approved:

- Yellow River / Bohai Delta (BHR) (incorporating Beijing, Tianjin, and surrounding area)
- Yangtze River Delta (YRD) (Shanghai, Hangzhou, Nanjing, etc.)
- Pearl River Delta (PRD) (Guangzhou, Shenzhen, and surrounding area)
- Chengdu-Chongqing Economic Zone (includes the traditional Third Line defense enterprise and research base of Mianyang)
- Guanzhong-Tianshui Economic Zone or West Triangle Economic Circle
- Beibu Gulf (Guangxi) Economic Zone (also referred to as the Little Beibu Gulf, encompassing Beihai, Qinzhou, Fangchenggang, Nanning, Changzuo, and Yulin)

As evidenced by contemporary S&T and defense industry policies and plans, Beijing clearly believes that adopting a similar approach for the defense sector as has performed reasonably well for commercial industry will: (1) promote and hasten interactions between and among key innovative actors—defense sector researchers, industry, academia, and government officials—creating critical, new defense clusters of innovation; (2) foster dual-use technology development efforts through sharing of S&T resources, services, and infrastructure; (3) facilitate domestic and foreign technology transfers to, from, and across the defense sector; and (4) maximize opportunities for serendipitous or improvisational innovation by co-locating key innovative actors and institutions where they already reside or will reside (i.e., in clusters).[47] Accordingly, recent regulatory reforms were made to the FDI Catalogue to permit greater foreign investment in selected defense industrial sectors and areas of advanced S&T research, to promote more advanced forms of technology transfer by both domestic and foreign firms (e.g., establishing R&D centers, research contracts, management consulting services, and industry associations), and to incentivize investments in and around new or existing zones or parks where, it is expected, other defense, commercial, and S&T enterprises will also locate their ventures or institutes. In short, Beijing seeks to build on a proven commercial development model in advancing its defense industrial innovative capabilities.

If the same model is followed down to the enterprise level, in fact, one can expect to see Chinese defense enterprises following a development strategy similar to their earlier commercial counterparts—attempting to form strategic partnerships and joint ventures with a range of foreign investors and experts possessing up- and downstream industrial and technological know-how. Such was an early strategy employed by China's now well-known commercial enterprises Lenovo, Huawei, and Datang. By partnering with foreign companies involved in every aspect of the industry—from research to production to marketing and services—several of the then-nascent Chinese companies were able to relatively quickly learn the business and industry-wide processes and dynamics, as well as gain the technical understanding needed to integrate diverse sources of technology. This strategic partnering approach allowed Chinese venture partners to, before long, compete with these same foreign investors, who then were permitted to establish wholly foreign-owned enterprises or WFOEs in China. Foreign WFOEs were then encouraged to begin joint R&D programs with certain Chinese partners and, later, as WFOEs to conduct more advanced R&D for the global, regional, and China markets. The regulatory limits placed on the number of available Chinese partners with which foreign investors could choose to partner were what allowed some Chinese ventures to effectively employ a tactic aimed at maximizing foreign technology transfers by playing prospective investors off one another in their bids to gain early access to the China market via a Sino-foreign joint venture. In this way, the Chinese partner could pick and choose among a variety of prospective, eager foreign partners and strategically partner in ways that could help the Chinese firm vertically develop and integrate their business into a full-scale competitor.[48] As the US Department of Defense noted in its 2006 annual report on China's military power, "where technology targets remain difficult to acquire, foreign investors are attracted to China via contracts that are often written to ensure Chinese oversight, with the eventual goal of displacing foreigners from the companies brought into China." It appears that a similar dynamic is at play (or at least planned and to some extent being attempted) today in the defense sector, with the defense conglomerates and their subsidiaries cast to play the lead role.

As presently envisioned, the 10 defense conglomerates will become the innovation centers of gravity in China's DIS, taking over much of the strategic industrial development oversight role and the technological development planning previously performed by government officials.[49] The degree to which this greater autonomy and interaction by the defense conglomerates and their subsidiaries with actors clustered in innovation zones, centers, and parks occurs or does not occur will be a key indicator of whether or not and to what extent China's reforms have been effective. At the same time, this and related S&T reforms are also aimed at promoting more efficient use and sharing of resources across the defense sector, employing various mechanisms such as a nationwide IT network, libraries and databases, shared industry and S&T roadmaps, and more, in an expanded, nationwide knowledge innovation system designed to connect the defense and military universities to the civilian sector and to better leverage the latter for defense industrial and S&T development.[50] Recent reform efforts have sought also to better leverage China's elite civilian universities for the training of defense-sector and military personnel in advanced science and technology fields and to serve as the primary site for development of "fundamental, cutting edge, and generic technologies."[51]

Theme 4: Adopting a strategic "grid" approach to connecting innovation centers and their respective scientists, researchers, industry executives, entrepreneurs, government officials, and others working in dispersed regional locations and within clusters at the local, provincial, regional, and central government levels and connected via information communications technologies

No degree of innovation planning and oversight will succeed in China or elsewhere without actual interactions among the key actors in any DIS—representatives of the defense industry, the military, government-funded researchers, academic institutions, and the commercial marketplace both domestic and international. One of the fundamental challenges to China's defense innovation efforts has long been geographic distance and subsequent disparity among defense sectors, which together have effectively limited collaboration among these actors, institutions, and processes. Those defense industries with access to the more vibrant commercial sectors—generally located along China's coastal zones—(i.e., IT and shipbuilding) have tended to fare better than those without sufficient outlet to the commercial sectors and/or coastal zones, primarily those tied down in the interior and third-line defense areas (e.g., aerospace and aviation).[52] Beijing's strategy is two-fold: to enhance *intra*regional interactions (to develop the "regional innovation system embodying individual features and advantages") as national defense innovation nodes and to expand *inter*regional—particularly coastal-inland—connections in order to promote and hasten defense innovation capacities across all sectors. This cross-regional linkage of innovation clusters or nodes constitutes a grid that joins these various regional nodes through information networks in order to aid the development of a more productive, nationwide defense innovation system.[53] The regional innovation clusters will compose the national nodes in China's grid approach to connecting and developing its innovative system of systems; they are intended to improve cross-regional as well as cross-sector, civil-military innovation coordination and collaboration.

Theme 5: Instituting a regular cycle of structural and institutional reforms in the defense sector (by instituting a period of organizational disaggregation followed by a period of industry consolidation, then another cycle of disaggregation, and so on) as a means of promoting continuous institutional and innovative dynamism in the defense industry sector

While the defense conglomerates are expected to be granted greater autonomy from state planners in order to foster sectorwide defense innovation, the state plans to maintain a critical policy role, namely overseeing and guiding the above-mentioned cycles of regularized industry restructuring reforms. The plan appears to be to institute regular, repeated cycles of institutional consolidation followed by disaggregation then renewed consolidation, to make the defense industry more likely to be continuously innovative and vested corporate interests less likely to become systemic obstacles to innovation. This approach, according to Gu Shulin and other Chinese analysts discussing China's NIS and DIS, is being pursued strategically as a deliberate effort to foster industry and sectoral reform and competition (versus what could at times appear, and might well be, haphazard reforms in response to persistent failures). This strategic "transformation" approach applies to both industry and research institutes and aims at "recombination learning" via market-oriented reforms, reorganization, and technical and management training, as well as the institutional restructuring of the defense sector.[54] This regularized creative-destructive institutional reform cycle is meant to shake up incentive structures in the defense industry, in order to promote greater efficiencies and effectiveness and to fill critical capability gaps that might otherwise go unaddressed by status quo–oriented defense conglomerates.[55] The 12th FYP seems to support this approach, suggesting that there will be further defense sector restructuring and consolidation to come during the five-year period, including the promotion of increased privatization and of mergers and acquisitions.[56] Shortly following the FYP's release, for instance, China Aviation Industry Corporation (AVIC) announced a consolidated reacquisition of six subsidiaries, which is expected to "expand its research and development and production activities into airborne electronic equipment, control systems, and airborne lighting equipment."[57]

Theme 6: Promoting more cross-disciplinary and cross-sector research, overseen by the defense conglomerates in what some have termed a "matrix" approach to industrial development and defense innovation[58]

Present plans to enhance China's defense industrial production and innovation capabilities call for the defense conglomerates to play a leading role in fostering sectorwide—and now also cross-sector—innovation. The highest-level group of companies or conglomerates will be charged with overseeing not only all aspects of vertical development in their industry sector but also in any strategic, cross-cutting (horizontal) industry sectors that might complement and enhance new forms and directions of innovation. Take, for example, the Chinese Aerospace Science and Technology Corporation (CASC), which, according to reports outlining its plans through 2015, "will implement strategic management at two levels, that is to say, CASC Group will formulate, implement and supervise the overall strategy; and all CASC subsidiaries will formulate and implement their own business development strategies under guidance of the overall strategy to improve their market-oriented strategic development capability. CASC will actively perform its corporate social responsibility."[59] This new industrial plan emphasizes the need for the group-level holding company to have insights and, where beneficial, investment not only in civil-military aerospace sectors, but also in other industry sectors, such as information technology and automotive. This approach, while not entirely new (in terms of overseeing vertical, industry-sector and project-level research), expands on earlier plans by including more *cross-sector* oversight by the defense conglomerates themselves.[60]

The lack of such cross-cutting industry interactions in the past is viewed as having been a serious limitation on defense industry evolution. This new approach—termed a "matrix" management approach in some Chinese analyses—reflects the state's plan, as often articulated in Hu Jintao's era, to make enterprises "the main players in the market." According to this matrix-style approach, the defense conglomerates are intended to become, in some respects, like their Western equivalents, the defense-sector prime contractors (like Lockheed Martin, General Dynamics, Northrup Grumman, EADS, British Aerospace, etc.). China's prime conglomerates will coordinate their respective industry sectors, including inputs from China's now-more-competitive commercial enterprises, who have become key suppliers and partners to the PLA.[61] Notably, however, this defense innovation effort could easily conflict with the theme of structural reform cycles outlined in the previous section.

China's defense laboratories are also expected to play a greater role in enhancing cross-sector and cross-disciplinary research, as well as in facilitating technology transfer and talent exchange between the defense industries and civilian research systems. "Key point research facilities such as the National Defense Science and Technology Key Laboratories have been designated as a way to concentrate defense science and technology resources. . . . their numbers now appear to be increasing in both quantity and variety."[62] Research by Francis shows that "there are now at least three different variations on the defense key laboratory model": Defense Science and Technology Key Laboratories, Defense Science and Technology Key Disciplines Laboratories, Defense Science and Technology State Key Laboratories. "National Defense Science and Technology State Key Laboratories are comprehensive laboratories, engaging in defense major basic research programs, strategic high technologies research, and systems integration research, whereas National Defense Science and Technology Key Laboratories are specialized laboratories, engaging in exploratory, innovative, and crux technologies basic and applied research. National Defense Key Discipline Laboratories conduct basic defense discipline and advanced technology field research into new principles, new methods, and new technologies."[63]

Theme 7: Leveraging international S&T expertise by instituting additional incentive programs to promote advanced scientific and technological research and entrepreneurial opportunities for mainland and overseas Chinese citizens and for selected foreign talent and foreign investors in ways that promote spillover of advanced S&T expertise, practices promoting academic integrity and quality assurance, interdisciplinary cooperation and flows of personnel, increased patenting capabilities, and other innovation-oriented activities

China's current DIS plans recognize the importance of human resources and seek to exploit talent wherever it resides, whether in the commercial or defense sectors, academic or research institutions, at home or overseas. Defense universities, labs, and enterprises have received state funding for the express purpose of attracting domestic and foreign expertise through a variety of formats (e.g., lectures, fellowships, collaborative and joint projects, coauthorship of scientific papers and journal articles). Although direct connections between the defense industry and foreign scientists and researchers might be limited by mutual security concerns, a growing number of joint university programs between Western and Chinese academic institutions and Western university satellite campuses in

China have emerged in recent years. These programs provide the opportunity—at least in theory—for greater socialization of Chinese defense researchers and scientists working at or with China's civilian universities and their foreign counterparts.

Theme 8: Focusing on incremental innovation in the short term by prioritizing defense innovation efforts on filling existing gaps in China's present force structure (to catch up and be comparable to modern military powers) while also pursuing more advanced forms of innovation for the long term

Although China's long-time strategy has been to "take the road of leapfrog development" and to "accelerate the revolution in military affairs with Chinese characteristics,"[64] based on China's indigenous innovation strategy as well as re-cently unveiled weapons platforms and defense technologies, it appears that China has been taking an incremental approach to achieving its defense innova-tion aspirations, prioritizing its efforts on programs and platforms that fill critical gaps in China's existing force structure as compared to other modern militaries (e.g., developing late-generation fighters, undersea warfare capabili-ties, modern surface ships and aircraft carriers) while simultaneously pursuing longer-term, fundamental research.[65] While China's actual defense development strategy is hard to confirm, such an approach is considered the norm for develop-ing countries, is in line with more recent interpretations in the West of the meaning of indigenous innovation, and would seem to fit China's past record of adopting a generally gradual approach to developing new technologies, demon-strating a deliberate, yet steep, technology learning curve and adapting existing and new (mainly new-to-China) technology to serve China's particular needs.[66] This near-term incremental, longer-term fundamental approach is suggested in the MLTP, which cites the goal for defense S&T as being "basically meeting the needs in developing modern arms and associated information technology, and providing S&T support for safeguarding national security" while also seeking to catch up to the world's leading powers by 2020.

Interestingly, no mention is made in the 2010 *Defense White Paper* of techno-logical leapfrogging, although it has been explicitly cited since at least as far back as the 2000 iteration and appeared as a heading in the 2008 *Defense White Paper*, under which it stated, "China is working to develop new and high-tech weaponry and equipment . . . in an all-round way, so as to change the mode of formation of war-fighting capabilities. Persisting in laying stress on priorities, China distinguishes between the primary and the secondary, and refrains from doing certain things, striving to achieve leapfrog development in key areas." Even here there is an indication that some prioritization is taking place in defense technology innovation and that any leapfrogging will likely be confined to selected areas (e.g., space exploration or nanotechnology). If so, this suggests that China's near-term strategy is, in fact, to primarily pursue incremental innovation by design, as well, perhaps, as by necessity. If so, this strategy could put China's defense innovation efforts in a somewhat different light than is sometimes depicted—as simply a failure to achieve more radical innovation. It could also simply reflect a more realistic assessment of China's ability to achieve in the near term its military modernization objectives.

Defense Innovation: Making the Wheels Turn

Taken together, the above themes paint a picture of an overarching Chinese defense innovation system and strategy that envisions a DIS as part of a cross-indigenous and exogenous series of systems of innovation systems. In other words, China's DIS strategy is a key component of China's national innovation system but is connected also to the other layers of a system of innovation systems linking international, regional, industry, civil-military, knowledge-based, and other systems. While Beijing continues to amend its top-down strategies, plans, and policies as needed, its main challenge in realizing a more productive and efficient DIS is effectively incentivizing more collaborative and innovative interactions among various communities, actors, and institutions at the bottom of the system and across the civil-military divide, that is, the scientists and researchers, enterprises and industries, provinces and regions, and domestic and international actors. Beijing hopes that these interdependent innovation ecosystems—akin to wheels turning at the base of its DIS—will form a more collaborative, innovative, bottom-up dynamic able to move the entire defense innovation system into high gear. In order to facilitate this lower-level, organic interaction, the Chinese government is implementing the many new mechanisms, institutions, and processes described above.

Conclusions

China's efforts to develop a more modern, effective, and efficient defense innovation system are not without some significant challenges. The most prominent challenge is the one that current reforms seek to address: how to foster greater and regular collaboration among innovators themselves, whether they are working in academic circles (military or civilian), commercial industry, or defense industries;

in research labs funded by public, private, or international funds; are foreign or domestic; and are scientists, researchers, or industry experts. In China these communities historically have been separated by institutional stovepipes, distinct regulatory systems, geographic distance, and cultural differences. Employing top-down strategic plans, programs, and guidelines to make these actors interact in more innovative ways will not suffice, but Beijing seems to have recognized this and is focusing its present reform efforts largely on putting into place a more innovation-friendly defense industrial ecosystem, then connecting this with other innovation systems across the country, across the civil-military divide, and across international boundaries. This more holistic, interconnected system-of-innovative-systems approach could, indeed, lead to more organic innovative interactions among actors found at the edges or bottom of an innovation organizational chart. But it is still relatively early days in China's efforts to develop this sort of DIS alongside its NIS and other related innovation systems. Recent Chinese interlocutors have noted that progress on breaching the civil-military and foreign-domestic barriers to defense innovation, in particular, remains problematic and slow-going and that overcoming long-time vested interests of government, industry, and scholars in current modes of operation will be difficult.[67]

Furthermore, defense industrial decisions made today typically will not reap rewards for many years or decades to come. Even then, efforts to incentivize defense innovation, though perhaps theoretically astute and strategically well considered, might not actually match whatever economic, industrial, societal, cultural, or financial environment emerges down the road. Consequently, the success or failure of China's efforts to establish a complex system of innovation systems and to maximize advanced defense technology development capabilities will depend on a mix of theory, reality, and chance; nor are traditional scientific and technological metrics (e.g., patents, scientific publications, spending on R&D) likely to be clear indicators of whether or not China's innovative wheels are, indeed, turning and gaining traction as a result of cross-cutting innovative interactions.

In today's globalized industrial, technological, and scientific age, one thing has become clear. Those national innovation systems that are most adaptable in terms of sources, processes, and the sort of actors collaboratively involved in innovative activities appear to be weathering real-world fluctuations better than those that are more rigidly designed, insular, or dependent on either a top-down, government-designed model *or* a laissez-faire, bottom-up approach to innovation by the entrepreneurial class. Systems that incorporate elements of both a strategic top-down approach *and* a vibrant, bottom-up entrepreneurial and innovative foundation open to international innovative inputs appear to be faring best, which is a key reason why this approach constitutes China's clear objective in developing its DIS and in linking these efforts to other national and international innovation systems.[68] But only time will tell whether such an ambitious, multisystemic change will succeed. To the extent it does, China can be expected to realize success in achieving incremental product innovations and, potentially over the longer term, more radical process innovations.

NOTES

This chapter stems from research conducted by a study group originally composed of Ed Francis, Micah Springut, and Kathleen Walsh (chair), with guidance and substantive input from Tai Ming Cheung. The group was tasked with characterizing China's DIS concept. Portions of this chapter were originally drafted and presented at the Summer Training Workshop on the Relationship between National Security and Technology in China (June 20–25, 2011) and the Workshop on Chinese Military Innovation (June 28–29, 2011) of the Institute on Global Conflict and Cooperation. The majority of the original research and drafting for the workshop paper were done by Ed Francis and Kate Walsh. The author is grateful for the substantive contributions made to the conference draft by Ed Francis; where his contributions are specifically included here, the draft conference volume is referenced. The author is grateful also for comments on the paper by Tai Ming Cheung and Richard P. Suttmeier. The views and any errors presented herein are those of the author alone and do not represent official policy or views of the US Government, Department of Defense, US Navy, or US Naval War College.

1. For the purposes of this chapter, the generic definition of *defense innovation* offered by Tai Ming Cheung is sufficient: "the transformation of ideas and knowledge into products and processes for military or dual use." Tai Ming Cheung, "Defense Innovation: The State of the Field and the Systems of Innovation Approach," presentation to the Conference on New Approaches to Defense Industrial Innovation, Singapore, February 28, 2011.

2. Many Chinese writings reference the main NIS theorists, Freeman, Lundvall, Edquist, Nelson, et al. See Chris Freeman, *Technology Policy and Economic Performance: Lessons from Japan* (London: Pinter, 1987); B-Å. Lundvall, ed., *National Innovation Systems: Towards a Theory of Innovation and Interactive Learning* (London: Pinter, 1992); Charles Edquist, ed., *Systems of Innovation: Technologies, Institutions, and Organizations* (Washington, DC: Pinter Press, 1997); Richard R. Nelson, ed., *National Innovation Systems: A Comparative Analysis* (New York: Oxford University Press, 1993); andOrganization for Economic Cooperation and Development, *National Innovation Systems* (Paris: OECD, 1997).

3. OECD, *National Innovation Systems* (Paris: OECD, 2007).

4. Ibid. See also J. A. Schumpeter, *The Theory of Economic Development*, trans. Redvers Opie (New York: Oxford University Press, 1934;originally published in German in 1911); and Andrew D. James, "The Place of the UK Defense Industry in its National Innovation System: Co-Evolution of National, Sectoral, and Technological Systems," Occasional Paper #25, in Judith Reppy, ed., *The Place of the Defense Industry in National Systems of Innovation* (NY: Cornell University Press, 2000) accessed online at http://www .einaudi.cornell.edu/peaceprogram/publications/occasional_papers/Natl-sys-25.pdf.

5. Theo J. A. Roelandt and Pim den Hertog, "Summary Report of the Focus Group on Clusters" (Paris: OECD, 1999); and Edquist, *Systems of Innovation*, 3–15.

6. In *Run of the Red Queen*, Dan Breznitz and Michael Murphee contend that China is pursuing (by dint of accidental industrial policy outcomes) two innovation systems at once: one national and the other regional. The contention made here is, rather, that Beijing policy makers have expanded this dual-, now multisystem, approach to innovation beyond the national and regional dimensions. Breznitz and Murphee, *Run of the Red Queen: Government, Innovation, Globalization, and Economic Growth in China* (New Haven: Yale University Press, 2011): 2–3.

7. The MLTP cites the goal of achieving an "innovation-oriented society by 2020"; in other documents the word *nation* is used rather than *society*.

8. Edquist, *Systems of Innovation*.

9. Judith Reppy, "Competing Institutional Paradigms: Conceptualizing the Role of Defense Industries in National Systems of Innovation," in Judith Reppy, ed., *The Place of the Defense Industry in National Systems of Innovation* (Ithaca, NY: Cornell University Press, 2000):1–12, esp. 2–3.

10. Gao Changlin, "Chinese Science and Technology Indicators System: Toward an Innovation-Based Nation," presentation to the OECD-MOST Indicator Workshop in Chongqing, PRC (October 19–20, 2006), accessed online at www.oecd.org/dataoecd/29 /4/37737643.pdf. This list of components and system-of-systems approach is in line with the views of the Chinese Academy of Sciences (CAS) on developing an NIS, which CAS separates into four distinct "subsystems," namely: knowledge innovation, technological innovation, knowledge dissemination, and knowledge application. See CAS, "A National System of Innovation to be Built for Welcoming the Era of Knowledge Economy," *Bulletin of the Chinese Academy of Sciences* 12, no. 3 (1998). Other materials present a similar approach, sometimes listing a national defense innovation system as a separate component. See, for instance, Yang Qiquan, "The Development Strategy and Innovation System in China," presentation to the Chinese Academy of Science and Technology for Development conference in Moscow, October 1, 2009, slide 14, accessed online at www .issras.ru/conference_2009/docs/Qiquan_Yang.pdf.

11. Gao Changlin, "Chinese Science and Technology Indicators System.

12. OECD, *Managing National Systems of Innovation* (Paris: OECD, 1999).

13. The reliance on foreign investment or inputs is not unusual and can be advantageous, particularly given China's stage of technological development. In a study on Japan's innovation challenge to US competitiveness, the author states, "During America's early industrialization, immigrant engineer-entrepreneurs played a significant role in technology and enterprise development." John H. Dunning, *Multinational Enterprises and the Global Economy* (Wokingham, England: Addison-Wesley, 1993), as cited in Na-

tional Research Council Committee on Japan, *Maximizing U.S. Interests in Science and Technology Relations with Japan* (Washington, DC: National Academies Press, 1997).

14. The original notion of an NIS as depicted by Freeman did presume national boundaries, although this has since been the subject of much debate. Freeman, *Technology Policy and Economic Performance*; Reppy, *The Place of the Defense Industry in Naitonal Systems of Innovation*, 1. Others have termed China's approach more of a global innovation system, suggesting that China abandoned the borders-limited NIS model in the early 1980s. See Jon Sigurdson, "Regional Innovation Systems (RID) in China," Working Paper 195 (July 2004), 5, http://swopec.hhs.se/eijswp/papers/eijswp0195.pdf.

15. Reppy, *The Place of the Defense Industry in National Systems of Innovation* (2000); James, "The Place of the UK Defense Industry in its National Innovation System"; and Cheung, "Defense Innovation."

16. Efforts to create a new scholarly framework have been attempted more recently. See, for instance, Tai Ming Cheung, Thomas G. Mahnken, and Andrew L. Ross, "Frameworks for Analyzing Chinese Defense and Military Innovation," in *New Perspectives on Assessing the Chinese Defense Economy: 2011 Industry Overview and Policy Briefs*, Tai Ming Cheung, ed. (San Diego: University of California San Diego, 2011): 77–80.

17. A saying attributed to Alexandre Dumas. John Bartlett, *Bartlett's Familiar Quotations*, 10th ed. (1919), accessed at http://www.bartleby.com/100/777.41.html.

18. Based on author interviews with innovation experts in China, December 2011. Notably, all of these states are relatively open with regard to publicly outlining their innovation strategies, policies, and plans yet are distinct in terms of the role played by the state vis-à-vis the private sector. See, for instance, publicly available studies, such as Government of Australia, *Venturous Australia: Building Strength in Innovation* (Melbourne: Cutler, 2008), also known as the "Cutler Review"; OECD, *OECD Reviews of Innovation Policy: Norway* (Paris: OECD, 2008); Research Council, *Innovation Strategy for the Research Council of Norway*, trans. Anna Godson and Carol B. Eckmann (Oslo: Research Council, 2011); Government of Canada, *Canada's Innovation Strategy: New Ideas, New Opportunities* (Ottawa: Information Distribution Center, 2002); United Kingdom Department for Business and Innovation Skills, *Annual Innovation Report 2010* (London: NESTA, 2011); and Committee on Global Science and Technology Strategies and Their Effect on U.S. National Security, *S&T Strategies of Six Countries: Implications for the United States* (Washington, DC: National Academies Press, 2010).

19. See Royal Society, *Knowledge, Networks and Nations: Global Scientific Collaboration in the 21st Century* (London: The Royal Society, 2011); Committee on Global Science and Technology Strategies, *S&T Strategies of Six Countries*; Committee on Comparative Innovation Policy: Best Practice for the 21st Century, of the Board on Science, Technology, and Economic Policy, "Innovative Flanders: Innovation Policies for the 21st Century—Report of a Symposium," Charles W. Wessner, ed. (Washington, DC: National Academies Press, 2008); and OECD, *National Innovation Systems* (1997).

20. The original conference version of this study included extensive research and analysis of these institutions and their changing roles in the emerging defense innovation system; the research was conducted primarily by Ed Francis. Due to space constraints, many of these details are not included here but nonetheless play an important role in

understanding China's defense innovation efforts. Where these insights appear in the chapter, the draft conference volume is referenced.

21. US Department of Defense, *China Military Power* (2007): 26–27 online at http://www.defense.gov/pubs/pdfs/070523-china-military-power-final.pdf.

22. See, for instance, Gu Shulin, "Policy Process and Recombination Learning: China in the 1980s and 1990s," presentation to the World Bank–sponsored event, Innovation Policies and Institutions for the Knowledge Economy: An Asian Senior Policy Forum and Study Tour to Korean Innovation Institutions, Seoul, South Korea, November 29, 2006.

23. Breznitz and Murphee suggest that, in fact, Chinese firms complain about too little formal Chinese government guidance in policy making as well as institutionalization that is *ad hoc vice* strategic in nature. Breznitz and Murphee, *Run of the Red Queen*, 10–11.

24. China reached an R&D spending level of 1.8 percent of GDP in 2010, with a goal of reaching the R&D/GDP ratio of 2.2% by 2015 on the way to 2.5 by 2020. "China to Spend 2.2% of GDP on R&D by 2015," *Xinhua*, March 5, 2011.

25. CAS, "Creation 2050: Science, Technology, and China's Future" (June 2009). The CAS oversees 117 institutions, of which 50 are state key labs, 29 research institutes and observatories, and 31 open laboratories; it also supervises several "mega-science" programs and facilities and two universities. See CAS, *Science and Technology in China: A Roadmap for 2050—Strategic Reports of the Chinese Academy of Sciences*, ed. Lu Yongxiang (Secaucus, NJ: Springer, 2010), xiv; "China Issues Long-Term Roadmap for Development of Science and Technology," *Xinhua News Agency*, June 10, 2009; and Yang Zurong, "Interpretations of 'Innovation 2050': S&T and China's Future," *Jiefangjun Bao*, June14, 2009; CAS website: http://english.cas.cn/ST/BR/br_introduction/200909/t20090914_37733.shtml; IAP, "The Chinese Academy of Sciences," member database, online at http://interacademies.net.

26. CAS, *Science and Technology in China: A Roadmap*, xiv–xvi.

27. "Strive to be a Powerhouse in China's S&T Development—2010 Annual Meeting of CAS in Beijing," *Bulletin of the Chinese Academy of Sciences* 24, no. 1 (2010): 1–4. The Chinese Academy of Engineering also was mentioned as a key actor, playing a more central coordinating role in discussions in China in December 2011. Whether the CAS's role has changed fundamentally or not is debatable, however, and the above-described role could, as suggested in comments by Peter Suttmeier, reflect simply normal interacademy contests for influence.

28. See Jane Qiu, "China Sets 2020 Vision for Science," *Nature* 470, no. 15 (February 1, 2011); and *University World News*, March 19, 2011, online at http://www.universityworldnews.com/article.php?story=2011031918623523.

29. The 12th FYP (2011–2015) also stresses several specific defense S&T and industry goals, including: "build advanced military industrial core capabilities"; "achieve breakthroughs in key defense projects, including phases 2 & 3 of China's lunar exploration program, manned space station, and high-resolution earth observation systems"; "promote informatized research and production"; "perfect the dual-use development system"; "expand international cooperation, increasing import of advanced technologies,

equipment, energy, and raw materials and intensifying talent recruitment"; and "strengthen military industry core talents buildup." "Report on 2011 Defense Science, Technology, and Industry Work Meeting," *Keji Ribao* (January 3, 2011).

30. Office of the State Council, "China's Medium- and Long-Term National Plan for Science and Technology Development 2006–2020" (2006).

31. Seth Drewey and William Edgar, "Focus: China Gambles with Private Sector," *Jane's Defense Weekly*, November 1, 2005; Ben Vogel, "China to Subsidise Private Sector Defense Activities," *Jane's Defense Weekly*, August 16, 2006.

32. Jon Grevatt, "China Draws Up Industry Reforms in Bid to Raise Competitiveness," *Jane's Defense Industry*, July 1, 2007.

33. The Chinese National Development and Reform Commission (NDRC) outlines state economic plans, industrial plans, and the catalogue of investments (i.e., those encouraged, restricted, or eliminated; permitted sectors are no longer listed), the most recent of which was published in April 2011 in support of 12th FYP goals. See "China Unveils New Industrial Policy Guideline to Restructure Economy," *IHS Global Insight: Country and Industry Forecasting*, April 26, 2011; Jon Grevatt, "China Drafts FDI Plan for Defense Sector," *Jane's Defense Weekly*, April 8, 2011.

34. See, for instance, discussion over the right level of foreign technology imports as detailed most recently in Micah Springut, Stephen Schlaikjer, and David Chen, *China's Program for Science and Technology Modernization: Implications for American Competitiveness*, report prepared for the US-China Economic and Security Review Commission (USCC) (Arlington, VA: CENTRA Technologies, 2011), esp. 84.

35. The 2010 document was titled "Several Opinions of the State Council on Encouraging and Guiding the Healthy Development of Private Investment." Information on the 2010 and 2011 policies is found in Jon Grevatt, "China Plans Guidelines to Drive Private Sector Defense Development," *Jane's Defense Industry*, March 15, 2011.

36. Ibid.

37. Ed Francis and Kathleen Walsh, "China's Defense Innovation System: Making the Wheels Spin," draft conference paper, IGCC Summer Training Workshop on the Relationship between National Security and Technology in China, June 20–25, 2011, and Workshop on Chinese Military Innovation, June 28–29, 2011.

38. "Chinese Defense Industry: Chinese Puzzle," *Jane's Defense Weekly*, January 14, 2004.

39. Jon Grevatt, "China Accelerates Defense Technology Research," *Jane's Defense Weekly*, September 26, 2007.

40. Francis further notes that "labs can be situated at a number of different types of host institutions, including defense industry enterprises, defense industry universities under MIIT, and civilian universities." Francis and Walsh, "China's Defense Innovation System.

41. Ibid.

42. Joanne Chien, "Overview of China's 12th Five-Year Plan," *(Taipei) Digitimes Research*, January 31, 2010; see also *Xinhua News Agency*, December 30, 2010.

43. There are today various types of investment and innovation-oriented zones and services, including: Science & Technology Industrial Parks (STIPs), which are also re-

ferred to as High-Technology Development Zones (HTDZs), National Economic and Technological Development Zones, Provincial-level STIPs / HTDZs, Civil-Military Integration Industry Zones or Civil-Military Integrated Industrial Bases, Regional Ocean Economic Zones, University Science Parks, CAS Science Parks, S&T Business Incubators, Productivity Promotion Centers, and Technology Trading Agencies. See Zhou Ding, "Regional Practice for Developing Hi-Tech Industrial Clusters," in "Fostering Innovation in Hi-Tech Clusters: Proceedings and Papers Presented at the Workshop on Fostering Innovation Through Strengthening of Hi-Tech Clusters," conference hosted by the Asia and Pacific Center for Transfer of Technology (APCTT), New Delhi, India, 2010, 73–82, accessed online at http://nis.apctt.org/PDF/HTC_Report_Final.pdf; Luo Hui, "Sub-National Innovation System Practices in China," presentation to the National Workshop on Subnational Innovation Systems and Technology Capacity-Building Policies to Enhance Competitiveness of SMEs, in Jakarta, Indonesia, April 3–4, 2007, accessed online at www.unescap.org/tid/projects/sisindo_s2; and "China's First Ocean Economic Zone Signs Deal Worth 38 Billion Dollars," *Xinhua*, February 23, 2011.

44. Provincial-level civil-military integration (CMI) zones have been established subsequently in a number of other locations, including Shaanxi, Sichuan, Hunan, Jiangxi, and Hubei provinces, and Chongqing municipality. Zhang Guofeng, "A Look at the Development of Industry Zone Establishment and Civil-Military Fusion Development," *Defense Science and Technology Industry*, no. 12 (2009): 42; Francis and Walsh, "China's Defense Innovation System."

45. Francis and Walsh, "China's Defense Innovation System" (2011); Zhang Guofeng, "A Look at the Development of Industry Zone Establishment," p. 43.

46. MOST, "Major S&T Findings to Auction," *China S&T Newsletter*, News Briefs, no. 613, March 20, 2011.

47. An example of this dual commercial-military approach to fostering defense innovation is the Dual-Use R&D Integration Institute. Established in Guangdong, the institute is specifically dedicated to integrating commercial and military technologies and will collaborate with area universities and defense and high-tech firms in order to "encourage advanced civilian scientific and technological achievements applied to defense research and production, and promote technical development of weapons and equipment, to reduce costs and improve efficiencies." The Guangdong institute is expected to be one of several strategically located institutions devoted to similar activities. Jon Grevatt, "China Creates Institute to Integrate Dual-Use Technologies," *Jane's Defense Weekly*, April 7, 2011.

48. Kathleen A. Walsh, *Foreign High-Tech R&D in China: Risks, Rewards and Implications for US-China Relations* (Washington, DC: Stimson Center, 2003).

49. See "Main Functions and Responsibilities of SASAC," accessed at http://www.sasac.gov.cn/n2963340/n2963393/2965120.html in April 2010; and Francis and Walsh, "China's Defense Innovation System."

50. China's 2002 *Defense White Paper* notes that "informationization and networking of teaching have been promoted, and an information network platform for the armed forces' teaching and scientific research has been initially put in place, giving shape to a training information network linking PLA's colleges and schools and having nearly

100,000 websites and centers." Information Office of the State Council, *China's National Defense in 2002* (Beijing: State Council, 2002); and Francis and Walsh, "China's Defense Innovation System."

51. "China Top Legislator Urges Universities to Speed Up Innovation," *Xinhua,* March 7, 2011.

52. The Pentagon's assessment in 2009 was, "Progress across China's defense industry sectors has been uneven. Production trends and resource allocation appear to favor missile and space systems, followed by maritime assets (both surface and sub-surface), aircraft, and ground force materiel. In all areas, however, China is increasing the quality of its output and surge production capabilities." US Department of Defense, *Military Power of the People's Republic of China,* 2009 (Washington, DC: Office of the Secretary of Defense, 2009), 36.

53. Reference to developing a research "grid" structure is made in CAS, *Science and Technology in China: A Roadmap,* xii, among other citations. The concept is not unlike the Advanced Research Projects Agency network or ARPAnet, the US Defense Department–funded communications network that was the precursor to the Internet.

54. Gu, "Policy Process and Recombination Learning."

55. Ibid.

56. Jon Grevatt, "China's 12th Five-Year Plan Calls for Accelerated Industry Development," *Jane's Defense Weekly,* March 8, 2011.

57. The April 2011 reconsolidation followed two reconsolidations in 2010. Jon Grevatt, "China's AVIC Announces Restructuring Plan," *Jane's Defense Weekly,* April 1, 2011.

58. The matrix and grid approaches to S&T management are cited in "Strive to be a Powerhouse in China's S&T Development—2010 Annual Meeting of CAS in Beijing," *Bulletin of the Chinese Academy of Sciences* 24, no. 1 (2010):1–4.

59. Zhang Huiting, "CASC to Build a New Aerospace Industrial System by 2015," *Aerospace China* (Autumn 2008): 2–5.

60. Among the late 1990s reform efforts was promotion of matrix management for oversight of R&D projects by the defense conglomerates (as opposed to the former "chief designer" system), with China Aerospace Science and Industry Corporation's Fourth Academy serving as the model for turning around inefficient, cost-overrun weapons projects. See Tai Ming Cheung, *Fortifying China: The Struggle to Build a Modern Defense Economy* (Ithaca, NY: Cornell University Press, 2009), 151–152.

61. "Chinese Defense Industry: Chinese Puzzle," *Jane's Defense Weekly,* January 14, 2004.

62. Francis and Walsh, "China's Defense Innovation System"; "Increase Innovation Capacity, Promote Sustainable Development: National Defense Science and Technology Key Laboratory On Site Experience Exchange Proclamation and Implementation Meeting Summary," *Defense Science and Technology Industry* (August 2009).

63. Francis and Walsh, "China's Defense Innovation System."

64. Cited in the 2008 *DefenseWhite Paper* and reiterated by Hu Jintao at 17th Party Congress. Jon Grevatt, "Chinese President Pledges Increase in Pace of Military Modernization," *Jane's Defense Industry,* November 1, 2007.

65. See Gu, "Policy Process and Recombination Learning."

66. Cheung notes that, "in late-industrializing states such as China, the focus of technological development and innovation diverges markedly from that in industrialized economies. These states emphasize absorption and incremental innovation rather than the development of new or radical products or processes." Cheung, *Fortifying China*, 11.

67. Based on author interviews with innovation experts in China (December 2011).

68. Committee on Global Science and Technology Strategies, *S&T Strategies of Six Countries*; and Committee on Comparative Innovation Policy "Innovative Flanders."

Chapter Seven

Locating China's Place in the Global Defense Economy

Richard A. Bitzinger, Michael Raska, Collin Koh Swee Lean, and Kelvin Wong Ka Weng

Introduction

This chapter starts with the premise that the global arms industry is a hierarchical system, and that a nation's position as an arms producer in this hierarchy is dictated by the relative level of its indigenous capabilities for independent defense-related research and development (R&D) and manufacturing.[1] Although there are no generally agreed upon criteria for how arms-producing nations are compartmentalized, it is customary to divide the global defense industry into three or four tiers. Keith Krause, for example, sees three tiers. He defines the first tier of arms suppliers as the "critical innovators" at the technological frontier of arms production, and he confines this group to the United States and the former Soviet Union. He places most of Western Europe into a second tier of "adapters and modifiers" of advanced military technologies. Finally, Krause puts all remaining arms-producing countries into a third-tier of "copiers" and "reproducers" of existing defense technologies.[2] Andrew Ross accepts Krause's definition of the first tier (i.e., the United States and the USSR), but he places China, along with the major arms producers in the industrialized world (specifically France, Germany, Italy, Japan, Sweden, and the United Kingdom), into his category of second-tier producer-states. Ross then puts most other arms-producing countries (i.e., the developing, newly industrialized, and smaller industrialized nations) into his category of third-tier producers (e.g., Brazil, Israel, India, South

Korea, and Taiwan). Finally, Ross has a fourth tier of countries, ones with only very limited capabilities for arms production (e.g., Mexico and Nigeria).[3]

In this chapter, we define the first tier as comprising those states with the capacity for across-the-board development and manufacture of advanced conventional weaponry. This tier consists of just a handful of countries: the United States and the four largest European arms producers (Britain, France, Germany, and Italy). Increasingly, these four European weapons states have achieved Tier 1 status mainly through the amalgamation of their defense industrial capabilities, via collaborative programs or the creation of pan-European defense enterprises and joint ventures. Russia may or may not fit into this grouping, based mainly on its inheritance of the Soviet military-industrial complex; at the same time, Russia's defense industrial capacities have atrophied considerably over the past 20 years, due to a lack of funding to maintain its defense R&D base. Like some other analysts, we subdivide the tiers. Given the US preponderance of defense industrial capabilities—especially when it comes to defense R&D, which in turn is powered by a huge military R&D budget (approximately $81 billion in FY2009, more than the rest of the world's defense R&D budgets combined)—it seems more fitting to describe the United States as a *Tier 1a* country and the others as *Tier 1b* producer-states. The second tier comprises a rather catholic group of countries. The first grouping within this tier (Tier 2a) consists of those industrialized countries possessing the capabilities for advanced but quantitatively limited (i.e., niche) defense production, such as Australia, Canada, Israel, Norway, Japan, and Sweden. The second subgrouping (Tier 2b) consists of developing or newly industrialized countries containing modest (but in some cases, expanding) military-industrial complexes, such as Argentina, Brazil, Indonesia, Iran, South Africa, South Korea, Taiwan, and Turkey. Finally, there are Tier 2c producers, such as India; these are developing industrial states with large, broad-based defense industries but nevertheless still lacking a sufficiently capable R&D and industrial capacities to develop and produce highly sophisticated conventional arms. At the bottom, in Tier 3 of the hierarchy we are using, are various states that possess very limited and generally low-tech arms-production capabilities, such as the manufacture of small arms or the licensed assembly of foreign-designed systems. Countries in this group include Egypt, Mexico, and Nigeria.[4]

China has traditionally been placed into the category of a Tier 2c arms producer (see Figure 7.1). China possesses one of the oldest, largest, and most diversified military-industrial complexes in the developing world. By the late 1990s,

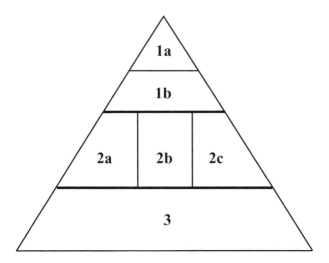

Figure 7.1. A hierarchy of global arms industries. Data from Richard Bitzinger, Michael Raska, Collin Koh Swee Lean, and Kelvin Wong Ka Weng, "Locating China's Place in the Global Defense Industry," SITC Policy Brief No. 28, September 2011 (La Jolla, CA: IGCC); adapted from Keith Krause, *Arms and the State: Patterns of Military Production and Trade* (Cambridge: Cambridge University Press, 1992), 26–33; and Richard A. Bitzinger, "Towards a Brave New Arms Industry?" Adelphi Paper 356 (London: International Institute for Strategic Studies / Oxford University Press, 2003), 6–7.

the Chinese defense industrial base was an agglomeration of approximately 1,000 enterprises, each comprising multiple factories, research units, trading companies, schools and universities, 200-plus major research institutes, and employing some 3,000,000 workers, as well as 300,000-plus engineers and technicians.[5] In particular, China is one of the few countries in the developing world to produce nearly a full range of military equipment, from small arms to armored vehicles to fighter aircraft to warships and submarines (with plans to construct aircraft carriers), in addition to nuclear weapons and intercontinental ballistic missiles. At the same time, the Chinese military-industrial complex has suffered from a number of shortcomings that in turn have inhibited the translation of breakthrough technologies and design into reliable weapons systems. As recently as the late 1990s, China still possessed one of the most technologically backward defense industries in the world; most indigenously developed weapons systems were at least 15 to 20 years behind those of the West—basically comparable to 1970s-era, or at best early 1980s-era, technology—and quality control was consistently poor. China's defense research and development base was regarded to be deficient in several critical areas, including aeronautics, propulsion (such as jet engines), microelectronics, computers, avionics, sensors and seekers, electronic warfare, and advanced materials. Furthermore, the Chinese military-industrial complex had traditionally been weak in the area of systems integration—that is, the ability to design and develop a piece of military equipment that integrates hundreds or even thousands of disparate components and subsystems.[6] Consequently, aside from a few pockets of excellence, such as ballistic missiles, the Chinese military-industrial complex has appeared to demonstrate few capacities for designing and producing relatively advanced conventional weapons systems. Especially when it comes to combat aircraft, surface combatants, and ground equipment, the Chinese generally have confronted considerable difficulties in moving prototypes into production, which has resulted in long development phases, heavy program delays, and low production runs.

This pattern could be changing, however. Progress in reforming the Chinese military-industrial complex over the past decade or so has been palpably evident, in terms of the quality and capabilities of new weapons systems and of the increased tempo of defense development. At issue, therefore, is how well China's defense industry is performing *vis-à-vis* other arms-producing states. Assessment of this comparative performance is particularly critical for two reasons. For one thing, the technological goalposts of weapons development are constantly moving; as certain nations, particularly the United States, advance the state of the art in defense technology, they create new metrics for defining what is meant by "advanced" military systems. So, the first question to ponder is whether or not China is keeping pace—or better yet, closing the gap—with the overall progress in military technological-industrial development? Secondly, a nation's status in the global hierarchy of arms-producing states is not permanent; positioning is relative, depending on the ongoing performance of a nation's defense industrial base. Consequently, countries can rise or fall along this scale. Russia is obviously on the fence as a future Tier 1 producer-state, while one could argue that South Korea could eventually become a Tier 2a state, much like Japan.

Figure 1 captures only a static position of an arms-producing state within the global arms industrial hierarchy. It is useful to conceptualize the trajectory of dynamic change within this hierarchy, as in Figure 7.2. Defense innovation trajectories can be projected by a synthesis of three interrelated dimensions: (1) *paths*—emulation, adaptation, and innovation; (2) *patterns*—speculation, experimentation, and implementation; and (3) *magnitude*—exploration, modernization,

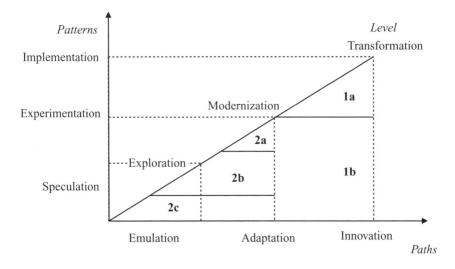

First tier: Innovators	1a	**Critical Technological Innovators** Having a state-of-the-art technological edge in weapons R&D
	1b	United States + Western Europe (UK, France, Germany, Italy)
Second tier: Adapters	2a	**Adapters and Modifiers** Small but advanced defense industry
	2b	Australia, Canada, Czech Republic, Norway, Japan, Sweden, Israel, South Korea, Singapore,
	2c	South Africa, Taiwan, and Turkey
Third tier: Emulators		**Copiers and Reproducers** Low-technology arms producers Egypt, Syria, Mexico, North Korea, Nigeria

Figure 7.2. Conceptualizing defense innovation trajectories and a taxonomy of global defense industries. Data from Richard Bitzinger, Michael Raska, Collin Koh Swee Lean, and Kelvin Wong Ka Weng, "Locating China's Place in the Global Defense Industry," SITC Policy Brief No. 28, September 2011 (La Jolla, CA: IGCC); based on Michael Raska, "RMA Diffusion Paths and Patterns in South Korea's Military Modernization," *Korean Journal of Defense Analysis* 23, no. 3 (2011): 369–385; Andrew L. Ross, "On Military Innovation: Toward an Analytical Framework," SITC Policy Brief no. 1 (2010): 14–17; Theo Farrell and Terry Terriff, eds., *The Sources of Military Change: Culture, Politics, Technology* (Boulder: Lynne Rienner, 2002); Thomas G. Mahnken, "Uncovering Foreign Military Innovation," *Journal of Strategic Studies* 22, no. 4 (1999): 26–54; and Keith Krause, *Arms and the State: Patterns of Military Production and Trade* (Cambridge: Cambridge University Press, 1992).

and transformation.[7] Military emulation paths involve importing new tools and ways of war through imitation of other military organizations. Adaptation is defined as adjustments of existing military means and methods; multiple adaptations over time may lead to innovation. Military innovation involves developing new military technologies, tactics, strategies, and structures.[8] Theo Farrell and Terry Terriff argue that "it is only when these new military means and methods result in new organizational goals, strategies, and structures that innovation, adaptation, and emulation lead to major military change."[9]

Similarly, as also illustrated in Figure 7.2, the character of defense innovation evolves in three distinct but often overlapping phases: speculation, experimentation, and implementation.[10] The speculation phase can be defined as employing novel ways of solving existing operational problems or acknowledging the potential of emerging technologies. As speculation turns into greater awareness, military services establish experimental organizations, battle laboratories, and units tasked with experimenting with new concepts, force structures, weapons technologies, and warfare methods. With the broadening and deepening of experimentation processes, a consensus emerges, and the military leadership and services decide to adopt, adapt, and later refine selected experimental operational concepts, warfare methods, organizational force structures, or new generations of weapons systems and technologies. The implementation phase includes a range of indicators: the establishment of new military formations, doctrinal revision to accommodate new ways of war, resource allocation supporting new concepts, development of formal transformation strategy, establishment of innovative military units, new branches and career paths, and ultimately, field training exercises with new doctrine, organizations, or technologies.[11]

By triangulating defense innovation paths and patterns, it is possible to ascertain the pace, direction, and magnitude of defense industrial innovation in three distinct levels: (1) exploration, (2) modernization, and (3) transformation.[12] Exploration includes both speculation and emulation, with initial attempts to develop new areas of technological expertise; military modernization involves continuous upgrades or improvements of existing military capabilities through the importation or indigenous development of weapons systems and supporting assets;[13] transformation can be characterized in the context of a discontinuous or disrupted defense innovation.

In this framework, one can locate the level and sophistication of a country's defense industrial base and can broadly define the relative level of states' indigenous capabilities for independent defense-related research and development and manufacturing. The global defense industry, then, consists of Tier 1 critical innovators at the technological frontier of arms production, Tier 2 adapters and modifiers of advanced military technologies, and Tier 3 copiers and reproducers of existing defense technologies.[14]

The Shipbuilding Industry

Asia has in recent years witnessed a boom in its shipbuilding industries. China has begun to lead the key regional players in this field, progressively churning out modern ocean-going civilian vessels. Prior to the 1980s, whole platforms built by China were based on existing Soviet designs while on-board components were also reverse-engineered Soviet equipment. This borrowing was observed in most Chinese warship programs. From the late 1960s to the 1980s, China operated the *Type-051 Luda* destroyer, a local copy of the Soviet *Kotlin*, whereas during the same period Japan built successive indigenous classes of destroyers. China's *Type-053 Jianghu*-series frigates were based on the Soviet *Riga* model, and it was not until the early 1990s that plans were laid down for the *Type-053H2G Jiangwei-I*. Similarly, the mainstay of China's littoral combatants, the *Type-021 Huangfen*, is a copy of the Soviet *Osa-I*. Prior to the 1990s, the only indigenously built Chinese diesel-electric submarine was the *Type-035 Ming*, which was a locally improved version of the Soviet *Romeo*, previously supplied to China in large quantity.

In amphibious-landing ships, the *Type-072 Yukan*, operated in the 1980s, was based on the *Shan*, which were actually American WWII-vintage vessels inherited from the Nationalists who fled to Taiwan. China's naval science and technology (S&T) research essentially stagnated at mere reverse-engineering with minimal improvements until the governmental imperative for modernization to keep up with technological trends came down in the late 1980s. Without access to modern Soviet naval technologies at that time, and since relations with the West were improving, China sought and managed to acquire a number of crucial systems from European suppliers, including marine propulsion, integrated combat management systems (CMS),[15] electronic warfare (EW), and radar and sonar systems, to rectify capability shortfalls afflicting China's fleet. These foreign models provided crucial starting points for China's indigenization process in these naval S&T innovations.[16]

PROGRESS IN CHINA'S NAVAL SHIPBUILDING

China, by our measures, overtook Japan in destroyer design during 2000–2010. It all began with the *Type-052A Luhu*, China's first truly modern indigenously

built destroyer, whose onboard system requirements largely exceeded its indigenous S&T capacities, thus necessitating extensive use of foreign technology.
However, China was apparently dissatisfied with the *Luhu*, which was intended
as a test-bed for subsequent designs.[17] The *Luhu* spawned the *Luhai*, whose basic
hull design led to that in the *Luyang* series. The new-construction ("newcon")
Type-052C Luyang-II is interesting, as it incorporates many adapted technologies:
a modern combat management system together with advanced phased aperture
radar (APAR), which resembles the Aegis SPY-1;[18] a modified *Luhai* hull, incorporating stealth characteristics; an integrated EW suite that includes a new "hard-
kill" system (which reportedly doubles as an ASW mortar) an innovation first
observed in Sweden's Elma Alecto system; a true area-defense missile capability
exceeding that aboard Russian-supplied *Sovremenny* destroyers; and finally, new
close-in weapon system (CIWS) resembling the Dutch-developed Goalkeeper.
Compared to contemporary Japanese destroyers, such as the *Atago*, Chinese
newcon DDGs (missile-carrying destroyers), such as the *Luyang-II*, apparently
incorporate more indigenous S&T content by playing catch-up in CMS, EW, radars (especially APAR), and sonar and probably fared better in area-defense
surface-to-air missiles (SAMs) and CIWSs.

With regard to frigates, China has consistently occupied the bottom ranks. Essentially, China's FFG (missile-carrying frigates) program development resembled
the DDG program. Like the *Luhu*, the *Jiangwei* series introduced many foreign-
sourced systems, despite attempts to indigenize some on-board components. However, the *Jiangwei-I* was deemed unsuccessful, too; its HQ-61 SAM may have been
judged to be a failure, since the superseding *Jiangwei-II* reintroduced the HQ-7
(French Crotale look-alike) and was built in larger numbers. Nonetheless, the *Jiangwei* series's overall success spurred the *Jiangkai* series—China's most modern
newcon FFG.[19] Interestingly, the *Jiangkai* appears to incorporate more foreign, in
particular Russian, content, such as radar, sonar, and medium-range SAMs.[20] Its
stealth features are apparently based on the French *La Fayette*. Again, China's S&T
innovations, based on indigenization of foreign models, were observed in CMS,
EW, and anti-ship cruise missiles (ASCMs) in its frigate program.

China's diesel-electric submarine program appears to follow an approach similar to that of its surface warships. After the *Type-035 Ming*, the *Type-039 Song* became China's first-ever attempt to build a modern SSK (diesel-electric submarine) adopting Western influences. Essentially, the *Song* introduced new features,
such as CMS, modern digital sonar, and submerge-launched missiles,[21] and it
benefited from German diesel engines, French sonar, and influences from the

French *Agosta* design.[22] The most significant S&T progress can be seen in the *Type-041 Yuan*. China apparently preferred the stubbier *Kilo* hull design, and it probably gleaned significant insights from the Russian boat that was sold to it in large numbers in the 1990s.[23] The *Yuan* also incorporates air-independent propulsion (AIP), but other than these features, Chinese S&T achievements have been in sonar—which could be indigenous hybrids combining French and Russian features—CMS, EW, and radar, much in the same vein as Japan's approach. In contrast to its surface warship programs, China reportedly made more inroads into submarine propulsion, even if the indigenous AIP is based on foreign models.[24] However, it seems clear that China remains at the preliminary SSK indigenization stage—still behind the Western and Russian builders, though slowly catching up with Japan. Arguably, however, the *Yuan's* apparent success has spurred development of a follow-on improved boat.[25]

Explaining Observed Chinese Naval S&T Trends 1980–2010

One could observe that from 1980 to 2010 China's naval S&T innovation continued to lag behind that of the established Western builders and, through technological leapfrogging, played incremental catch-up with Japan. Its progress might be considered comparable with that of two Asian peer competitors, India and the ROK. Synthesizing the various warship program trends over the period 1980–2010 provides a rough general positioning of China's naval S&T innovation vis-à-vis other countries (see Figure 7.3).[26] The comparison is made by positing China relative to Western Europe (collectively France, Germany, the Netherlands, and the UK), Northern Europe (collectively Finland, Norway, and Sweden), the US, Russia, and the three Asian peer competitors. This positioning of China's naval S&T innovation recognizes the differences amongst disparate warship programs and is thus necessarily subjective in nature.

Political-Military and Economic Imperatives

Post–Cold War strategic imperatives spurred the build-up of China's navy and consequently provided an impetus for indigenous naval S&T development. The overarching need to safeguard national maritime interests, such as protection of vital sea routes China depended upon for its socioeconomic development, as well as geopolitical contention in disputed maritime territorial zones were probably some of the key strategic drivers that sustained political will in the long run to support naval S&T developments. For instance, the *Luhu/Luhai* DDG program was listed as among the few top-priority, core defense industrial projects under

a. 1980s

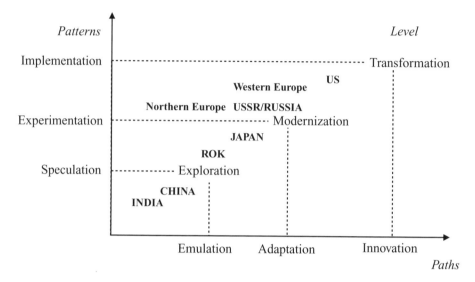

b. 1990–2010

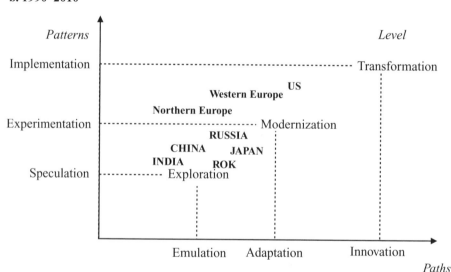

Figure 7.3. China's naval S&T innovation in comparative perspective. Based on Richard Bitzinger, Michael Raska, Collin Koh Swee Lean, and Kelvin Wong Ka Weng, "Locating China's Place in the Global Defense Industry," SITC Policy Brief No. 28, September 2011 (La Jolla, CA: IGCC); Michael Raska, "RMA Diffusion Paths and Patterns in South Korea's Military Modernization," *Korean Journal of Defense Analysis* 23, no. 3 (2011): 369–385.

China's 6th Five-Year Plan in 1999.[27] Also, in trying to attain greater self-sufficiency in its naval S&T, Beijing has apparently devoted huge efforts to promoting R&D through measures such as manpower restructuring and creation of new research initiatives.[28] The Chinese political leadership seems dissatisfied with the level of innovation demonstrated in the country's state-owned strategic industries, including shipbuilding; it has urged deepening of reforms.[29] A commonly mentioned driving force behind China's naval S&T is its recent economic growth, which benefited defense outlays to fund both acquisition of foreign equipment and indigenous naval S&T development. The double-digit defense budget growth is likely to be sustained as long as China's economy continues to bloom, in stark contrast to the economic woes being experienced by established Western naval builders. Under austere budgetary scenarios in the foreseeable future, there will probably be further defense industrial rationalization and multinational collaborations, in order to share cost burdens, judging by a recent report from the Stockholm International Peace Research Institute.[30] This would risk causing Europe's naval S&T development to stagnate. Meanwhile, economic growth may enable Asia's emerging NSBIs, such as China, India, and the ROK, to invest in their naval S&T capabilities.

General Expansion in Chinese Shipbuilding

The growth in China's NSBI is also spurred by the general growth of the national shipbuilding industries. The quality of its commercial ships has improved in recent years, reflecting indigenous efforts combined with adoption of foreign (Japan and ROK) best practices, such as quality control, modular construction, advanced design software, and precision machine-tooling, which found their way to naval construction.[31] Chinese yards building newcon warships are also engaged in commercial shipbuilding, thus allowing transfer of best practices from the latter to the warship production. The improving quality of Chinese NSBI can be exemplified by recent warship sales to Thailand, which was initially displeased with the poor quality of four modified *Jianghu* (*Chao Phraya*) frigates in the 1990s but later appeared satisfied with a pair of *Jianghu* (*Naresuan*) ships constructed after feedback was passed to the Chinese. Lately, Thailand turned to China again for *Pattani* offshore patrol vessels. This might be an isolated case, but it could be assumed that China's NSBI had indeed benefited from commercial shipbuilding practices. Nonetheless, problems with on-board component quality probably constitute stumbling blocks to China's warship export prospects. With regard to certain warships, Chinese NSBI performance is not all that

rosy, if one takes the case of the *Yuzhao* construction cycle as an example; it requires almost four years from construction to delivery, deemed slow by modern
standards and considering that the ROK built and delivered an even larger
amphibious assault ship, the *Makassar*, to Indonesia within three years.[32] The in-
efficiency within Chinese NSBI could be attributed to its lack of warship design-
production integration. It continues to practice the old-style "throw-it-over-the-wall"
approach, whereby warship design is undertaken by a separate entity, China Warship Design Institute, but construction is done by shipyards. The huge drawback
with this arrangement is that the teams from each stage fail to communicate with
the next and later stages in the development process, and the delays in transmitting
specifications from one stage to another will be costly in the long run in terms
of lost time and the lost opportunity to incorporate advanced methods and technologies in the production process.[33] By contrast, modern Western, Japanese,
and ROK NSBIs integrate design and production processes.

Access to Crucial Foreign Naval Components

Prior to the 1989 Western arms embargo, China had secured valuable access
to key foreign technologies to help kick-start indigenous naval S&T. The availability of at least one modern example of each crucial component might have
sufficed as a basis for China's S&T development in each of these areas, serving
the aim of attaining self-sufficiency. Chinese indigenous naval S&T work could
have been based on these "technological seeds," so as to leapfrog technological
barriers that would otherwise have to be overcome by painstaking years of original local R&D. European naval technologies enabled China to institute its newcon warship programs, best manifested in the *Luhu*, *Jiangwei*, *Houjian*, and *Song*
series, which served as test-beds for subsequent designs. However, the Chinese
quest for key warship components could not be considered smooth-going. There
have been reports that Washington exerted pressure upon Ukraine not to transfer to China crucial gas-turbine technologies that are critical for building large
oceangoing warships.[34] Some commentators also pointed out that, due to its
heavy reliance on foreign components, even though Chinese NSBI could assem-
ble a small number of large-tonnage warships, the fast-paced serial construction
of large numbers of units would have to wait until China could indigenously produce all essential components.[35] An example has been the slowing down of the
Luyang program due to difficulty encountered in absorbing Ukraine's DA80/
DN80 gas-turbine technologies.[36]

Access to Whole Foreign Naval Platforms and Know-how

China never had the chance to purchase complete Western naval platforms before imposition of the arms embargo. However, the end of the Cold War opened the Russian arms route, satisfying China's quest for modern examples to help spur its indigenous naval S&T. In the 1990s, two primary naval purchases were made that would provide key recompense for China's S&T weaknesses.[37] Russia's sale of *Sovremenny* destroyers and *Kilo* SSKs—all vastly superior to warships in Chinese service—not only bridged operational gaps but also provided crucial naval S&T insights badly needed by China.[38] For instance, from the *Sovremenny* class, China's naval S&T could have gained insights into CMS, radar, targeting datalink, medium-range SAMs, fire control systems, sonar, and EW suites, some of which were later copied, possibly improved upon, and then transplanted into newcon Chinese surface warships. Given the apparent snags in China's indigenous SSK design, the *Kilo* could have provided insights into hydrodynamic design, digital sonar, and CMS for the *Yuan*, for instance.[39]

It is mainly from Russia, former Soviet Republics, and France that China managed to access foreign naval technical know-how to enhance its indigenous naval S&T.[40] By studying this foreign technology, China could obtain first-hand access to crucial naval technical parameters. For example, China's SPY-1-like Type-346 Dragon Eye APAR aboard the *Luyang-II* was said to have been developed with technical assistance from Ukraine's Kvant Bureau.[41] Otherwise, China might have taken many more years to cross the technological barrier from planar-array—which it is still trying to master—to APAR. Naval stealth technology could also not have been developed successfully in China without access to foreign sources. The French reportedly transferred the stealth know-how of the *La Fayette* frigate to the Chinese after the scandals that rocked France's sale of similar frigates to Taiwan caused significant disquiet in Beijing.[42] Another notable area where Chinese indigenous naval S&T has benefited from access to foreign technical know-how is air-independent propulsion (AIP).[43] Access to such high-end technologies certainly helped propel China's nascent AIP-related R&D, which reportedly began during the 1990s in China's national scientific institutes.[44]

Leveraging Dual-Use COTS Technologies

Development of modern naval components, particularly those with open-architecture such as CMS and data-links, can be enabled by dual-use commercial off-the-shelf technologies.[45] China's naval S&T almost certainly leveraged its blooming domestic IT (information technology) industries for the necessary hard- and software for either evolutionary developments of existing foreign models or purely for original naval S&T innovation. A notable example is combat management system development—China's naval S&T weakness. Beijing reportedly imported France's Thomson-CSF TAVITAC CMS in the 1980s and developed it into an indigenous ZKJ-3C, installed aboard the *Jiangwei*, which also utilized Pentium computer technology and Ethernet. Subsequent ZKJ-series ships might have benefited even more from dual-use technologies, considering that after Tiananmen Square, the Chinese found it difficult to obtain further examples of foreign CMS.

Apparently, the Chinese have enjoyed success in leveraging foreign technology. For instance, the visual display units (VDUs) aboard the *Luyang-II*, instead of the traditional stovepipe displays in earlier-era warships, were reportedly provided by local IT plants, such as Huawei; and those VDUs were said to have exploited dual-use technologies such as Pentium-III ruggedized computers, 100-megabyte Ethernet, and Windows for the local area network architecture aboard the destroyer.[46] China's NSBI has apparently begun producing customized computer systems for possible warship production, thanks to commercial off-the-shelf technologies.[47] Besides in high-tech warship electronics, dual-use technologies are leveraged in other aspects, such as hull designs. Notably, China's connections with the Australian firm INCAT provided catamaran, wave-piercing commercial hull concepts that were later adopted by Chinese NSBI for the *Houbei*.[48]

Defense Technological Espionage

The final driver for China's indigenous naval S&T could be its defense technological espionage overseas, a strategy not unique to Beijing or even its Asian competitors.[49] The clandestine acquisition of vital foreign technical data could allow the shortcutting of R&D bottlenecks. A recent case that gives an inkling of China's naval technical espionage is the alleged theft by a petty officer in the Japan Maritime Self-Defense Force of crucial Aegis data, and complications relating to his Chinese wife.[50] Though China might have obtained Ukrainian APAR technical assistance, it is plausible that the Type-346 warship had been unsatisfactory thus far and Beijing sought more advanced foreign examples, such as Western APAR models, which it has not been able to obtain legally due to the arms embargo.[51] This hypothesis is likely, since the *Luyang-II* program stopped at only two units. Moreover, the complexity of developing an APAR and an Aegis-like integrated combat system could mean that Chinese naval radar scientists and engineers continued to face hurdles in their quest for a destroyer design more advanced than the *Luyang-II*.[52] Another area where China has apparently conducted espionage is underwater warfare, probably to supplement its indigenous anti-submarine warfare (ASW) and submarine capabilities, which constituted problematic capability gaps for a long time.[53]

SECTORAL FINDINGS

Overall, China's naval S&T progress has been remarkable but short of impressive. Decades of indigenous naval S&T development might have placed Chinese NSBI at least on par with its Asian competitors but not at the same level of sophistication as established Western naval S&T leaders. Moreover, China owes its naval S&T successes to a mixture of strategies that overshadows original R&D efforts:[54] acquiring non-Western military technical assistance and, where feasible, procuring whole platforms from which to glean valuable technical insights to facilitate or catalyze indigenous naval S&T efforts. This is not to say that China did not devote efforts to indigenous R&D. On the contrary, it has been doing so for the past four decades. However, such efforts fall short of full-fledged original R&D ventures; they have been merely incremental evolutions from existing foreign components. To bolster these systems' capabilities and promote self-sufficiency, China extensively utilized its domestic commercial shipbuilding and civilian IT industries to facilitate its naval S&T programs. These programs are decidedly slanted towards shipboard electronics such as CMS, radar, sonar, and defensive systems, even though there is an apparent effort to institute a blanket indigenous naval S&T effort on as broad range of systems as possible, with the ultimate objective of attaining self-sufficiency in naval S&T on all fronts. While ASCMs and shipboard artillery remain China's indigenous naval weapon S&T strongpoint, only in recent times have nascent inroads been made into SAMs and torpedoes. However, like marine propulsion, these R&D areas in China are still limited to copying or at best modifying existing foreign models. Only CMS, radar, sonar, and EW systems have attained better indigenous S&T progress, although these benefited from access to Western and Russian naval technologies from the 1980s to 1990s. Current levels of naval S&T allow China to possess, at best, capabilities that are short of unique and extensive compared to established competitors.

The process of naval S&T development in China is comparable to that of Asian competitors such as India[55] and the ROK. Some similarities are: (1) the initial starting point of relying solely on importation of foreign platforms and vital components; (2) focus on selected areas, largely inclined towards shipboard electronics;[56] (3) leveraging of civilian shipbuilding in naval construction; (4) reliance on existing foreign models to catalyze indigenous naval R&D, short of extensive original R&D; and (5) infusion of dual-use technologies wherever possible, primarily in shipboard electronics. Japan was in such a stage in the 1980s while the other three Asian players later played catch-up through the abovementioned strategies. Compared to India, Japan, and the ROK, China has relatively limited options. It has a small pool of ready and willing technological providers, but this pool apparently has been increasingly unable to satisfy China's thirst for more advanced naval capabilities, which its indigenous S&T is as yet incapable of satisfying. The apparent urgency of China's desire to bridge technological gaps with its rivals may have motivated its turn to clandestine measures, such as defense technological espionage.

In sum, China may have achieved remarkable progress in naval S&T development, but this feat would not have been possible without a confluence of the non-technical and technical factors discussed above. It is difficult to predict China's ability to sustain, enhance, and expand this existing capacity, which is dependent upon a continued economic growth that will allow it to persist in capital-intensive R&D, or its ability to cross the barrier from reverse-engineering and improvement of existing foreign models into original R&D. Some technological gaps remain unclosed, for instance marine propulsion for oceangoing warships.

Based on the current trajectory, it seems unlikely that China can catch up with the established naval S&T leaders unless the latters' defense S&T capabilities erode over time under financial constraints. The lifting of the Western arms embargo in the future might serve to catalyze China's naval S&T even further, given its current progress.[57] China has already used its access to crucial foreign naval technologies to spur indigenous S&T development, and it is harnessing a range of methods to enhance this capacity. However, China's naval S&T limitations clearly also remain real and yet to be rectified.

The Aviation Industry

China's commercial and military aviation industries have gradually advanced from reverse-engineering Soviet aircraft to developing and producing indigenous models. These include improved versions of older aircraft and modern fourth-generation fighters. If recent developments are any indication, China's aviation industries are poised to break into the fifth-generation aircraft market with the ongoing development of J-20 and J-31 fighters. This section explores the development of China's aviation industrial base from the 1980s to present. In doing so, it will briefly discuss the creation of the Chinese aviation industry in the 1950s and identify key developments until the period of critical and sweeping industry reforms in the 1990s. Second, it will provide a comparative analysis of the Chinese military aviation industry against major international competitors—France, Russia, United States—as well as smaller or less advanced regional competitors—South Korea, India, and Japan—and attempt to compare and contrast this group. Finally, the section highlights the progress and challenges of the Chinese aviation industry today and in the future.

OVERVIEW OF THE CHINESE AVIATION INDUSTRY

Like many other would-be aviation powers, China's goal since the start of its aviation industry in the 1950s has been self-reliance. However, without an aviation history to begin with, Beijing attempted to lay the foundation for an indigenous aviation industry by acquiring foreign aircraft and subsystems (mainly Soviet products) and reengineering these for knowledge. However, these early efforts were derailed by the isolation imposed by the Cultural Revolution and the subsequent freeze in Sino-Soviet relations. Even in more recent years, China's aerospace sector has remained relatively static, impeded by the unfavorable trinity of political chaos, underfunding, and limited access to new foreign technology. The defense systems they have produced have been unimpressive. The weaknesses of China's aviation production capabilities are evident in the lack of technological sophistication of many of these systems, the relatively protracted research and development and production timelines for most indigenously built products, and China's continued reliance on foreign nations for major aircraft platforms and systems.[58]

Since the early 1990s, China's political and military leadership has coped with the aviation sector's inability to produce world-class products. In 1999, China reorganized its then 440,000 aircraft sector employees into two large corporate conglomerates, placing most military and large aircraft development in the Aviation Industries of China 1 (AVIC 1) and tasking AVIC 2 with the development of trainers and helicopters, aiming to spur greater domestic competition. AVIC, however, turned out to be a monolithic bureaucracy that exercised control over still-existing aircraft and component companies. As a result, redundancy became particularly acute. However, sweeping structural and financial reforms launched by the government changed the landscape of the aviation industry, seemingly for the better. In 2008 and 2009, AVIC 1 and 2 were merged into a single entity, AVIC, with around 420,000 employees and 100 aviation-related companies. The merger of AVIC 1 and AVIC 2 brought significant benefits to the firm. In July 2009, AVIC appeared on Fortune's Global 500 ranking list for the first time, at the 426th spot, and reported a profit of US$568 million from sales revenue of US$21.7 billion.[59] In October 2010, AVIC's chief executive, Lin Zuoming, stated that "accelerated international development" was a priority of the firm, aiming to generate a revenue of CNY 1 trillion (US$149 billion) by 2017, a five-fold increase over the CNY 200 billion earned in 2009.[60]

Structurally, AVIC is aggressively expanding its stake in aviation-related industries. Since 2009, it has brokered partnerships with local governments across China to improve its own capabilities as well as to spur private innovation. It has agreements with cities in central China, the northeastern and southern provinces, and in Beijing to set up R&D and production facilities. For example, it signed a US$1.5 billion deal with the centrally located Chongqing municipal government in December 2010 to jointly develop an aviation industrial base in the province. The deal aims to grow expertise in critical aircraft subsystems such as avionics, and visual and communications technologies.[61] It has also imported high-precision and technologically advanced machine tools, electronics, and other components that can be used in the production of military aircraft. Moreover, a number of financial initiatives launched by the government have allowed defense industrial businesses to access commercial and foreign funds for defense production purposes. Defense firms are now allowed to tap into resources from other companies, internal funds, and foreign investment for product development. Analysts point to the Chengdu FC-1/JF-17 Thunder project, which was subsidized by Pakistani funds.[62] The collaboration was reasonably successful, with both nations procuring a number of platforms for their air forces. Pakistan has recently accepted delivery of Chinese-made Thunders and has set up indigenous production of future platforms, reportedly preparing for an expansion of its Thunder fleet with upgraded avionics.[63]

The government's effort to boost its aviation industry's global competitiveness is set to continue. The 12th Five-Year Plan for national economic development started in 2011 and looks set to extend industrial reforms and boost indigenous capabilities and to market its state-owned defense firms in the international market. Reforms are focused on the adaptation of dual-use technologies for defense purposes and the acceleration of capabilities through indigenous R&D programs. Finally, government-led initiatives will also aim to enhance China's presence in international markets, particularly Western ones, both to supply local industries with greater access to the dual-use technologies they require and to create additional funds that can be channeled towards defense R&D.[64]

Another potential thrust in the government's approach is an improved military-corporate collaboration with its top engineering and research institutions. In May 2010, the China Aerospace Science and Industry Corporation signed an agreement with the Harbin Institute of Technology, renowned for its role in China's manned space program and for aircraft carrier design, to set up five new research laboratories in a bid to hasten R&D. A recent US congressional hearing noted that, while most Chinese aerospace universities and departments are heavily involved in state-funded research for military programs, formal military-corporate relationships may be a new development. Tighter collaboration between the industry and relevant research institutions may boost the competitiveness of both aviation firms and universities.[65] However, China's ability to stimulate aviation production will still be limited by its reliance on foreign sourcing for advanced aircraft engines and avionics, as well as the availability of skilled personnel.[66] For example, the limitations of China's defense industries are reflected in the long production cycles for major defense systems. For example, the Chengdu J-10 multirole aircraft, its most advanced indigenously produced military aircraft, was under development for two decades. The J-10 has just entered series production despite the fact that the program was initiated in the early 1980s, and the design is largely derived from Israel's cancelled Lavi fighter program (which in turn was based on US F-16 technology).[67] Some have noted that AVIC's subsidiaries, like Chengdu and Shenyang, have split into military and civil branches, but these companies remain united by a single leadership, and military and civilian assembly lines remain co-located, to ease the sharing of skills and technology. These reorganizations also will not change existing Chinese policies aimed at "combining the military and civilian" to ensure maximal mutual benefit.[68]

SECTORAL FINDINGS

Developed in near-secrecy for most of the decade following its 1998 test flight, Chengdu Aviation Corporation's J-10 multi-role fighter is set to enter the global market. Following a development history that extends from the 1960s and includes five years of service with the People's Liberation Army Air Force (PLAAF), the J-10 is now being marketed internationally, offering capabilities approaching Lockheed Martin's F-16C Block 60, at half the price. Despite a history of Israeli and Russian design assistance and dependence on the Russian-made Salyut AL-31FN engine for its propulsion, the J-10 is touted by China as an indigenous product.[69] China has brokered a deal to sell 36 J-10s to Pakistan for US$1.4 billion, at about US$40 million per unit. It is not known whether the price includes maintenance support, repair, and training.[70]

Following global trends, China has invested heavily in new materials that enable the manufacture of lighter, stronger airframes and that allow the higher temperatures generated by high-performance engines. A recently released biography of a Chengdu Aircraft Company designer explained how he and his colleagues developed initial composite materials for use in the J-10 and how they managed to hire a California-based laboratory to test their product. Composite material fabrication has also been an increasing part of the airline component production work that Airbus and Boeing have subcontracted to China. In early October 2009, Xian Aircraft International acquired Austria's Fischer Advanced Composite Components, a major supplier of airframe and interior composite-based components. An ability to build large composite material airframes and aircraft skin of sufficient strength would greatly improve China's ability to produce stealth, fifth-generation aircraft designs, as well as modern and efficient civil and military transports.

Russian aviation industry officials who exhibited at the Zhuhai air show maintain that ample opportunity for military-technical cooperation exists between the two nations. PLAAF commander-in-chief General Xu Qiliang and other senior military officials told major Russian exhibitors that they saw "at least five more years of close cooperation" between the defense industries of the two nations.[71] Despite the cozy relationship that was painted by Xu, Russian sources had reservations, referring to charges that China had produced illegal copies of the Sukhoi Su-27 (Shenyang J-11B) and the naval variant of the Sukhoi Su-33 (Shenyang J-15).[72]

Given the developments anticipated in China's civilian aviation industry, it is also poised to grow beyond its current status (see Figure 7.4). China's civilian aircraft fleet will more than triple in size by 2030, spurred by continued economic growth and increasing trade activities. According to US aviation firm Boeing, China will need 5,000 new commercial airplanes. worth at least US$600 billion, over the next 20 years. The firm believes that small and intermediate passenger aircraft, such as the Boeing 787 Dreamliner and 777, will compose a substantial part of these new acquisitions; it projects around 1,040 deliveries. Boeing also forecasts that Chinese air carriers will acquire about 400 cargo aircraft by 2030 to support domestic logistics.[73]

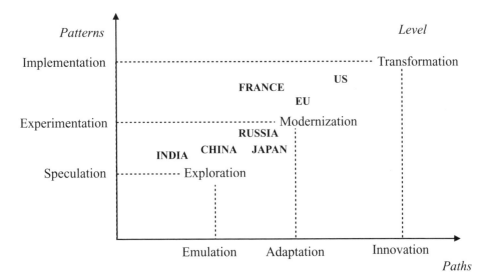

Figure 7.4. China's aviation industry in comparative perspective, as of 2012. Based on Richard Bitzinger, Michael Raska, Collin Koh Swee Lean, and Kelvin Wong Ka Weng, "Locating China's Place in the Global Defense Industry," SITC Policy Brief No. 28, September 2011 (La Jolla, CA: IGCC); and Michael Raska, "RMA Diffusion Paths and Patterns in South Korea's Military Modernization," *Korean Journal of Defense Analysis* 23, no. 3 (2011): 369–385.

The Engine Conundrum

One of the key deficiencies in China's aviation industry is the aero-engine sector, particularly its inability to produce the turbofan jet engines used to power modern military aircraft and transports.[74] As a result, Sino-Russian collaboration could once again feature in a variant of the J-10's AL-31FN engine. Defense intelligence firm HIS Jane's reported a possible joint effort that would incorporate Chinese-developed improvements to modernize the J-10's Russian-made AL-31FN jet engine to equip the new J-10B aircraft.[75] Even as the prospect of continued dependency on Russian engines remains likely for the near future, Chinese efforts into advancing indigenous jet engine technology are increasing. In early 2009, the AVIC Commercial Aircraft Engine Company was set up with the intention of developing a large, high-bypass, turbofan engine by 2016. It is now building a 30 hectare research and development facility in Shanghai, which indicates that there is a potential for this new organization to actually relocate existing large aircraft engine expertise from major engine development centers in

Chengdu and Shenyang or to build a new engineer cadre. Military turbofan research and production remain at Chengdu and Shenyang, which likely have had long-standing programs exploring large, high-bypass, turbofan technology. If the design makes its way into production, the engine is expected to convert civilian airliner designs for military purposes and to power new, large, military aircraft platforms such as transports and, potentially, bombers.[76]

Legislative Tweaks and Continued Investments in Infrastructure

The momentum is showing no signs of abating. In December 2010, AVIC signed an agreement with the Chongqing municipal government to jointly develop an aviation industrial base in the region. The industrial base will be managed by AVIC and will aim to spur technology firms in Chongqing to participate in the R&D and production of aviation-related systems for both military and commercial purposes. The base is expected to specialize in integrated circuit technologies and to focus on developing avionics systems, as well as display and communications equipment.[77]

A notable aspect of the Chinese aviation industry is the close integration of the civilian and military aviation sectors and the potential for commercial advances to fuel developments in the military sector. China's defense industry has benefited from integration with China's rapidly expanding civilian economy and science and technology sector, particularly elements that have access to foreign technology. Progress within individual defense sectors appears to be linked to the relative integration of each—through China's civilian economy—into the global production and research and development chain. The investment is showing nascent signs of payoff. Since 2008, China has not made any major acquisitions from Russian firms.[78]

Prospects for Domestic-Foreign Joint Ventures in Military Aviation

China's military industrial planners have long leveraged the domestic civilian sector to advance military-related industries. Early attempts to integrate processes useful to both the civilian and military industrial sectors—such as computer-aided design, manufacturing technologies, and raw materials—yielded little utility for the Chinese military-industrial complex.[79] Military and civilian aviation technologies do not overlap in all areas. A recent RAND Corporation study noted:

> Many military-specific aerospace technologies, such as low-observable technology, low-bypass afterburning turbofan engines, electronic countermeasures, and signals-intelligence satellites, do not have civilian counterparts. Similarly,

many civilian aerospace technologies do not have military applications. Nonetheless, there are areas of overlap, including computer-aided design and computer-aided manufacturing technologies, precision machining, composite materials, high-bypass turbofan engines, flight-control systems, space launch vehicles, communications satellites, and imagery satellites.[80]

Some analysts assert that technological know-how and material from collaboration with foreign partners on civilian projects may end up providing China with the means potentially to fast forward its military aviation industry. In recent months, industry leader General Electric has announced that it will sign a deal with AVIC to provide advanced avionics equipment for the Chinese C919 civilian airliner project. While General Electric executives maintain that the technology they are sharing remains strictly nonmilitary, critics nevertheless point out the possibility that it will aid Chinese military aviation development through trickle-down effects.[81]

The Space Launch Sector

Since the great space race between the United States and the former Soviet Union during the Cold War, aerospace has traditionally been considered the "international geostrategic high ground."[82] While the United States has been in the first tier of space-related programs and technologies for decades and achieved dominance in both the civil and military uses of space, the accelerating globalization of space marketplace activities over the past two decades has intensified both international competition and international cooperation in the development of space-related capabilities.[83] The 2011 unclassified version of the US National Security Space Strategy Summary points to three key trends it says are shaping the current and emerging space environment: "space is becoming increasingly congested, contested, and competitive."[84] Indeed, according to a study by Euroconsult, more than 50 countries are currently investing in domestic space programs.[85] Some nations invest in space for the domestic and international respect concomitant with technological advances in space; others aim to leverage economic, commercial and military benefits derived from communications services, imagery, and applied sciences. With more nations joining the "Space Club," there is a growing awareness that space is vital to national security, as space assets are increasingly vulnerable to a range of threats that may deny, degrade, deceive, disrupt, or destroy these assets.[86] Military forces recognize the force multiplier effects of space assets like secure communications, reconnaissance, navigation, force tracking, and remote coordination and operation of military assets.[87] Simultaneously, the global diffusion of space-related technologies and knowledge broadens the international competitive pressures to develop innovative space capabilities. The globalization of space today is thus driven by a wide range of factors—economic and political as well as military objectives aimed at enhancing geopolitical leverage, military competitiveness, and technological development.[88]

According to the 2010 Space-Competitiveness Index (SCI), the globalization of space is unfolding more broadly and rapidly than previously assumed.[89] "As countries continue to collaborate in space, competition is growing more intense. Dominant actors are increasingly challenged by a second and third tier of space leaders, and the competitive gaps among all nations are narrowing."[90] In 2009, world government expenditures for *civil* space programs totaled US$36 billion, a 9 percent increase over 2008. Spending for *defense* space programs (classified and nonclassified) is estimated to have climbed to US$32 billion in 2009, a 12 percent increase compared to 2008. In 2010, world government spending on space set a historic record, with civil and defense government spending combined at US$71.5 billion and projected to remain at around US$70 billion until 2015. In this context, 90 percent of world expenditures in the *civilian* space sector are concentrated in six countries/regions—USA, Europe, Russia, China, Japan, and India (see Tables 7.1, 7.2, and 7.3).[91]

One of the most ambitious countries in the increasingly competitive space industry is China. Over the past two decades, China has substantially invested in advancing its civil and military space platforms and capabilities, supported by extensive organizational infrastructure, research and development facilities, and an increasingly more capable defense industrial base. With space investments exceeding US$2 billion, China in 2010 became the second largest spender on space in Asia after Japan (US$3.8 billion), and it is narrowing the gap.[92] In 2010, China conducted as many launches (15) as the United States, second only to Russia (31). While many aspects of China's vast space programs remain classified, Beijing has publicized its technical prowess and space ambitions in areas such as launch vehicles, launch schedules, satellites, human space flight, as well as command and control, anti-satellite technologies, and sensor capabilities.

China, as a rising great power, views the exploration of space not only as the cornerstone of China's national science and technology innovation efforts but also as an important catalyst for achieving its national development goals and its vital political, economic, and security interests.[93] Politically, China's space programs may amplify Beijing's geopolitical influence and freedom of action; militarily, they may enable the PLA to accelerate its ongoing transformation drive;

Table 7.1 Selected Civilian Space Program Expenditures (US$ mil.)

	2007	2009	2010
USA	17,297	20,083	20,316
ESA	3,974	5,073	4,378
EU	311	735	882
France	1,798	2,436	2,277
Germany	1,017	1,245	1,226
Italy	969	940	1,010
UK	438	406	480
Spain	373	324	346
Belgium	213	237	232
Russia	1,280	2,719	2,804
Japan	2,126	2,340	2,230
China	1,300 (e)	1,269 (e)	1,432 (e)
India	926	906	1,257
Canada	338	298	377
Brazil	118	85	198
South Korea	317	208	228
Israel	11 (e)	11 (e)	11 (e)
Australia	7	36	63

Source: Euroconsult (2007, 2009, 2010) "World Prospects for Government Space Markets."

Table 7.2 Worldwide Orbital Launch Activity (2010)

	Commercial Launches	Noncommercial Launches	Total Launches
Russia	13	18	31
USA	4	11	15
China	0	15	15
Europe	6	0	0
India	0	3	3
Japan	0	2	2
Israel	0	1	1
South Korea	0	1	1
TOTAL	23	51	74

Source: Futron (2010) "Space Competitiveness Index 2010—A Comparative Analysis of How Countries Invest in and Benefit from Space Industry."

Table 7.3   Orbital Launch and Spacecraft Manufacturing Trends
(2000–2009)

	Successful Orbital Launches	Spacecraft Manufactured
Russia	251 (40%)	222 (22%)
USA	213 (34%)	415 (40%)
Europe	66 (11%)	188 (18%)
China	61 (10%)	69 (7%)
Japan	20 (3%)	51 (5%)
India	14 (2%)	24 (2%)
Israel	2 (>0%)	9 (1%)
Iran	1 (>0%)	
South Korea	1 (>0%)	5 (1%)
Rest of the world		44 (4%)
TOTAL	629	1,027

Source: Futron (2010) "Space Competitiveness Index 2010—A Comparative Analysis of How Countries Invest in and Benefit from Space Industry."

economically, they propel economic and technological advancement and increase revenues for China's space industrial base. In other words, China's aerospace capabilities are seen as vital to China's rise, power projection, and global influence.[94]

Following the Soviet example, China has not differentiated among its military, civilian, and commercial use of space. The State Council and the Commission for Science, Technology, and Industry for National Defense (COSTIND) oversee the China National Space Administration (CNSA), which has an annual budget estimated at around US$1.7 billion (2010) and is responsible for China's civil space policy as well as space-related intergovernmental agreements. The State Council and COSTIND also oversee the China Aerospace Science and Technology Corporation and the China Aerospace Science and Industry Corporation, both of which are responsible for heavy-lift launch vehicles, missile and spacecraft research, and satellite development and manufacturing.[95] Meanwhile, the PLA's General Armament Department (GAD) of the Central Military Commission is responsible for development and acquisition necessary to meet the operational requirements set by the General Staff Department (GSD). The GAD also manages the launch, tracking, and control of all space vehicles and civilian and military satellites, and it coordinates technical aspects of China's unmanned and manned space activities, including China's manned spaceflight Project 921, which includes military-related missions.[96]

With the launch of the Shenzhou-5 ("Divine Vessel") carried by the Long March-2F rocket on October 15, 2003, China became the third nation (after the US and Russia) to complete a successful manned space mission. Since then, China has carried out four additional manned missions as part of the manned spaceflight Project 921, including Shenzhou 6 (SZ-6) in October 12–17, 2005, with two "taikonauts" on board, and Shenzhou 7 (SZ-7) spaceflight September 25–28, 2008. The SZ-7 demonstrated another technological milestone for the Chinese manned space program when its two crewmembers performed the country's first extra-vehicular activity (EVA), one wearing a Chinese-made Feitian EVA suit. By the end of the SZ-7 mission, China had demonstrated all seven elements of Phase One of Project 921: launch site system, astronaut system, measurement and control system, manned delivery rocket system, manned spacecraft system, landing system, and spacecraft application system. In 2013, China is on track to complete Phases Two and Three of the Project 921, with orbital rendezvous docking missions (Shenzhou 8, 9, and 10), completion of a 60-ton orbital space station by 2020, and possibly fielding of a reusable launch vehicle by 2025.[97]

Parallel to the Project 921, China's space science program has centered on the robotic lunar exploration program, Chang'e, formally announced in 2003.[98] On October 24, 2007, China successfully implemented the first phase of the program—launching the Long March 3A rocket carrying the Chang'e 1 lunar-orbiting spacecraft. The Chang'e 1, China's first deep-space mission, lasted for 16 months, until March 2009, and succeeded in its primary task, to map the entire surface of the Moon in 3D high-resolution imagery. The data would be used to identify potential landing spots for a future soft-lander.[99] On October 1, 2010, China launched a follow-on probe, the Chang'e 2, carried by a more powerful Long March 3C rocket, which placed it on a direct transfer orbit to the Moon. The Chang'e 2 featured higher-resolution cameras, different scientific instruments, improved tracking, and lunar orbiting capability at only 100 km altitude. The second and third phases of the Chang'e program envision deploying lunar rovers for limited surface exploration at Sinus Iridium (Bay of Rainbows) landing site, possibly in 2013 (Chang'e 3), followed by an automated lunar-sample return flight (Chang'e 4) around 2017 and a possible manned lunar landing sometime in 2025–2030.[100]

The accelerating progress in China's aerospace sector can be viewed in the broader context of reforms in China's defense industry. Since the late 1990s, Beijing has gradually introduced elements of competition, autonomy, entrepreneurship, and decentralization into China's defense industrial base, with the aim of overcoming the entrenched monopoly of China's traditional defense industrial conglomerates and transforming them into global prime contracting defense firms by the end of next decade.[101] For example, the State Council divided the China Aerospace Corporation (CAC) in 1999 into two nominally independent companies: China Aerospace Science and Technology Corporation (CASC), responsible mainly for research, design, manufacture, and launch of space systems and strategic and tactical missiles,[102] and the China Aerospace Machinery and Electronics Corporation (CAMEC), specializing primarily in the development and production of guided missile systems and precision-guided munitions. In 2001, CAMEC became the China Aerospace Science and Industry Corporation (CASIC).[103] More importantly, the CASC and CASIC, together with their vast network of subsidiaries and manufacturing suppliers, are increasingly competing for contracts in the global commercial space launch vehicle (SLV) market and are leveraging their commercial technological and R&D advances and business practices in their production lines.[104] The CASC, for example, has been active in developing satellites, launcher, and propellant technologies and provides commercial launch services through its China Great Wall Industry Corporation (CGWIC).

Notwithstanding the existing export controls and restrictions on the transfer of military technologies, China has been able to tap into a range of dual-use technologies through select partnerships with Western primes. The competitive nature of the global SLV market, worth over $250 billion a year, provides greater incentives for both the CASC and the CASIC not only to increase their revenues but, more importantly, to enhance their capabilities through global commercial technology transfers and services. At the same time, Western firms increasingly seek to bypass the existing export-controls and restrictions. For example, satellite manufacturers such as Thales Alenia Space and Astrium Satellites are producing more payloads without US-made components for operators who can then include the CGWIC in their portfolio of launch services providers.[105] In addition, the "Big Three" global satellite operators, Intelsat, SES, and Eutelsat, have encouraged the entry of CGWIC into the market as an alternative to existing launch services providers, to constrain rising prices through increased competition and to expand manifest launch slot opportunities.[106] As of mid-2011, China operated a total of 70 satellites in orbit, ranking third after the United States and Russia, with 440 and 100 respectively.[107]

In the military aerospace area, China has been making progress by selectively enhancing its strategic and tactical missile capabilities. While many analysts have traditionally downplayed the modernization of Chinese long-range missile and nuclear forces as relatively conservative, incremental, and slow,[108] recent advances in technology, training, and doctrinal evolution, coupled with ongoing defense in-dustrial reforms, intensive state investment, and growing sophistication of China's space capabilities in select areas, has substantially revised baseline assumptions of China's defense aerospace industry capabilities.[109] Notwithstanding the continu-ing veil of secrecy, Chinese development of strategic and tactical ballistic missiles is well into its third generation of comprehensive, targeted, and stealth moderniza-tion. The latest generation of China's strategic and theater missile technologies can be characterized as advanced and can be benchmarked with the fourth generation of missile systems developed by the United States and Russia. Based on available reports, China is diversifying its inventory of missiles in terms of strike capabilities and mobility and is formulating new asymmetric warfare concepts and doctrine to ensure the effective retaliatory purpose of China's missile forces.[110] As Robert Hewson noted, "China has the ability to produce all the key subsystems demanded by modern missiles, including small jet power-plants, various seekers and guidance systems, and long-range data-links. The result is an ever expanding family of weap-ons designed for land, sea, and air launch that, on paper at least, are capable of dispatching every conceivable type of target."[111]

Specifically, China is developing, testing, and deploying not only a new generation of solid-propellant, road-mobile intercontinental ballistic missiles (ICBMs), such as the DF-31 and DF-31A, equipped with nuclear payloads, but also designing and developing new classes of conventionally armed short-range ballistic missiles (SRBMs) and medium-range ballistic missiles (MRBMs), such as DF-21 variants, that are mobile, use solid-propellant rocket engines with short system reaction time, and have longer range, more accurate guidance, and the ability to exploit vulnerabilities in ballistic missile defense systems. As part of its missile and nuclear force modernization towards greater range, survivability, accuracy, and responsiveness against a wider range of targets, China is also focusing on development and deployment of its sea-launched ballistic missiles (SLBMs), such as the JL-2, testing the DF21-D as an anti-ship ballistic missile (ASBM) for maritime strikes, and further developing its anti-satellite weapon capabilities (ASAT).[112] In this context, China is developing new solid-fuel motors, diversifying its range of warheads and increasing their accuracy, and enhancing ballistic-missile defense countermeasures, such as penetration aids (decoys, chaff, jamming, thermal shielding, and possibly MaRVs as well as MIRVs).[113]

Overall, the trajectory of China's ballistic missile production shows a gradual, phased, albeit progressive qualitative transition from a copier and reproducer of

Soviet ballistic missile technologies (first generation) from the late 1950s to early 1980s, to adapter and modifier of smaller, mobile, solid-propellant ballistic missile systems and their follow-on systems (second generation) throughout the mid and late 1980s, to independent producer and technological innovator of selected missile systems and related aerospace technologies in the 21st century.

Similar arguments can be made in the broader context of China's aerospace industry, which shows a gradual advancement in the development and production of space launch vehicles (SLVs) over the past three decades. In particular, China's SLV path reflects a gradual shift from emulation and experimentation toward adaptation and implementation of its scientific, commercial, and military applications. In a comparative perspective, while China's expanding space architecture, civil-military space programs, and rocket sector are far from achieving dominance, China is poised to challenge traditional space leaders—the US, Russia, and the EU, as seen in Figure 7.5.

In this context, China's SLVs—the Long March (LM) or the Chang Zheng (CZ) series of rockets have evolved from the Dong Feng (DF) ballistic missiles programs. The first DF generation can be linked to the broader strategic blue-

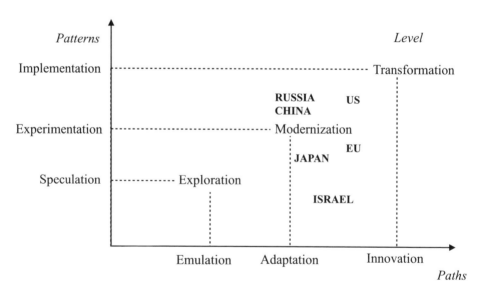

Figure 7.5. China's aerospace industry in comparative perspective, as of 2012. Based on Richard Bitzinger, Michael Raska, Collin Koh Swee Lean, and Kelvin Wong Ka Weng, "Locating China's Place in the Global Defense Industry," SITC Policy Brief No. 28, September 2011 (La Jolla, CA: IGCC).

print announced in 1965 by the First Academy (Carrier Rocket Research Academy) to build "four types of ballistic missiles in eight years" (*banian sidan*): (1) DF-2A MRBM, (2) DF-3 IRBM, (3) DF-4 IRBM, and (4) DF-5 ICBM.[114] One of these missiles, the DF-4 IRBM, provided the baseline design and rocket propulsion for the first Long March launch vehicle (LM-1 or CZ-1), first launched on April 24, 1970, carrying the first Chinese satellite into a low Earth orbit.[115] Since then, China has developed a number of versions in the LM series; three main variants are currently in use: (1) LM-2F, developed to launch the Shenzhou manned space missions; (2) LM-2C and LM-4B, designed to launch satellites into low Earth orbit (LEO)and Sun-synchronous orbit (SSO); and (3) LM-3A, LM-3B, LM-3BE, and LM-3C, developed to launch heavy payloads into geostationary transfer orbit (GTO).

The LM-3A, LM-3B, LM-3BE, and LM-3C currently represent the main launch vehicles for China's GTO/GEO space missions. Their design and system configuration have evolved from the LM-3 platform, a three-stage SLV, of which the first and second stages were based on the LM-2C. The third stage of the LM-3, however, used cryogenic propulsion with LOX/LH2 as propellants, giving the third stage engine a restart capability. The first launch of the baseline LM-3 occurred on January 29, 1984, which made China the third user of cryogenic propulsion after the US and European Space Agency. While the LM-3 was phased out in 2000 after 13 flights, its design and technologies have shaped the trajectory of the follow-on variants in the LM-3 series (see Table 7.4).

In 2011, China is believed to have embarked on a full-scale technology development program on new heavy-lift Long March rockets, the LM-5 series, designed to overcome the limitation of existing SLVs in terms of cost and reliability. The new rocket family will have a modular design—a common core stage and various strap-on boosters and upper stages, using nontoxic fuels (LOX/kerosene)—have larger and diverse combinations of boosters, and feature a 5-meter fairing covering payloads from 1.5 metric tons LEO to 14 metric tons GEO. The LM-5 is expected to be launched in 2014 from the newly constructed Wenchang Space Center on the Hainan Island.[116]

Conclusions

Any sector-by-sector, comparative analysis of the global arms industry is bound to be a massive undertaking. The amount of information that has to be delivered in order to inform these assessments is inevitably close to being a "data dump." At the same time, it is beyond the scope of even a chapter as long as this

Table 7.4 Selected Variants in the Long March Series of Space Launch Vehicles

	LM-2C	LM-4B/LM-4C	LM-2F	LM-3A	LM-3B	LM-3BE	LM-3C
Height (m)	43.0	48.0	58.3/52.0	52.5	54.8	56.3	54.8
Diameter (m)	3.35	2.90/3.35/3.80	3.80/4.20	3.35	4.00	4.00/4.20	4.00
Launch mass (t)	245	250	498	241	426	456	345
Lift-off thrust (kN)	2,962	2,962	5,923	2,962	5,923	5,923	4,443
Stage-1 propellant	N_2O_4/UDMH						
Stage-2 propellant	N_2O_4/UDMH						
Stage-3 propellant	N/A	N_2O_4/UDMH	N/A	LOX/LH_2			
Main mission	LEO/SSO	SSO	LEO	GTO			
Launch capability (kg)	3,850/900	2,230/2,950	8,080/8,600	2,600	5,100	5,500	3,800
Launch Site	JSLC/TSLC/XSLC	JSLC/TSLC	JSLC	XSLC	XSLC	XSLC	XSLC
First orbital launch	Nov. 26, 1975	Oct. 5, 1999	Nov. 20, 1999	Feb. 8, 1994	Feb. 14, 1996	May 14, 2007	Apr. 25, 2008
Launch record	32:32 S	13:13 S	7:7 S	19:19 S	12:10 S, 1F, 1 PF	3:3 S	6:6 S

Sources: "Long March (Chang Zheng)," Jane's Space Systems and Industry (October 8, 2010); China Great Wall Industry Corporation (2010).

Taiyuan (LM-4B/LM-4C Site), Jiuquan (LM-2F Site), Xichang (LM-3A, LM-3B, LM-3BE, LM-3C Site)

to address every defense industrial sector; missing from this chapter are critical analyses of the ground ordnance, defense electronics, tactical missile, and non-fighter aircraft industries. This chapter can only provide some insight into the progress that China's defense industry has made over the past 20 years or so and where it appears to stand and be moving within the global hierarchy of arms-producing nations, as well as the continuing challenges it faces.

Overall, Chinese S&T progress has been remarkable to date, especially in the areas of naval shipbuilding, fighter aircraft, and space launch vehicles. Consider China's naval shipbuilding industry: successive warship designs are becoming increasingly better and more comprehensively equipped, and the decades of indigenous naval S&T development in China may have placed it at least on par with its Asian peer competitors. However, it has not yet brought China to the level of sophistication of the established Western naval S&T leaders or even Russia. As far as the means of achieving the recent successes are concerned, China's naval S&T relies heavily on a mixture of leveraging strategies which overshadows comparatively meager efforts in original R&D, particularly the acquisition of non-Western military-technical assistance and, where it is possible to do so, the procurement of whole naval platforms from which China can glean valuable technical insights to facilitate or catalyze indigenous naval S&T efforts.[117] These measures were consistently observed prior to post-Tiananmen Square Western arms embargo in 1989, when China absorbed a considerable influx of Western naval technologies at an unprecedented scale. When this became no longer possible, it resorted to piecemeal efforts to acquire such technologies, though the key strategy apparent in the 1990s was its heavy reliance on Russia for key naval components, which came embedded in whole platforms that also served the purpose of capability gap fillers in the PLA Navy.

This is not to say that China did not plough efforts into indigenous naval technological R&D. It did, and has been doing so for the past few decades. Such efforts remain short of a full-fledged S&T venture into original R&D; they are restricted to incremental improvements of and evolutions from existing foreign components. To bolster the capabilities of these systems and self-sufficiency in the future and to develop more capable systems and platforms, the Chinese made extensive use of its domestic commercial shipbuilding, bolstering warship construction techniques, and of its IT industries, providing for dual-use technology infusion into the naval S&T programs. Such indigenous programs are decidedly more tilted towards shipboard electronics. There is an apparent attempt by China to institute a blanket indigenous naval S&T effort on as broad a range of systems as possible, probably with the ultimate objective of attaining self-sufficiency in naval S&T on all fronts—sensors, weaponry, propulsion, and the other key warship components. As far as weaponry is concerned, anti-ship missile armaments, and to a lesser extent shipboard artillery, remain the strong-point of Chinese naval weapon S&T innovations. However, like marine propulsion, many areas of naval R&D are limited to copying or modifying foreign models. Only combat management systems, radar, sonar, and electronic warfare systems attained better progress as far as Chinese naval S&T development is concerned, but, again, these benefited mostly from the 1980s acquisition of Western and, later, Russian naval technologies. Without adequate attention to original naval R&D, China's naval weapons S&T development will continue to revolve around mere reverse-engineering and local modifications of SAM and torpedo armaments. Based on the current trajectory, it seems unlikely that China can catch up to the established naval technological leaders in terms of original naval R&D unless economic growth continues to fuel persistent defense fiscal appropriations for indigenous naval S&T development and unless the stagnation in European defense S&T continues unabated.

Similar observations can be made about the fighter aircraft and space launch vehicle sectors. Undeniable progress has been observed in these areas of the Chinese defense industry, especially with regard to other Tier 2 countries. Given the vast amounts of resources Beijing has plowed into its defense technology base, this is not surprising. China has increased its defense budget at least fivefold (in real, that is after-inflation, spending) over the past 15 years, and it is now the second largest defense spender in the world. Its military expenditures in 2011 totaled nearly $92 billion, outstripping the United Kingdom, France, Russia, and Japan. More important, it probably has the world's second highest defense R&D budget; although the precise figure is classified, it is not inconceivable that Chinese expenditures on military R&D approach $6 billion. In other words, China simply throws more money at its defense development, and this has begun to reap tangible benefits over the past decade. If one looks at such products as the J-20 fighter aircraft or the DF-21D anti-ship ballistic missile, it would appear that China's military-industrial complex has certainly exceeded the capacities of its fellow Tier 2c country India and it is approaching the niche capabilities of Tier 2a arms-producing states. The big question is, is China approaching the capacities and capabilities of a Tier 1b state? In other words, it is becoming a "critical innovator," as Krause puts it?

In many senses, the answer is still no. The global centers of innovation *overall* are still located in the United States, Western Europe, and Japan. These countries still dominate when it comes to the cutting-edge of modern technology: microelectronics, biotechnology, aerospace, software, etc. However, the center of *defense-specific* innovation is increasingly shrinking, and to just one country, the United States. This point is particularly apropos of Western Europe, where defense innovation is languishing. Again, this is largely the result of funding: European military spending has been more or less stagnant since the end of the Cold War, more than 20 years ago. Total Western European defense R&D spending is only around $12 billion, less than one-sixth that of the United States. And while this figure is about twice China's military R&D budget, European defense research and development is uneven among the constituent countries (France's defense R&D expenditures in 2009 were $5.4 billion, the largest in Europe, and Britain's were $3.9 billion; together, these two countries accounted for nearly four-fifths of all European military R&D spending) and is generally allocated to duplicative, competing programs; consequently, the "buying power" of European military R&D spending is diluted, inhibiting European technology development and defense innovation.

Consequently, should the overall process of defense innovation slow, China might have an opportunity to catch up. Certainly, in its pursuit of a fifth-generation fighter aircraft (e.g., the J-20) it is poised to overtake Europe. China may not supplant Europe as a defense innovator, but it appears to be gaining capacities to at least match Europe in certain niche areas. At the same time, critical weaknesses remain. China appears still to have only limited indigenous technological capabilities, relative to the West, in areas such as propulsion and defense electronics. It remains more of a "fast follower" than an innovator in many areas of defense science and technology (although this may be irrelevant if China is only looking to gain asymmetrical niche advantages). Finally, China's continued use of a state-owned enterprise system for arms manufacturing means relying upon a means of production that has traditionally proved suboptimal, to say the least, when it comes to injecting innovation into the process of weapons development.

Two axioms that have long been used with regard to Chinese military modernization remain true: "China has come a long way," and "China has a long way to go." Although they approach the point of being clichés, they are nonetheless useful, and depending on the *order* in which they are said, they can speak volumes on how we interpret Chinese progress in raising the level of its defense industry relative to global competitors. Both are true, but one must inevitably be more true than the other.

NOTES

1. See Stephanie G. Neuman, "Industrial Stratification and Third World Military Industries," *International Organization* (Winter 1984): 191–197.

2. Keith Krause, *Arms and the State: Patterns of Military Production and Trade* (Cambridge: Cambridge University Press, 1992), 26–33.

3. Andrew L. Ross, "Full Circle: Conventional Proliferation, the International Arms Trade and Third World Arms Exports," in Kwang-il Baek, Ronald. D. McLaurin, and Chung-in Moon, eds., *The Dilemma of Third World Defense Industries* (Boulder, CO: Westview Press, 1989), 1–31.

4. Richard A. Bitzinger, *Towards a Brave New Arms Industry?* Adelphi Paper #356 (London: International Institute for Strategic Studies/Oxford University Press, 2003), 6–7.

5. John Frankenstein, "China's Defense Industries: A New Course?" in James C. Mulvenon and Richard H. Yang, eds., *The People's Liberation Army in the Information Age* (Santa Monica, CA: RAND, 1999), 191–192.

6. Evan S. Medeiros, Roger Cliff, Keith Crane, and James C. Mulvenon, *A New Direction for China's Defense Industry* (Santa Monica, CA: RAND, 2005), 4–18.

7. Andrew L. Ross, "On Military Innovation: Toward an Analytical Framework," SITC Policy Brief no. 1 (2010): 14–17; Theo Farrell and Terry Terriff, eds., *The Sources of Military Change: Culture, Politics, Technology* (London: Lynne Rienner, 2002); Thomas G. Mahnken, "Uncovering Foreign Military Innovation," *Journal of Strategic Studies* 22, no. 4 (1999): 26–54; Michael Raska, "RMA Diffusion Paths and Patterns in South Korea's Military Modernization," *Korean Journal of Defense Analyses* (23) no. 3 (2011): 369–385.

8. Theo Farrell and Terry Terriff, eds., *The Sources of Military Change: Culture, Politics, Technology*, (London: Lynne Rienner, 2002).

9. Ibid.

10. Mahnken, "Uncovering Foreign Military Innovation," 26–54.

11. Ibid.

12. Ross, "On Military Innovation," 14–17.

13. Ashley J. Tellis, Michael Wills, eds., *Strategic Asia 2005–06: Military Modernization in an Era of Uncertainty* (Seattle: National Bureau of Asian Research, 2005), 15.

14. Krause, *Arms and the State*.

15. Naval CMS (combat management systems) are command and control systems located on warships that assist the command team in execution of its mission. Their main capabilities encompass situational awareness around the ship (or a naval force) using sensors, recognition of threats against the ship or force, and response to those threats using actuators such as missile and gun systems. Other capabilities of a naval CMS include those frequently called command support capabilities and which in general are concerned with the preparation of the ship's mission. They also include the preparation and supervision of diverse plans as well as reception and interpretation of communica-

tion from external parties (other vessels or shore-based parties). See Jacek Skowronek and J. H. van't Hag, Business Unit Combat Systems, Thales Naval Nederland, "Principles of Future Architecture for Naval Combat Management Systems," paper presented at the *RTO IST Symposium on Technology for Evolutionary Software Development*, held in Bonn, Germany, September 23–24, 2002, published in RTO-MP-102: 11–12.

16. Chinese new-construction, missile-carrying destroyers are a mix of local designed and manufactured systems, foreign imports with production rights, illegally copied import equipment, and illegal examples with no local production capability at all. Ronald O'Rourke, *China's Naval Modernization: Implications for U.S. Navy Capabilities— Background and Issues for Congress* (CRS Report for Congress, November 18, 2005), 21.

17. Bernard D. Cole, "Right-sizing the Navy: How Much Naval Force Will Beijing Deploy?" in Roy Kamphausen and Andrew Scobell, eds., *Right Sizing the People's Liberation Army: Exploring the Contours of China's Military* (Strategic Studies Institute, September 2007), 528. The Chinese apparently also experienced teething problems with integrating so diverse a set of systems aboard the Luhu. See Richard D. Fisher, Jr., *China's Military Modernization: Building for Regional and Global Reach* (Praeger Security International, 2009), online e-book version.

18. *China's Military Modernization and U.S. Export Controls, Hearing before the U.S.-China Economic and Security Review Commission*, 109th Congress, 2nd sess. (March 16–17, 2006), 52.

19. The hull form of the *Jiangkai* is apparently in line with the most modern of frigate hull designs, with a V-shaped cross-section and a relatively small length-to-width ratio. This makes its wave resistance better and renders it incredibly suitable for accompanying distant sea fleets heading out for actions and for better sea-keeping than the *Jiangwei*; not to forget also its stealth features, which resemble those aboard the French *La Fayette*. "WWP Article Views Capabilities of PLA Navy's Type 054A Guided-Missile Frigate," article by Li Guoqiang, member of the Chinese People's Political Consultative Conference and director of the Hong Kong Culture Association, *Wen Wei Po Online*, January 2, 2010.

20. "China's Navy: Drive for Modernisation," *Strategic Comments* 14, no. 1 (January 2008): 1; and Yihong Chang, "China Launches New 'Russianised' Frigate," *Jane's Navy International*, November 1, 2006.

21. Apparently, the Chinese encountered problems regarding integration of diverse foreign systems with the initial prototypes of the *Song* class of frigates (a problem which also afflicted the *Luhu* and *Jiangwei* classes) but later rectified them, so much so that they were confident enough to mass produce the improved Type-039A variant. See Cole, "Right-sizing the Navy," 534–35; Fisher, *China's Military Modernization*; and Massimo Annati, "China's PLA Navy: The (R)evolution," *Naval Forces* 25, no. 6 (January 2004): 66–67.

22. Unlike the earlier Soviet-type SSKs, the *Song* class has a hydrodynamically sleek, teardrop hull and is much quieter because of its asymmetrical seven-blade skew propeller, anechoic rubber dampening tiles on the hull, and shock absorbency for the engine to reduce its acoustic signature, features that would become the standard for subsequent newcon Chinese SSK designs. O'Rourke, *China's Naval Modernization*, 130. See also "Top Ten Chinese Military Modernization Developments," *International Assessment and Strategy Center*, March 23, 2005.

23. It might also be possible that the *Yuan* design received Russian technical inputs from the *Amur-1650* SSK. "Top Ten Chinese Military Modernization Developments."

24. Chinese R&D into AIP technologies apparently dated back to the 1970s, and it had apparently conducted advanced research in the areas of fuel cells, closed-cycle diesel engines similar to the French MESMA, and Swedish-style Stirling engines. China was also known to have tested a Stirling AIP aboard a submarine and has undertaken long-standing Stirling R&D at the 711 Institute of the China Shipbuilding Group, which has built a 100-kW output Stirling AIP. The Dalian Institute of Chemical Physics, part of the Chinese Academy of Sciences, has apparently developed 100-kw and 1000-kw fuel-cell engines, and academic literature indicates significant Chinese R&D into closed-diesel engines that use argon gas to absorb exhaust, a technology used by the French-designed MESMA AIP system. Fisher, *China's Military Modernization.*

25. The improved *Yuan* class reportedly incorporates the Russian *Amur-1650*'s stouter hull with a reduced aft taper, an elongated sail, and hull-mounted retractable hydroplanes similar to the Project 636M *Kilo*, though unlike these Russian designs, the new Chinese SSK incorporates a hydrodynamic sail with elements such as an intricately faired leading edge with concave and convex curves. Moreover, a model released by China Shipbuilding Corporation showed that this new-generation SSK currently under development is structurally very close to the German *Type-212A* and uses an X-rudder configuration, which brings it on par with the Japanese *Souryu* class. See "Indian Monthly Reports on Chinese Navy's Force Modernization, Fleet Expansion," report by Prasun K. Sengupta: "Sustained Build-Up," *Force Online*, December 6, 2010; and "Kanwa: Third 'Yuan' Class Diesel Submarine Launched," *Kanwa Asian Defense Review*, November 20, 2008.

26. The three-dimensional model draws on the following works: Ross, "On Military Innovation"; Farrell and Terriff, *Sources of Military Change*; Mahnken, "Uncovering Foreign Military Innovation"; and Raska, "RMA Diffusion Paths."

27. "China's Cruise Missile Development Reported," *BBC Monitoring Service: Asia-Pacific*, August 17, 1999.

28. See "PLA Navy Armament Academy Builds Equipment Research 'National Team,'" by staff reporter Si Yanwen, *Jiefangjun Bao Online*, September 15, 2009.

29. "Vice Premier Asks SOEs to Promote Reform, Innovation," *Industry Updates* (China Daily Information Company), September 29, 2009; and Wang Ying, "Innovation Urged in Shipping Industry," *China Daily*, September 9, 2010.

30. "Global Weapons Spending Slows as Europe Slashes Military Budgets," *Deutsche Welle*, April 12, 2011.

31. Fisher, *China's Military Modernization.* Modular construction, according to O'Rourke, is increasingly widespread in Chinese NSBI. See O'Rourke, *China's Naval Modernization*, 133–34. See also, Keith Crane, Roger Cliff, Evan Medeiros, James Mulvenon, and William Overholt, "China's Defense Industry," in *Modernizing China's Military: Opportunities and Constraints*, RAND Report prepared for the US Air Force (Santa Monica: RAND Corp., 2005), 180.

32. Of the *Yuzhao* LPD's building cycle of 45 months, 3 months are for fundamental project design, 6 months for technological assessment, 8 months for engineering design, 7 months for building preparation, 12 months for actual construction, another 5 months

for equipment installation, 2 months for sea tests, and finally, 1 month for delivery. See Andrei Chang, "Kanwa: The Role of PLA's LPD and Heavy-Duty Hovercraft in Landing Operations at the Taiwan Strait," *Kanwa Asian Defense Review*, August 12, 2008. By contrast, the *Makassar* LPD was ordered by Indonesia from ROK in 2000 and the first ship was delivered in 2003.

33. Thomas J. Eccles and Henry S. Marcus, "Integrating Design and Production: A Case Study of the Naval Submarine Program," *International Journal of Production Economics* 28 (1992): 108.

34. Chang, "Kanwa."

35. "Problems in PLA Navy's Large Battleship Construction," *Kanwa Defense Review*, September 12, 2005.

36. Ibid.

37. See, for instance, Charles Hutzler, "Beijing Strategy Needs Foreign Arms—Deal with Russia Highlights Shortcomings of Chinese Weapons Makers," *Asian Wall Street Journal*, June 28, 2002.

38. This move might have indicated the persistent Chinese limitations in their indigenous capabilities for integrating the most complex sets of warship systems. See O'Rourke, *China's Naval Modernization*, 41.

39. It was speculated that the *Yuan* class could be a Chinese attempt to reverse-engineer the *Kilo* class. Cole, "Right-sizing the Navy," 535.

40. Even Israel is believed to have assisted China, albeit covertly, in its defense S&T. In 2002 it was reported that Israel might have helped China in the R&D of YJ-62 long-range AShM. "Israel Assisting Chinese SAM Program," *Forecast International Defense Intelligence Newsletters*, April 22, 2005.

41. Richard Fisher, Jr., People's Liberation Army Leverage of Foreign Technology to Achieve Advanced Military Capabilities, Testimony Before the U.S.-China Economic and Security Review Commission, March 16, 2006: 12. http://www.strategycenter.net /research/pubID.251/pub_detail.asp.

42. Ibid.

43. China reportedly obtained German fuel-cell technology to develop a future AIP system, while Russia's Rubin Design Bureau could have provided similar examples or closed-cycle diesel and hydrogen-based AIP systems offered by the Malachite Submarine Design Bureau. See "Top Ten Chinese Military Modernization Developments." Lately, it was reported that China had produced a "technically advanced" fuel-cell. Stephen Chen, "China: Fuel Cell Breakthrough for Diesel Submarines," *South China Morning Post* (scmp. com), August 7, 2010.

44. Fisher, *China's Military Modernization.*

45. The essential point about COTS technologies is that they provide generic component parts even for bespoke systems, for instance, man-machine (or human-computer) interfaces. Controls and displays (knobs and dials) previously employed for dedicated functions are now replaced by visual display units (VDUs) that enable common architecture and hardware to be used for various functions, with the characteristics of the displays being defined by software. The use of COTS technology in this situation provides significant cost benefits. See M. Farrow, "Naval Applications for Commercial Off the Shelf Technology," Paper 9 presented at the Third International Naval Engineering

Conference and Exhibition 1996, Warship Design: What Is So Different? Organized by the Institute of Marine Engineers in association with the Royal Netherlands Navy and sponsored by Jane's Navy International, April 10–12, 1996: 97. For China's leveraging of COTS technologies for shipboard data-links, for instance, see Bussert, *Signal*, 2009.

46. Bussert, *Signal*.

47. In 2004, the Number 707 Research Institute of China Shipbuilding Industry Corporation was reported to have developed a ruggedized computer capable of operating in very harsh environmental conditions including extremely high temperatures and humidity. "China Developed Ruggedized Computer," *Xinhua's China Economic Information Service*, April 23, 2004.

48. The Chinese chose INCAT's AMD-350 hull design as the basis for developing the *Houbei*. Bussert, *Signal*. The catamaran hull design is pivotal to the *Houbei* since it provides for an exceptionally fast (probably 45 knots) yet stable and low-profile platform comparable to that of the *LCS-1*. Patch, 2010: 48–53.

49. For example, the ROK's indigenous development of a shipboard three-dimensional naval radar system reportedly involved a spy scandal implicating the French representative of Thales in the ROK in 2006. "Fleet of the Future," *Defense Technology International*, February 1, 2009.

50. "Police, MSDF to Probe Secret Aegis-ship Data Leakage," *Kyodo News*, April 4, 2007; and "Ex-MSDF Officer's Guilty Verdict over Aegis Info Leakage to Stand," *Kyodo News*, March 3, 2011.

51. This appeared to be the same Chinese sentiments expressed even in earlier indigenous attempts, such as the *Jiangwei* class. See "China's Navy: Drive for Modernisation," 1.

52. It has been pointed out that developing the software for signal processing and tracking a hundred air, surface, and submarine targets may take even longer for China than merely developing an APAR. Integration to various indigenous ships' guns and missiles and other sensors, as well as other ships' data management and weapons, might take longer. Thus, the *052C* destroyers' Type-346 APAR may be limited to 1940s-era radar tasks of detecting and tracking air and surface targets for their own ships' weapons. See O'Rourke, *China's Naval Modernization*, 21.

53. The director of the acoustic noise laboratory at Russia's Pacific Oceanography Institute was put on trial in Vladivostok for allegedly trying to smuggle secrets to the Chinese. Lyle Goldstein and Bill Murray, "China's Subs Lead the Way," *United States Naval Institute: Proceedings* 129, no. 3 (March 2003): 58–61. Another case happened in 2005 when a Japanese engineer working at Japan Defense Agency's Technical Research and Development Institute passed secret submarine data to China. "Mole Handed over Submarine Data—Counter-Espionage," *Intelligence Online*, April 15, 2005.

54. The inclination towards development activities which led to lack of funds for basic R&D has been a problem observed in the Chinese defense industries in general, not just the naval S&T sector. See, for instance, *S&T Strategies of Six Countries: Implications for the United States*, National Research Council of the National Academies, Committee on Global Science and Technology Strategies and Their Effect on US National Security; Standing Committee on Technology Insight—Gauge, Evaluate, and Review; Division on Engineering and Physical Science (Washington, DC: National Academies Press, 2010).

55. Some of the problems encountered by China in naval S&T are also experienced by India. In many ways, the trajectory of naval S&T development appears similar for both countries. Read Rajeshwer Nath, "Towards Modern Ship Design and Shipbuilding in India," *Military Technology* 10 (2005): 72–80, for a detailed account of India's NSBI progress to date.

56. For a detailed, English translation of a Chinese write-up on China's indigenous S&T on naval EW systems, read "Xinhua Depicts Naval Engineer's Research in Electronic Warfare Equipment," report by Renmin Ribao reporter Feng Chunmei and Xinhua News Agency reporter Chen Wanjun, "I Will Shake the Sea and Air with Thunderbolts—Profiling Doctor Yang Chao, High-Level Engineer and Military Representative Stationed at Naval Research Institute," *Xinhua Domestic Service*, April 19, 2006.

57. It has been argued that, while lifting of export controls to China might lead to the emergence of new S&T and R&D possibilities for its defense industrial sectors, this might diminish China's current enhanced capabilities at system integration due in part to necessity of technologically integrating diverse sources of dual-use foreign technology into new locally made products or components. *S&T Strategies of Six Countries*, 31–32.

58. Keith Crane et al., *Modernizing China's Military: Opportunities and Constraints* (Santa Monica: RAND, 2005), 141.

59. Wendell Minnick, "China's Aviation Corp. Makes Global Splash," *Defense News*, July 20, 2009, http://www.defensenews.com/story.php?i=4195521&c=FEA&s=T1C, accessed February 8, 2011.

60. Ibid.

61. Jon Grevatt, "Chinese Invest $1.5bn in Development of Aviation Industry Base in Chonqing," *Jane's Defense Weekly*, December 30, 2010.

62. Ibid., 169.

63. Robert Wall, "Pakistan Expands Fighter Force," *Aviation Week and Space Technology*, December 22, 2010, http://www.aviationweek.com/aw/generic/story_channel .jsp?channel=defense&id=news/awst/2010/12/20/AW_12_20_2010_p31-277626.xml& headline=Pakistan%20Expands%20Fighter%20Force, accessed March 15, 2011.

64. Jon Grevatt, "China's Five-Year Plan Aims to Put Defense Industry on Global Stage," *Jane's Defense Weekly*, December 30, 2010.

65. United States–China Economic and Security Review Commission, "China's Emergent Military Aerospace and Commercial Aviation Capabilities," *Hearing Between the US-China Economic and Security Review Commission*, released May 20, 2010: 82–83.

66. Office of the Secretary of Defense, *Annual Report to Congress: Military and Security Developments Involving the People's Republic of China 2010*, August 2010, p. 45, http://www.defense.gov/pubs/pdfs/2010_CMPR_Final.pdf, accessed January 8, 2011.

67. Ibid., 142.

68. Richard D. Fisher Jr., "China's Aviation Sector: Building Toward World Class Capabilities," Testimony for the US-China Economic and Security Review Commission Hearing on China's Emergent Military Aerospace and Commercial Aviation Capabilities, International Assessment and Strategy Centre, May 20, 2010.

69. Richard D. Fisher Jr., "Chinese Chengdu J-10 Emerges," *Aviation Week*, January 14, 2010, http://www.aviationweek.com/aw/generic/story_generic.jsp?channel=defense

&id=news/dti/2010/01/01/DT_01_01_2010_p65-188015.xml&headline=Chinese %20Chengdu%20J-10%20Emerges, accessed February 8, 2011.

70. Tarique Niazi, "J-10: The New Cornerstone of Sino-Pakistani Defense Cooperation," *Jamestown Foundation China Brief* 9, no. 25 (December 16, 2009).

71. Reuben F. Johnson, "Russian Defense Industry Still Sees Cooperation Opportunities with China," *Jane's Defense Weekly*, November 25, 2010.

72. Ibid.

73. Xinhua News Agency, "China's Aircraft Fleet to Triple by 2030," http://news.xinhuanet.com/english2010/china/2011-09/08/c_131115693.htm, accessed September 8, 2011.

74. Medeiros et al., *New Direction for China's Defense Industry*, 170.

75. Johnson, "Russian Defense Industry."

76. Fisher, "China's Aviation Sector."

77. Grevatt, "Chinese Invest $1.5bn in Development."

78. Jeremy Page, "China Clones, Sells Russian Fighter Jets," *Wall Street Journal*, Business Section, December 4, 2010.

79. Richard Bitzinger, "Civil-Military Integration and Chinese Military Modernisation," *Asia-Pacific Centre for Security Studies* 3, no. 9 (December 2004): 2–3.

80. Roger Cliff, Chad J. R. Ohlandt, David Yang, *Ready for Takeoff: China's Advancing Aerospace Industry* (Santa Monica: RAND Corp., 2011), 120.

81. David Barboza, Christopher Drew, and Steve Lohr, "G.E. to Share Jet Technology with China in New Joint Venture," *New York Times*, January 17, 2011, http://www.nytimes.com/2011/01/18/business/global/18plane.html, accessed January 21, 2011.

82. Andrew Erickson, "Seizing the Highest High Ground: China's Aerospace Development and Its Larger Implications," East-West Center Working Papers, International Graduate Student Conference Series, No. 3 (Honolulu, HI, 2004).

83. The Industrial College of the Armed Forces, "Space Industry—Final Report," National Defense University, Washington, DC, 2009.

84. US Department of Defense, "National Security Space Strategy—Unclassified Summary," Washington, DC, 2011, 1.

85. Euroconsult, "Governments Worldwide Invest a Record $68 billion in Space Programs," press release (February 23, 2010). Available at: http://www.euroconsult-ec.com/news/press-release-33-3/29.html.

86. Ibid., 3.

87. SatMagazine, "InSight: Futron—The Space Competitiveness Index Update," *SatMagazine*_(December 2009). Available at: http://www.satmagazine.com/cgi-bin/display_article.cgi?number=1856883389.

88. Marc Kaufman, "Dominance in Space Slips as Other Nations Step Up Efforts," *Washington Post* (July 9, 2008).

89. Futron, "Space Competitiveness Index (SCI)—Global Military Space," *MilSat Magazine* (2009). Available at: http://www.milsatmagazine.com/cgi-bin/display_article.cgi?number=875113067.

90. "U.S. Space Edge Erodes, Non-Traditional Players Ascend, and Competition Intensifies," Futron press release (July 20, 2010).

91. Euroconsult, "Worldwide Government Spending on Space to Flatten over the next Five Years," press release (February 16, 2011). Available at: http://www.euroconsult-ec.com/news/press-release-33-1/42.html.

92. James Moltz, "China's Space Technology: International Dynamics and Implications for the United States," statement presented before the US-China Economic and Security Review Commission (May 11, 2011). Available at: http://www.uscc.gov/hearings/2011hearings/written_testimonies/11_05_11_wrt/11_05_11_moltz_testimony.pdf.

93. David J. Thompson and William R. Morris, "China in Space: Civilian and Military Developments," Air War College Maxwell Papers 24,(Maxwell Air Force Base, AL, 2001); Joan Johnson-Freese, "China's Space Ambitions," IFRI Proliferation Papers (Paris and Brussels: IFRI, 2007).

94. Kevin Pollpeter, *Building for the Future: China's Progress in Space Technology During the Tenth 5-Year Plan and the U.S. Response* (Carlisle Barracks, PA: Carlisle Strategic Studies Institute, 2008).

95. Key subsidiaries include the China Academy of Launch Vehicle Technology, responsible for the CZ-2 and CZ-3 series; the Shanghai Academy of Space Flight Technology, which developed the LEO CZ-2D and CZ-4; and the Academy of Space Chemical Propulsion Technology, responsible for liquid rocket engines. The China Great Wall Industry Corporation is responsible for marketing launch services on international space markets.

96. Mark Stokes, "Implications of China's Military and Civil Space Programs," statement presented before the US-China Economic and Security Review Commission (May 11, 2011). Available at: http://www.uscc.gov/hearings/2011hearings/written_testimonies/11_05_11_wrt/11_05_11_stokes_testimony.pdf.

97. In April 2011, the China Manned Space Engineering Office unveiled a blueprint of the future orbital station, which will comprise an 18.1-meter core module and two 14.4-meter lab modules. The 60-ton space station is smaller than the International Space Station (419 tons), and Russia's Mir Space Station (137 tons), the latter of which served between 1996 and 2001.

98. J. Johnson-Freese, "China's Space Ambitions," *IFRI Proliferation Papers* (2007).

99. ESA, "Chang'e-1—New Mission to Moon Lifts Off," *ESA News* (October 24, 2007). Available at: http://www.esa.int/esaCP/SEMPM53Z28F_index_0.html.

100. "Chang'e Series," *Jane's Space Systems and Industry* (October 12, 2010).

101. Jon Grevatt, "China Draws-up Industry Reforms in Bid to Raise Competitiveness," *Jane's Defense Industry* (June 25, 2007).

102. The CASC has eight large R&D and production complexes. By the end of 2009, CASC had total assets of RMB 153.3 billion. In 2009, its operating revenue nearly reached RMB 70 billion and its total profit was over RMB 7 billion. In 2010, the company has been focusing on the construction of a new aerospace industrial system to accelerate the development of its businesses, covering space systems, defense systems, aerospace technology applications, and aerospace services.

103. CASIC consists of seven research academies, two R&D and manufacturing bases, and a number of research institutes and factories. The corporation has six publicly listed companies and over 150 member firms, with nearly 100,000 employees in total.

The corporation offers a range of defense and aerospace products and services, covering missiles, spacecraft, telecommunications and electronic systems, and special vehicles and machinery. See "China Aerospace Science and Industry Corporation (CASIC)," *Chinese Defense Today* (2011), available at: http://english.casic.cn/n189298/n189314/index .html.

104. Medeiros et al. *New Direction for China's Defense Industry.*

105. A recent example of this is the Eutelsat W3C satellite built by Thales Alenia Space and Astrium Services, which has been contracted to fly on an LM-3 in 2011. This spacecraft would previously have been considered addressable and open for capture by commercial launch service providers such as Arianespace and ILS, which Eutelsat has favored in recent procurements.

106. Federal Aviation Administration, "2011 Commercial Space Transportation Forecasts," FAA Commercial Space Transportation (AST) and the Commercial Space Transportation Advisory Committee (Washington, DC, 2011).

107. Richard Fisher, "Final Frontier—China's Emerging Military-Space Architecture," *Jane's Defense Security Report* (September 13, 2011).

108. M. Taylor Fravel, Evan Medeiros, "China's Search for Assured Retaliation," *International Security* 35 no. 2 (2010): 48–87.

109. Michael S. Chase, Andrew S. Erickson, and Christopher Yeaw, "Chinese Theater and Strategic Missile Force Modernization and its Implications for the United States," *Journal of Strategic Studies* 32 no. 1 (2009): 67–114.

110. Christian Le Miere, "China Develops Nuclear Capability," *Jane's Intelligence Review* (May 27, 2009).

111. Robert Hewson, "Dragon's Teeth: Chinese Missiles Raise their Game," *Jane's Navy International* (January 1, 2006).

112. Mark Stokes, *China's Evolving Conventional Strategic Strike Capability* (Arlington, VA: Project 2049 Institute, 2009).

113. Anthony Cordesman and Martin Kleiber, *Chinese Military Modernization and Force Development—Main Report* (Washington, DC: Center for Strategic and International Studies, 2006), 84.

114. John Wilson Lewis and Hua Di, "China's Ballistic Missile Programs: Technologies, Strategies, Goals," *International Security* 17, no. 2 (1992): 16.

115. The LM-1 was basically a DF-4 missile with an extra solid-fuel third stage. It could place a 300kg payload into a 440km orbit.

116. "Space Launch Vehicles—Orbital, China: Long March 5 (CZ5)," *Jane's Space Systems and Industry* (May 6, 2011).

117. The inclination towards development activities which led to a lack of funds for basic R&D has been a problem observed in the Chinese defense industries in general, not just the naval S&T sector. Read for instance, *S&T Strategies of Six Countries.*

Chapter Eight

Organization as Innovation

*Instilling a Quality Management System in China's
Human Spaceflight Program*

Kevin Pollpeter

Space industries, regardless of nationality, confront unique challenges in successfully bringing programs to fruition. These challenges are primarily due to the medium in which spacecraft operate and the technologies needed to send them into orbit.[1] Indeed, the launch, space, and reentry environments are extremely harsh and place great stress on technologies. It is possible that no other type of technology poses the same degree of difficulty as that encountered in transporting spacecraft from the Earth's surface to orbit and back again.[2]

This chapter explores the elements required to successfully develop space technologies; it examines the research and development factors involved in human spaceflight programs. Based upon a variety of sources on spacecraft manufacturing and systems engineering and on histories of US human spaceflight programs, it develops a theory of spacecraft research and development. It posits that the difficulty of developing successful space systems places a great emphasis on reliable technologies, exacting manufacturing process, and strict and documentable quality assurance measures. In addition to these technological and manufacturing factors, space programs often require support from a country's top leadership as well as adequate funding.

This hypothesis is then tested using histories and technological and systems engineering accounts of China's human spaceflight program. It finds that China's space industry had been following the same principles in developing human-rated spacecraft and launch vehicles as its US counterpart. However, because China's space program inherited a legacy industry that was underfunded, unfamiliar with modern systems engineering, technologically backwards, and generally lacking a commitment to quality, China's human spaceflight program did not become mature until at least 2005—13 years after the approval of the human spaceflight program and two years after China's first manned flight.

This 13-year struggle holds important implications for both China and the United States. Many discussions of China's technological advancements center on the role of foreign cooperation and technology transfer. This chapter does not intend to diminish the role of these factors. It contends, however, that these factors, while necessary, are not sufficient to fully explain the success of China's human spaceflight program. Also required was top-level political support, adequate funding, and a systems engineering approach that emphasized a commitment to quality through a comprehensive program of standardized components, testing, manufacturing processes, and documentation. Over the long term, as China increasingly relies on its own technology to build spacecraft, these factors will play a more prominent role in determining the success of its space program and will ultimately determine China's ability to manage a sustainable space technology development program. Moreover, technological accounts of China's human spaceflight mission make clear that the lessons learned from planning, designing, and manufacturing China's human-rated space capsule and launch vehicle will be disseminated to the broader Chinese defense industrial community as well as to the civilian economy.

Factors in Successful Space Programs

This section covers the characteristics that make space programs unique and the ways in which their challenges are addressed. These characteristics range from political to technical. In examining these factors, this chapter relies on textbooks written for aerospace engineers on spacecraft design and systems engineering and on histories of the US Apollo space capsule program, the Saturn V rocket program, and the Space Shuttle. The histories in particular illustrate just how difficult space programs are. Consequently, simply listing these characteristics masks the exactness, persistence, and ingenuity that go into spacecraft manufacturing.

Political Support

The first characteristic of large-scale space programs is the necessity of political support. Many studies have revealed that, due to the overarching role of the government in funding space programs and the large budgets needed to support such programs, top-level political support is required for the success of a space program. Reflecting on the US space program, former NASA Chief Historian Roger Launius has concluded, "Before an initiative has any chance of political success, it must be endorsed by the president . . . the president has been and continues to be the crucial player in the effort to define the overall space program. Without the president, no large-scale project could be placed on the national political agenda."[3]

The classic example of high-level political support for a space program is President John F. Kennedy's decision to conduct manned lunar missions. The Apollo Program should not be mistaken for a pure science and technology program, however, as the decision to send men to the moon was ultimately made on the basis of Cold War strategy. Presidential candidate Kennedy portrayed the United States as lagging behind the Soviet Union in its economy and science and technology level. Most notable was his depiction of the Soviet Union as leading the United States in the number of intercontinental ballistic missiles each country held. To remake the United States into the leading super power, Kennedy committed to making the United States a nation that was not "first but, first and, first when, first if, but first PERIOD."[4]

Upon entering office, however, Kennedy found that his assessments of Soviet power were erroneous. The so-called "missile gap" was actually in the United States' favor, and the superiority of the Soviet economy was based on a comparison of the US economy during a particularly difficult recession and inflated Soviet economic data.[5] Even in the field of space technology, a 1961 NASA report had concluded that the United States led the Soviet Union in every area of space science.[6] Nevertheless, the ability of the Soviet Union to carry out space spectaculars such as the launch of the first satellite, Sputnik, in 1957 and the launch of the first human into space in 1961 fueled the perception that the Soviet Union was the greater super power. Such feats, in particular the 1961 Yuri Gagarin flight, mobilized the president to find ways to counter this perception, which ultimately resulted in the Apollo program.

President Richard Nixon's decision to approve the Space Shuttle, as the follow on to the Apollo program, is also an example of the necessity of top-level leadership in ensuring the success of space programs. Unlike his two predecessors, Nixon had no real interest in space exploration, but he did not want to be known as the president that killed the space program.[7] Funding for the program became problematic, however. The proposed costs of developing a completely new type of launch vehicle and spacecraft were large, and they were coming during a time of increasing concerns over budget deficits brought about by social spending and the Vietnam War. Despite these concerns, the debate over the Space Shuttle centered more on the speed and annual costs of the program rather than on the more fundamental question of its utility. The initial plan for the space shuttle called for \$10–12 billion[8] to develop a reusable spacecraft that would fly 20 times per year.[9] The final plan, however, was approved at a cost of \$5.15 billion[10] to build a spacecraft that would make no more than 8 flights per year. Even at this reduced level, presidential approval was required. Ultimately, the president approved the Space Shuttle on the grounds that it would revolutionize spaceflight by making it cheaper and routine.[11]

Presidential approval alone, though, is not sufficient to ensure the success of large space programs. Large space efforts take place over many years and must be able to survive multiple presidential administrations if they are to reach a successful conclusion.[12] National leaders cannot simply make declarations and expect space programs to be approved. One instructive case is President George W. Bush's 2004 announcement that the United States would develop and test a new Crew Exploration Vehicle by 2008 and make the first flight by 2014, would resend astronauts to the moon by 2020, and would prepare the way for eventual human missions to Mars. The Bush plan did not survive the Obama administration, which ultimately canceled plans to return humans to the moon and decided instead to concentrate on incentivizing commercial companies to accomplish missions in low earth orbit and that NASA should develop technologies to send humans to a nearby asteroid.

LARGE AND COMPLEX SYSTEMS

Space programs can be large, complex endeavors that require vast numbers of personnel and organizations working on different systems and whose work must be coordinated, scheduled, and provided with technical data. The Apollo-Saturn program, for example, has been estimated to have involved 20,000 companies and 300,000 people.[13] The Saturn V program alone involved Boeing, North American Aviation, Douglas Aircraft, and IBM simply as the lead contractors, while the command module was manufactured by North American Aviation and the lunar module by Grumman. The Saturn V was composed of approximately 3 million parts, the command and service modules 2 million parts, and the lunar module 1 million parts.[14] Indeed, "William Mrazek, a top official in Marshall Spaceflight Center's Industrial Operations Division, once remarked that the Apollo program was possibly the greatest engineering program in history, overshadowing the Manhattan Project that produced the atomic bombs of World War II and outranking the efforts of the builders of the Egyptian pyramids."[15]

USE OF PROVEN DESIGNS AND TECHNOLOGIES

Taking a conservative approach to spacecraft design is one of the most basic steps by which to ensure spacecraft reliability. Once a spacecraft is in orbit, it cannot be repaired and must remain in good working condition for the length of its service life, which can be up to 15 years. Launch vehicles, on the other hand, are used only once; and when they fail, they tend to do so catastrophically. Because of this, customers are reluctant to acquire new, unproven technologies, unless dictated by mission requirements. As a result, a disincentive against innovation exists in the space industry due to the higher level of risk inherent in new technologies[16] and may be the reason why launch vehicle technology has remained stagnant for many years.

LAUNCH VEHICLES

The type of launch vehicle used to transport a craft into space is the most constraining design factor. Except for certain spacecraft, in particular human-rated ones, rockets will not be designed to the specific needs of the spacecraft.[17] Unlike aviation, in which aircraft can be as small as ultralights or as large as the double-decker Airbus 380, the physics of spaceflight demand that spacecraft be launched on relatively large rockets capable of producing large amounts of thrust. The Delta IV Heavy launch vehicle, for example, is 72 meters high and 5 meters in diameter and can produce up to 744,737 pounds of thrust, which can deliver a nearly 29,000-pound payload into geosynchronous transfer orbit.

As a consequence of this constraint, spacecraft engineers must instead design the spacecraft so that its mass and dimensions fit the capabilities of the launch vehicle. The restrictions on mass and volume then limit the selection and design of deployable structures, such as antennae and solar panels, and can influence the choice of materials.[18]

LAUNCH ENVIRONMENT

Launch imposes a highly stressful environment on spacecraft. A launch vehicle's engines produce severe acoustics and vibration, especially just after lift-off as the rocket engine noise is reflected from the ground. Aerodynamic buffeting will also occur as the vehicle rises through the Earth's atmosphere. In addition, a spacecraft will experience an atmospheric pressure drop as it increases in altitude.[19]

SPACE ENVIRONMENT

Vacuum and Temperature Effects

In all of the elements on board a spacecraft, material strength and fatigue life and electrical, mechanical, and thermal systems are affected by a high-vacuum environment.[20] The space environment can subject spacecraft to extremes of temperature that range from minus 73 degrees Celsius in the dark to 77 degrees Celsius in the light. This can result in fatiguing of spacecraft materials as they expand and contract during the cycles between dark and light.[21] Most spacecraft equipment, however, was originally designed for terrestrial use and designed to operate most effectively at or around room temperature.[22] Consequently, spacecraft must use both passive and active thermal control methods to ensure that equipment operates in required temperature ranges. Passive thermal control methods include the "selection of surface properties, the control of conduction paths and thermal capacities, and the use of insulation systems."[23] Active controls consist of heaters and coolers designed to maintain the proper temperature throughout operation.[24]

Orbit Radiation Effects

Solar radiation, such as that produced by solar flares and other cosmic sources, can reduce the life of spacecraft. Ultraviolet radiation can cause certain materials to become brittle and can cause electrical and optical changes that affect thermal characteristics and opacity. For example, UV radiation can reduce the power generation of solar arrays by darkening the cover glass of solar arrays.[25] Radiation-hardened parts and shielding are the two main methods of reducing the effects of radiation.[26]

Micrometeroids and Orbital Debris

Micrometeroids and orbital debris can damage or debilitate a spacecraft when it collides with them at high speed. Micrometeroids are small, naturally occurring particles. Orbital debris, on the other hand, are pieces of expended launch vehicles or spacecraft that remain in orbit after their useful lives. Micrometeroids and orbital debris can be extremely dangerous and even minute pieces can be lethal to a spacecraft and potentially its occupants. In 1983, for example, the outer layer of a windshield of the Space Shuttle Challenger was chipped by a fleck of paint.[27] To prevent such damaging collisions, the exterior structures of spacecraft can be hardened or thermal blankets can be added. In some cases, a "meteor bumper" can be affixed to the structure of the spacecraft to absorb the impact of meteoroids and debris.[28]

Atmospheric Reentry

The most risky aspect of spaceflight is reentry. While reentry technology is mature, it remains very demanding. In addition, reentries cannot be aborted and they offer few chances for astronauts to escape. Whereas astronauts can escape a space capsule before or during launch, few passenger escape mechanisms exist for a reentering spacecraft.[29]

During entry into the atmosphere, a spacecraft's speed must be reduced from Mach 25 at the beginning of reentry to subsonic speeds as it nears landing. In the process, a great amount of heat is generated on the surface of the spacecraft, and it must be dissipated. An added danger is the possibility that parachutes will fail to effectively deploy. It is indicative of the dangers of reentry that, out of 286 total human spaceflight missions, only one fatal accident has occurred during launch—the 1986 Challenger mission. In contrast, there have been three fatal reentries—Soyuz 1, Soyuz 11, and Columbia. The one notable failure of the Shenzhou program occurred during the reentry of the Shenzhou II capsule. While the cause of that failure has never been announced, it is possible that a malfunction occurred with the drogue chute that is intended to slow the spacecraft before the main chute is deployed.

In the mitigation of heat buildup through design of the spacecraft, the three basic approaches are heat sinks, radiative cooling, and ablative shielding. Heat sinks use a large mass of materials with a high melting point to absorb heat. Radiative cooling allows the outer skin of a spacecraft to become extremely hot, and the heat is then transferred to the atmosphere. The Space Shuttle uses this kind of heat dissipation system.[30] Ablative shielding involves the use of special materials that draw heat away from the spacecraft by breaking away during reentry.

QUALITY ASSURANCE AND TESTING

Among the major challenges in building a reliable space system are the low production volumes and the expense and difficulties in testing components or systems designed for use in space. These challenges hinder manufacturers' ability to identify systemic flaws and limit the opportunities to find solutions. For example, flight testing for the Apollo missions involved just 10 missions over a 3-year period, only 5 of which were manned. Aircraft testing, on the other hand, has the benefit of many hours of test flights using multiple test aircraft.

The original Boeing 747 flight test program used 5 airplanes, lasted 10 months, and required more than 1,500 hours of flying.[31]

Indeed, no space system has flown enough to allow failure probabilities to be well established.[32] NASA required each Apollo mission to provide .999 percent probability of crew safety (1 in 1,000 chance of fatality) and .99 percent probability of mission success (1 in 100 chance of aborting the mission). However, as Thomas Kelly, head of the lunar module effort for Grumman, wrote, "From a designer's point of view these probabilities were not much help. In practical terms they could not be demonstrated because the allowable failure rates were so low that to prove them would require hundreds or even thousands of repetitive tests."[33]

The extremes of the launch, space, and reentry environments coupled with the impracticality of conducting real world testing place a great stress on the testing of components, subsystems, and systems. In fact, testing of components is the only method of demonstrating the integrity of both the design and the construction of the machine and of verifying its ability to operate over its design life. The success of the Saturn program is said to be owed "to two basic philosophies: (1) the stringent reliability and quality assurance programs during manufacture, and (2) exhaustive ground testing." Indeed, the test phase of the Saturn program accounted for as much as 50 percent of the total effort, in terms of allotted man-hours and physical resources.[34]

The main way to test the reliability of both launch vehicles and spacecraft is to subject the systems to higher levels of stress than will be encountered during the mission, from lift-off to end-of-life. In order to simulate the vacuum of space, components, systems, and even entire spacecraft are placed in a vacuum chamber. The microgravity of space is simulated by suspending components from their center-of-mass.[35] Vibration testing, conducted on large vibrating tables to simulate the experience of launch, is conducted at 1.5 times the expected vibration level, while thermal testing is conducted at ±10°C of the predicted orbit temperatures.[36] Any test failure must be examined and analyzed and the component retested until the reason for the test failure is found.[37] Testing has to be done on each component of the spacecraft throughout the manufacturing process. The Apollo command module and the lunar module had more than 2,500 test points while the Saturn had 5,000.

In addition, whole systems must also be tested, often in building-block fashion. For example, the Saturn rocket test launches initially used live lower stages attached to dummy upper stages and progressively worked up to using all live stages and then test flights carrying the command and service modules and the lunar module.[38]

Reliability is also enhanced through the use of redundancy. Redundancy in this application is defined as the "provision of extra components or systems by means of which the desired task can be accomplished despite the failure of the first component or system. . . . Redundancy can be provided within components, among components, across subsystems, and at the whole system level."[39] Because reliability is even more important in crewed spacecraft, redundancy is automatically built in. The Space Shuttle had five main computers and "three subsets of most avionics and control subsystems."[40]

Manufacturing processes must be tightly controlled. During manufacture, oxygen and humidity can corrode materials and pins in electrical connectors. Airborne particulates can cause wear in mechanisms and can plug small holes. Dust particles dislodged by the microgravity of space can look like stars to a star sensor or tracker on the spacecraft. To minimize contamination, spacecraft and their subsystems are assembled and tested in "clean rooms," in which dust and humidity are carefully controlled.[41]

Space program manufacturing processes are very exacting and require highly skilled workmanship. For example, the nearly one kilometer of welded joints on the S-II stage of the Saturn V had to be flawless, and many had to be accurate to 0.33 mm. "Minuscule cracks, tiny bits of foreign material in the weld seams, moisture, or other apparently innocuous imperfections could leak volatile propellants or cause catastrophic weaknesses under the pressures and loads experienced in flight."[42] Moreover, the welds had to be surgically clean. "Theoretically, if a worker left a fingerprint on the inside of a liquid oxygen (LOX) tank," the oil from the fingerprint could react with the LOX and cause an explosion.[43]

The stresses placed on spacecraft during launch and reentry and in space also require space technology manufactures to institute strict reliability and quality control standards. The size and complexity of space programs require that a systematized process of design, testing, and manufacturing be installed and rigidly enforced. Documentation is the primary way of ensuring compliance with quality control procedures. All work done must be approved through documentation, including work orders, drawings, test preparation sheets, or test plans, and then it must be inspected.[44]

Systems Engineering

The necessity of managing the design, manufacture, testing, budgeting, and quality control processes conducted by each of the many organizations and large numbers of personnel working on different systems, when each party may have different competencies and competing views on how to meet specified goals, has given rise to the need for a scientific approach to systems engineering. Systems engineering here is defined as "the art and science of developing an operable system capable of meeting mission requirements within imposed constraints including (but not restricted to) mass, cost, and schedule."[45]

Systems engineering seeks to resolve conflict in an effective and productive manner and involves dealing with people as much as dealing with technical issues.[46] The ultimate goal of systems engineering in this case is to build a reliable spacecraft that is able to successfully complete a mission and last for the required amount of time. Subsidiary goals are to ensure that systemic failures are weeded out and that only random failures will occur.[47]

Systems engineering is performed at all levels of space program management by the government and contractors. Usually, the best program management is characterized by a close and interactive relationship between contractors and the client. The experience of NASA's management of the Apollo-Saturn program is instructive in this regard. Initially, NASA, using US Air Force management methods, provided a relatively loose program oversight. However, because of the complexity of the program, "it became clear that close and continuous surveillance of the contractor operation was required on an almost daily basis."[48]

Initially, contractor reaction to this monitoring was not favorable, but it was eventually perceived to be of mutual benefit and now is considered one of the reasons why the program was successful. The Apollo-Saturn program frequently used the phrase "government-industry team" to describe the relationship.[49]

RESULTS

Despite all of the quality assurance methods and procedures that are used to ensure successful launches of spacecraft, the success rate of launch vehicles and satellites remains far below what is required of other technologies. For example, a 2004 study by the business consulting firm Frost and Sullivan concluded that the most reliable satellite, as determined by the ratio of insurance claims to successful deployments, was Boeing's BSS 376, which had a reliability rating of 89 percent.[50] Similarly, the reliability of launch vehicles remains far below what would be expected in the aviation industry, for instance. The Delta family of launch vehicles manufactured by Boeing has a 95.7 percent success rate. The Arianne 5, built by the European company Astrium, has a 92.9 percent success rate. These success rates demonstrate that while many advances have occurred in the space industry, it continues to be a relatively high-risk venture.

The Chinese Human Spaceflight Program

This section examines China's human spaceflight program in light of the factors identified in the previous section. In doing so, it explores the political, organizational, budgetary, technical, and manufacturing challenges China's space industry faced to successfully send humans into space. Sources used in this analysis of the development of the Shenzhou space capsule and the Shenjian (Long March 2F [LM-2F]) launch vehicle include news reports, histories, and technical accounts. Technical accounts in particular were useful, as they were written to disseminate lessons learned to China's space professionals. The most useful sources were on the development of the LM-2F, so most of this section discusses the development of the launch vehicle.

While these sources may not present as complete a picture of China's human spaceflight program as the volumes written on the Apollo and Saturn programs, they do make it evident that those involved in the program worked to fulfill the same combination of requirements that make large space programs successful. These include securing the support of the top political leadership and an adequate budget, identifying a vision, choosing a relatively simple design, developing a qualified workforce, and instituting a strict quality assurance program involving standards, testing, standardization, documentation, and inspections. As with the US space program, the requirements of ensuring and maintaining a commitment to quality necessitated a close relationship between the prime contractors, China Academy of Space Technology and the China Academy of Launch Vehicle Technology, and their suppliers. This entire process appears not to have matured until China's second human spaceflight mission—a full 13 years after the approval of the project in 1992.

POLITICAL SUPPORT

As with US human spaceflight programs, one of the main factors in determining the success of China's human spaceflight program has been the support of China's top political leadership. This has not always been guaranteed, however, and it is easy to overlook the intense debates that have occurred within China's authoritarian system over space policy issues. China's Communist Party follows the practice of democratic centralism in which debate is allowed to occur up until a decision has been made. Once a decision is made, factions are expected to join ranks and carry out the decision. The struggle to approve the human spaceflight program is a textbook example of this practice.

Human spaceflight was first proposed in China in 1986, after the approval of China's major science and technology funding program, the National High-Technology Development Plan, also known as the 863 Program. At this time, Chinese scientists, seeing that the Soviet Union was operating the space station Mir and the United States was planning to build its own space station, believed that in order for China to be a great power it also had to have a space station.

Feasibility studies for a human spaceflight program were approved by the 863 Program within months of the funding plan's initiation. Securing support to go beyond feasibility studies, however, was difficult. Human spaceflight was universally recognized as an expensive endeavor, and many argued that China would be better off spending resources on other projects. China's worsening economy in the late 1980s bolstered opposition arguments. Hopes of moving beyond feasibility studies were further dashed as the leadership dealt with the fallout of the 1989 Tiananmen Massacre. Recognizing that such an expensive and complicated program required unanimous support from the Chinese leadership, in the winter of 1991 top officials from the Aviation and Space Ministry made an end run around the bureaucracy by giving their proposal to the brother-in-law of then-paramount leader Deng Xiaoping. After reading the proposal, Deng approved the project. While his exact response is unknown, it was rumored that Deng had said that there were two things he would regret not living to see: one was the Three Gorges Dam, the other, human spaceflight.[51]

Deng's approval did not result in formal bureaucratic approval of the project, however. The human spaceflight program had to undergo an additional two years of extensive feasibility analysis in which both the political justifications and technical issues were examined. During this time, proponents of the human space program refined the justification that underlay their rationale for human spaceflight and for China's space program overall. This justification centered on the concept of comprehensive national power, defined as a country's ability to exercise political, economic, scientific, and military power.[52] Proponents argued that human spaceflight contributed to each of these areas by increasing China's international stature, producing high technology and high-technology jobs, promoting space science, and providing remote sensing capabilities.

Though the program underwent extensive feasibility testing over two years, Deng's approval had removed all opposition to the program. Li Peng, the country's premier and an opponent of human spaceflight, set aside his opposition soon after Deng gave his support to the program. In August 1992, the proposal received unanimous approval from the Central Special Commission, an organization that approves and oversees large-scale strategic technology projects. In September 1992 the proposal was approved by the Politburo Standing Committee, China's highest leadership body, which gave it the project name 921, after the month and day (September 21) it was approved.

Top leadership support was followed by monetary support. Initially, the program was allocated 9 billion yuan, but costs had risen to 18 billion yuan by the time of the first test flight in 2003. As one person involved in the project stated, "in most programs when more funding was sought, they always received less than what was asked for. However, with the human spaceflight program the leadership voluntarily increased the funds."[53] Nevertheless, statements from those involved in the program suggest that, while funding was adequate, it was by no means plentiful. At one point, some personnel in China's space industry worked without pay.[54] Additionally, Li Jinai, then head of the PLA General Armament Department, has stated that the space industry would have conducted more test launches of the Shenzhou space capsule had it not been for lack of funds. [55]

Despite these difficulties, 19 years after the approval of the Shenzhou program, statements by President Hu Jintao commemorating launches of the Shenzhou demonstrate continued top-level support for China's space program. While Jiang Zemin presided over the approval and development of the Shenzhou program, it was President Hu Jintao who attended the first manned space launch, Shenzhou 5, spoke to the orbiting astronauts carrying out the Shenzhou 6 and 7 missions, and gave prominent speeches to members of the Shenzhou program following the completion of the Shenzhou 6 and 7 missions. In each speech, Hu praised the missions for promoting China as a science and technology power and expressed appreciation to those involved in the missions.[56]

SCALE

China's human spaceflight program is one of the country's largest and most complex technology efforts and has been described as one of the three great projects conducted by China during the late twentieth century, along with the Three Gorges Dam and the Beijing to Kowloon rail line.[57]

The project involved a total of 3,000 work units and 110 academies, research institutes, and factories, including the Chinese Academy of Sciences, the Chinese Academy of Space Technology (CAST), the Chinese Academy of Launch Vehicle Technology (CALT), the Shanghai Academy of Space Technology (SAST), and the Ministry of Information Industry (MII). Approximately 300,000 personnel from the aviation, shipbuilding, armaments, mechanical electronics, chemical, metallurgy, textile, and construction industries took part.

The project required the coordination of seven systems: those to do with the astronaut; the space capsule; the capsule application; the carrier rocket; the launch site telemetry, tracking, and communication; and the landing site.[58] Successfully bringing these systems into being involved activities that had never been performed by China's space industry, including large-scale ground testing such as zero-altitude emergency-escape tests, thermal tests, speed tests, and return vehicle separation tests. Not surprisingly, delays in one system often affected progress on other systems.[59]

The project also necessitated the development of new technologies.[60, 61] The LM-2F alone has 55,000 electronic components that incorporate 55 new technologies, 10 of which are said to reach world technology levels.[62] These include an escape system, a malfunction monitoring system, a space capsule interface, the use of computer-aided design, precision milling and new materials, new types of low-density heat materials, and the research and manufacturing of long-lived reliable manned space capsule sensors.[63]

ORGANIZATION

In order to effectively manage a program as large and complex as the human spaceflight program, a two-pronged command system was established, made up of a commander and a chief designer. The commander is responsible for overall space capsule quality and safety, while the chief designer is responsible for the space capsule design, production, testing, and experimentation.[64] The program then established the China Manned Space Engineering Office, which serves as the lead organization during the development phases.[65]

CAST and CALT established offices for the management of space capsule and launch vehicle research and manufacturing. CAST's office was divided into two independent units, each headed by a manager. One team conducted testing at the launch site and conducted launches. The other team was responsible for the research and development of the space capsule in Beijing.[66] The human spaceflight program also established quality control organizations at multiple levels. For example, CAST established a quality management organization responsible for quality assurance planning, inspecting delivered products, conducting other inspections, and reviewing critical technologies.[67] A materials manager also participated in quality assurance by implementing quality control regulations for materials.[68]

PERSONNEL DEVELOPMENT

One of the most important factors in developing any type of spacecraft is the quality of the workforce. Whereas the early US space program could draw upon expertise developed during the first missile programs and a vibrant aviation industry, the Chinese defense industry was moribund at the time of the approval of the Shenzhou program and offered no such reservoir of talent. Aerospace engineers from the previous "two bombs, one satellite" generation were retiring or had passed away and many who remained lacked the skills needed for a human spaceflight program.[69]

China's space industry also faced challenges persuading qualified personnel to hire on with the program. China's rapidly expanding economy had caused an exodus of highly skilled employees from state-owned enterprises, and most of these job candidates wanted to work for foreign companies. In Beijing, for example, Sino-foreign joint ventures, enterprises with Sino-foreign cooperation, and wholly foreign-owned enterprises hired 51.2 percent of all job candidates.[70]

To fill this gap, China's space industry hired large numbers of recent graduates. In fact, the space program continues to recruit heavily from universities, with a focus on domestic schools, not on graduates with degrees from abroad. The chief designer and commander of the LM-2F, as well as the designers of all its subsystems, were educated in mainland Chinese institutions. Overall, 90 percent of personnel are graduates from Beijing University of Aeronautics and Astronautics, Nanjing University of Aeronautics and Astronautics, Beijing Polytechnic University, Northwest Industrial University, National Defense Science and Technology University, or Harbin Engineering University. In addition to tapping the pool of fresh graduates in any given year, the state also selects a large number of technical leaders and experts from different agencies to fill research, manufacturing, and managerial jobs.[71]

But in the mid-1990s, not only attracting but retaining these graduates was difficult. Between July 1994 and October 1996, Jiuquan Satellite Launch Center launched only one satellite, and many people working there asked to be transferred. Responding to these pressures, CALT came up with a strategy for attracting and retaining personnel. This strategy was based on three principles: nurturing and using young employees, caring for the middle-aged ones, and respecting and taking care of the old ones. CALT also singled out outstanding employees for distinction and career growth.

But it was not until 2005 when CALT finally instituted a new strategy to attract and retain talent. CALT endeavored to become more attractive to employees by establishing a good team environment, providing advancement opportunities, and providing good living conditions. The first aspect of this strategy was to implement a core talent program centered on developing approximately 200 personnel made up of 50 technically competent leaders with strong management and leadership skills, 50 personnel who show the potential to be innovative, 50 technicians knowledgeable of advanced processes and manufacturing technologies, and 50 managers and investment analysts with good market analysis, planning, and operations skills.

The second part of the strategy was to develop approximately 1,000 elite personnel through local training, studying abroad, on-the-job training, performance evaluations, and incentives.

The third part of the strategy was to expand opportunities for personal growth, focusing on developing talent, identifying employees with potential, giving people's talents full play, and enhancing opportunities for advancement in leadership and nonleadership positions.[72]

Keeping It Simple

One major factor ensuring the success of the program was the decision to develop a space capsule. In 1987, five years before the human spaceflight program was formally approved, 2,000 personnel from more than 60 work units conducted an analysis of alternatives involving six spacecraft proposals.[73] These proposals included both powered and unpowered space planes, cooperation with foreign partners, and a space capsule. Space plane advocates argued that China should be at the cutting edge of space technology. Space capsule advocates, on the other hand, argued that space capsules were more practical and that much of the technology used in China's recoverable satellites—command and control systems, reentry technology, heat shield technology, and carrier rockets—could be applied to the human spaceflight program. They also proposed leveraging China's existing rocket technology, the LM-2E, to launch the space capsule.[74]

After the alternatives were vetted, it was determined that space planes were too costly, required too much maintenance, and were more risky than space capsules. Space capsules, like the Soviet Soyuz space capsule in particular, were more appropriate for China's skill and technological level and had a long history from which the Chinese could learn.[75]

Quality Assurance

The story of the space programs' efforts to improve its quality assurance processes spans 13 years, during which standards and technical conditions for human-rated components were successively made more stringent. Similar to vehicles in the Apollo program, which required a 0.99 reliability rating and a 0.999 crew safety rating, the LM-2F was required to have a 0.97 reliability rating and a 0.997 crew safety rating. Early in the human spaceflight program, it became apparent that the quality assurance procedures used on previous space projects could not be used on the human-rated program. Simply put, the reliability required to safely send humans into space and then safely return them could not have been met by China's then-existing standards, but the human spaceflight program inherited the same lackluster processes, procedures, and commitment to quality used in China's previous space technology efforts.

Initially, China's space industry had used an older set of standards called the "seven specials." These were broad standards developed during the 1970s and 1980s that covered personnel, equipment, materials, ordering, inspections, and processes. These standards could not meet the reliability requirements for human-rated launch vehicles, possibly because they did not include detailed operational specifications. As a result, it was determined that all components and systems should adhere to a military standard and, in cases where no military standard existed for a certain component, by a reinforced seven specials.[76]

Issuing standards was one thing; implementing them was another. Most factories could not manufacture components and systems to the national military standards, only to the strengthened seven specials.[77] To correct these deficiencies, in 1993 CALT organized a meeting of experts from more than 58 work units to improve overall understanding of quality assurance and the role of standards in quality assurance and to strengthen the specifications for components.[78]

This group of experts decided that the seven specials had to be improved and that second- and third-tier suppliers must explicitly follow the national military standards. A major revision of these standards gave CALT the role of assuring quality among space program suppliers. This responsibility included approving the quality assurance plans and production processes of suppliers, inspecting their factories, and inspecting and approving finished components.[79]

Even these efforts, however, appear to have been insufficiently strict to raise the quality to the levels necessary for human spaceflight, and it was agreed in

March 1995 that quality standards needed to be raised again.[80] This was an important step. In the next month CALT issued the component requirements for the LM-2F and organized a conference in which CALT and 11 other units signed more than 60,000 component supply contracts with 51 suppliers.[81] These contract signings were followed up, between December 1995 and March 1996, with the inspection of 36 suppliers.[82] These inspections revealed a number of problems, including poor management of local suppliers, insufficient investment in technology, and outdated design, production, and inspection processes.

To address these problems, the China Aerospace Science and Technology Corporation (CASC) finalized a component list that provided regulations for design and disseminated quality management processes that covered the purchasing, inspection, and production of components to every work unit in the supply chain. The ultimate goal was to have the same components or components of equal capabilities and quality assurance procedures used by all organizations working on the LM-2F. To ensure that these regulations and processes were followed, CASC reviewed the design, craftsmanship, and testing procedures of each factory.[83] In doing so it required suppliers to draw up documentation for:

- Organizational structure and quality assurance systems
- Personnel training
- Product reliability planning and assessment
- Original materials and parts selection and control
- Production processes quality control
- Management of instruments and equipment
- Management of components
- The use of standardized indicators and management methods
- Information quality and feedback management[84]

In 1996, measures to strengthen quality assurance processes were accompanied by the establishment of the Component Reliability Center by the China Aerospace Company in CALT. Its responsibilities included improving the quality of electronic components and manufacturing standardization, developing a product list, organizing purchasing rules and application guides, conducting inspections of the components on the selection and purchasing lists, supervising manufacture, checking on the delivery of components, and performing acceptance tests of components.[85] The center was able to reduce the rejection rate of domestic components from 13.89 percent in 1997 to 1.3 percent in 2006 and that of imported components from 2.3 percent to 0.6 percent.[86]

Despite these improvements, rejection rates continued to be too high for human spaceflight. In 1997, CALT inspections of 40 companies resulted in the rejection of 1,766 of 246,864 components, including 101 entire batches.[87] These inspections identified problem areas in the use of components during the design stage and highlighted the need for more stringent screening of components.[88]

In March 1999, in what appeared to be preparation for the first launch of the LM-2F, CALT promulgated the document LMS-1999, "Electronic Component Technical Conditions." This document based technical specifications on the seven specials and used some of the military standards and other national standards to determine other technical specifications. Manufacturers devised nearly 400 additional component specifications, which were then reviewed and amended by CALT. As a result of these efforts, a preliminary standardized system of human-rated launch vehicle and astronautic components took shape.[89]

It was not until six years after the first technical specifications were promulgated, however, that they were finalized, in the 2005 edition of the "Electronic Component Technical Conditions" (LMS-2005). After the Shenzhou 6 launch, CALT conducted an overarching analysis of electrical components and revised the quality assurance regulations and the electrical component list. This process delisted components that had been eliminated or retired or were no longer in production and added nine more components to the 32 that were in the 1999 edition.[90] LMS-2005 appears to have effectively eliminated the role of the seven specials as a standard as it revised these standards to correspond to national military standards.[91] This procurement specification system then became China's astronautic component standards system.[92]

In addition to disseminating the new standards to suppliers, the requirements of LMS-2005 were also made known to purchasers. The new standards required purchasing documents to clearly state product specifications, quality levels, delivery checks, packaging methods, and that the products conformed to LMS-2005 technology conditions. Inspection reports were to be conducted on received products, and these reports would be kept on file by the component control center.[93]

STANDARDIZED MANAGEMENT

In the process of establishing quality assurance, an emphasis was placed on standardization. One of the main issues was the standardization of terminology. An extensive amount of coordination required the use of a common lexicon between the LM-2F project and the other systems of the human spaceflight project, as well as among the LM-2F subsystems. To that end, the 921-4 technical terminology team was formed to collect the terms, jargon, and definitions used by CALT during previous launch vehicle development programs and compile them into a document entitled "Human Spacecraft and Space Program Terminology." This standardization of terminology facilitated coordination between technical and management personnel because it provided a uniform technical linguistic platform.

A second issue was the standardization of manufacturing processes, components, metal materials, and nonmetal materials. In response to issues involving electrical components, for example, a team made up of CALT personnel and suppliers classified all the electrical connectors. The team collected operation manuals of all the electrical connectors listed in the standards, and on the basis of analyzing the manuals and electrical connector malfunctions, the team was able to issue the document "Standard Use and Operation of Electrical Connectors," which was used to guide the development of the first LM-2F.

Software also needed to be standardized. In the course of the LM-2F development program, comprehensive program management was applied for the first time to software development. Rules on software programming were established that stipulated software filing requirements and product coding.

A third aspect was standardization of documents. During many of its inspections, CALT discovered discrepancies and nonstandard ways of filling out documents. Design drawings were also found to have been done in nonstandardized ways, and CALT had to take great pains to rectify the drawings before they were copied and disseminated. Based on this, CALT devised standards for preparing documents. [94]

TESTING

Testing played an important role in ensuring reliability for both the launch vehicle and the space capsule. CALT conducted large-scale ground testing of the LM-2F that included testing of the entire rocket, vibration testing, large-scale design finalization testing, and trial runs of ground equipment and moving systems. Also done were comprehensive testing of electrical systems and electrical system integration, explosive testing, static testing of the rocket structure, static and dynamic testing of the escape system, reliability testing of important components, grid fin deployment testing, and testing of launch site systems.[95]

One example provides insight into how the LM-2F development team approached testing and resolved issues discovered as a result. The LM-2F rocket is designed to ignite for 300 seconds during launch. In order to ensure the reliability of the rocket engines, however, tests were conducted lasting 1,000 seconds. It was 480 seconds into one of these tests that a rocket exploded. After two to three months of investigation, it was determined that a crack or dimple in the turbine had caused an uneven burn in the rocket engine, and that had led to the catastrophic failure. After this, the rocket team wrote a new design plan, set new design standards, and examined the manufacturing units' methods for finding flaws.[96]

The capsule system also underwent extensive testing. The explosive locks that are used to separate the capsule modules in preparation for reentry were subjected 100 times to stand-alone tests and more than 10 times for their ability to separate the return module from the propulsion module. Electrical systems were also tested to ensure that they could work for 100 hours without problems. In total, from August 1996 to May 1997, every system of the capsule was extensively and successfully tested.[97] While testing the capsule, Chinese engineers, aware that reentry is the most risky part of a human spaceflight mission, paid particular attention to the reliability of the return module.[98]

To simplify the capsule testing process, which had become increasingly complex, the program used four capsules for experimentation. One capsule was used for vibration tests, a second for structural strength testing, and a third for testing the heat shield. The fourth capsule was used to test the electronics.[99] In addition, flight testing was done in a step-by step fashion in which each step involved more complex tasks. The Shenzhou 1 launch tested the space capsule's control systems and the interfaces between systems. The Shenzhou 2 tested the capsule's environmental systems. The Shenzhou 3 conducted a complete test of the capsule's environmental systems. Shenzhou 4 completed testing of emergency rescue systems, and Shenzhou 5 was the first manned flight.[100]

Despite all this testing, there was concern that four test flights were not adequate to fully evaluate China's human spaceflight program, especially since a major malfunction occurred during the return of Shenzhou 2.[101] Then-head of CAST, Zhang Qingwei, stated, "The success of the [previous] launches does not mean that we have a thorough grasp of spacecraft technology."[102] GAD head Li Jinai has also acknowledged such concerns, by stating, "We had only conducted four unmanned test flights before carrying out the first human flight mission; many things could only be tested once. It was really worrisome that something unexpected would occur."[103] According to Li, to make up for the paucity of test launches, the human spaceflight program rigorously studied the Russian, US, and domestic space programs to identify previous problem areas and "rely on the wisdom of the scientists and technologists to compensate for material and technological limitations."[104]

To incorporate lessons learned into subsequent missions, the space capsule management team conducted a review session, a "hot wash," after each mission, to identify problems, determine the need for additional standards, and establish procedures for making technological revisions. Any suggested change had to undergo five procedural stages: thorough deliberation, approval by all parties involved, testing and verification, full-cycle review and approval, and complete execution.[105] Many times, hot washes uncovered the need for improvements. Many of the components used in the first Shenzhou flight had to be redesigned or reworked, including the solar panels, which underwent further vibration testing.[106] Extensive revisions were also conducted for the Shenzhou 5 mission. A total of 120 revisions were made to the Shenzhou 4 capsule design, including 90 hardware, 20 software, and 10 documentation revisions.[107]

Conclusions

China's human spaceflight program remains the country's largest and most complex technology program. In successfully sending astronauts into space, China surmounted numerous difficult challenges. This success is even more remarkable considering the relatively low technological base from which China started. Indeed, at the outset of the program, China's space industry was staffed by an aging workforce who were nearing retirement and saddled with poor work habits, outdated technology, and an insufficiently strict commitment to quality.

China overcame these challenges by following the same principles implemented by other nations. Like the US program, China's human spaceflight program had to receive high-level political support. The project had to be approved by the Politburo Standing Committee. This support continues to the present day.

Beyond the political aspects, a recurring theme in Chinese accounts of its space program is an ever-increasing commitment to quality. At the beginning, the leaders of the Shenzhou program realized that China's quality management system was not suitable to the requirements of human spaceflight.[108] China's space program did not manage individual projects nor did it use project management technology or properly control quality and costs.[109] Whereas the US space industry benefited from its relatively well-developed aerospace industry, which could draw upon a young workforce and extensive experience developing aircraft and missiles as well as the expertise of former German scientists who emigrated after World War II, China had no such benefits. The story of China's human spaceflight program is as much about developing an effective systems engineering program as it is about developing new technologies. China did develop new technologies for its Shenzhou space capsule and Shenjian rocket, but a successful human spaceflight program would not have been possible if a carefully managed system of testing and standards had not inculcated a commitment to quality in all parties, from prime contractor to third-tier suppliers.

This system, however, took 13 years to become fully developed. China did not finalize its component specification list until 2005, after it had already launched its first manned spaceflight in 2003. Nor has China's level of testing ever matched that of the US Apollo/Saturn program. The Saturn V launch vehicle used to send the Apollo spacecraft into orbit was tested in whole or in part 16 times before its first use on a manned mission. This testing started with the testing of the first stage, then multiple stages, then the complete rocket with mock versions of the Apollo command and service modules, and then launches with real command and service modules. China on the other hand, conducted no test launches of the LM-2F before the launch of Shenzhou 1 and conducted just four unmanned launches before sending an astronaut into space.

While China's quality assurance rigor may not have equaled that of the US Apollo program, its enhanced commitment to quality places the role of technology innovation in a broader context. Technological advancement is not just an accomplishment of talented individuals; it is also the product of a system led by an effective organizational structure implementing a strict quality assurance system made up of standards, testing, documentation, and inspections. As with the Apollo program, which formed a close government-industry team, China's human spaceflight program leaders realized that the Chinese Academy of Space Technology and the Chinese Academy of Launch Technology had to take a direct role in supervising the work of its second- and third-tier suppliers if the program was to be successful.

The role of organization in technological innovation also places China's attitude towards foreign cooperation and technology transfer in a new light. Many discussions of Chinese defense programs focus on the role of foreign cooperation and technology transfer as the single most important determinant of success.[110] The analysis in this chapter is not intended to diminish the role these two factors have played in the advancement of China's defense technology. In fact, China has acknowledged the critical support it has received from Russia in the area of human spaceflight technology.[111] Nevertheless, while foreign assistance may have been necessary, it alone has not been sufficient to guarantee success of the human spaceflight program.

Viewing technological innovation as a system rather than as an individual act demonstrates that China's greatest accomplishment may be not the development of new technologies but the organizational skills that were necessary to orchestrate a large number of institutions in a united effort to conduct the exacting business of spacecraft manufacturing. As China increasingly relies on domestically manufactured components and systems to manufacture spacecraft, the internal processes it has developed will play a more important role and will be a more reliable indicator of China's ability to sustain a successful space program. As a result, the lessons China has learned in developing a human-rated spacecraft and launch vehicle will have a more lasting effect on the space industry's ability to innovate than the role of technology itself.

NOTES

1. J. Barrie Moss and Graham E. Dorrington, "Launch Vehicles," in Peter Fortescue, John Stark, and Graham Swinerd, eds., *Spacecraft Systems Engineering,* 4th ed. (Chichester, UK: John Wiley & Sons, 2003), 211.

2. Ibid.

3. Roger Launius and Howard E. McCurdy, "Epilogue: Beyond NASA Exceptionalism," in Roger D. Launius and Howard E. McCurdy, *Spaceflight and the Myth of Presidential Leadership* (Urbana: University of Illinois Press, 1997), 243.

4. Michael R. Beschloss, "Kennedy and the Decision to Go to the Moon," in Roger D. Launius and Howard E. McCurdy, *Spaceflight and the Myth of Presidential Leadership* (Urbana: University of Illinois Press, 1997), 51.

5. Ibid., 52.

6. Walter A. McDougall, *The Heavens and the Earth: A Political History of the Space Age* (Baltimore: Johns Hopkins University Press, 1985), 317.

7. T. R. Heppenheimer, *The Space Shuttle Decision, 1965–1972: History of the Space Shuttle* (Washington, DC: Smithsonian Institution Press, 2002), 435; and Joan Hoff, "The Presidency, Congress, and the Deceleration of the U.S. Space Program," in Roger D. Launius and Howard E. McCurdy, *Spaceflight and the Myth of Presidential Leadership* (Urbana: University of Illinois Press, 1997), 93.

8. Ibid., 396.

9. T. R. Heppenheimer, *The Space Shuttle Decision, 1972–1981: History of the Space Shuttle* (Washington, DC: Smithsonian Institution Press, 2002), 362.

10. Heppenheimer, *The Space Shuttle Decision, 1965–1972,* 422.

11. Ibid., 435.

12. Launius and McCurdy, "Epilogue: Beyond NASA Exceptionalism," 243.

13. Roger E. Bilstein, *Stages to Saturn: A Technological History of the Apollo/Saturn Launch Vehicles* (Gainesville: University Press of Florida, 1980), xii.

14. Ibid., 288.

15. Ibid., 307.

16. Michael D. Griffin and James R. French, *Space Vehicle Design*, 2nd ed. (Reston, VA: American Institute of Aeronautics and Astronautics, 2004), 14.

17. Ibid., 193.

18. Ibid., 390.

19. John P. W. Stark, "The Spacecraft Environment and Its Effect on Design," in Peter Fortescue, John Stark, and Graham Swinerd, eds., *Spacecraft Systems Engineering*, 4th ed. (Chichester, UK: John Wiley & Sons, 2003), 12.

20. Griffin and French, *Space Vehicle Design*, 69, 72.

21. Ibid., 98.

22. Chris J. Savage, "Thermal Control of Spacecraft," in Peter Fortescue, John Stark, and Graham Swinerd, eds., *Spacecraft Systems Engineering*, 4th ed. (Chichester, UK: John Wiley & Sons, 2003), 355.

23. Ibid., 375.

24. Ibid., 379.

25. Stark, "The Spacecraft Environment and Its Effect on Design," 41.

26. Thomas A. Meaker, "Product Assurance," in Peter Fortescue, John Stark, and Graham Swinerd, eds., *Spacecraft Systems Engineering*, 4th ed. (Chichester, UK: John Wiley & Sons, 2003), 563–564.

27. Griffin and French, *Space Vehicle Design*, 95.

28. Ibid., 92.

29. Ibid., 273–274.

30. Ibid., 300.

31. "747 Fun Facts," accessed at http://www.boeing.com/commercial/747family/pf/pf_facts.html on May 13, 2011.

32. Griffin and French, *Space Vehicle Design*, 571.

33. Thomas J. Kelly, *Moon Lander: How We Developed the Apollo Lunar Module* (Washington, DC: Smithsonian Institution Press, 2001), 70.

34. Bilstein, *Stages to Saturn*, 183–184.

35. H. Mervyn Briscoe and Guglielmo S. Aglietti, "Spacecraft Mechanisms," in Peter Fortescue, John Stark, and Graham Swinerd, eds., *Spacecraft Systems Engineering*, 4th ed. (Chichester, UK: John Wiley & Sons, 2003), 527.

36. Meaker, "Product Assurance," 552.

37. Kelly, *Moon Lander*, 126.

38. Ibid., 324.

39. Griffin and French, *Space Vehicle Design*, 602.

40. Jerry Jon Sellers, *Understanding Space: An Introduction to Astronautics* (New York: McGraw Hill, 2005), 627.

41. Griffin and French, *Space Vehicle Design*, 50.

42. Bilstein, *Stages to Saturn*, 218.

43. Ibid., 203.

44. Kelly, *Moon Lander*, 176.

45. Griffin and French, *Space Vehicle Design*, 2.

46. Ibid.

47. Meaker, "Product Assurance," 558.

48. Bilstein, *Stages to Saturn*, 278.

49. Ibid.

50. Frost and Sullivan, "Commercial Communications Satellite Bus Reliability Analysis," accessed at http://www.lr.tudelft.nl/live/pagina.jsp?id=ed766dad-dc20-44b8-9153-c89014139d0b&lang=en on May 6, 2011.

51. "The Highest Leader Has the Final Say" (最高层领导拍板), *China Space News* (中国航天报), P34.

52. Huang Chunping and Hou Guangming, eds., *The Management of Human Spaceflight Carrier Launch Vehicle Systems Research and Development* (载人航天运载火箭系统研制管理) (Beijing: Science Press, 2007), 27–29.

53. "The Highest Leader Has the Final Say," P34.

54. Li Jingyuan, "China's First Space Project Component Astronautic Standard System," in Huang Chunping, ed., *The Great Cooperation: An Account of China's Human Spaceflight Program's Launch Vehicle Electronic Component Development* (大协作- 中国运载人航天工程运载火箭电子元器件发展纪实) (Beijing: Astronautics Press, 2007), 26–27.

55. Li Jinai, "An Unforgettable Historical Moment" (难忘的历史时刻), *China Aerospace News* (中国航天报), November 12, 2003, 2.

56. "Hu Jintao Speaks at a Meeting Celebrating the Successful Launch of Shenzhou 6" (胡锦涛在庆祝神州六号载人航天飞行圆满成功大会上的讲话), *China Aerospace* (中国航天), December 2005, 5–7; and "Hu Jintao Speaks at a Meeting Celebrating the Successful Launch of Shenzhou 6" (胡锦涛在庆祝神州七号载人航天飞行圆满成功大会上的讲话)," *China Aerospace* (中国航天), November 2008, 3–6.

57. Zhang Qingwei, "A Commentary on the Successes of China's Human Space Flight Program and Future Prospects," in China Aerospace Science and Technology Corporation Culture Department, *An Account of China's Space Flight: The Complete Story of China's First Human Space Flight* (中国飞天记: 首次中国在人航天飞行大揭秘) (Beijing: Guangming Press, 2003), 1.

58. Yuan Jiajun, *Shenzhou Space Capsule Systems Engineering Management* (神舟飞船系统工程管理) (Beijing: China Machine Press, 2006), 1–2.

59. Huang and Hou, *The Management of Human Spaceflight Carrier Launch Vehicle Systems Research and Development*, 16.

60. Huang Chunping, "The National Great Cooperation of Human Spaceflight Electronic Components" (载人航天电子元器件的全国大协作), in Huang Chunping, ed., *The Great Cooperation: An Account of China's Human Spaceflight Program's Launch Vehicle Electronic Component Development* (大协作- 中国运载人航天工程运载火箭电子元器件发展纪实) (Beijing: Astronautics Press, 2007), 5.

61. Huang and Hou, *The Management of Human Spaceflight Carrier Launch Vehicle Systems Research and Development*, 14.

62. Huang Chunping, ed., *The Great Cooperation: An Account of China's Human Spaceflight Program's Launch Vehicle Electronic Component Development* (大协作- 中国运载人航天工程运载火箭电子元器件发展纪实) (Beijing: Astronautics Press, 2007), in the "Graceful Bearing of the Rocket" section.

63. Huang and Hou, *The Management of Human Spaceflight Carrier Launch Vehicle Systems Research and Development*, 225.

64. Yuan, *Shenzhou Space Capsule Systems Engineering Management*, 129–130.

65. Ibid., 84.

66. Ibid., 88.

67. Ibid., 145.

68. Ibid., 130.

69. Huang and Hou, *The Management of Human Spaceflight Carrier Launch Vehicle Systems Research and Development*, 16.

70. Ibid., 328.

71. Ibid., 332.

72. Ibid., 329.

73. "The 863 Plan's Turn for the Better: The Competition between a Manned Space Capsule and a Space Plane" (863 计划带来转机：载人飞船与航天飞机大论战), *China Space News* (中国航天报), October 16, 2003, P33.

74. Ibid., P33.

75. Deng Ningfeng, ed., *Dream about the Milky Way Fulfilled* (天河圆梦) (Beijing: China Astronautics Press, 2004),148–150.

76. Sun Ningsheng, "Importance Attached to Electric System—Components" (重视电气系统的基础- 元器件), in Huang Chunping, ed., *The Great Cooperation: An Account of China's Human Spaceflight Program's Launch Vehicle Electronic Component Development* (大协作- 中国运载人航天工程运载火箭电子元器件发展纪实) (Beijing: Astronautics Press, 2007), 14.

77. Huang, "The National Great Cooperation of Human Spaceflight Electronic Components," 3.

78. Huang and Hou, *The Management of Human Spaceflight Carrier Launch Vehicle Systems Research and Development*, 282.

79. Ibid., 277.

80. Jinan Semiconductor Parts Laboratory, "Realize the Thousand-Year Dream of Spaceflight, Insure Quality" (实现千 年飞天梦，质量做保证), in Huang Chunping, ed., *The Great Cooperation: An Account of China's Human Spaceflight Program's Launch Vehicle Electronic Component Development* (大协作- 中国运载人航天工程运载火箭电子元器件发展纪实) (Beijing: Astronautics Press, 2007), 52.

81. Liu Xiaowei, "Nationwide Great Collaboration and Systems Management to Ensure Human Rocket Components Supply," (载人航天电子元器件的全国大协作), in Huang Chunping, ed., *The Great Cooperation: An Account of China's Human Spaceflight Program's Launch Vehicle Electronic Component Development* (大协作- 中国运载人航天工程运载火箭电子元器件发展纪实) (Beijing: Astronautics Press, 2007), 5.

82. Huang and Hou, *The Management of Human Spaceflight Carrier Launch Vehicle Systems Research and Development*, 282.

83. Liu Zhusheng, "Work Together to Raise Component Quality to a New Level" (共同努力，使元器件质量再上新台阶), in Huang Chunping, ed., *The Great Cooperation: An Account of China's Human Spaceflight Program's Launch Vehicle Electronic Component Development* (大协作- 中国运载人航天工程运载火箭电子元器件发展纪实) (Beijing: Astronautics Press, 2007), 8.

84. Huang and Hou, *The Management of Human Spaceflight Carrier Launch Vehicle Systems Research and Development*, 282.

85. China Academy of Launch Vehicle Technology Component Inspection Center, "Carry Forward the Cause and Forge Ahead into the Future, Create Brightness Again" (继往开来再创辉煌), in Huang Chunping, ed., *The Great Cooperation: An Account of China's Human Spaceflight Program's Launch Vehicle Electronic Component Development*

(大协作- 中国运载人航天工程运载火箭电子元器件发展纪实) (Beijing: Astronautics Press, 2007), 250–251.

86. Ibid., 255.

87. Huang and Hou, *The Management of Human Spaceflight Carrier Launch Vehicle Systems Research and Development*, 286.

88. Sun Ningsheng, "Importance Attached to Electric System—Components" (重视电气系统的基础- 元器件), in Huang Chunping, ed., *The Great Cooperation: An Account of China's Human Spaceflight Program's Launch Vehicle Electronic Component Development* (大协作- 中国运载人航天工程运载火箭电子元器件发展纪实) (Beijing: Astronautics Press, 2007), 15–16.

89. Li, "China's First Space Project Component Astronautic Standard System," 24.

90. Liu, "Nationwide Great Collaboration and Systems Management to Ensure Human Rocket Components Supply," 22.

91. Huang and Hou, *The Management of Human Spaceflight Carrier Launch Vehicle Systems Research and Development*, 332.

92. Huang, *The Great Cooperation*, "Graceful Bearing of the Rocket" section.

93. China Long March Rocket Technology Company, Quality Technology Component Control Center, "An Overview of Human Spaceflight Space Launch Rocket Component Quality Management Work" (载人航天运载火箭元器件质量管理工作总结), in Huang Chunping, ed., *The Great Cooperation: An Account of China's Human Spaceflight Program's Launch Vehicle Electronic Component Development* (大协作- 中国运载人航天工程运载火箭电子元器件发展纪实) (Beijing: Astronautics Press, 2007), 262.

94. Huang and Hou, *The Management of Human Spaceflight Carrier Launch Vehicle Systems Research and Development*, 254.

95. Ibid., 140.

96. Deng, *Dream about the Milky Way Fulfilled*, 86–90.

97. Ibid., 174–177.

98. Yuan, *Shenzhou Space Capsule Systems Engineering Management*, 143.

99. Deng, *Dream about the Milky Way Fulfilled*, 182.

100. Yuan, *Shenzhou Space Capsule Systems Engineering Management*, 3.

101. The Shenzhou 2 reentry is acknowledged to have had a serious problem. No photos of the returned capsule have been released.

102. "China's Manned Space Mission Stays on Course for October Launch," *Space Daily*, February 14, 2003.

103. Li, "An Unforgettable Historical Moment," 2.

104. Ibid.

105. Yuan, *Shenzhou Space Capsule Systems Engineering Management*, 58.

106. Deng, *Dream about the Milky Way Fulfilled*, 236.

107. Yuan, *Shenzhou Space Capsule Systems Engineering Management*, 59.

108. Ibid., 125.

109. Ibid., 18.

110. See, for example, Evan S. Medeiros, Roger Cliff, Keith Crane, and James C. Mulvenon, *A New Direction for China's Defense Industry* (Santa Monica, CA: RAND Corp., 2005).

111. Yi Yao, "China Emphatically Sketches Great Space Plan," *Liaowang*, October 21, 2002, 19.

Chapter Nine

China's Evolving Space and Missile Industry

Seeking Innovation in Long-Range Precision Strike

Mark Stokes

Despite past barriers that have impeded innovation, the People's Republic of China (PRC) is improving its ability to research, develop, and field innovative military capabilities and advanced weapon systems. Since the late 1990s, driven in part by an operational requirement to complicate the US ability to intervene in a Taiwan scenario, the PRC's defense industry has transformed itself, in order to overcome bureaucratic, technological, and cultural barriers to success.[1] While results have been impressive, China's defense industry as a whole still lags behind standards established by the United States, Europe, and perhaps even the former Soviet Union. Yet, surprising breakthroughs in disruptive or innovative technologies, including so-called "trump card" capabilities, could change strategic calculations in the Asia-Pacific region and beyond.[2]

While the industry has achieved successes in testing and deploying systems that appear to be technologically sophisticated, it is difficult to judge where breakthroughs in disruptive technologies could emerge. However, more than other sectors of its defense industrial complex, the PRC's space and missile industry has been and likely will continue to be the most capable of absorbing and diffusing advanced technology for the purposes of research, development, manufacturing, and maintenance of advanced weapon systems. Expanded collaboration between the People's Liberation Army (PLA), defense industry, and civilian universities has the potential to create synergies that could result in significant advances in key areas of defense technology. The organizational changes that have occurred within the space and missile industry are significant and also could permit rapid advances. More effective and efficient defense industrial management could allow China to emerge as a technological competitor of the United States in certain niche areas, such as long-range precision strike.

China's relative potential for technological breakthroughs and innovation in its space and missile industry is due to a number of factors. Perhaps most important is the historical legacy of China's space and missile program and record of success. Secondly, its organizational and management systems set the industry apart from other sectors. Political factors, such as the special status of the industry and its primary customer—the Second Artillery Force—and national pride in the space program are other contributing factors. Aerospace power is emerging as a key instrument of PRC statecraft, and operational priorities, such as long-range precision strike, favor the aerospace industry. Finally, cultural inclinations and decisive measures to overcome traditional cultural impediments to innovation further favor the space and missile industry.

This chapter examines China's space and missile industry and its potential for supplying the PLA with disruptive military technologies. As a side note, the terms *space and missile industry* and *aerospace industry (hangtian gongye)* are used interchangeably, bearing in mind that the aviation industry *(hangkong gongye)* is a separate and distinct sector. The chapter first outlines a theoretical foundation, including drivers for innovation, highlights key organizations involved in developing operational requirements and managing acquisition, and covers the general framework for research and development (R&D). It then provides an overview of the two defense industrial enterprises that make up the aerospace industry: China Aerospace Science and Technology Corporation (CASC) and China Aerospace Science and Industry Corporation (CASIC). The final section offers a discussion of the anti-ship ballistic missile program as an illustrative example of how the industry could be meeting PLA requirements in innovative ways.

Theoretical Foundation

China's future success in fielding innovative technologies depends upon a mix of demand-driven factors, such as operational requirements, and technology push from China's scientific and industrial community. Various organizations within the PLA, such as the General Staff Department (GSD), General Armament Department (GAD), and individual services, such as the Second Artillery, establish operational requirements and oversee basic preliminary research and

R&D contracts, manage acquisition programs, and ensure follow-on support for newly fielded systems.

Drivers for Innovation

There are at least three drivers shaping aerospace technology development: strategic interests, operational requirements, and availability of technology. Strategic interests have served as a primary impetus for China's prioritization of aerospace technology. Space technology often is viewed as a metric of national power, and China's reflects its expanding status within the international community. The ability to project power over significant distances, without necessarily having to operate from fixed overseas bases, could mark China as a leading global player. Policy makers view aerospace power as one aspect of a broader international competition in comprehensive national strength and in science and technology. Also, an assured ability to deliver nuclear payloads has long been a major strategic driver behind prioritization of aerospace technology. Observers appear concerned about vulnerability to first strike against China's nuclear deterrent. The PLA appears to be investing in an ability to deliver conventional munitions at increasingly long distances.[3] Publications are reflecting an interest in developing countermeasures against advanced US long-range precision strike capabilities, which are expected to be in place by 2025.[4]

Operational demands have pushed the development of aerospace technologies. Perhaps most important is the operational requirement associated with sovereignty and territorial claims around China's periphery. Looking horizontally beyond the country's immediate periphery and vertically into space, Chinese analysts view disruption of US ability to project conventional power as a legitimate force modernization requirement. In enforcing sovereignty claims over the past 20 years, conventional ballistic missiles have been one of the most effective tools of PRC political and military coercion, and perhaps the most visible and central element of the PRC's coercive strategy against Taiwan. Whoever dominates the skies over a given geographic space has a decisive advantage on the surface. Increasingly accurate and lethal ballistic and land attack cruise missiles have enabled the PLA to suppress air defenses and air operations even by relatively outmoded air forces. Over the coming 10 to 15 years, more advanced conventional air assets, integrated with persistent surveillance, a single integrated air and space picture, and survivable communications architecture, could give China greater confidence in enforcing a broader range of territorial claims around its periphery.

Finally, the aerospace industry, along with China's broader science and technology (S&T) elite, may prove to be the major driver, rather than strategic or operational interests. A more efficient and effective system for leveraging military-related technologies may be driving new operational and organizational concepts that best accommodate new capabilities, such as long-range precision strike and counterspace systems. If the technological capacity exists, the incentives to develop systems to expand the country's aerospace power may prove irresistible.[5]

DEFENSE INDUSTRIAL POLICY CONTEXT

China's defense technology community is organized as a number of state-owned enterprises responsible for space and missiles, nuclear technology, electronics and information technology, aviation, and shipbuilding, just to name a few. It is within this organizational context that China's potential for fielding disruptive military capabilities should be analyzed. Influenced in large part by Soviet defense industrial practices, China's defense industry has advanced significantly over the years.[6]

China's means of diffusing aerospace technology include formal and informal organizations intended to facilitate collaboration among the PLA, industry, and academia; enabling technological breakthroughs via innovative organizational changes within the PLA's acquisition and equipment system and aerospace industry; measures to apply systems engineering successes in one industry to another; and decisive steps taken to develop new internationally competitive industries involving large, complex systems, such as commercial aviation.[7] Indeed, China's defense R&D establishment is breaking down barriers that have hampered the country's ability to field complex an aerospace-related system of systems.

China's strategic and operational warfighting requirements play a role in driving aerospace technology innovation. The GSD and the armed services develop short-term (e.g., five years) to long-term (e.g., 15 or more years) operational requirements. Based on Central Military Commission (CMC) guidance, for example, the GSD First Department appears to establish operational requirements for satellite navigation. The GSD Second Department most likely develops electro-optical and synthetic aperture radar reconnaissance requirements, and the Second Artillery establishes conventional and nuclear force requirements.

The GAD develops, coordinates, and oversees defense acquisition and technology policy in order to satisfy operational requirements. It is most likely the approval authority for service-level R&D and acquisition contracting.[8] In the case of space launch operations, the GAD itself most likely establishes operational requirements. The GAD was created in a reorganization in 1998 intended to address shortcomings in oversight of defense technology development. Its predecessor, the Commission for Science, Technology, and Industry for National Defense (COSTIND), was split into military and civilian functions, with the General Armament Department absorbing defense acquisition functions of COSTIND and the GSD Equipment Bureau.[9]

The GAD S&T Committee (STC) functions as the CMC's principal advisory group addressing China's long-term defense technology development. The STC is supported by at least 20 national-level technology working groups and defense R&D laboratories around the country. Presumably, the purpose is to leverage and pool resources to review technological progress and to advise on resource allocation. Examples of individual GAD-led technology working groups are:

- General missile technology[10]
- Precision guidance technology[11]
- Computer and software technology
- Satellite technology
- Radar sensor technology
- Micro-electromechanical systems (MEMS) technology[12]
- Communications, navigation, and tracking technology[13]
- Integrated military electronics and information systems technology[14]
- Simulation technology
- Stealth technology[15]
- Opto-electronics technology
- Aircraft technology
- Target characteristics and signal control
- Inertial technology

To further encourage innovation, GAD has expanded its Key National Defense S&T Laboratories network. As a major component of the PLA's National Defense Innovation System, at least 45 PLA GAD-certified labs are housed in selected research institutes and civilian universities. Their purpose is to foster civilian, defense industry, and military collaboration; develop key strategic technologies; and foster innovation in dual-use technologies. For example, Key National Defense S&T Labs have been established at Shenzhen University for automated target recognition and at the CASC 12th Research Institute for missile guidance and control. One of four specialized C4ISR labs has been established within

CASIC's 17th Research Institute, and a multispectral image information processing technology lab has been housed within Huazhong University.[16]

Administrative oversight of China's defense industry is exercised by the Ministry of Industry and Information Technology (MIIT). Formed in the summer of
2008, MIIT oversees a restructured and downgraded COSTIND, which previously had a dual reporting channel to the State Council and the PLA. MIIT's
State Administration for Science, Technology, and Industry for National Defense
(SASTIND) is administratively in charge of defense industrial enterprises that
support military-related R&D and manufacturing. .

A primary focus of SASTIND is supposed to be fostering greater competition
within the defense industry in order to better meet the requirements of the PLA
and to encourage greater civil-military integration. SASTIND provides policy
guidance to 11 state-owned defense industrial enterprise groups responsible for
space and missiles, electronics, aviation, nuclear-related products, shipbuilding,
and other sectors. A key guiding principle is civil-military integration (CMI), the
process of combining the defense and civilian industrial bases so that common
technologies, manufacturing processes and equipment, personnel, and facilities
can be used to meet both defense and commercial needs. As a result, spin-on technology is prioritized, as is self-reliance and innovation.[17] In addition, programs that
cater primarily to civilian interests, such as China's manned space initiative, may
produce militarily useful technologies, such as thermal protection systems and
associated materials. Engineers engaged in civilian programs often have more
access to foreign expertise, which on occasion can assist in overcoming technical
bottlenecks at the component or subsystem level.[18]

With US and European defense industries serving as models, the Chinese defense industrial authorities have attempted to encourage competition among lead
systems integrators and contractors for subsystems, subassemblies, and components. An initial step taken in 1998 was dividing each defense industrial ministry into two independent enterprises. In 2007, Chinese authorities announced
guidelines for private, non–state-owned enterprises to market and bid for PLA
defense contracts for development, manufacturing, and logistics support for military systems. Supposedly, consideration also is being given to involving foreign-
owned enterprises as well.[19] However, it remains open to question how many
high-tech entities would voluntarily choose to enter the defense market. Defense
industry writings are open in expressing preference for the civilian market,
which yields more lucrative profit margins.[20]

China's university system appears to be playing a more prominent role in defense R&D. It is not surprising that defense R&D has been undertaken by certain civilian universities and academic institutions, such as the Beijing University of Aeronautics and Astronautics, Northwest Polytechnical University, and the Harbin Institute of Technology. Qinghua University in Beijing also has been known to be a key player in basic defense R&D. However, the networks linking China's defense R&D community and traditionally civilian universities appear to be expanding significantly. For example, Xiamen and Sichuan Universities have been heavily involved in military opto-electronics R&D. Zhejiang University has been instrumental in developing components for kinetic kill vehicles (KKV). Nanjing University has been granted R&D funding for specialized passive stealth coatings for reentry vehicles.

Civilian universities and subordinate research centers also are expanding cooperative relationships with counterparts in the United States, Taiwan, Europe, Russia, and the Ukraine. Chinese technical journals credit a major US university with helping the 863-409 working group to overcome a specific technical problem related to space interceptor KKV development. Collaboration with Ukraine's Academy of Sciences helped civilian researchers develop advanced heat-ablative materials for boost-glide reentry vehicles.

R&D Strategy

China's defense R&D strategy has its roots in a directive issued by former state science and technology director Nie Rongzhen in the 1960s. The strategy, named Three Moves in a Chess Game, calls for the presence of three variants of each model or system in the R&D cycle at any one time. Under this concept, the variants should be in three increasingly advanced stages of R&D: (1) preliminary research; (2) system R&D involving design, development, testing, design reviews, and then finalization of the design; and (3) low-rate initial production.[21]

Preliminary Research

Chinese defense industries stress preliminary research as the foundation for follow-on stages of development. Preliminary research allows the mastering of mature technologies, which in turn reduces R&D time and risk.[22] For example, because of substantial preliminary research work, one unidentified medium-range ballistic missile system took only 21 months to design, quite a feat compared to other systems, some of which have taken up to a decade to complete. One focus preliminary research can have is generic technologies applicable to multiple systems across various enterprises, including telemetry, aerodynamics, synthetic aperture radar, millimeter wave radar, global positioning system (GPS) exploitation, hypersonics, and artificial intelligence. A second potential focus is basic technologies applicable to a specific system, for instance, a movable spot beam antenna for a communications satellite or a new missile propulsion system. The PLA GAD's Integrated Planning Department's Preliminary Research Bureau or similar organizations within the armed services function as supervisory bodies.[23]

Preliminary research can be funded by various means. The primary source within GAD is the Weapons and Equipment Basic Research Fund. The fund awards grants for two-year projects valued at around 50,000 to 2 million renminbi. Other funding sources include the GAD-managed Defense Technology Cross-Enterprise Fund, Defense Technology Key Laboratory Fund, CASC Innovation Fund, and CASIC Support Fund. Additionally, preliminary research has been supported by the National 863 Program, the National 973 Program, and the National Natural Sciences Program.

The 863 Program, ostensibly managed by the Ministry of Science and Technology (MOST), is a particularly important source of funding. GAD manages selected aspects of China's 863 Program on behalf of MOST.[24] The 863 Program has attempted to cut across organizational boundaries and break down stovepiped R&D efforts within China's defense S&T community. China's answer to the US Strategic Defense Initiative (SDI) and Europe's Eureka program, the 863 Program has served as a funding source for a range of R&D programs and as a mechanism to leverage the talent that resides in China's university system.[25] According to one estimate, 70 percent of the members of expert groups that manage individual technology development areas received advanced degrees from American, European, and other foreign universities.[26] In many cases overlapping with the GAD S&T Committee, the 863 Program involves expert working groups with many members also serving as GAD advisors.[27]

The 863 Program had its share of successes as its first phase drew to a close in 2001. In 2002, China's State Council approved a second phase of the program, extending it to 2017. However, the PLA appears to have viewed the 863 Program as insufficient to bridge the gap between R&D and targeted military applications. One of the detractions, at least from the PLA's perspective, may have been the leading role that civilian S&T authorities play. While the PLA's defense R&D community was granted authority over funds associated with three of the 863 Program's focus areas (advanced defense technology, aerospace, and lasers), China's civilian S&T authorities presumably have retained overall management of the 863 Program and resource allocation authority for each focus area, which they have based on overall national needs rather than specific requirements of the PLA.

Preliminary research contracts are tendered on a competitive basis.[28] Organizations that execute basic research contracts can be PLA-affiliated units, defense industry actors, or civilian education institutions. Because published technical articles are a metric of international technological competitiveness, the findings of many preliminary research projects funded under the 863 Program and other grants are published in a wide range of professional journals—after a security review. Approximately 45 percent of preliminary research projects flow directly into the model R&D stage, while a different 40 percent are used as a foundation for follow-on preliminary research projects. Only 14 percent of preliminary research projects are civilian in nature.[29]

Systems R&D

After completion of preliminary research, a review process determines if risks have been sufficiently mitigated to move the project into the R&D stage. The systems R&D phase is lengthy, costly, and closely monitored by the GAD. Each model R&D program that emerges from the preliminary research phase requires a new GAD-managed contract. Although it may vary by industry, the systems R&D phase is usually divided into four subphases. In a general systems design phase, a chief designer is appointed to monitor various subsystem design and R&D efforts. Chief designers and deputy chief designers managing subsystems rely heavily on computer aided design and other modeling and simulation tools. In the prototype phase, the design is revised after a series of ground tests, to ensure that the model meets technical specifications. A system enters the flight testing phase after successful ground tests, beginning with simple ones and traversing a series of increasingly complex tests. After successfully completing flight testing, the system is reviewed by a design certification board and, if approved, will enter small batch production.

R&D programs involve a division of administrative program management and technical leadership. The chief designer and up to six deputy chief designers coordinate the technical aspects of R&D, including coordinating with a vast supply chain. The chief designer usually is a senior director within an academy's design department. However, a senior engineer from CASC or CASIC headquarters may lead larger, more complex systems engineering projects. Deputy chief designers are generally responsible for major subsystems R&D and final assembly or manufacturing. Typical subsystems could include a solid-fueled motor subsystem; guidance, navigation, and control subsystem; warhead or post-boost vehicle subsystem; and ground equipment subsystem. Deputy chief designers often are selected from research institutes or factories rather than from within the chief designer's departmental chain of command.

The second position in the dual command structure is responsible for administrative program management. The program manager ensures that timeliness standards are being met, monitors quality, schedules testing, and manages the program budget. Design and program management teams work closely with PLA acquisition managers to ensure economy of effort, timely production, and cost-effective use of resources.[30]

While the GAD is responsible for acquisition and technology policy, PLA's service-level equipment departments have been granted greater leeway in overseeing preliminary research, R&D, and testing. Within these departments, equipment research academies appear to play a central role in program management and oversight of industrial R&D and manufacturing contracts. For example, the Second Artillery Equipment Research Academy was formed in December 2003 to better leverage available technologies for the purpose of force modernization and to integrate activities of stovepiped research institutes. Its five subordinate research institutes conduct feasibility studies, develop concepts for new missile systems, and oversee industrial R&D and testing. The first known tender of competitive bids for an R&D contract appears to have been in 2002. Program management of larger, more complex systems is handled within offices reporting directly to equipment research academy leadership, while subsystems are managed within equipment research institutes.[31] The Second Artillery Equipment Department also hosts defense industrial representative offices in selected CASC and CASIC academies, industrial research institutes, and factories.

The Second Artillery Equipment Department also oversees test and evaluation units that are responsible for integrating new weapon systems into the operational inventory. As a new missile variant is being developed and tested, a select group of field grade officers forms a regimental-level operational test and evaluation "seed unit." The unit familiarizes itself with the R&D design team, suppliers, and assembly plant. Members from the unit also develop tactics and maintenance procedures, as well as simulation systems, to ensure the smooth introduction of the new variant into the operational inventory. Adjustments to the design can be made based on the unit's recommendations in the course of operational testing. The seed unit that is introducing a new missile variant in the

Second Artillery is often attached to an existing brigade equipped with a similar airframe for administrative, training, and other support. The unit transitions to a new location and is upgraded to brigade status once it is equipped with new missiles and attains full operational capability.[32]

In short, an aerospace program that is in the R&D phase is assigned a chief designer, a small handful of deputy chief designers, and a program manager. The chief designer and his deputies coordinate the efforts of dozens of suppliers, while the program manager manages budgetary and other administrative issues. The R&D phase draws to a close once a design is finalized after successful flight testing and approved by a PLA GAD or service-led program review committee. After design finalization, a missile system enters low-rate initial production and, in the case of the Second Artillery, is assigned to test and evaluation units. The Three Moves on a Chessboard R&D strategy has the potential for pushing new technologies onto operational users in an incremental fashion even in the absence of a clear operational requirement. Assuming that technologies are sufficiently mature, a follow-on variant can enter the R&D phase when full-rate production begins and initial units are equipped with the basic variant.

The Space and Missile Industry

A group of senior-level executives who are well under the age of 50 have led the most extensive shifts in China's capacity for military technology innovation, and they have taken place within space and missile industry. The aerospace industry enjoys a historical legacy with a proven record of success, well-established channels and methods for overcoming technological bottlenecks, and the prestige needed to recruit some of China's best and brightest. For almost 50 years, China's space and missile industry has enjoyed an unrivaled status that has given it an advantage over other industries.

Its prestige is in part rooted in historic, iconic figures, such as the father of China's space and missile industry and China's best-known technological icon, Qian Xuesen. A leader in shaping the industrial organization and culture in the late 1940s and early 1950s, Qian was a China-born, US-educated aerospace engineer and a founding member of the US Jet Propulsion Lab. As a significant part of the US Army Air Corps team who secured and recruited leading members of Germany's ballistic missile design team at the conclusion of World War II, Qian worked on a number of advanced aircraft and missile programs and helped produce the US Air Force's first long-range aerospace planning document, entitled *Toward New Horizons*. The study upon which the statement was based established

an innovative research and development agenda that guided US Air Force investment throughout the Cold War. Qian also developed some of the initial theories
associated with trans-atmospheric hypersonic cruise vehicles.

Qian's work was cut short, however, when he was accused of espionage and
deported to China in 1955. Upon return to China, Qian Xuesen volunteered to
organize a team of foreign-trained engineers and establish an aerospace research
and development organization. In 1956, Qian shaped a plan that bears a striking
resemblance to the US Air Force's *Toward New Horizons*, which prompted China
to adopt a long-range perspective in its aerospace weapons development. The
plan emphasized atomic energy, missiles, computer science, semiconductors,
electronics, and automation technology. Qian also exploited foreign—especially
US—technical materials as guides for indigenous development. Most importantly,
Qian convinced the Chinese government in its formative stage that missile
development should take precedence over other parts of the defense industry,
aviation in particular. Today, Qian Xuesen has been eulogized as a defense technology innovator and an icon who established the long-term foundation for China's aerospace R&D and manufacturing.

Based on a track record of success, China's aerospace industry appears to be a
model of organizational management. An increasingly competitive environment,
mixed with a system that encourages cross-enterprise cooperation, appears to
have helped overcome generations of cultural conditioning that stifled creativity
and impeded major technological breakthroughs within the defense industry.
The space and missile industry has long been viewed as more advanced than
China's aviation industry, which has been criticized for its underdeveloped R&D
and manufacturing management practices.[33] The assignment of space and missile
industry leaders to key national defense and aviation industry positions, specifically the country's large passenger aircraft program, reflects the lack of confidence that senior PRC political leaders have in the aviation establishment.[34]

Today, the two key industrial groups that make up the space and missile industry include China Aerospace Science and Technology Corporation and China
Aerospace Science and Industry Corporation. With the GAD and Second Artillery as primary customers, CASC oversees space launch vehicles and strategic
ballistic missiles, spacecraft, and satellites. CASIC specializes in conventional
defense and aerospace systems, including tactical ballistic missiles, anti-ship and
land attack cruise missiles, air defense missile systems, direct ascent anti-satellite
interceptors, small tactical satellites and associated tactical satellite launch
vehicles.[35]

Both CASC and CASIC are organized in a manner similar to US defense corporations, with a corporate-level structure and various business divisions, referred to as academies. Like US defense industrial business divisions, each academy focuses on a core competency, such as medium-range ballistic missiles, short-range ballistic missiles, intercontinental ballistic missiles and satellite launch vehicles, cruise missiles, and satellites. While US defense companies tend to specialize further within a business division, CASC and CASIC academies are organized into R&D and/or design departments; research institutes focusing on specific subsystems, subassemblies, components, or materials; and testing and manufacturing facilities. Each academy is accountable for profit and loss and includes an information collection and dissemination institute that diffuses technical information attained from abroad and within China.

Establishment of a new design department or research institute focused exclusively on a next generation military technology indicates a significant investment of resources and relative priority of that particular technology. For military-industrial coordination and quality control, the Second Artillery Equipment Department and other acquisition authorities maintain at least 18 representative offices in key CASIC and CASC research, development, and manufacturing centers.

CHINA AEROSPACE SCIENCE AND INDUSTRY CORPORATION

Spun off from CASC in July 1999 as a second major aerospace industrial enterprise, China Aerospace Science and Industry Corporation (CASIC) employs more than 100,000 engineers, technicians, and workers within its headquarters, academies or business divisions, subordinate design departments, research institutes, factories, and commercial enterprises. CASIC's product lines include air and missile defense, cruise and conventional ballistic missile systems, operationally responsive tactical microsatellites, and related subsystems and components. The CASIC S&T Committtee is a key advisory group for the PLA, State Council, and CASIC leadership. While academies and subordinate institutes appear to conduct independent international business transactions, CASIC's principal export management enterprise is the China Precision Machinery Import-Export Company.

CASIC First Academy. Established on July 1, 2002, as part of a CASIC reorganization, CASIC First Academy (also known as Academy of Information Technology) is one of a number of entities within China focused on operationally responsive tactical microsatellites that ostensibly could be launched on solid-fueled launch vehicles. The First Academy also engages in R&D satellite applications and GPS/inertial guidance units. Its most prominent products, the Qinghua-1 (HT-1) 50kg microsatellite, which operates in a sun synchronous orbit, and the 25kg NS-1 microsatellite, are serving as tests for MEMS-based guidance and navigation systems. One institute under the First Academy specializes in space-based and missile-borne electronic countermeasure research and development.[36]

CASIC Second Academy. Established alongside the First Academy in 1957, the Second Academy is China's main designer and producer of air and space defense systems and is demonstrating a growing emphasis on integrated air and space defense. It consists of a design department, ten specialized research institutes, a simulation center, three factories, and nine independent commercial enterprises. The PLA Air Force is a core customer, and the academy's most prominent defense products include the Hongqi-series of surface to air missile systems, including the missile, radar, and associated ground equipment. The Second Academy also probably designed, developed, and produced the KKV systems that were tested in January 2007 and January 2010.[37]

CASIC Third Academy. Also known as China Hai Ying (Sea Eagle) Electro-Mechanical Technology Academy, the Third Academy was established in 1961 and engages in research, design, development, and production of 20 different types of cruise missiles. The Third Academy has a design department, 10 research institutes and 2 factories, with more than 3,000 employees. Its traditional core customer has been the PLA Navy. However, its land attack cruise missile program has enabled a closer working relationship with the Second Artillery and Air Force. In the 1970s and 1980s, China's aviation industry made an attempt to enter the cruise missile development and production field. Today, however, it appears that the Third Academy has a near monopoly on the Chinese cruise missile market.

CASIC Fourth Academy. Established in 2002, the Fourth Academy has more than 5,000 employees and specializes in design, development, and manufacturing of the DF-21 medium-range ballistic missile (MRBM) and associated variants.[38] The Fourth Academy's business model marks an evolutionary departure from previous aerospace industrial practices.[39] Under its "small core, large collaboration" (*xiaohexin, daxiezuo*) philosophy, the Fourth Academy specializes in systems integration programs involving a complex supply chain. In the case of the DF-21C, for example, the Fourth Academy oversaw more than 20 subcontractors, of which fewer than half were within CASIC.

CASIC Sixth Academy. The Sixth Academy is CASIC's primary business division dedicated toward the design, development, and manufacturing of solid rocket motors.[40] Employing 5,000 workers in four research institutes and two factories, the CASIC Sixth Academy is situated in Hohhot, Inner Mongolia. With roots dating back to October 1956, when Qian Xuesen proposed development of solid-propelled missile systems, it began R&D in 1965. Its primary product has been 1.4 meter–diameter motors for the DF-21/JL-1 medium-range ballistic missile. Research institutes and factories in the Sixth Academy focus on specific facets of solid-fueled motors, such as casings, nozzles, grains, and igniters.

In theory, the Sixth Academy's main competitor would be its parent organization—the CASC's Fourth Academy, based in Xian. In 2002, China's senior leadership directed that the CASC Fourth Academy spin off its Hohhot subsidiary and create two competing divisions to vie for contracts related to advanced solid-propulsion systems, as well as restartable hybrid liquid-solid engines. As a new entrant to the defense market, the CASIC Sixth Academy reportedly raised private capital to cover R&D expenses for a new solid-fueled motor used for operationally responsive satellite launch vehicles.

CASIC Ninth Academy. The CASIC Ninth Academy, also known as 066 Base, was created in August 1969 as a third-line industry, specifically supplying the Third Academy with cruise missile components. A key landmark was establishment of a design shop in October 1975.[41] Its most prominent product is the DF-11 (NATO Designation: CSS-7) short-range ballistic missile. Based on a 1993 decision, 066 Base began work on an extended-range variant, the DF-11A, with the goal of doubling the range while keeping the same accuracy. The motor was viewed as the key subsystem. An initial static test of a new motor on February 24, 1995, resulted in failure. A second test in June 1995 based on an adjustment to the motor design succeeded. An initial design concept flight test was conducted on August 28, 1996. After a successful flight test on October 6, 1997, another test a few days later encountered problems. A test on June 24, 1998, discovered a problem with the warhead. However, the missile was successfully flight tested on August 15, 1998. The 066 Base is believed to have expanded its scope of work, and probably developed a follow-on variant to the DF-11A, notionally the DF-11B. Some 066 Base engineers have been cited as having conducted R&D into terminal guidance systems.[42]

Jiangnan Aerospace Group (061 Base). Founded in 1964, Jiangnan Aerospace Group, also known as 061 Base, employs more than 6,000 people, of whom 650 are technicians. Headquartered in Guizhou and with subordinate entities in Suzhou, 061 Base functions as a primary supplier of specialized missile components and software. Its 20 institutes and factories develop and produce missile-related guidance, navigation, and control software, composite materials, and a range of components, including aerospace-qualified fasteners, gyroscopes, autopilot systems, batteries, micromotors, and fuel gauges.[43]

Hunan Space Bureau (068 Base). The 068 Base was established in 1970 in Hunan's Shaoyang area as a third-line production complex. Currently centered in Changsha, its core competencies include special materials and components, such as magnets, diamond coatings, and antennas. More recently, the base has become a key center for R&D and production of reconnaissance platforms operating in near space.[44]

CHINA AEROSPACE SCIENCE AND TECHNOLOGY CORPORATION

The China Aerospace Science and Technology Corporation is China's other aerospace enterprise. Focused on strategic ballistic missile and space systems, CASC employs more than 100,000 engineers, technicians, and workers. Its functional business divisions specialize in ballistic missiles and space launch vehicles, large solid-fueled motors, liquid-fueled engines, and satellites. A new division was established in 2008 that consolidated CASC institutes and factories specializing in inertial measurement units, telemetry, and missile-related microelectronics, such as high-performance digital signal processors and field programmable gate arrays that are needed for long-range precision strikes at high speeds and extreme temperature conditions. A key advisory group for PLA, State Council, and CASC leadership is the CASC S&T Committee. In addition to a dedicated export management and international contracting entity (China Great Wall International Corporation), CASC also includes a unique business division that produces specific types of satellites, launch vehicles, and even, in the past, air defense systems.

CASC First Academy. Established on November 16, 1957, the CASC First Academy, also known as China Academy of Launch Technology, was the first organization dedicated to the design, development, and manufacturing of ballistic missile and space launch vehicle systems. Among its products are China's entire inventory of liquid-fueled ballistic missiles (e.g., the DF-4 and silo-based DF-5 ICBMs) and solid-fueled systems (e.g., DF-15 SRBM and DF-31/DF-31A ICBM). CASC First Academy short-range ballistic missile (SRBM) systems appear to have been in competition with designs developed by the CASIC 066 Base, and indications exist that CASC First Academy is developing MRBM designs to compete with CASIC Fourth Academy. The First Academy is also a leading organization in

China's manned space program. Subordinate research institutes specialize in guidance, navigation, and control subsystems, reentry vehicles, and launchers.[45]

The First Academy houses one of the defense technology establishment's most recent organizational innovations—a new design shop focused exclusively on hypersonic cruise vehicles operating in the realm of near space. The 10th Research Institute, also known as the Near Space Flight Vehicle Research Institute, specializes in the design and development of hypersonic flight vehicles that transit the upper atmosphere rather than adopting a traditional ballistic trajectory. The establishment of a separate research institute within China's premier launch vehicle and ballistic missile academy that focuses on one capability serves as a prominent indicator of the priority that senior civilian and military leaders place on the new generation of long-range precision strike vehicles.[46]

CASC Fourth Academy. Established in 1962, the Fourth Academy is responsible for solid rocket motor research, development, and manufacturing. It has more than 7,000 employees. Also known as the Academy of Aerospace Solid Propulsion Technology, the CASC Fourth Academy consists of a design department, five research institutes, and three production facilities involved in all aspects of solid rocket motor development. In addition to R&D on solid-fueled motors for the DF-31, DF-31A, JL-2, and possibly the DF-41, the Fourth Academy may be designing, developing, and producing motors for use on larger solid-fueled launch vehicles. Sources indicate work on a 2.5 meter–diameter motor and work on high-energy composite propellants. The Fourth Academy would be roughly analogous to Aerojet or Alliant Techsystems (ATK) Space Systems.

CASC Fifth Academy. Established in February 1968, the Fifth Academy, or China Academy of Space Technology (CAST), is China's primary organization engaged in satellite design, development, and manufacturing. Based in Beijing's northwestern suburbs, CAST's institutes, factories, and other enterprises are centered around its design department. Institutes specialize in attitude control, on-board communications and sensor subsystems, vacuum and cryogenic technologies, antenna systems, and modeling and simulation.[47]

CASC Sixth Academy (067 Base). With roots dating back to 1965 and established in its current form on April 26, 2002, the Sixth Academy (also known as Academy of Space Propellant Technology) is China's primary organization engaged in research, development, and production of liquid-fueled propulsion systems. Originally centered in the Qinling Mountains west of Xian, the 067 Base employs around 10,000 people in four research institutes and one factory; it is now headquartered in Xian. Among its more recent products are the YF-77 and

YF-100, currently China's most powerful liquid oxygen and kerosene rocket engines. It also is a key organization in the development of the LM-5 heavy-lift launch vehicle, expected to operate from Wenchang Satellite Launch Center on Hainan Island.

Sichuan Aerospace Corporation (062 Base). Established in 1965, the 062 Base employs 15,000 people and is a key CASC manufacturing hub for space systems and subsystems. Among its products are navigation, guidance, and control components, with a special interest in terminal guidance radar systems (including millimeter wave radar seekers). Subordinate factories also produce engine-related assemblies and support 068 Base with near space vehicle propulsion systems.

CASC Eighth Academy. Established in August 1961, the Eighth Academy (also known as the Shanghai Academy of Space Technology) is the Chinese aerospace industry's largest and most diverse business division. Employing around 16,800 people, the Shanghai space industry was in large part formed with the transfer there of several defense industry research institutes in the mid-1960s. One of its design departments focuses on launch vehicle systems, and another on weather, synthetic aperture radar, and electronic reconnaissance satellites. As a result, the Eighth Academy has some incentive to compete with CASC First Academy and Fifth Academy. The Eighth Academy is believed to have subcontracting relationships with key institutes under China Electronics Technology Corporation.

CASC Ninth Academy. The Ninth Academy, formed in part on the basis of China Aerospace Times Electronics Corporation, was created in March 2003 (and recreated in February 2009). It marked the consolidation of research and manufacturing entities involved in electronic components, on-board computers, and inertial guidance systems. Most of these entities had been subordinated to the CASC First Academy. It employs 15,000 personnel. One of its primary institutes designs and develops military-standard very large scale integrated circuit ceramic packages and mounts, radiation-hardened ICs, digital signal processors, and analogue to digital and digital to analogue converters. The CASC Ninth Academy may serve as a main supplier of sensitive microelectronic components used on Chinese missile and space systems, to a greater extent than China's defense electronics industry.

CASC Eleventh Academy. The Eleventh Academy was formed on the basis of the 701st Research Institute, or the Beijing Institute of Aerodynamics. Employing around 1,000 people, its primary function is aerodynamic testing; but it also designs, develops, and produces a range of components. Its relationship with the GAD's China Aerodynamic Research and Development Center in Mianyang is unknown.

    Shenzhen Academy of Aerospace Technology. Established in 2000, the Shenzhen Academy of Aerospace Technology is a joint venture between CASC, the Shenzhen City government, and Harbin Institute of Technology. It specializes in radio frequency identification, digital trunking communication systems, GPS vehicle location, radio frequency monitoring systems, as well as systems integration services. Shenzhen is expected to develop and produce a number of navigation satellites on behalf of the Fifth Academy.[48]

In summary, China's aerospace industry, made up of two large enterprises, is well established as a leader in defense industrial technology globally. The industry has been experimenting with various organizational structures, appearing to introduce competition in some cases while continuing to allow monopolies in other areas. One key organizational reform has been spinning off lower tier component and subassembly suppliers previously subordinate to lead systems integrators, such as the CASC First Academy, and reassigning them under separate, competing business divisions. In addition to traditional competitions in SRBM and satellite design, competitions now appear to exist in the design, development, and manufacturing of control and guidance packages and propulsion systems.

    A final note: a prominent characteristic of both CASIC and CASC is the relative youth of its leadership. Almost all corporate-level and academy executives are well under 60 years old, and most are in their 40s. The older generation they replaced appears to have moved into science and technology advisory board positions. One explanation is that much of China's education system, particularly the institutions specializing in aerospace engineering (Harbin Institute of Technology, Beijing University of Astronautics and Aeronautics, etc.), ground to a halt during the Cultural Revolution from 1966 until 1978. As a result, the generation now leading the aerospace industry received their undergraduate degrees in the early- to mid-1980s, served as senior designers on major programs in the 1990s, then moved into management positions in the first decade of the 2000s, after about 20 years of engineering and mid-level management experience. Few from this generation appear to have been educated in the United States or Europe. However, a large portion of the engineers and managers now working in R&D centers and design departments, research institutes, and manufacturing facilities likely have had more international experience.

Case Study: The Anti-Ship Ballistic Missile

The innovative capacity of the aerospace industry may best be illustrated by the design and development of complex long-range precision strike systems such as the anti-ship ballistic missile (ASBM). Judging from the technological foundation established by national-level technology development efforts such as the 863 Program, the PLA appears to have issued a requirement for technology to disrupt US carrier battle group operations in the wake of the 1996 Taiwan Strait crisis. One senior Chinese space engineer with direct access to details on both the ASBM and anti-satellite (ASAT) programs confirmed that their guidance and control packages share the same technologies.[49]

As an initial step in developing innovative means to satisfy operational requirements, the PLA's General Staff Department, the armed services, and the General Armament Department most likely sponsored a series of preliminary conceptual studies. Studies published by the aerospace industry and engineering organizations within the Second Artillery indicate that an ASBM capability appears to be only one facet of a longer-term vision outlined by GSD, Second Artillery, and GAD planners. Based on a broad survey of available literature, indications exist that operational concepts drove a phased approach for developing a conventional global strike capability by 2025.

The initial phase appears to involve a rudimentary capability to strike stationary and mobile targets on land and at sea at a range of up to 2,000 kilometers which was to be available by the conclusion of the 11th Five-Year Plan (2006–2010). A second phase would seek to extend these capabilities to a range of 3,000 kilometers by the conclusion of the 12th Five-Year Plan (2011–2015). Among the options for achieving the capabilities are a more advanced solid motor and a flatter "boost-glide" trajectory. A third phase would focus on extending a conventional precision strike capability out to 8,000 kilometers before the end of the 13th Five-Year Plan in 2020, and a global precision strike capability by the end of the 14th Five-Year Plan in 2025.[50]

The Chinese R&D community probably has been gradually accumulating the enabling technologies for an ASBM capability for more than 20 years. Like China's ASAT and anti-ballistic missile programs, the technological foundation for an ASBM has been the 863 and 973 Programs. Preliminary research for the ASAT kinetic kill vehicle was funded under the 863-4 Program. At least one funding source for ASAT guidance and control research during the late 1990s and earlier this decade appears to be the 863-409 program (and possibly the 863-706 program). Presumably, common technologies include passive imaging infrared terminal guidance and automated target recognition software. Among the research entities involved during the initial R&D of an ASAT kinetic kill vehicle—euphemistically referred to as a space interceptor—was the aerospace industry's Harbin Institute of Technology.[51]

CASC First Academy produced one particularly compelling conceptual design study that appeared to have validated the feasibility of penetrating midcourse missile defense systems and striking moving targets at sea. Confident of potential success, the GAD and the Second Artillery notionally began to evaluate potential lead systems integrators. Third Academy cruise missile designers highlighted the feasibility of an alternative option—extended-range cruise missiles flying a modified high-altitude trajectory—for striking large, slow moving targets at sea. The tone and content of articles published on the subject implied a competitive environment. Journals associated with the shipbuilding industry echoed the views of cruise missile designers, but they also published feasibility studies on the use of submarine-launched anti-ship ballistic missiles.

Successful testing and fielding of a terminally guided MRBM—the DF-21C—by 2005 probably increased confidence that it would be possible to modify the DF-21 guidance, navigation, and control system to enable engagement of maritime targets. Under the leadership of the CASIC Fourth Academy's design department's chief designer, Hou Shiming, the DF-21C was revised to incorporate a terminal guidance package that uses on-board computers to correlate stored images with land marks and that theoretically could achieve a circular error probability of 50 meters or better.[52] The 1,800 kilometer–range US Pershing 2 missile appears to have been used as a model, including the critical technologies for a maneuverable reentry vehicle and automated target recognition software.[53] Fourth Academy director Li Yue probably served as program manager. The first successful flight test of the terminally guided DF-21C MRBM was on December 19, 2002. The test revealed problems with the reentry vehicle, and a second test took place about six months later, in June or July 2003. All in all, the DF-21C program took two years from the time a decision was made to initiate formal R&D until design finalization in 2003.[54] The CASIC Fourth Academy is said to have overseen more than 20 subcontractors, of which fewer than half were within CASIC.

It is likely that the GAD's S&T Committee and other advisory boards offered formal opinions to the Central Military Commission as part of the final decision making process. Among potential lead systems integrators considered for the ASBM may have been the three business divisions with proven records in producing ballistic missile systems: CASIC Fourth Academy, CASC First Academy, which had been a key player in design feasibility studies, and the CASIC 066 Base. In the end, the CASIC Fourth Academy may have been selected for R&D and manufacturing based on the selected ASBM airframe, the DF-21. Theoretically speaking, a proven guidance, navigation, and control package capable of acquiring and engaging maritime targets could be integrated with other ballistic missile systems, such as the DF-11, DF-15, new MRBM variants, or perhaps even longer-range systems, assuming that speed could be controlled and external cueing systems were available to support targets at longer ranges.[55]

With CMC approval and the Second Artillery Equipment Department overseeing R&D and manufacturing contracts, the CASIC Fourth Academy's design department most likely served as lead systems integrator. The engineers of the Second Artillery Equipment Department's Equipment Research Academy ostensibly exercised technical oversight of the R&D and manufacturing. A deputy director of CASIC or the Fourth Academy notionally could serve as program manager; that person would manage the Second Artillery–GAD contract, coordinate scheduling of developmental flights with GAD and Second Artillery sponsors, and ensure that timelines and milestones were met. Leveraging a broad supply chain probably residing within CASIC and CASC, the chief designer would serve as technical leader of a design team responsible for various subsystems and tasks, such as solid rocket motor, guidance, navigation, and control subsystems, launcher, testing, and manufacturing.

The engineering tasks associated with guidance, navigation, and control would presumably be most challenging. Technical studies outline integration of an autonomous high-altitude target acquisition system and low-altitude terminal guidance system using millimeter wave and/or infrared imaging. Engineers recorded challenges associated with on-board sensors that needed to be able to withstand extreme environmental conditions (extreme heat, extreme cold, and gravity forces), process information at lightning speed, and generate sufficient radio frequency power to acquire and track a moving target at sea as early as possible in its flight.[56]

One CASC First Academy simulation from 2001 modeled a ballistic missile for optimal altitudes and for activating a high-altitude target acquisition system. If a missile started a glide and speed control measures at 200 kilometer altitude, at 80 kilometers in altitude, the reentry vehicle would activate its on-board radar system to acquire the target and allow for more refined course corrections. However, in a published discussion about the model, engineers note that the high-altitude engine burn time would be too long, thus exposing the reentry vehicle to missile defenses. The authors argue for a shorter glide duration.[57]

One particularly innovative technology the Chinese aerospace engineers appear to be developing is missile-borne synthetic aperture radar (SAR) for autonomous navigation, target acquisition, and tracking of mobile targets from high altitudes.[58] Like most radar systems, a SAR system transmits a radiofrequency pulse toward a target or area, and then collects the reflected signal. However, SAR helps to create a comprehensive image by observing the target from a variety of angles. A digital signal processor helps to store the images. The range of a SAR sensor would depend upon a range of factors, such as transmitter power, frequency used (e.g., S-, C-, X-, or Ka-Band), antenna dimensions, detector sensitivity, as well as the size of the target. With microelectronics, power sources, and computing as enabling technologies, Western technical analysts view SAR's ability to provide a high-resolution image in any weather at long ranges as an optimal solution for precision strike.[59]

China's aerospace industry appears to be investing significant resources into fielding a missile-born SAR capability that would be integrated with satellite positioning and inertial navigation systems. Intimately connected to China's air- and space-based SAR programs, the advantages of missile-borne SAR include all-weather capability, high resolution, extended-range imaging, and autonomous guidance. During flight, a SAR seeker could penetrate cloud cover to acquire a maritime surface target and could then turn it over to another active or passive seeker in the terminal flight phase. An on-board SAR system would be activated after slowing the missile down to below hypersonic speeds (e.g., below Mach 5, depending on various factors).[60] A number of technical studies also discuss integrated high-altitude and low-altitude guidance systems.[61]

Obstacles to utilizing SAR for missile navigation and guidance include the high speed of the missile, sudden changes in speed and motion, and high "squint" angles. As a general rule, the SAR sensor should operate while the vehicle is on a linear, constant-altitude flight path. As a result, missile-borne SAR presents significant technical challenges. Chinese engineers highlight the need for a highly accurate and high-speed inertial measurement unit to compensate for the motion of the missile and the unpredictable quality of SAR components. Engineers also have developed electronic warfare simulations to improve survivability of on-board SAR systems.[62] In terms of cost, technical commentators have noted that a radar package may be the most expensive aspect of an extended-range precision strike program.[63]

The deputy chief designer for an ASBM's guidance, navigation, and control subsystem, including a missile-borne SAR system, would ostensibly be under the purview of CASIC's 17th Research Institute, CASC's 12th Research Institute in its First Academy, or 066 Base's Hongfeng Machine Factory in Hubei. The supply chain may rely on a wide range of vendors, including component suppliers, such as the CASC Tenth Academy for microprocessors. The CASIC Sixth Academy may supply solid rocket motors for the DF-21D ASBM, and indications exist that modifications to the DF-21C solid rocket motor may have been necessary. It is likely that final assembly of the missile is carried out at the CASIC Fourth Academy's 307 Factory in Nanjing.

With the selection of the design team and establishment of the supply chain responsibilities, the Second Artillery probably formed a test and evaluation, or "seed," unit consisting mostly of specialized engineers. The seed unit may have been collocated with a well-established operational DF-21 brigade, and its members may have spent substantive time with the chief designer's team in Beijing, as well as with key institutes and factories throughout the country which support the ASBM program. Upon completion of successful CASIC developmental flight testing, the Second Artillery seed unit, in conjunction with the aerospace industry design team and Equipment Research Academy, would conduct operational flights of the missile system. Once the system's design is finalized and enters low-rate initial production, the seed unit would transform into an operational launch brigade and relocate to permanent garrison locations. At the same time, the GAD and Second Artillery may initiate formal R&D on a follow-on variant.

Conclusions

In sum, the PRC's aerospace industry appears increasingly capable of meeting long-term PLA operational demands. Through its participation in key advisory groups, such as the GAD S&T Committee and 863 Program, the industry may push adoption of innovative technologies even in the absence of strategic or operational demands. Given the political support defense technology is receiving at senior levels, with a more efficient and effective organization system it may prove a key force in propelling innovative technological advances, such as long-range precision strike and counterspace systems. Success in design, fielding, and supporting a terminally guided ballistic missile capable of engaging moving targets may serve as a prime example of China's emerging innovative capacity in defense technology.

NOTES

1. In his detailed study of China's defense economy, Tai Ming Cheung, identifies several barriers to success. These include: compartmentalization, decision-making fragmentation and rigidity as a result of central planning, insufficient information sharing, lack of incentives for innovation and protection of intellectual property rights, the dispersed nature of many research and production facilities, and political infighting. See Tai Ming Cheung, *Fortifying China; The Struggle to Build a Modern Defense Economy* (Ithaca, NY: Cornell University Press, 2009), 36–40.

2. A disruptive technology or disruptive innovation is a technological innovation, product, or service that uses a "disruptive" strategy, rather than an "evolutionary" or "sustaining" strategy, and overturns the existing dominant technologies or status quo products in a market. See Joseph L. Bower and Clayton M. Christensen, "Disruptive Technologies: Catching the Wave," *Harvard Business Review*, January–February 1995; and Clayton M. Christensen, *The Innovator's Dilemma* (Cambridge, MA: Harvard Business School Press, 1997).

3. See China's Defense White Paper (*China's National Defense in 2008*), January 20, 2009, at http://news.xinhuanet.com/english/2009-01/20/content_10688124_1.htm, accessed on August 29, 2009.

4. For a detailed assessment of US programs, see Xie Wu, "Four Major Challenges Facing an Accelerated US 'Prompt Global Strike Program,'" (美"快速全球打击" 难获快速发展 面临四大难题), *China Daily*, June 11, 2010, at http://www.chinadaily.com.cn/hqjs/jsyw/2010-06-11/content_446614_2.html.

5. For an overview of the technological imperative theory, see Barry Buzan and Eric Herring, *The Arms Dynamic in World Politics* (Boulder, CO: Lynne Rienner, 1998). Also see Hasan Ozbekhan, "The Triumph of Technology: Can Implies Ought," in Joseph P. Martino, ed., *An Introduction to Technological Forecasting* (New York: Gordon and Breach, 1972), 83–92.

6. For a detailed explanation comparing and contrasting the Soviet and Chinese defense industrial models, see Evan S. Medeiros, Roger Cliff, Keith Crane, and James C. Mulvenon, *A New Direction for China's Defense Industry* (Santa Monica, CA: RAND Corp., 2005), 18–22.

7. See Mark Stokes, "China's Commercial Aviation Sector Looks to the Future," *Project 2049 Futuregram*, March 2009.

8. More specifically, the GAD Comprehensive Planning Department (综合计划部) probably is responsible for overall force modernization planning and policy. Bureaus within the GAD Service probably function as coordinating bodies. For a good overview of GAD, see Harlan Jencks, "The General Armaments Department," in James C. Mulvenon and Andrew N. D. Yang, eds., *The PLA as Organization* (Washington, DC: RAND

Corp., 2002), http://www.rand.org/pubs/conf_proceedings/CF182/CF182.ch7.pdf. As of June 2011, the GAD director is Chang Wanquan. Born in January 1949, Chang Wanquan serves as GAD director. Chang has previously served as commander of 47th Group Army and Lanzhou and Beijing Military Region Chief of Staff, and subsequently Shenyang Military Region commander. He replaced Chen Bingde as GAD director in July 2007 and was appointed to the Central Military Commission in 2008.

9. Harlan W. Jencks, "COSTIND Is Dead, Long Live COSTIND! Restructuring China's Defense Scientific, Technical, and Industrial Sector," in James C. Mulvenon and Richard H. Yang. eds., *The People's Liberation Army in the Information Age* (Santa Monica, CA: RAND Corp., 2004), 59–77; Medeiros et al., *A New Direction for China's Defense Industry.*

10. Bao Weimin, director of the CASC First Academy's new 10th Research Institute (Near Space Flight Vehicle Institute), serves as director. He is dual-hatted as CASC First Academy S&T Committee director, and deputy director of the GAD Precision Guidance Experts Group.

11. The Precision Guidance Expert Group has been headed by Chen Dingchang, former CASIC Second Academy director. See "Introduction to Comrade Chen Dingchang," China Aerospace Science and Industry Corporation, September 20, 2008, at http://www.casic.com.cn/n16/n1250/n10984/n17506/17672.html. Bao Weimin serves as deputy director. The 863-801 program appears to be aligned with the GAD Precision Guidance Experts Group.

12. Qinghua University professor You Zheng leads the GAD MEMS technology expert group. He also served as chief designer for China's Naxing-1 [NS-1] and other microsatellite programs, a cooperative effort between Qinghua University and CASIC First Academy. Weighing just 25kgs, the NS-1 microsatellite was launched in April 2004 and is believed to have served as a major platform for testing of defense-related MEMS systems. See "You Zheng presentation," Qinghua University, June 21, 2010, at http://join-tsinghua.edu.cn/bkzsw/detail.jsp?seq=4003&boardid=35.

13. Among prominent members of the communications, navigation, and tracking technology working group is Xidian University's Li Jiandong.

14. China Electronics Technology Corporation director Wang Zhigang directs this GAD experts group.

15. Director of the GAD Stealth Technology Steering Group is Wu Zhe. Born in 1957, Wu is from the Beijing University of Aeronautics and Astronautics.

16. "Regulations for Leaders of Key National Defense S&T Labs," July 11, 2008; and "Management Methodology for Key National Defense S&T Labs," July 11, 2008, COSTIND announcements.

17. For a good summary of China's evolving defense industrial policy, see Tai Ming Cheung, "The Remaking of the Chinese Defense Industry and the Rise of the Dual-Use Economy," testimony before the US-China Economic and Security Review Commission Hearing on China's Proliferation and the Impact of Trade Policy on Defense Industries in the United States and China, July 13 2007. Also see Tai Ming Cheung, "The Chinese Defense Economy's Long March from Imitation to Innovation," *Study of Innovation and Technology in China*, Policy Brief No. 3, September 2010, at http://igcc.ucsd.edu/research/security/SITC/SITCpolicybrief03.pdf.

18. Among various sources, see Cheung, "Remaking of the Chinese Defense Industry and the Rise of the Dual-Use Economy," For another good overview of China's defense industrial reforms, see Medeiros et al., *A New Direction for China's Defense Industry*. Also see James Mulvenon and Rebecca Samm Tyroler-Cooper, "China's Defense Industry on the Path of Reform," Defense Group Inc. (DGI) Center for Intelligence Research and Analysis, report prepared for the US-China Economic and Security Review Commission, October 2009, at http://www.uscc.gov/researchpapers/2009/DGIReportonPRCDefenseIndustry—FinalVersion_10Nov2009.pdf.

19. Jiang Wei, "China Opens Military Industry to Private Businesses," *China Daily*, August 7, 2007. Taiwan has taken similar measures. The military there has an inherent mistrust of local defense industry, whether state-owned or private. However, when given a choice, it has demonstrated a bias towards state-owned.

20. China's defense industry is said to have made a profit of U.S. $2.6 billion in 2006, representing a 50% year-on-year increase over 2005.

21. Among various references, see Zhang Qingwei and Yin Xingliang, "Qian Xuesen's Road to China Aerospace Technology Development" (钱学森为中国航天指出正确技术发展道路), *Guangming Daily*, November 7, 2005, at http://www.gmw.cn/01gmrb/2005-11/17/content_332447.htm; and "Commemorating the Birthday of Marshal Nie Rongzhen and the Founding of the Aerospace Industry," *Xinhua*, November 20, 2009, at http://zt.xinhua023.com/2009/yrz110/2009-11/20/content_429123.htm.

22. Chen Guolin, Wu Pengwei, Leng Wenjun, Chen Guolin, and Wu Pengwei, "Discussion of National Defense Science and Technology Preliminary-Research Management" (国防装备预先研究管理初探), *Ship Science and Technology*, December 2007, 180–183.

23. The GAD Integrated Planning Department is responsible for developing and coordinating China's national-level defense-related five-year and longer-range plans, establishing priorities, and managing the portion of the overall defense R&D budget allocated for basic research. The Second Artillery Equipment Department has a similar second-level department that oversees R&D and preliminary research contracts.

24. The GAD-managed areas of the 863 Program are referred to as *junkou* (军口). For an excellent overview of the 863 Program, see Evan A. Feigenbaum, "Who's Behind China's High-Technology 'Revolution'?" *International Security* 24, no. 1 (Summer 1999).

25. For example, Zhejiang University has been actively involved in two related basic research programs, the 863-801 and 863-805 programs (863-801主题以及863-805重大专项主题).

26. Feng Jing, "863 Program Spurs Science and Technology," *Beijing Review*, March 29, 2001.

27. For example, the 863 Program's Precision Guidance Expert Group has been headed by Chen Dingchang, former CASIC Second Academy director. See "Introduction to Chen Dingchang," at http://www.casic.com.cn/n16/n1250/n10984/n17506/17672.html. Bao Weimin, director of the CASC First Academy's new 10th Research Institute, serves as deputy. Other key players in this group include Yao Yu, head of the Harbin Institute of Technology; Yin Xinliang, former Second Academy director, CASIC director, and currently deputy chairman of CASIC's S&T Advisory Group; Zhang Tianxu, an automatic target recognition expert from Huazhong S&T University's Institute for Pattern Recognition and Artificial Intelligence; and Zeng Guangshang from the CASC First

Academy's 18th Research Institute. The 863-801 program appears to be aligned with the GAD Precision Guidance Experts Group, with Yao Yu, for example, serving on both the 863-801 and Precision Guidance Expert Groups. Another expert, Long Teng from Beijing Ligong University, also has been on the 863-801 expert group and also sits on the GAD Radar Surveillance Experts Group (总装备部雷达探测专业组) and Satellite Application Expert Group (总装备部卫星应用专业组). He Songhua from Hunan University has been on a number of GAD committees, with a particular focus on millimeter wave seeker technology, and also was a consultant to the CASIC Second Academy's Second Design Department.

28. "Regulations for Contracting Defense S&T Preliminary Research Projects," COSTIND announcement, May 17, 1989.

29. *China Today: Defense Science and Technology* (Beijing: National Defense Industry Press, 1993), 155–156.

30. See General Work Regulations on Weapons Systems R&D Designer System and Program Management System (武器装备研制设计师系统和行政指挥系统工作条例). The regulations have been in place since 1984 and are unlikely to have changed since then.

31. For general background on the academy, see "How Did the Second Artillery Corps Create More than 6,000 S&T Results?" (二炮 6000余项科研成果是如何创造的？), *PLA Daily*, February 11, 2009, at http://news.xinhuanet.com/mil/2009-02/11/content_10798697. htm, accessed on May 30, 2010.

32. See "Report on Second Artillery Representative Offices" (来自二炮军代室的报告), *PLA Daily*, April 25, 2001, at http://health.eastday.com/epublish/gb/paper200/1 /class020000007/hwz274633.htm. The Second Artillery's Equipment Research Academy and the research labs within the Second Artillery's Engineering Academy provide support to Second Artillery headquarters staff in the development of technical requirements documentation. For example, the academy's Operations Support Department has produced a number of studies on anti-ship ballistic and anti-satellite technologies. Authors of articles on ASBM and ASAT requirements include Tan Shoulin, Wang Minghai, Li Xinqi, Zhang Daqiao, and Tang Baoguo. Most are affiliated with the Engineering Academy's 603th Instruction and Research Lab. The Department of Automated Control's 303 Lab has performed technical analysis on near space flight vehicles.

33. See "Reforming the Aviation Industrial System from the Perspective of the Space Industrial Management System" (从航天 工业管理体制特点看航空工业体制改革), China National Space Administration website, January 20, 2009, at http://www.cnsa.gov.cn /n615708/n2259527/167282.html. For an outstanding perspective on shifts in the aviation industry, see Tai Ming Cheung, "Remaking Cinderella: The Nature and Development of China's Aviation Industry," testimony before the US-China Economic and Security Review Commission, Hearing on China's Emergent Military Aerospace and Commercial Aviation Capabilities, May 20, 2010, at http://www.uscc.gov/hearings /2010hearings/written_testimonies/10_05_20_wrt/10_05_20_cheung_statement.php.

34. See Kevin Pollpeter, "The Stars of China's Space Program: The Rise of a 'Space Gang'?" *China Brief* 7, no. 17 (September 19, 2007); and Mark Stokes, "China's Commercial Aviation Sector Looks to the Future," *Project 2049 Futuregram*, March 13, 2009.

35. For background on CASIC, see http://www.casic.com.cn/n16/index.html. The CEO and president of CASIC is Xu Dazhe. Born in 1956 and with roots in the CASC First

Academy's 15th Research Institute and 211 Factory, Xu moved up the ladder within the First Academy and CASC. He was appointed as head of the First Academy in 2000. In 2007, senior industry leadership promoted him to CASIC to assume the senior position. His senior deputy is Gao Hongwei, also born in 1956 and with roots in the 066 Base and Third Academy (cruise missiles). Other deputies include Cheng Wen, Fang Xiangming, Li Yue, and Cao Jianguo.

36. The mentioned institute is the 8511 Institute, formed in 1978 in Nanjing. It is the aerospace industry's main electronic and infrared countermeasures entity and manages an integrated test and manufacturing facility in Nanjing's Jiangning Science Park.

37. Zhang Yiqun, assigned to the CASIC Second Academy Second Design Department, is a possible subsystem designer for the anti-satellite missile defense KKV. Cited as a deputy chief designer of an unnamed system, Zhang was granted a national "model worker" award in April 2010. For one account, see "Preliminary Analysis on China's Ground-Based Mid-Course Missile Defense Intercept Technology" (中国 "陆基中段反导拦截技术试验" 初步分析), Chinese Military Network, January 13, 2010, at http://military.china.com/zh_cn/critical3/27/20100113/15774945.html.

38. The CASIC Fourth Academy director is Pan Xudong, who replaced the 47-year-old Shen Weiwei sometime in 2008. Shen had previously served as the Third Academy's deputy director. Yang Xiling and Yang Shaohua are deputy directors. Unlike other academies within China's space and missile industry, few details on the Third Academy's executives are available.

39. The Fourth Design Department was formerly subordinate to the Second Academy, one of the few academies that has managed more than one subordinate design department.

40. See http://www.casic.com.cn:81/n16/n40241/n489066/n490094/n490261/541465.html.

41. "Xiong Wei Explores the Infinite Possibilities of Life" (熊 玮 探寻人生的无限可能), *China Space News*, July 13, 2007, at http://www.china-spacenews.com/n435777/n435778/n435788/34605.html, accessed on May 29, 2010.

42. See "Making Friends with Researcher Wu Chunfeng from CASIC Ninth Academy" [航天科工集团第9研究院研究员武春风校友], Alumni Profiles, Harbin Institute of Technology, at http://today.hit.edu.cn/articles/2010/06-04/0614513311.htm. Wu is an advisor to the Second Artillery on terminal seeker technology.

43. The 302 Research Institute at 061 Base functions as one of five software development centers under CASIC. Its core competency may be surface-to-air missile components, which would make it a key supplier for CASIC Second Academy. Suzhou is located within a regional cluster of microelectronics R&D and production entities. As a supplier of components, it may face competition from other entities inside CASIC itself. For example, one manufacturing entity directly under the cognizance of CASIC headquarters, the 694 Factory (Xinyang Aerospace Fastener Co.), also specializes in aerospace fasteners, with particular focus on titanium alloy technology.

44. The 068 Base opened its Near Space Flight Vehicle Development Center in 2005 and an Advanced Materials and Equipment Development Center in June 2009.

45. Among the programs currently under development are said to be the LM-5 and possibly the DF-41. The LM-5 is said to be designed to lift a 25-ton payload to low earth

orbit (LEO) or a 14-ton payload into geostationary transfer orbit (GTO). New facilities are said to be under construction in the Tianjin area, in order to transport the vehicle to its new launch site on Hainan Island. One of the senior designers of the DF-31 was Liu Baoyong, who worked in the First Academy's First Design Department. Among the programs currently under development are said to be the LM-5 and possibly a new mobile solid-fueled ICBM.

46. The 10th Research Institute's director, who served as a chief designer of a major solid-fueled ballistic missile system, also heads the PLA's GAD General Missile Technology Expert Working Group and serves as deputy director of the GAD Precision Guidance Expert Working Group.

47. CAST's Dongfanghong Satellite Company appears to be a significant commercial entity. The enterprise is a publicly traded company that offers satellite-related solutions to military and civil users. Its activities include manufacturing of satellite ground equipment and providing satellite services, such as satellite integrated applications, satellite navigation, satellite remote sensing and image transmission, satellite communication, and television broadcasting. It has eight subsidiaries, including ones in Xiamen, Yungang, and Xian.

48. The Shenzhen Academy has a relationship with a number of organizations, including the Bauman Institute in Russia, Samara State Aerospace University, Russian Academy of Sciences (Far East Branch), Far East Technical University, Novosibirsk State Technical University, National Technical University of Ukraine, and Saint Petersburg Electrotechnical University.

49. See "Qi Faren: Anti-Satellite Technology Can Be Used to Attack Aircraft Carrier," *Ming Pao*, March 5, 2007, A4.

50. For further background, see Mark Stokes, "China's Evolving Conventional Strategic Strike Capability: The Anti-Ship Ballistic Missile Challenge to U.S. Maritime Operations in the Western Pacific and Beyond," Project 2049 Institute Occasional Paper, September 2009.

51. The 863-4 series of projects is referred to as Advanced Defense (先进防御). A grouping of special research topics under an 863 subject area is known as a *zhuanti* (Key 863-409 group members include Chen Dingchang and Huang Chunping from Harbin Institute of Technology, Yang Guoguang from Zhejiang University, and Xiao Wen from the CASC First Academy, who served as deputy designer of the 409 KKV. Others include Shi Xiaoping from Harbin Institute of Technology, Lin Xiangdi from the Southwest University of Science and Technology, Wan Ziming from the Second Academy Second Design Department, and Zhou Jun from Northwest Polytechnical University, who played a leading role in establishing his university's Opto-Electronic and Imaging Precision Guidance Lab (光电和图像精确制导实验室). "Report on Recent Research Advances in Micro-Optics" ('微光学的应用及其最新研究进展'学术报告), announcement, China Jiliang University College of Information Engineering, September 11, 2006, at http://xxgcxy.cjlu.edu.cn/ReadNews.asp?NewsID=609. Chinese engineers on technical bulletin board sites indicate that the KKV "space interceptor" may have been a 35kg microsatellite equipped with experimental imaging infrared and millimeter wave terminal homing package.

52. Born in November 1937, Hou had previously served under Huang Weilu as deputy chief designer of the JL-1 sea-launched ballistic missile. He became head of the

Fourth Department in 1993. See "Space Personalities," Hou Shiming, at http://www
.54sh.com/special/universe/hangtianrenwu3.html.

53. See for example, Huang Pinqiu, "Initial Analysis on the Pershing 2 Missile War-head," *Missiles and Space Vehicles* (1994), 1. Huang was from the CASC First Academy's
14th Research Institute.

54. See "Extreme Urgency: The Fourth Academy Succeeds in Finalizing Design of a
Key Conventional Program Within Two Years" (十万火急: 航天四院重点常规型号两年实现定型),
China Space News, May 27, 2006. Also see "CASIC Fourth Academy Success in Certain
Key Program's Flight Test," *China Space News*, August 20, 2003. A key senior designer
inside the Fourth Department is Zhong Shiyong. Janes reported that a DF-21 test involv-
ing missile defense countermeasures took place in July 2002.

55. For general discussions on terminal guidance systems, see Zhang Yiguang and
Zhou Chengping, "Technological Trends Associated with Surface-to-Surface Ballistic
Missile Precision Guidance," *Tactical Missile Control Technology*, no. 4 (2004): 58–60.
The authors are from the 066 Base's design department and Huazhong University.

56. See for example Chen Haidong and Yu Menglun, "Concept for Maneuvering
Re-Entry Vehicle Integrated Guidance" (机动再入飞行器的复合制导方案研究), *Journal of
Astronautics* 22, no. 5 (September 2001): 72–76.

57. Ibid.

58. For one of the best overviews of SAR, see Gao Feng, "The Application of Radar
Homing Technology in Long-Range Precision-Guided Missiles" (雷达寻的技术在远程精确制
导导弹中的应用), *Aerospace Shanghai*, no. 5 (2004): 25–29. Gao is from the Shanghai Academy of Space Technology (CASC Eighth Academy) 802nd Research Institute. This organization specializes in missile guidance systems. Among other various sources, see Zou
Weibao, Ren Sicong, and Li Zhilin, "Application of SAR in Combined Navigation System
for Vehicle," *Aerospace Control*, no. 1 (2002); Jiang Jinlong, Mu Rongjun, and Cui Nai-
gang, "Application of SAR in Terminal Guidance of Ballistic Missile," *Journal of Ballistics*,
no. 2 (2008); and Zhang Junchang, Hou Yibin, Zou Weibao, and Gao Shesheng, "Study of
Tactical Ballistic Missile with Integrated Guidance System SINS/GNSS/SAR," *Journal of
Projectiles, Rockets, Missiles and Guidance*, no. 4 (2000). For a design study associated
with a DSP for SAR signal processing (TS203), see He Zhiming, Zhu Jiang, and Zhou Bo,
"Research on Real Time Signal Processing of Missile-Borne SAR System," *Journal of Electronics and Information Technology* 30, no. 4 (April 2008). The authors are from the University of Electronic Science and Technology. CASIC's Third Academy 35th Research
Institute also is said to be involved in missile-borne (弹载) SAR guidance R&D, as are
engineers from the PLA Navy and PLA Air Force. For the aviation community, the Lei-
hua Electronic Technology Research Institute in Wuxi appears to be doing work in use of
SAR for air-to-air missiles.

59. William H. Licata, "Missile Seekers for Strike Warfare beyond the Year 2000,"
paper presented at the NATO Research and Technology Organization (RTO) SCI Lec-
ture Series Technologies for Future Precision Strike Missile Systems, Tbilisi, Georgia,
June 18–19, 2001; Bucharest, Romania, June 21–22, 2001; Madrid, Spain, June 25–26,
2001; Stockholm, Sweden, June 28–29, 2001.

60. For general overviews of SAR systems, see Wang Qiang, Huang Jianchong, and
Jiang Qiuxi, "The Chief Development Trends of Synthetic Aperture Radar" (合成孔径雷达

的主要发展方向), *Modern Defense Technology* (April 2007): 81–88. The authors are from the PLA's Institute of Electronic Engineering in Hefei, Anhui province. Also see Qin Yuliang, Wang Jiantao, Wang Hongqiang, and Li Xiang, "Overview of Missile-Borne Synthetic Aperture Radar" (弹载合成孔径雷达技术研究综述), *Signal Processing* (April 2009): 630–635. The authors are from the National University of Defense Technology, which hosts the National Laboratory for Precision Guidance and Automated Target Recognition (精确制导自动目标识别国家重点实验室).

61. See for example, Chen and Yu, "Concept for Maneuvering Re-Entry Vehicle Integrated Guidance," 72–76.

62. Zhang Hongrong, Tang Yuesheng, Wu Guan, and Long Sun, "SAR Deceptive Jamming Signal Simulation," conference paper presented at the 1st Asian and Pacific Conference on Synthetic Aperture Radar, 2007. *APSAR 2007*, November 5–9, 2007, 61–64. The authors are from the East China Research Institute of Electronic Engineering in Hefei.

63. In one Chinese analysis, the ASBM radar is judged to be as sophisticated and costly as the AN/APG-77 active electronically scanned array (AESA) radar. With the radar accounting for about half of the cost, the authors estimate that the unit cost of an ASBM including the launcher would be US $5-10.5 million. See Qiu Zhenwei and Long Haiyan, "A Discussion of China's Development of an Anti-Ship Ballistic Missile," *Modern Ships*, no. 12 (2006) 12(B); and Qiu Zhenwei and Long Haiyan, "930 Seconds—A Discussion on China's Development of an Anti-Ship Ballistic Missile (Operational Scenario)," *Modern Ships*, no. 7 (2007) 1(B).

Conclusions

Tai Ming Cheung

China's national leaders fervently believe that the possession of an advanced, innovative, and self-reliant defense technological and industrial base is an essential pillar in the building of the country's great power status. They fear that without such a capability, the country would be strategically vulnerable and lack the means to defend itself and its vital interests. This is why so much sweat and treasure have been devoted to the construction of a modern and capable defense economy since the late 1990s.

This investment began to bear fruit in the second half of the last decade with the emergence of an impressive array of high-technology weapons systems. There are now so many projects under way that the Chinese defense industry appears to be on steroids. The aviation sector is simultaneously engaged in the development or production of more than half a dozen combat and transport aircraft, while the shipbuilding industry has at least four active nuclear and conventional submarine programs along with R&D and construction of aircraft carriers, destroyers, and numerous other surface warships. The space industry is also pursuing a highly ambitious across-the-board development, including manned, lunar, anti-satellite, and satellite projects. The enormous scale and intensity of this technological and industrial undertaking has not been seen since the Cold War days of intense US-Soviet technological and military rivalry. The pace, breadth, and nontransparent nature of China's activities is causing growing anxiety among its neighbors and the United States.

It is important, however, to distinguish between the expansive nature of China's defense technological and innovative activities and their quality and effectiveness. One of the principal conclusions of this volume is that, while China has made considerable efforts since the late 1990s to revamp its defense innovation capabilities, the results so far are mixed. While the space and missile industries have made impressive progress and are able to engage in incremental and architectural types of innovation, many other sectors continue to engage in a mixture of high-end imitation and lower-end innovation activities. They include the aviation, shipbuilding, and ordnance sectors.

A good example is the development of China's aircraft carrier program and the J-15 fighter aircraft that will operate from the decks of these vessels. The PLA Navy's first aircraft carrier, the *Liaoning*, is a rebuilt vessel purchased from the Ukraine in the mid-1990s. Chinese officials argue that the *Liaoning* should be viewed as a wholly indigenously developed product because all of the ship's key systems, equipment, and armaments, such as engines, radar, command and control facilities, and aircraft landing equipment, were sourced domestically.[1] They also claim that the J-15 was designed and developed in China and is not a reverse-engineered version of the Russian Su-33 fighter that China successfully acquired in 2001. A commentary from Xinhua News Agency, China's official news service, dismissed foreign reports that the J-15 was a Russian copy as "groundless and sour."[2] While the technological capabilities of the *Liaoning* and J-15 are likely to have been enhanced with Chinese subsystems and components, the fact remains that the Chinese shipbuilding and aircraft industries required the initial architectural platforms from Russia and Ukraine as starting points for developing their own variants. This would qualify as a case of creative adaptation rather than truly home-grown innovation.

The uneven state of development of the defense industry is likely to continue for the foreseeable future, with pockets of excellence existing in a broader landscape of technological mediocrity. However, more of these innovation clusters are likely to appear and to expand in size and capability, especially over the medium to long term. This will eventually lead to the overall transformation of the Chinese defense economy from a follower to a Tier 1 front-runner.

How long this transformation takes will depend on the continuing support of the top leadership. If senior policy makers remain committed to the goal of building a world-class defense S&T system, funding remains plentiful, and military end-user demand continues to be strong, the development of the defense economy's innovation capabilities will continue on an upward trajectory and could even accelerate. The fifth generation of civilian and military leaders that have taken charge of the country since the 18th Party Congress in 2012 appear to firmly subscribe to the vision defined by their immediate predecessors and enshrined in the various medium- and long-term S&T planning guidances issued since 2000, stating that having a world-class indigenous innovation capacity is critical to China's long-term national security and economic competitiveness. An ideological theme that Party general secretary and Central Military Commission (CMC) chairman Xi Jinping highlighted shortly after he took office at the 18th Party Congress was the importance of "rejuvenation" and "revival of the Chinese nation."[3] These nationalistic sentiments suggest that Xi will embrace the techno-nationalistic philosophy that has been a cornerstone of China's approach to defense science and technology innovation since the 1950s.

Moreover, if China's leaders were to view the country's national security as coming under serious threat once again, as happened between the 1950s and 1970s, there could be another concerted drive to attain breakthroughs in critical defense technological capabilities. Several events since the 1990s have boosted the strategic priority of the development of the defense S&T system in the eyes of the Chinese authorities. Cross-strait tensions between Beijing and Taiwan beginning in the early 1990s led the PLA and the defense industry to ramp up their defense modernization efforts, amid fears that Taiwan was moving towards independence. This led to a concerted effort to develop ballistic missile and precision strike capabilities along with more regular conventional forces such as armored fighting vehicles, combat aircraft, and warships.

The next key event was the US bombing of the Chinese embassy in Belgrade in May 1999. The Chinese leadership's reaction was to sharply intensify efforts to develop strategic weapons systems, or what the PLA terms "Assassin's Mace" or *Shashoujian* (杀手锏) capabilities. According to Gen. Zhang Wannian, who was a CMC vice chairman during the Belgrade Embassy crisis, the CMC convened an emergency meeting immediately following the bombing, and one of the key decisions made at the meeting was to "accelerate the development of *Shashoujian* armaments."[4] Zhang pointed out that Jiang Zemin was especially insistent on the need to step up the pace of development of *Shashoujian* mega-projects (重大工程), saying that "what the enemy is most fearful of, this is what we should be developing."[5] As the "enemy" was the United States, the implication was that the defense and strategic science, technology, and innovation systems should be engaged in developing asymmetric capabilities targeting US vulnerabilities. These leadership calls appear to have been turned into a major weapons technology and engineering development program, known as the 995 Project.[6]

A new major threat dynamic appears to have emerged since the beginning of the 2010s, with a sharp rise in maritime, especially territorial, tensions between China and several of its neighbors and with the United States announcing a strategic rebalancing back to the Asia-Pacific region, and in particular East Asia. A key plank of the US pivot is the development of a new Air-Sea Battle doctrine that is designed to thwart China's efforts to curtail the US military—especially naval—presence through an anti-access/area denial strategy. With China and Japan at loggerheads over the Diaoyu/Senkaku Islands in the East China Sea and rattling increasingly sharp sabers at each other, alongside standoffs between China and Southeast Asian countries over the Spratly Islands in the South Chins Sea, the Chinese leadership is calling for the PLA and the defense industry to step up their "preparations for military struggle, comprehensively improve deterrent and combat capabilities under informationized conditions, and safeguard the sovereignty, security, and development interests" of China.[7] Under this new, more dangerous threat environment, the defense technological and innovation base may enjoy even greater access to resources and be encouraged to become more aggressive in pursuing technological breakthroughs and surprises, especially in areas such as asymmetric (cyber, space, missiles) warfare and long-range naval and air power.

But the improvement of defense science, technology, and innovation capabilities is time-consuming and painstakingly slow, even for urgent, high-priority programs. As Kevin Pollpeter has pointed out in his study of the space industry, the development period for the Shenzhou space program was 13 years, which was significantly longer than counterpart projects in the United States and Soviet Union. Much of this time was spent on grappling with organizational and project management issues. This lengthy gestation period also appears to be the case in other defense sectors, such as aviation, where combat aircraft projects take between 15 and 20 years from research to production. This suggests that the stated overall goal of becoming a top-tier defense S&T power may take considerably longer than the early 2020s mark China hopes to meet, although a growing number of areas may close the gap to the top more quickly than anticipated.

China also appears to be pursuing two distinct innovation development strategies that stress different comparative advantages. The first model is what can be called the "good enough" approach, in which the central goal is affordability and the ability to field substantial quantities of arms that would overwhelm a more advanced but qualitatively smaller adversary. This is a widely adopted business model, known as *Shanzhai*, used by Chinese companies, especially smaller firms, to produce low-cost high-volume versions of foreign products that lack their quality and capabilities but are much cheaper and meet the needs of the average Chinese consumer. This "good enough" strategy also appears to be the principal approach that the PLA and Chinese defense industry are currently pursuing, which fits very well with its asymmetric anti-access/area denial strategy.

The second innovation pathway is the high-end, high-cost "gold-plated" approach, in which the goal is to develop sophisticated although hugely expensive weapons that are able to match those of the United States and other advanced rivals. This is more of a long-term aspirational strategy, as the Chinese defense industry presently lacks the necessary scientific and technological capabilities to effectively carry out higher-end innovation. However, Chinese defense S&T institutes are conducting R&D into increasingly advanced, cutting-edge emerging technologies and weapons that may eventually find their way into production, although in small quantities because of their high cost. This includes directed energy laser weapons, robotic systems, and miniature and nano-based systems.

Policy Implications for the United States and the Asia-Pacific Region

China's defense technological rise carries a host of policy implications for the United States, the Asia-Pacific region, and even the world. One of the overarching issues is whether China's growing defense technological capabilities are fundamentally transforming the nature of the military balance in the Asia-Pacific region, igniting arms spirals and intensifying security dilemmas. There does appear to be growing evidence of action-reaction dynamics taking place in response to China's arms modernization.[8] Countries such as Vietnam, Japan, and the United States have been taking steps to beef up their regional defense capabilities through weapons acquisitions or adjusting their military strategies and force deployments. This is leading to a deepening sense across Asia-Pacific that the regional security situation is being undermined.

Another major issue for the United States is how to counter the Chinese "good enough" approach, which sacrifices quality for quantity. The cornerstone of US weapons development strategy over the past few decades has been to build capabilities that are technologically far superior to those of its rivals with little regard to cost. This emphasis on high-end innovation has been extremely expensive, though, and in a new era of tight fiscal constraint in the aftermath of the 2008 global financial crisis, the Pentagon is struggling to afford many of the gold-plated weapons that it has been developing. The F-22 Raptor fighter is a prime example of an unrivaled weapon that the US Air Force has been able to purchase in far smaller numbers than it had wished because of cost issues. There is a growing reality that the F-35 Joint Strike Fighter may also be prohibitively expensive for the air force to acquire in the large volumes that had originally been planned. The navy, outer space, and other areas of the US defense establishment are also confronting this affordability challenge.

Regional countries such as Japan and Taiwan with much lower levels of military technological capabilities than the United States face an even tougher challenge from the Chinese "good enough" approach, as they cannot compete either on quality or quantity. They will need to find radically different ways to deal with China's rising military technological capabilities. One possible option that these countries may pursue is asymmetric strategic acquisition of more affordable low-tech weapons, such as long-range precision strike capabilities, that can deter the Chinese.

China and the United States are also looking to seek strategic advantages through cross-domain synergies and cross-domain deterrence, in which one side seeks to counter threats in one arena, such as space or cyber warfare, by relying on different types of capabilities, such as sea power or nuclear weapons. Cross-domain synergy is a central idea in the US 2012 Joint Operational Access Concept, which is a key component of its Air-Sea Battle doctrine. The principal facets of US cross-domain synergy, which is currently more conceptual than operational, include the fuller and more flexible integration of space and cyber-security operations into the traditional air-sea-land battle space and the creation and exploitation of advantages in one or more domains, to disrupt enemy anti-access / area denial capabilities in other domains.

The Chinese equivalent of cross-domain synergy is integrated joint operations (IJO, 体化联合作战), which the PLA has adopted as its operational doctrine since the early 2000s. IJO activities refer to operations carried out in multidimensional ground, sea, air, outer space, and electromagnetic battle domains by highly integrated joint forces.[9] This means that service boundaries and operating domains between the navy, air force, Second Artillery, and ground forces are increasingly blurred. So far, however, the PLA has lacked the technological capabilities to conduct IJO, as they require highly sophisticated command, control, communications, computers, intelligence, surveillance and reconnaissance (C4ISR) systems. These technical barriers appear to be falling with the advances in the Chinese defense industry, which is now able to supply hardware like integrated command and battle management platforms that will allow the PLA to carry out coordinated attacks against physical targets using long-range precision strikes along with attacks against information networks using electronic warfare and cyberwarfare assets.[10]

NOTES

1. "Liaoning Ship's Main Systems, Equipment Feature Independent Manufacture, Refit," *Liberation Army Daily*, September 12, 2012.

2. "Skepticism To China's Carrier-Borne Jet Should Be Mute," *Xinhua News Agency*, November 12, 2012.

3. "China's New Boss Xi hits Nationalist Note with Talk of 'Revival'," *Reuters News Service*, December 6, 2012.

4. Zhang Wannian Writing Team, *Biography of Zhang Wannian* (张万年传) (Beijing: Liberation Army Press [解放军出版社], 2011), 416.

5. Ibid., 419.

6. There is no official Chinese acknowledgement of the 995 Project, but there are occasional allusions to it in media reports, writings by Chinese military analysts, résumés of Chinese scientists, and project listings of university laboratories and companies engaged in defense-related work. See, for example, Zeng Li, "Investment in Defense Science and Technology," *Science and Technology Daily* (科技报), April 30, 2009.

7. "Hu Jintao, Xi Jinping Attend Enlarged Meeting of Central Military Commission, Deliver Important Speeches," *Xinhua Domestic Service*, November 17, 2012.

8. Desmond Ball, "Arms Modernization in Asia: An Emerging Complex Arms Race," in Andrew T. H. Tan, ed., *The Global Arms Race: A Handbook* (Milton Park, Abingdon, UK: Routledge, Taylor & Francis Group, 2010), 30–51.

9. Liu Jixian, "Innovation and Development in the Research of Basic Issues of Joint Operations," *China Military Science* (中国军事科学), March 2009, 1–17.

10. See ibid. and Cortez A. Cooper, "Joint Anti-Access Operations China's 'System-of-Systems' Approach," Testimony to the US-China Economic and Security Review Commission, January 27, 2010, p. 6.

Contributors

Daniel Alderman is a research associate at Defense Group, Inc. His research interests include China's defense industry reforms, civil-military relations, and military modernization. Previously, he served as an assistant director at the National Bureau of Asian Research. He has an M.A. in Asian studies from George Washington University's Elliott School of International Affairs.

Richard A. Bitzinger is a senior fellow at and director of the Military Transformations Program at the S. Rajaratnam School of International Studies, Nanyang Technological University, Singapore. He has previously worked at the RAND Corporation, the Asia-Pacific Center for Security Studies, and the US Central Intelligence Agency. He is the editor of *The Modern Defense Industry* (2009).

Tai Ming Cheung is the director of the Institute on Global Conflict and Cooperation at the University of California, San Diego, and the leader of IGCC's Minerva project, titled "The Evolving Relationship Between Technology and National Security in China: Innovation, Defense Transformation, and China's Place in the Global Technology Order." He is a long-time analyst of Chinese and East Asian defense and national security affairs. Cheung was based in Asia from the mid-1980s to 2002, covering political, economic, and strategic developments in greater China. He was also a journalist and a political and business risk consultant in northeast Asia. Cheung manages IGCC's Northeast Asia Cooperation Dialogue, a Track Two program that brings together senior foreign ministry and defense officials as well as academics from the United States, China, Japan, South Korea, North Korea, and Russia for informed discussions on regional security issues. He received his Ph.D. from the War Studies Department at King's College, London University in 2006.

Lisa Crawford graduated from the George Washington University in 2009 with a B.A. in international affairs and Asian studies, with an emphasis on China. She spent two years as a research associate at Defense Group, Inc., and is currently pursuing an M.A. in global marketing at the Thunderbird School of Global Management in Glendale, Arizona.

Debra Geary is a research associate at Defense Group, Inc. Her work focuses on Chinese science and technology research and development. She received a B.A. in economics and Asian studies with a focus on Chinese studies from Mount Holyoke College. She also studied Chinese at Beijing Language and Culture University and Beijing Foreign Studies University. She is pursuing an M.A. in International Commerce and Policy from George Mason University.

Eric Hagt was the director of the China Program at the Center for Defense Information in Washington, DC, 2004–2011. He led a variety of research projects on US-China relations and established and edited *China Security*, a quarterly journal dedicated to understanding China's strategic rise. He earned an M.A. at University of California, Berkeley, and is currently a Ph.D. candidate in the China Studies Center at the Johns Hopkins University School of Advanced International Studies.

Collin Koh Swee Lean is an associate research fellow at the Military Studies Programme, Institute of Defense and Strategic Studies, a constituent unit of the S. Rajaratnam School of International Studies, Nanyang Technological University, Singapore. His research interests include military and security affairs in the Asia-Pacific as well as Scandinavian defense affairs. Koh is pursuing the study of naval arms control and nonprovocative defense in particular.

Brian Lafferty is a research analyst at Defense Group, Inc., where he specializes in primary source research on China's defense-related science and technology development. His current research interests include China's defense-related S&T institutional networks, China's civil-military integration, the internal security role of the People's Liberation Army, and PLA remuneration policies. He has a Ph.D. from Columbia University, where his dissertation highlighted the importance of the PLA's role as an internal security guarantee after 1989 and the impact this has had on China's defense spending.

Thomas G. Mahnken is currently Jerome E. Levy Chair of Economic Geography and National Security at the US Naval War College and a senior research professor at the Philip Merrill Center for Strategic Studies at the Johns Hopkins University School of Advanced International Studies. Mahnken served as US deputy assistant secretary of defense for policy planning 2006–2009. He is the author of *Competitive Strategies for the 21st Century: Theory, History, and Practice* (2012), *Technology and the American Way of War since 1945* (2008), and *Uncovering Ways of War: U.S. Intelligence and Foreign Military Innovation, 1918–1941* (2002), among other works.

Joe McReynolds is a research analyst at the Center for Intelligence Research and Analysis at Defense Group, Inc. His research centers on Chinese cyberwarfare capabilities and defense science and technology development. He has traveled widely across East Asia and has lived in Nagoya, Guilin, and Beijing.

Kevin Pollpeter is deputy director of the Program on the Study of Innovation and Technology in China at the University of California Institute on Global Conflict and Cooperation at the University of California, San Diego, where he specializes in Chinese science and technology issues with a focus on China's space program. Previously, he was the deputy director of the East Asia Program at Defense Group, Inc., where he specialized in Chinese national security issues with a focus on China's space program. He has also served in research positions at the Center for Nonproliferation Studies at the Monterey Institute of International Studies of Middlebury College and the RAND Corporation. Pollpeter is the author or coauthor of numerous works on Asian security issues. He holds a B.A. in China studies from Grinnell College and an M.A. in international policy studies from the Monterey Institute of International Studies. He is currently pursuing a Ph.D. at King's College London.

Susan M. Puska, Colonel, US Army (retired), is president and CEO of Kanava International, a woman-owned, venteran-owned small business focused on geopolitical and economic research and analysis and management capacity building. She served as an army attaché in the US Embassy, Beijing, during 1992–1994 and 2001–2003. She holds an M.B.A. from George Mason University and an M.A. from the University of Michigan. She received a certificate from the Hopkins-Nanjing Center for American and Chinese Studies and is a graduate of the US Army War College. She has published widely on Chinese military topics, including China's military activities in Africa, crisis management, logistics, and training. She is currently researching the Chinese General Armament Department and the history of US-China military relations.

Michael Raska is a research fellow in the Military Transformations Program at the S. Rajaratnam School of International Studies, Nanyang Technological University, Singapore. His research and publications focus on East Asian security and defense issues, including theoretical and policy-oriented aspects of military innovation, force modernization trajectories, and military strategy. He holds a Ph.D. in public policy from the Lee Kuan Yew School of Public Policy, National University of Singapore.

Andrew L. Ross is director of special science, engineering, and policy research initiatives; director of the Center for Science, Technology, and Policy; and professor of political science at the University of New Mexico. Ross's work on US grand strategy, national security and defense planning, regional security, weapons proliferation, security and economics, and public policy has appeared in numerous journals and books. His current work focuses on the US grand strategy debate, military innovation, and nuclear policy, strategy, and force structure.

Aaron Shraberg is a research associate at Defense Group, Inc. His research focuses on China's science and technology policies and its defense technology research and development. From 2004 through 2006, he volunteered in China with the US Peace Corps. Shraberg has a B.A. from the University of Kentucky and an M.A. from George Washington University's Elliott School of International Affairs.

Mark Stokes is the executive director of the Project 2049 Institute. Previously, he was the founder and president of Quantum Pacific Enterprises, an international consulting firm, and vice president and Taiwan country manager for Raytheon International. A 20-year US Air Force veteran, Stokes also served as team chief and senior country director for the People's Republic of China, Taiwan, and Mongolia in the Office of the Assistant Secretary of Defense for International Security Affairs. He holds a B.A. from Texas A&M University and graduate degrees in international relations and Asian studies from Boston University and the Naval Postgraduate School. He is a fluent speaker of Mandarin.

Kathleen (Kate) Walsh is associate professor of national security affairs and teaches policy analysis in the National Security Affairs Department of the US Naval War College and is an affiliate of the China Maritime Studies Institute. Her research focuses on China and the Asia-Pacific region, particularly security and technology issues, and she has authored numerous publications. She has an M.A. in international security policy from Columbia University and a B.A. in international affairs from the Elliott School of International Affairs, George Washington University.

Kelvin Wong Ka Weng is an associate research fellow at the S. Rajaratnam School of International Studies, Nanyang Technological University, Singapore. He is with the Military Studies Programme at the school's constituent unit, the Institute of Defense and Strategic Studies. Wong holds an M.A. in strategic studies from the Australian National University.

Index

Page numbers in *italics* indicate figures.

France, 169, 170, 181, *189*; army maneuvers of, used to test innovation, 28; innovation studies of, 19

Geely Group, 34
General Armament Department, 6, 11, 25, 149, 194, 242–43, 244–45, 261; Audit Department, 100; authority and influence of, 47; compensation strategy in, 76; Comprehensive Planning Department, 99–100; creating competitive market for weapons procurement, 124; creation of, 67; decision-making layers in, for S&T projects, 71–72; dependence of, on the defense industry, 76–77; enacting administrative rules, 51; as gatekeepers for private defense firms, 125; implementing bureaucracies in, 74; involvement in defense Project Design Stage, 49; involvement in weapons research and development, effects of, 57–58; as link in technology-push, demand-pull process, 94; linkages of, in MRO system, *95*; Logistics Department, 100; making final determination on contracts, 75; managing growing numbers of actors, 73; military representative system, overhaul of, 77; MROs and, 88, 89–90, 92, 101; patronage in, 74–75; promoting stronger oversight role, 88; relation of, with the defense industry, 58; responsible for acquisition and technology policy, 250; rivalries of, with other departments, 52–53; working groups of, 245
General Logistics Department, 52–53, 88, 89, 105n24
General Political Department, 104
General Staff Department, 52–53, 88, 89, 101, 194, 242–43, 244
Germany, 169, 170; army maneuvers of, used to test innovation, 28; Blitzkrieg doctrine of, 34, 37; Troop Office in, 27
global arms industry, 169–75
global innovation system, 137
global technology, leveraging of, 5
"good enough" approach, 276–78
grid approach, for innovation centers, 154–55
Guo Boxiong, 53

Han Yanlin, *69*
Harbin Institute of Technology, 187, 247, 259, 261
heat sinks, 219
Hongfeng Machine Factory, 264
Hou Shiming, 261
Huawei, 153
Huazhong University, 246
Hu Jintao, 53, 101; CMI strategy under, 109, 110, 111; leadership under, 9; official doctrine under, shifting to S&T, 146; praising China's space program, 225
human resources, importance of, 157–58
Hunan Space Bureau, 256

imitation, types of, 30–33
imitation-to-innovation, depiction of, *32*
implementation, as innovation process, *26*, 29–30, 172, *173*, 174, *178*, *189*, 198
incremental innovation, 30, *32*, 33, 35–36, 39, 62, 63, 158
independent regulatory system model, 50
India, 79–80, 138, 169, 170, 177, *178*, 183–84, *189*
indigenous innovation, 33, 136, 140
industrial systems, technological innovation in, 54–57
information warfare, 39
innovation, *189*, *198*; agents of, 15–16; architectural, 62; characteristics of, 15; cross-sector, 156; defense-specific, 203; defined, 16–18; discontinuous, 36–38; disruptive, 36–38, 62–63; distinguished from invention, 16; diversity of, 16; impact of, 35–39; incentivizing, 160; incremental, 22, 35–36, 62, 63, 158; indigenous, 136, 140; inputs to, 24–26; large-scale, 21–22; major, 42n31; matrix of, 36, *37*; merit of, calculating, 29; military, 172, *173*, 174, *178*; models of, 3–4; national security, types of, 17; organizational barriers to, 20; outputs of, 24, 30–35; processes of, 24, 26–30; sectorwide, 156; strategies for, target of, 115; studies of, 18–21, 137; systems for, 4; types of, 30–35
Innovation 2020 (CAS), 146
innovation zones, 151–52, 153, 154–55